RELIGIOUS EXPERIENCE
and the
KNOWLEDGE
of GOD

RELIGIOUS EXPERIENCE

and the

KNOWLEDGE

of GOD

The Evidential Force *of* Divine Encounters

Harold A. Netland

Baker Academic

a division of Baker Publishing Group
Grand Rapids, Michigan

Published by Baker Academic
a division of Baker Publishing Group
PO Box 6287, Grand Rapids, MI 49516-6287
www.bakeracademic.com

Printed in the United States of America

Library of Congress Cataloging-in-Publication Data
Names: Netland, Harold A., 1955– author.
Title: Religious experience and the knowledge of God : the evidential force of divine encounters / Harold A. Netland.
Description: Grand Rapids, Michigan : Baker Academic, a division of Baker Publishing Group, [2022] | Includes bibliographical references and index.
Identifiers: LCCN 2021030951 | ISBN 9780801099649 (paperback) | ISBN 9781540965318 (casebound) | ISBN 9781493434893 (ebook) | ISBN 9781493434909 (pdf)
Subjects: LCSH: Christianity—Psychology. | Experience (Religion) | God (Christianity)—Knowableness.
Classification: LCC BR110 .N48 2022 | DDC 261.5/15—dc23
LC record available at https://lccn.loc.gov/2021030951

Baker Publishing Group publications use paper produced from sustainable forestry practices and post-consumer waste whenever possible.

22   23   24   25   26   27   28   7   6   5   4   3   2   1

To Keith Yandell (1938–2020)

Contents

Acknowledgments

I have been thinking about the issues in this book for a long time, as they have been part of classes I have taught at Trinity Evangelical Divinity School (TEDS) and elsewhere over the past twenty-five years. The comments and questions of many people over the years have helped me to sharpen my own thinking and, at times, to modify my views on some issues. I cannot possibly mention everyone here, but special acknowledgment is due to my excellent students at TEDS, especially those in the religious epistemology classes. I am also very grateful for colleagues and friends who were willing to read and comment on drafts of these chapters, including Doug Geivett, Wilson Jeremiah, David Luy, Tom McCall, Justin Mooney, Doug Sweeney, Stephen Williams, and David Yandell. Once again, I am deeply grateful to Jim Kinney, Wells Turner, and the fine production team at Baker Academic for their professionalism, encouragement, and guidance at each stage of the writing, editing, and publication process.

I was blessed in having Keith Yandell (1938–2020), for many years professor of philosophy at the University of Wisconsin–Madison, as a friend and colleague (he taught part time at Trinity for many years). The issues in this book were subjects of spirited discussions with Keith on many occasions. I learned much from him. It is with deep appreciation for Keith as an exemplary Christian thinker and a wonderful human being that I dedicate this book to him.

Introduction

In 1985 my wife Ruth and I moved from the lovely city of Kyoto, Japan, to a community in western Tokyo. We were expecting our first child and did not yet know many people in the area. One day my wife returned from the maternity clinic excited because she had met an American who, like Ruth, was a graduate of the University of Minnesota. Americans were unusual in that part of Tokyo, so Ruth invited her to our home for coffee, anticipating an afternoon of fun conversation about Minnesota and things they had in common. But when the woman came to visit Ruth, the conversation began on a surprising note. Upon entering our home, she immediately turned to Ruth and said, "Let me tell you how I found perfect peace and happiness in Soka Gakkai Buddhism." She proceeded to give a powerful account of how meditation and practicing Buddhist precepts had completely transformed her life. Ruth was shocked. "Change a few key words here and there," she remarked, "and it could have been a beautiful Christian testimony!" The woman had met her Japanese husband while he was an international student at the University of Minnesota. Through his influence, she became a Buddhist, and now the couple was living in Tokyo, where she served as a leader in the local Soka Gakkai community.

There are a number of intriguing aspects to this encounter. The woman, a white American from the Midwest, was a convert to Buddhism. She is just one of a growing number of Americans who embrace religions such as Hinduism, Buddhism, or Islam, traditions generally not associated with American society. But the American religious landscape today is fluid and very diverse, with conversions and deconversions flowing in many directions.

1

Furthermore, in her witness to Ruth, the woman immediately went into her personal story about what Buddhism had done for her, how it met her needs by providing peace and happiness. She gave a Buddhist testimony. Many Western converts to Buddhism provide eloquent testimonies about the transformative effects that Buddhist teaching and practice have had on their lives.[1] But listening to reports like these can be disconcerting for Christians who have been taught that such experiences are unique to Christianity and that a personal story about how Jesus changed one's life is the most powerful evangelistic tool we can employ. The idea that Buddhists, Hindus, and Muslims also have compelling personal testimonies just doesn't seem right.

At the heart of this woman's story was personal experience. She did not launch into esoteric arguments supporting the Four Noble Truths or the doctrine of dependent co-origination. Nor did she appeal to the divine inspiration of Buddhist sutras, since there is no God in Buddhism to inspire sutras. She simply shared her experience of finding peace, meaning, and happiness through Buddhist meditation. This, too, has parallels with the approach of many Christians who place a premium on a personal experience of God and minimize, if not ignore entirely, any appeal to evidence or reasons in support of Christian teachings.

But if personal experience is the sole or even primary factor in determining whether to accept particular religious claims, there would be little for Ruth to say in response to the woman's testimony. Her experience provided what she was looking for. Relying only on personal experience, an appropriate response to her would be, "I'm so glad that you have found something that meets your needs and gives you peace and meaning. As for me, I've found meaning and peace in Jesus." End of conversation. Unless one appeals to *reasons* for religious commitments that are independent of the experience itself, there is little one can say to the woman about why she should abandon Buddhist teachings and accept Jesus as Lord.

Religious experiences are significant, for in one form or another, they are a common and important part of life for many people around the world today. Despite the significant increase in those who self-identify as nonreligious, most people worldwide continue to have religious affiliation of some kind and engage in religious activities. Experiences, both personal and corporate, ordinary and unusual, are a central part of vibrant religious communities.

1. See Vickie MacKenzie, *Why Buddhism? Westerners in Search of Wisdom* (London: Element, 2002).

Experiences are an important aspect of the Christian tradition as well. Christians do not generally speak of having "religious experiences" but they do pray to God, meditate on Scripture, have feelings of guilt due to sin and then experience God's forgiveness upon repentance, worship God through song and liturgy, hear God's voice of guidance in perplexing times, experience God's special peace during trials, and so on. All of this involves experience. Nor is this surprising, for the ongoing daily exercise of faith entails undergoing many kinds of experiences.[2] Simeon Zahl observes that, "To a significant degree, the question of Christian experience of God is the question of God's presence as it is perceived in human lives in various forms and under various conditions and with various effects."[3]

In addition to ordinary experiences, there are also the more unusual and dramatic experiences of those who have visions of Jesus or dreams in which God is said to communicate directly to them. Scripture itself is full of examples of God or angelic beings appearing in dreams or visions to individuals or groups. The history of Christianity is replete with examples of those claiming to have directly encountered God, Jesus, or an angelic being in a vision, dream, or other perceptual experience. Many people around the world today report experiences in which Jesus appears to them.[4]

A testimony—a personal account of how one's conversion to Jesus Christ through the supernatural work of the Holy Spirit results in a dramatically changed life—gives voice to an especially important kind of experience. The narrative of personal transformation, expressed powerfully in the dramatic statement of the blind man in John 9:25—"One thing I do know. I was blind but now I see!"—has always been significant for Christians. But it took on special meaning in the early modern era with the rise of the Puritans and Pietists.[5] The testimony of a transformed life,

2. Oliver D. Crisp, "Faith and Experience," in *The Oxford Handbook of Evangelical Theology*, ed. Gerald R. McDermott (New York: Oxford University Press, 2010), 69.

3. Simeon Zahl, *The Holy Spirit and Christian Experience* (Oxford: Oxford University Press, 2020), 53.

4. See Phillip H. Wiebe, *Visions of Jesus: Direct Encounters from the New Testament to Today* (New York: Oxford University Press, 1997); Wiebe, *Visions and Appearances of Jesus* (Abilene, TX: Leafwood, 2014). See also Tom Doyle, *Dreams and Visions: Is Jesus Awakening the Muslim World?* (Nashville: Nelson, 2012); and Craig S. Keener, *Miracles: The Credibility of the New Testament Accounts* (Grand Rapids: Baker Academic, 2011), 2:870–84 ("Appendix E: Visions and Dreams").

5. See D. Bruce Hindmarsh, *The Evangelical Conversion Narratives: Spiritual Autobiography in Early Modern England* (New York: Oxford University Press, 2005).

accompanied by ongoing personal experiences of God's presence, has become a central feature of modern Protestant, and especially evangelical, Christianity.

Moreover, for many Christians, it is precisely this personal experience of God that provides the grounds for confidence in the truth of the gospel and one's acceptance by God. The conviction that comes from personal experience is captured nicely in this early twentieth-century hymn:

> You ask me how I know He lives?
> He lives within my heart.[6]

Something very important is captured in this hymn. There is a sense in which Christians can legitimately claim to know the reality of God because of their experiences of God. Any biblically faithful perspective should acknowledge this. But, as we shall see, this affirmation must be qualified in certain ways and needs to be appreciated within a broader epistemic framework of beliefs that itself requires justification. One of the purposes of this book is to tease out some of the epistemological implications of this claim about the role of personal experience of God in the justification or support of Christian commitments.

When thinking of experiences of God, it is tempting to focus on the dramatic or "peak" experiences of the great spiritual giants and treat these as paradigmatic for what theistic experience is like. But this can be misleading. It is crucial that we are also attentive to the more ordinary and mundane experiences of life in which believers encounter God. In her excellent ethnographic study, *When God Talks Back*, anthropologist T. M. Luhrmann offers a rich exploration of ordinary American evangelicals' understandings of their relationship with God. Based on sustained observation and extensive interviews with evangelicals in the Vineyard Christian Fellowship, Luhrmann elucidates the thinking of many Christians about a personal relationship with God: "Many Americans not only believe in God in some general way but experience God directly and report repeated contact with the supernatural. . . . These Christians speak as if God interacts with them like a friend."[7] Similarly, Dallas Willard, reflecting on typical experiences of ordinary Christians, says, "Many might be surprised

6. "He Lives." Text and music by Homer A. Rodeheaver, 1933. Copyright renewed by The Rodeheaver Company, 1961. *The Hymnal for Worship and Celebration* (Waco: Word Music, 1986), 220.

7. T. M. Luhrmann, *When God Talks Back: Understanding the American Evangelical Relationship with God* (New York: Knopf, 2012), xi, xix.

to discover what a high percentage of serious Christians—and even non-Christians—can tell of specific experiences in which they are sure God spoke to them."[8] These experiences of ordinary people in the routine patterns of life, no less than the dramatic experiences of the great saints, constitute the raw data on which theoretical accounts of experiences of God should be constructed.

Some Epistemological Issues and Approaches

Experience plays a significant role in people coming to accept Christian commitments and to have confidence in the truth of the gospel. Religious experiences serve many different functions, both positive and negative, but an important one is helping to provide some justification for certain beliefs and practices. These experiences can take a bewildering variety of forms and come with varying degrees of clarity or intensity, but they provide some support for religious commitments. William Alston observes that for ordinary Christians,

> somehow what goes on in the experience of leading the Christian life provides some ground for Christian belief, makes some contribution to the rationality of Christian belief. We sometimes feel the presence of God; we get glimpses, at least, of God's will for us; we feel the Holy Spirit at work in our lives, guiding us, strengthening us, enabling us to love other people in a new way; we hear God speaking to us in the Bible, in preaching, or in the words and actions of our fellow Christians. Because of all this we are more justified in our Christian beliefs than we would have been otherwise.[9]

Alston's point is not that Christians consciously construct formal arguments for the rationality of Christian beliefs using aspects of their experience as premises; most Christians don't do anything of the kind. But he is highlighting the fact that for many believers there is a relation between what they take to be experiences of God and their conviction that basic Christian teachings "make sense" or are "reasonable" and thus should be accepted. Moreover, there is an important sense in which this *ought* to be the case. Alston comments, "If I could not find any confirmation of the Christian

8. Dallas Willard, *Hearing God: Developing a Conversational Relationship with God* (Downers Grove, IL: InterVarsity, 2012), 21.

9. William P. Alston, "Christian Experience and Christian Belief," in *Faith and Rationality: Reason and Belief in God*, ed. Alvin Plantinga and Nicholas Wolterstorff (Notre Dame: University of Notre Dame Press, 1983), 103.

message in my own experience, I would be less justified in accepting that message than I am in fact."[10] And surely Alston is correct in this.

So there is an epistemological relation of some kind between experience and the adoption of religious beliefs. But, of course, experience can be deceptive. Even in our ordinary experience of the physical world not everything is as it seems. The stick in the water appears bent (because of water's refractive property) until we pull it out and see that it is actually straight. Similarly, not all of our religious experiences are as they initially appear. Sometimes what seems to be the case proves to be delusory. Moreover, religious experiences are used to justify conflicting religious commitments, so we cannot simply accept uncritically any claims based on experiences. In other words, we need to be able to make responsible judgments about religious experiences, determining which should be accepted and which should not. And in working through these issues, we confront some of the more complex and controversial questions at the heart of contemporary religious epistemology.

A comprehensive discussion of the epistemology of religious experience would examine the nature and role of experience in all the major religions, comparing and contrasting phenomena from the many cultures and traditions. It would also be based on rich ethnographic and phenomenological studies of such experiences, something that scholars are only now beginning to amass. This book makes no pretense of being genuinely comprehensive in scope; its purpose is more modest: we are concerned primarily with some epistemological issues arising from theistic experiences, especially within the Christian tradition.

In considering the epistemology of theistic experiences, it is important to distinguish two kinds of questions. First, there are issues arising from within a confessional commitment to the Christian faith: From within the Christian framework, how does one distinguish genuine experiences of God from those that are not? In the Christian tradition this question is often expressed in terms of the work of the Holy Spirit: How does one distinguish the witness of the Holy Spirit from experiences that are not of the Spirit? These questions, internal to the Christian faith, are answered largely in terms of authoritative resources such as Scripture, the creeds, and the mainstream teachings of the church. Theologians have given the testimony or witness of the Holy Spirit a great deal of attention, but until recently there has been little discussion of this by Christian philosophers.[11] Although theological

10. Alston, "Christian Experience," 103.
11. There is increasing attention to the subject. See William Abraham, "The Epistemological Significance of the Inner Witness of the Holy Spirit," *Faith and Philosophy* 7, no. 4 (October 1990): 434–50; William Alston, "The Indwelling of the Holy Spirit," in *Divine Nature*

and philosophical issues overlap, my interest in these questions is not primarily theological but rather philosophical.

A second kind of question concerns the possible role of religious experience in justifying central Christian claims: To what extent and in what ways can religious experience provide evidence for the truth or rationality of Christian theism? Does experience provide reasons for belief, either for the person undergoing the experience or for others? These questions can be asked either from the perspective of a committed Christian who is interested in the evidential force of such experiences for beliefs he or she already accepts, or from the vantage point of a skeptic or unbelieving inquirer interested in the epistemic implications of religious experiences. In the chapters that follow, I am primarily interested in questions of this sort, although we will also give some attention to issues in the first category (identifying genuine experiences of God), especially as they pertain to the inner witness of the Holy Spirit.

"Evidence" is a tricky word because it is used in different ways. It is sometimes understood in a narrow sense to mean whatever is used in a formal argument to support a conclusion. An appeal to evidence in this sense involves constructing an argument where the evidence, presented in the premises, is intended to support the conclusion. But this is an unnecessarily restrictive understanding of evidence. In ordinary life, something can serve as evidence in support of a belief even though we do not—and probably could not—construct a formal argument to that effect. Our appeal to evidential factors is often immediate and noninferential. Johnny's mother walks into the kitchen and sees the peanut butter jar open and bread crumbs and smudges of peanut butter and strawberry jam on the counter, and she immediately thinks, "Johnny made a peanut butter and jelly sandwich again and did not put things away." Seeing the peanut butter and jam on the counter provides the evidential grounds for her judgment, although she does not go through a formal process of deriving the conclusion from the premises. Following Stephen Evans, it is helpful to think of evidence broadly as "whatever makes some truth evident to

---

and Human Language (Ithaca, NY: Cornell University Press, 1989), 223–52; Marilyn McCord Adams, "The Indwelling of the Holy Spirit: Some Alternative Models," in *The Philosophy of Human Nature in Christian Perspective*, ed. Peter Weigel and Joseph G. Prud'homme (New York: Peter Lang, 2016), 83–99; Paul Moser, "The Inner Witness of the Spirit," in *The Oxford Handbook of the Epistemology of Theology*, ed. William J. Abraham and Frederick D. Aquino (New York: Oxford University Press, 2017), 111–25; Simeon Zahl, *Holy Spirit and Christian Experience*; and R. Douglas Geivett and Paul K. Moser, eds., *The Testimony of the Spirit: New Essays* (New York: Oxford University Press, 2017).

us";[12] evidential factors can be used in the premises of a formal argument but they need not be. We will be using "evidence" in this broader sense in what follows.

In discussing the ways in which religious experience provides epistemic support for certain commitments, William Hasker distinguishes between what he calls the perceptual model and the explanatory model.[13] The perceptual model draws an analogy between our five senses and perception of the physical world and our intellectual faculties and perception of God and maintains that if the deliverances of the former are justified, then those of the latter should be accepted as well. The explanatory model, by contrast, regards religious experiences as something requiring explanation and argues that the reality of God is the best explanation for these phenomena. This approach typically makes use of the inference to the best-explanation (or cumulative-case) argument in accounting for religious experiences. Both approaches will be considered in the chapters that follow.

Our ordinary perception of objects—seeing a tree or a desk or a cat— usually involves one or more of the five senses. Despite some nagging philosophical questions, there is a broad consensus that the five senses can generally be relied on for a trustworthy understanding of the world. But can we also use sensory experience to perceive God? Some influential philosophers argue that we can. Just as we are generally justified in trusting the input of our senses in our experience of the physical world, so too we can be justified, in appropriate circumstances, in trusting our experienced perceptions of God. Some significant recent work by Christian philosophers adopts this approach. The epistemic support provided by religious experience in this case is immediate and noninferential; it is not the product of an inferential process or argument.

The perception model can be further divided into two approaches. One popular move in recent decades comes from the influential proposal by Alvin Plantinga that, in appropriate circumstances, certain beliefs about God can be "properly basic" and thus be epistemically entirely acceptable apart from any corroborating evidence or argument. Plantinga draws an analogy between such beliefs and other properly basic beliefs that we typically hold. A second approach within the perception model is advocated by

12. C. Stephen Evans, "Religious Experience and the Question of Whether Belief in God Requires Evidence," in *Evidence and Religious Belief*, ed. Kelly James Clark and Raymond J. VanArragon (New York: Oxford University Press, 2011), 39.
13. William Hasker, "The Epistemic Value of Religious Experience: Perceptual and Explanatory Models," in *The Rationality of Belief and the Plurality of Faith*, ed. Thomas D. Senor (Ithaca, NY: Cornell University Press, 1995), 150–69.

philosophers such as Richard Swinburne, who appeal to the principle of
credulity to justify certain kinds of religious experience. We will consider
both of these approaches.

Some philosophers within the perception model, following a long tradition within Christian theology, appeal to a special "spiritual sense" through
which we are able to perceive God. There is a rich tradition of theologians
using sensory language to depict human encounters with the divine, and
the term *spiritual senses* is often used to denote the faculty through which
believers apprehend spiritual truths and experience nonphysical realities
such as God and angels.[14] We will consider how this theme is expressed in
the works of Jonathan Edwards and John Wesley.

We will also give attention, especially in chapter 7, to what Hasker calls
the explanatory model, which develops an inference to the best-explanation
argument for the justification of religious commitments based on the phenomena from theistic experiences. The widespread occurrence of theistic
experiences across time and cultures, along with the distinctive nature of
these experiences, can be regarded as phenomena demanding some explanation. The reality of God is then offered as the most reasonable explanation
for these phenomena.

Much of the discussion in scholarly literature is concerned with the evidential force of the experience for the person who has the experience. But
there is also the question about the force of the evidence for others who
hear reports about the experience. Although related, these are separate issues, and as Doug Geivett explains, what might function noninferentially
as evidence for the person having the experience could also be part of a
formal argument in the case of the observer.

> A subject's belief in God may be grounded in an awareness of God who is
> present to the subject, either directly or indirectly, in his/her experience. But
> a nonbelieving recipient of a report of this experiential awareness will natu-
> rally want a reason to believe that the subject's experience was a bona fide
> experience of God, an experience where God was actually present (directly
> or indirectly) to the subject, if the subject's experience is to count as evidence
> for the nonbelieving recipient of testimony regarding the experience. What
> is *non-inferential evidence* for the believing subject of a religious experience
> is, for the nonbelieving outside observer, data for a potential *inference* to the
> existence of God.[15]

14. See Paul L. Gavrilyuk and Sarah Coakley, eds., *The Spiritual Senses: Perceiving God in
Western Christianity* (Cambridge: Cambridge University Press, 2012).

15. Doug Geivett, "The Evidential Value of Religious Experience," in *The Rationality of Theism*, ed. Paul Copan and Paul K. Moser (London: Routledge, 2003), 177. Emphasis in original.

We must be attentive to the different ways in which experiences can provide evidence, both immediate and inferential, for the subject and outside observers.

Religious experiences sometimes produce a high degree of confidence in certain beliefs. And yet, experience can be a notoriously unreliable guide to truth, and this applies to religious experience as well. If we were never mistaken in our judgments about religious experience, epistemological issues concerning them would not arise. But we are sometimes mistaken. So the questions are there, and they are not restricted to philosophers or agnostic skeptics. Believers also struggle with doubt. Many believers claim to have experiences of God, but they do so with the realization that they might well be mistaken. Reflecting on her interactions with evangelicals in the Vineyard Christian Fellowship, who believe that they *do* experience God's presence, Luhrmann states, "And they doubt. They find it hard to believe in an invisible being—let alone an invisible being who is entirely good and overwhelmingly powerful. Many Christians struggle, at one point or another, with the despair that it all might be a sham."[16] Or, as comedian Lily Tomlin puts it, "Why is it that when we speak to God we are said to be praying but when God speaks to us we are said to be schizophrenic?"[17]

Although technical terms and key concepts are defined as they appear in the following chapters, three terms in particular—*truth*, *rationality*, and *veridicality*—should be clarified at the outset. Each term is controversial and contested, but since they recur throughout the book, it is important that the reader understand how I am using them.

Truth is a property of propositions or statements such that a statement is true if and only if the state of affairs to which the statement refers obtains. Otherwise, it is false. Or as William Alston puts it, a statement "is true if and only if what the statement says to be the case actually is the case."[18] This is closely related to what is often called the correspondence theory of truth, which maintains that "for a statement to be true, there must be some appropriate *correspondence* between true statements and actual features of the world."[19] Thus, "The heavy rainfall last night resulted in flooding in the basement" is true if and only if the heavy rainfall last night did indeed cause

16. Luhrmann, *When God Talks Back*, xiii.
17. Quoted in Willard, *Hearing God*, 22.
18. See William P. Alston, *A Realist Conception of Truth* (Ithaca, NY: Cornell University Press, 1996), 5.
19. Paul K. Moser, Dwayne H. Mulder, and J. D. Trout, *The Theory of Knowledge: A Thematic Introduction* (New York: Oxford University Press, 1998), 65. Emphasis in original.

flooding in the basement. "On the third day, Jesus of Nazareth was raised from the dead" is true if and only if on the third day Jesus of Nazareth was raised from the dead. This notion underlies our ordinary and commonsense understanding of truth and is taken for granted by most religious believers in their acceptance of the claims at the heart of their traditions.

Although we have a commonsense understanding of rationality that we use in ordinary life, it is difficult to specify precisely what the term means and the conditions of its applicability. Whereas truth is a property of propositions or statements, rationality is a characteristic of persons. Statements are true or false, but persons are rational or irrational in their beliefs. Let S stand for a person and P represent a belief. Whether S is rational in believing P is not merely a matter of the content of P but also other contextual factors, including the relevant circumstances of S at the time of belief, S's background beliefs, and the reasons or grounds S has for believing P. Although we like to think that there is a tight correlation between rationality and truth, so that what is rational to believe is also true, in principle it is possible for it to be rational to believe something that is false. Given their other beliefs at the time, for example, it was rational for people in Europe in the tenth century to believe that the earth is flat.

We can distinguish stronger and weaker forms of rationality. A strong notion of rationality includes rationality norms that make accepting the relevant belief obligatory. To fail to accept P is then irrational or unreasonable. For example, belief in the reality of the external world or the general reliability of memory is typically regarded as perfectly rational, and failure to accept these beliefs indicates cognitive malfunctioning of some sort. It is not just that we are somehow *permitted* to believe in the reality of the external world. To the contrary, the expectation is that people who are rational and whose cognitive faculties are operating properly *will* believe in the reality of the external world.

But there is a weaker form of rationality such that it can be rational for a person in certain circumstances and with particular background beliefs to believe P even if others, in their own circumstances, can also be rational in not believing P. This sense of rationality is person-relative and context-dependent to an extent that the strong version is not. Whereas the stronger sense of rationality involves what we might call *epistemic obligation*, the weaker sense involves *epistemic permission*. With a weak sense of rationality, given appropriate circumstances and background beliefs, it can be rational for a person to believe what in fact is false. It can be rational for S to believe P, while it might also be rational for R, in quite different circumstances, not to believe P. When we come to discussions of what it is reasonable to believe with respect to religious experiences, it is important to clarify whether we are thinking in terms of strong or weak rationality.

The final concept to be introduced here is veridicality. Roughly, veridicality is to experience truthful propositions or statements. The term *veridical* connotes accuracy, truthfulness, or veracity, so that a veridical experience is one that is not illusory or deceptive. A perceptual experience is an experience in which a person perceives a particular object or event or state of affairs. Perceptual experiences are veridical if the perceived object really is present or if the event really occurs or if the state of affairs really is as it seems to the subject. For example, if I have an experience in which I perceive a red ball on top of a table, the experience is veridical if and only if there really is a red ball on top of the table. If not—perhaps a projector is projecting an image of a red ball on the table—the experience is illusory.

Experiences occur and are understood under certain "descriptions" as we make sense of what is presented to us.[20] In making sense of experiences, we make judgments about them, and it is here that the notion of veridicality is especially relevant. Imagine that I have a stick in my hand, and I then place half of it under water. I then have a visual image of the stick, half of which is above water and half submerged beneath the water. The portion of the stick outside the water appears straight, but the part in the water appears crooked. If I conclude that the stick under the water *is* crooked, then my experience of the stick is not veridical, since the stick itself remains straight and merely appears to be crooked. The visual image presented to me is real enough, but my experience of the submerged stick as crooked is not veridical. This example is straightforward enough, although there are many less clear-cut cases in which determining whether an experience is veridical is more problematic. Much of the debate in the epistemology of experience deals with clarifying what criteria are appropriate for distinguishing veridical experiences from those that are not.

Overview of the Chapters

This book provides an overview of some key issues in current debates about the epistemology of religious experience and argues that certain kinds of experience can provide some positive support for some religious claims.

20. See Caroline Franks Davis, *The Evidential Force of Religious Experience* (Oxford: Clarendon, 1989), 25.

Theistic experiences in particular—what are taken to be experiences of God—can provide evidential support for some Christian beliefs, both for the person having the experience and for others.

In defending this position, I adopt what is sometimes called a critical-trust approach to theistic experience: what seems to be an experience of God can be accepted as such, so long as there are no compelling reasons to conclude otherwise.[21] We generally accept something like the critical-trust approach with respect to sense experience or memory or our experience of other persons. I see no persuasive reason to conclude that it cannot be applied to theistic experiences as well. What are taken to be experiences of God can provide evidential support for certain Christian beliefs for those who have the experiences as well as for others who hear about them. This does not mean that all purported experiences of God are to be accepted uncritically; there are appropriate checking procedures, both from within the Christian tradition itself and from broader epistemological principles, that enable us to distinguish what ought to be accepted from what should not.

Moreover, I argue that the acceptability of any particular religious experience depends in part on the broader epistemic context within which the experience occurs, including the background beliefs of the person having the experience or of those hearing reports of the experience. Ultimately, the question of the acceptability of an experience cannot be determined apart from considering the truth or rationality of the broader set of beliefs within which the experience is understood. This indicates the importance of what is often called "natural theology" in the assessment of religious experience. Some form of natural theology that addresses the question why we should accept basic Christian claims about God is unavoidable.

Chapter 1 clarifies the meaning of "religious experience" by exploring the concepts of experience, religion, and religious experience and by showing how our current understanding of religious experience has been shaped by intellectual developments that have arisen since the early modern period. Some basic types of religious experience are also introduced. Chapter 2 continues the consideration of various kinds of religious experience and emphasizes the role of interpretation in different types of experiences. The

---

21. I take the term "critical-trust approach" from Kai-Man Kwan's excellent *The Rainbow of Experiences, Critical Trust, and God: A Defense of Holistic Empiricism* (New York: Bloomsbury Academic, 2011), although as we shall see in chapter 3, a number of philosophers have adopted this approach to religious experiences.

importance of background beliefs in interpreting and evaluating experiences is also noted.

The critical-trust approach to religious experience is introduced and defended in chapter 3. According to this approach, what seems to be an experience of God can be accepted as such unless there are compelling reasons to conclude otherwise. The ways in which influential philosophers such as Richard Swinburne and William Alston have developed this approach are examined. Some of the major criticisms of this approach to religious experience are also considered and responded to.

Chapter 4 provides a historical interlude by exploring the views of two of the most significant modern Protestant thinkers, Jonathan Edwards and John Wesley, on experiences of God. Both men lived during a time of intellectual upheaval as well as spiritual renewal and awakening, and both had to address questions about discerning the work of the Holy Spirit in the lives of believers. The manner in which they responded to accusations of "enthusiasm" and the perspectives they developed on the inner witness of the Spirit have had a significant influence on later Christians, especially evangelicals.

Some of the themes from Edwards and Wesley have found fresh expression among contemporary philosophers associated with Reformed epistemology. Chapter 5 looks at the ways in which thinkers such as Alvin Plantinga and William Lane Craig have used the notion of the witness of the Holy Spirit in conjunction with the claim that for the Christian, in appropriate circumstances, belief in God can be "properly basic." Some of the possibilities and limitations of these claims are examined.

No discussion of religious experience is complete without reference to mysticism because mystical experience is often portrayed as being at the heart of religious experience. Chapter 6 shows how the concept of mysticism used today is largely the product of movements and developments of the past several centuries. Special attention is given to the work of William James and Rudolf Otto, as well as to the more recent debate between the "perennialists" and the "constructivists" over interpretation in mystical experience.

Chapter 7 takes up the thorny set of issues stemming from religious diversity and disagreement and their implications for the critical-trust approach to religious experience. After examining some of the epistemic implications of religious disagreement, I argue that some form of natural theology is necessary if we are to apply the critical-trust approach to theistic experiences. My own view is that the most helpful form of natural theology is an inference to the best-explanation argument, and the phenomena from theistic experiences can form an important part of the data that require explanation. The chapter concludes by looking at two arguments that might be formulated on the basis of theistic experiences. Although as formal arguments neither is particularly impressive, I contend that elements from each argument can be taken and used effectively in a cumulative-case argument for Christian theism.

1

Religious Experience
Mapping the Conceptual Territory

Just what counts as a religious experience? This might seem easy to determine, but there is an astonishing variety of experiences that could be regarded as religious. Experiences of God or of supernatural beings, such as angels or spirits, are typically treated as religious.[1] Visions of Jesus or the Virgin Mary are religious, as is the experience of *sunyata* (emptiness) in Buddhism or *samadhi* (the insight into one's unity with Brahman) in Hinduism. The experience of making ritual offerings to Tu Di Gong, the earth deity, in a Chinese village to ensure a good crop is religious, as is chanting the mantra *namu-myoho-renge-kyo* (I take refuge in the Lotus of the Wonderful Law Sutra) in Nichiren Buddhism. But not every human experience can qualify as a religious experience. Having a vision of Lord Krishna while meditating is surely a religious experience, but for most people, paying the water bill is not. Praying in a mosque is religious, but mowing the lawn is not. Invoking the blessing of the *kami*

---

1. Saying that a person has an experience of God could be understood as meaning that the experience is veridical, and thus entailing that God exists and that the individual does actually experience God. In order to leave open the possibility that the experience might not actually be veridical, it is common to speak of an *apparent*, *putative*, or *purported* experience of God. Since, however, it is tedious to use such qualifiers every time we wish to refer to an experience that seems to be of God but might not be, I will omit them from what follows. Unless the context indicates otherwise, expressions such as "an experience of God" should be understood as referring to an experience the subject takes to be of God, regardless of whether it is veridical or even whether God exists.

(deities) in a Shinto purification ceremony is religious, but filling out one's income tax forms is not.

Other experiences are more ambiguous and harder to determine whether they are religious. For example, should the veneration of departed ancestral spirits be considered a religious experience? Although not typically discussed by Western philosophers, communication with ancestral spirits is common in much of the rest of the world. Western scholars do discuss experiences of paranormal phenomena such as near-death experiences, out-of-body experiences, clairvoyance, and telekinesis.[2] Are these religious too? What about the experiences of healing or cursing associated with shamans, witches, and other spiritual specialists? Though often studied by anthropologists and religious studies scholars, these phenomena are largely ignored by philosophers writing about religious experience.[3] Reports about miraculous events, especially miraculous healings, abound across religious traditions. Are these also religious experiences?[4]

Many experiences could be considered religious or just as easily be understood in nonreligious terms. Consider, for example, the experience of feeling one with nature while hiking in the mountains, or the experience of tranquility and joy derived from hearing beautiful music, or the experience of amazed gratitude and wonder at the birth of a child. For some, these are profoundly religious experiences. Others, though deeply moved by these experiences, would not regard them as religious. Some people interpret all of life as permeated with the presence and activity of God, so that even in harvesting crops or passing a history exam one experiences the gracious

2. See Gregory Shushan, "Extraordinary Experiences and Religious Beliefs: Deconstructing Some Contemporary Philosophical Axioms," *Method and Theory in the Study of Religion* 26 (2014): 384–416; Shushan, *Near-Death Experiences in Indigenous Religions* (New York: Oxford University Press, 2018); Ann Taves, "Psychology of Religion Approaches to the Study of Religious Experience," in *The Cambridge Companion to Religious Experience*, ed. Paul K. Moser and Chad Meister (Cambridge: Cambridge University Press, 2020), 25–54; and Fiona Bowie, "Miraculous and Extraordinary Events as Religious Experience," in Moser and Meister, *Cambridge Companion to Religious Experience*, 261–83.

3. See, e.g., Michael Winkelman, "Ethnological and Neurophenomenological Approaches to Religious Experience," in *The Study of Religious Experience: Approaches and Methodologies*, ed. Bettina E. Schmidt (Sheffield: Equinox, 2016), 33–51; and Edith Turner, "The Reality of Spirits: A Tabooed or Permitted Field of Study," *Anthropology of Consciousness* 4, no. 1 (1993): 9–12. One of the few analytic philosophers to take seriously reports of evil spirits and the demonic is Phillip H. Wiebe, *God and Other Spirits: Intimations of Transcendence in Christian Experience* (New York: Oxford University Press, 2004).

4. See, e.g., Kenneth L. Woodward, *The Book of Miracles: The Meaning of the Miracle Stories in Christianity, Judaism, Buddhism, Hinduism, and Islam* (New York: Touchstone, 2000); and Craig S. Keener, *Miracles: The Credibility of the New Testament Accounts*, 2 vols. (Grand Rapids: Baker Academic, 2011).

provision of God. What are understood by some as perfectly ordinary experiences can be taken by others to be manifestations of divine presence. Any acceptable understanding of religious experience must acknowledge not only the clear paradigm cases but also the more ambiguous experiences as well. In this chapter we will sort through some of the issues involved in identifying an experience as religious. We will also look briefly at how the concepts of religion and religious experience have been shaped by developments in the modern era and will suggest some general types of religious experiences.

Ann Taves notes that around the year 1900 European and American intellectuals in a range of disciplines became preoccupied with the notion of personal experience. Protestant and Roman Catholic theologians as well as religious studies scholars "turned to the concept of religious experience as a source of theological authority at a time when claims based on other sources of authority—ecclesiastical, doctrinal, and biblical—were increasingly subject to historical critique."[5] The increased prominence of religious experience in justifying one's religious commitments in the early modern period coincides with the growing religious skepticism of the time and disillusionment with traditional theistic arguments. Matthew Bagger states, "With all the more traditional avenues of theism's defense generally in disrepute, modern theologians and religious philosophers have repeatedly sought to justify religious belief rationally by reference to the individual's experience."[6]

The idea that religion is grounded in the religious experiences of key individuals became popular in the academic study of religion as well, and remained so until well into the twentieth century. But from the 1970s and '80s onward, the experiential approach to understanding religion has been sharply criticized.[7] In part this criticism was due to growing skepticism about the notion of religion itself; it became widely acknowledged that the current concept represents a modern construct that serves various agendas. Dissatisfaction with an experiential approach also stems from what today are seen as naive assumptions about the commonality of religious experiences across religious traditions and cultures, with insufficient attention given to their differences.

But giving more attention to the differences among religious traditions simply highlights the difficulty of determining the boundaries of the concept

5. Ann Taves, *Religious Experience Reconsidered* (Princeton: Princeton University Press, 2009), 3–4.

6. Matthew C. Bagger, *Religious Experience, Justification, and History* (Cambridge: Cambridge University Press, 1999), 1.

7. Stephen S. Bush, *Visions of Religion: Experience, Meaning, and Power* (New York: Oxford University Press, 2014), 23.

of religious experience. Robert Sharf observes that the current use of "religious experience" by religious studies scholars "is exceedingly broad, encompassing a vast array of feelings, moods, perceptions, dispositions, and states of consciousness."[8] There is no clear consensus on what is to be included or how we are to understand the nature of religious experiences. Yet despite its ambiguity, we cannot just dispose of the concept of religious experience. People do have experiences that are commonly identified as religious, and these experiences can be highly significant both for those who have them and for others. Taves wisely remarks, "After decades of critical discussion of the concept, we can neither simply invoke the idea of 'religious experience' as if it were a self-evidently unique sort of experience nor leave experience out of any sensible account of religion."[9]

In attempting to clarify the meaning of terms, it is always tempting to look for precise definitions. Definitions, of course, serve different purposes. Consider, for example, the definition of "religion" given by Ambrose Bierce in *The Devil's Dictionary*: "Religion: a daughter of Hope and Fear, explaining to Ignorance the nature of the Unknowable."[10] Although witty, this definition tells us more about Bierce's own views on religion than it does about the meaning of the term "religion." Acceptable definitions of "religion" and "religious experience" should accurately reflect current usage of the terms as well as the lived realities that they denote.

But we should not assume that the only, or even the best, way to clarify meanings is by providing unambiguous definitions. Some concepts can be clearly defined, while others cannot. Meanings can be clarified through means other than definitions. Moreover, we should not be misled by the difficulty of defining terms like "religion" or "religious experience." Many important concepts are very difficult to define, but we nevertheless are able to use them meaningfully in discourse.[11] Consider, for starters, the difficulty of defining the words "meaning," "knowledge," "justice," or "beauty." Even though precise definitions are almost impossible to provide, it does not mean that we cannot know the meanings of these terms or that we cannot, through careful description and contrast with other concepts, give accurate accounts of their meaning. Not all words lend themselves to tidy definition.

8. Robert H. Sharf, "Experience," in *Critical Terms for Religious Studies*, ed. Mark C. Taylor (Chicago: University of Chicago Press, 1998), 95.

9. Taves, *Religious Experience Reconsidered*, 8.

10. As cited in Hillary Rodrigues and John S. Harding, *Introduction to the Study of Religion* (New York: Routledge, 2009), 4.

11. See Joshua C. Thurow, "Religion, 'Religion,' and Tolerance," in *Religion, Intolerance, and Conflict*, ed. Steve Clarke, Russell Powell, and Julian Savulescu (New York: Oxford University Press, 2013), 155.

Even when use of a definition is appropriate, we should not expect greater precision than the subject allows. The meanings of some terms are vague because they are used to depict realities that are not very clear. Vagueness in a concept can be a necessary tool for effective communication when the reality one speaks of lacks clear boundaries. Consider the word "tall." Its meaning is imprecise and somewhat relative (Is 6'0" tall for a man? How about 5'10"?), and yet we have no problem understanding the word in general usage. As we shall see, there is some ambiguity and vagueness in the concept of religion, and therefore in the concept of religious experience as well. But, in part, this is because it is not always clear just what is to be included in the set of things designated religious. The problem, in other words, is not necessarily with the definitions as such, but rather that the realities these terms refer to are themselves messy and unclear.

The Concept of Experience

Since religious experiences are a kind of experience, let's begin by thinking about the concept of experience. On one level, of course, we all have a basic sense of what "experience" means, for experience is a fundamental and pervasive feature of human existence. The passing moments of each day include a vast array of experiences, some perhaps significant but most rather mundane. Even so, it can be difficult to characterize the notion of experience with any precision.

It is helpful to distinguish between an *event* and an *experience*. For example, a tree falling in the forest is an event but someone observing a tree falling in the forest has *the experience of seeing the tree fall*. The event itself is one thing, someone perceiving it is something else. Experiences, for our purposes, occur with people; they require a subject who undergoes the experience.[12] But we can also think of experiences themselves as events, for *a person having an experience* is an event. We normally think of experiences as momentary events of varying duration; they have a beginning and an end and occur at particular points of time.[13] We can, of course, consider experience in an extended sense as well, such as one's experience as a nurse in the oncology department or the accumulated experience of a lifetime. Unless

12. We can ignore here the complication posed by Buddhism, which acknowledges experiences but denies the reality of an enduring person who has experiences.

13. We will also ignore here the question whether there can be "timeless" experiences; that is, experiences that have no temporal duration. That there are such experiences is sometimes suggested by reports of mystical experience.

otherwise noted, however, we will use "experience" to refer to particular momentary events or a series of such events rather than in its more general or extended sense.

Experience typically involves awareness of an object or state of affairs. But in having an experience, must one be consciously aware of what the experience is about? Many philosophers include conscious awareness as a necessary feature of experience. Richard Swinburne, for example, maintains that "an experience is a conscious mental event."[14] Similarly, Caroline Franks Davis claims that an experience "is a roughly datable mental event which is undergone by a subject and of which the subject is to some extent aware."[15] Keith Yandell states that to have an experience "is to be in a conscious state which one is at least somewhat capable of describing."[16] The point here is that we do not normally speak of those in unconscious or comatose states as having experiences. But to say that having an experience requires being conscious does not mean that one is directly aware of everything that she experiences. One can have the experience of seeing the green lawn outside the window without being aware of just how long the grass is or the squirrel sitting in the grass.

Having an experience typically involves making a judgment of some kind about the experience.[17] This could include, among other things, judgments about the veridicality of the experience or how the person undergoing the experience should relate to the object of the experience. Judgments can be the product of careful deliberation and thought or they might be immediate and unreflective. Our judgments are often correct but they can also be mistaken. We should allow for degrees of clarity and explicitness in judgments, as they can be vague and often implicit. A closely related issue is that of interpretation in experience, something we will explore further in chapter 2. Experiences do not occur in a conceptual or social vacuum; we bring to them a range of prior assumptions, values, and dispositions, so that particular experiences are processed and understood in light of these factors.

Having an experience often involves an experience *of something*. That is, a person encounters or is made aware of an object or a particular state of affairs in the experience. In ordinary sensory experience the object might

14. Richard Swinburne, *The Existence of God*, 2nd ed. (New York: Oxford University Press, 2004), 293.

15. Caroline Franks Davis, *The Evidential Force of Religious Experience* (Oxford: Clarendon, 1989), 19.

16. Keith Yandell, "Religious Experience," in *A Companion to Philosophy of Religion*, ed. Philip L. Quinn and Charles Taliaferro (Oxford: Blackwell, 2000), 367.

17. George I. Mavrodes, *Belief in God: A Study in the Epistemology of Religion* (New York: Random House, 1970), 52.

be a tree or a desk—we see or touch the tree or desk. Given the "sharp-
ness" and "forcefulness" of ordinary sensory experience and our regular
engagement with the physical world in ordinary daily activities, we tend to
think of experience primarily in terms of what is delivered through the five
senses. Sensory experience is often perceptual as one perceives an object
through the senses. Much of twentieth-century analytic philosophy privileged sensory experience, giving it normative status and ignoring other,
nonsensory modes of experience. Philosophical discussions of religious
experience typically evaluate purported experiences of God in reference
to other kinds of experience that we generally accept as reliable. For many
philosophers, this means that sense experience provides the criteria for all
veridical experiences. As we shall see in subsequent chapters, this presents
challenges for those maintaining the veridicality of religious experiences. But
it is crucial to see that even in nonreligious contexts, we regularly experience
many things that are *not* accessible through the five senses—for example,
we remember a conversation from breakfast this morning, or we have a
sense of guilt over the misleading story given to a professor, or we see that
modus ponens must be a valid form of inference. These too are common
experiences, although none of them is derived through sense experience.

Kai-Man Kwan helpfully distinguishes six kinds of experience: experience
of the self, sense experience, interpersonal experience, moral experience,
aesthetic experience, and intellectual experience.[18] As we shall see, religious experience itself can include one or more of these kinds of experience
(e.g., a religious experience might include sense experience and/or moral
experience).

Experience of the self involves what is sometimes called the first-person
perspective, which underlies our ordinary experiences. Although the notion of the self bristles with controversy, the important point here is that
there is a basic awareness of one's self as a subject, the *I* underlying one's
other experiences and the agent of conscious activity. Whatever the actual
ontological status of this self, there is a subjective, first-person awareness
underlying the flow of one's conscious experiences, giving them experiential
unity. Moreover, this involves more than merely awareness of what is "out
there"; there is also a self-referential aspect to this consciousness. Not only
is there continuity of subjective awareness beneath the flow of experiences,
but the *I* as a subject can also reflect critically on this awareness, analyzing
it and constructing theories about it. Experience of the self can also take

18. Kai-Man Kwan, *The Rainbow of Experiences, Critical Trust, and God: A Defense of
Holistic Empiricism* (New York: Bloomsbury Academic, 2011), 8–9.

a more thoughtful nature, as one contemplates the purpose of life or the significance of one's experiences.

Sense experience is perhaps the kind of experience with which we are most familiar and which has generated the most philosophical debate during the past four centuries. In our daily activities, we are continually dealing with aspects of the physical world, and since we have access to the physical world largely through our five senses, it is not surprising that sense experience attracts so much attention. Moreover, given the stability of the physical world and the uniformity of the operations of the five senses for people in general, there is widespread agreement concerning the physical environment: water is wet and fire burns, regardless of historical context, ethnicity, culture, or language. To be sure, we can be "deceived" by the senses (e.g., the stick in the water is not actually bent), but as children mature and are socialized, they learn to make appropriate distinctions between veridical and illusory sense experiences. Not surprisingly, then, sense experience is often held up as the standard by which other forms of experience are to be assessed—the closer an experience approximates sense experience the more likely we are to regard it as reliable; the less an experience has in common with sense experience, the more skeptical we are about it. Experiences of something not detectable through the senses, such as God, are thus often regarded as problematic.

The third kind of experience identified by Kwan is interpersonal experience, that is, the direct experience of other persons. We accept that other persons exist and that we can directly experience them by talking with them, taking walks with them, loving them, or debating with them. To genuinely doubt whether other people exist is an indication of something seriously wrong with one's noetic faculties. But although we know that other people exist and that we can relate to them in many ways, it is notoriously difficult to demonstrate the reality of "other minds" in a non-question-begging manner. Repeated attempts to prove this reality on the basis of sense experience, for example, are widely regarded as unsuccessful. It is crucial to see that much more than simply sense perception is operative in our recognition of other persons. In identifying something as a person we do of course make use of the senses—we see a body, observe facial expressions, and hear a voice. But more than *just* sense perception is involved in my judgment that the physical object in front of me with the contorted facial expressions, flailing arms, and noisy demeanor is an angry person. Moreover, in typical cases, the judgment that this is a person is immediate and noninferential; only in questionable cases do we go through a process of considering the relevant evidence and then drawing the appropriate inference. Our recognition of other persons seems to be a basic experience—that is, an experience that is not derived from other more primitive experiences. This is significant, for theists hold that God also is a person, and thus experiences of God should, in some respects, resemble our experiences of other persons more so than our experiences of chairs or trees.

Intellectual experience includes the use of reason in a wide variety of ways, including in critical reflection on one's experiences and the ability to identify relationships between things, distinguish truth and falsity, and draw inferences from premises in an argument. There is an important distinction here between the epistemic, logical, and moral principles we use in making judgments and the experience of applying these principles in a particular judgment. Particular logical principles—the argument form *modus ponens*, for example—are one thing; the experience of applying logical principles in an actual inference is something else.

Moral experience is a basic feature of human life and includes awareness of fundamental moral principles and values, our obligation to do what is right, and feelings of guilt when we do what we know is morally wrong. Aesthetic experience is also an important part of human life, and it includes experiences of beauty through the visual arts, music, nature, and literature. The boundaries between these types of experiences are not hard and fast, and indeed elements of one or more types might be present together. In experiencing other persons, for example, we use sense experience as we perceive the body or hear the voice of another person. Moral experience typically involves experiences of others as well as some intellectual experience as we weigh various considerations in a given case, consult relevant moral principles, and decide the right course of action.

In addition to these types of experience mentioned by Kwan, we might also note the significance of memory, or the experience of remembering something, as another important kind of experience. Although it is distinct from the six types noted above, it can include experiences from each of them. Seeing cherry blossoms in bloom is one thing; remembering the experience of seeing the cherry blossoms is something else. It is difficult to exaggerate the significance of memory for our understanding of life and the world around us. Any experiences that are not *immediately present* to us are past experiences, and we have access to them through our memory. This applies to our religious experiences as well.

Our experiences as human beings are richly variegated, and we should resist attempts to reduce this diversity to just one or two basic types. In particular, we must be careful not to privilege sense experience in an unwarranted manner over other types of experience. Religious experiences are distinct from these types of experiences and cannot simply be reduced to any of them, although they can include elements from each.

The Concept of Religion

In order to understand what we mean by *religious experience*, we must have some grasp of what is meant by *religion*. But the concept of religion is controversial, with two issues in particular regarded as especially problematic: (1) it is said that the category is so ambiguous that it is unhelpful, and (2) the notion of religion itself as well as the concepts of world religions such as Hinduism and Buddhism are modern, Western constructs. Both issues are important, but we will begin by briefly addressing the second concern.

Philosophical discussions of religious experience generally focus on experiences within the so-called world religions—Christianity, Judaism, Islam, Hinduism, and Buddhism. But both the idea of world religions as such and the general category of religion as we use it today are to some extent constructions of modernity.[19] This is also the case with the concept of religious experience.

The idea of world religions, as distinct from merely local traditions, developed in conjunction with the modern conception of the world as one place that includes within it many diverse peoples and ways of living. The first use of the English term "world religions" was in the article "Religions" in the 1885 (ninth) edition of the *Encyclopedia Britannica*.[20] By the early twentieth century, the idea of a half dozen major world religions was becoming more widely accepted, so that theologian Ernst Troeltsch wrote an essay in 1923 in which he listed Christianity, Judaism, Islam, Buddhism, Zoroastrianism, and Confucianism as "the great world religions."[21] Interestingly, Hinduism was not included in the list, no doubt because the idea of Hinduism as a single identifiable religion was still taking shape. So the

19. See Tomoko Masuzawa, *The Invention of World Religions: Or, How European Universalism Was Preserved in the Language of Pluralism* (Chicago: University of Chicago Press, 2005); Talal Asad, *Genealogies of Religion: Discipline and Reasons of Power in Christianity and Islam* (Baltimore: Johns Hopkins University Press, 1993); Brent Nongbri, *Before Religion: A History of a Modern Concept* (New Haven: Yale University Press, 2013); Guy G. Stroumsa, *A New Science: The Discovery of Religion in the Age of Reason* (Cambridge, MA: Harvard University Press, 2010).

20. Tomoko Masuzawa, "World Religions," in *Encyclopedia of Religion*, ed. Lindsay Jones, 2nd ed. (Detroit: Gale, 2005), 14:9800.

21. Ernst Troeltsch, "The Place of Christianity among the World Religions," in *Christianity and Other Religions: Selected Readings*, ed. John Hick and Brian Hebblethewaite (Philadelphia: Fortress, 1980), 19.

concept of world religions, as well as the notions of Hinduism, Buddhism, and Islam as particular religions, is to some extent a recent, modern development. This is important to remember because discussions of religious experiences often give the impression that the so-called world religions are massive self-contained religious systems that have endured since ancient times and that each system has its own unique religious experiences. This can be very misleading.

Similarly, our current concept of religion is also to some extent a modern innovation. To say this is not, of course, to suggest that prior to the modern era there were no religious beliefs, practices, or institutions. Rather, the point is that our understanding of religion is in part a product of the intellectual and social changes that arose over the past four centuries, and in particular through European and North American encounters with the peoples of Asia, Latin America, and Africa. As Kevin Schilbrack puts it, "the concept of 'a' religion as a particular system of beliefs embodied in a bounded community was largely unknown prior to the seventeenth century, and the concept of 'religion' as a generic something which different cultures (or all cultures) share was not thought until the nineteenth century."[22] It does not follow from this, of course, that these concepts are somehow illegitimate or ought to be abandoned. As with any modern concept, their appropriateness depends on their ability to help us understand the realities to which they refer.

Our modern understanding of religion developed from the changes brought about by the growing European (and later, American) awareness during the sixteenth through twentieth centuries of two sets of binary oppositions. The first was the growing distinction between Christendom in Europe and the "secular" domains of intellectual and social life. From the sixteenth century onward there has been in Europe and North America an increasing tendency to differentiate religious from nonreligious domains in intellectual, social, and political life. Brent Nongbri observes, "What is modern about the ideas of 'religions' and 'being religious' is the isolation and naming of some things as 'religious' and others as 'not religious.'"[23]

22. Kevin Schilbrack, "Religions: Are There Any?," *Journal of the American Academy of Religion* 78, no. 4 (December 2010): 1113–14.
23. Nongbri, *Before Religion*, 4. But this should not be exaggerated. As Martin Riesebrodt notes:

> Even if we recognize the specific character of the concept of religion in Western modernity, this in no way means that the concept of religion expresses a cognitive distinction that is specifically Western. The distinction between religious and nonreligious is lacking neither in the premodern West nor in non-Western cultures, and the religious in the sense of institutions that are associated with superhuman powers has

The idea of religion as a distinctive sphere of human life, set apart from other aspects of public life, is thus related to the much-debated notion of secularization, especially as this relates to European societies. We can think of secularization as the (supposedly) empirically observable historical process of social, intellectual, cultural, and political change brought about by modernization resulting in the transformation of traditional religious patterns. At the heart of such changes are the increased fragmentation, differentiation, and pluralization of society and the decline, in some sense, of the social influence of religion.[24] Whether secularization is occurring is an empirical question to be answered through careful historical, social, and cultural observation. Although we cannot examine further the debates over the nature and extent of secularization, we can observe that societies and religious traditions have changed in significant ways under modernization and globalization and that this has affected how people think about religion and religious experience.

The second binary opposition behind the modern notion of religion is the distinction between Christianity and what increasingly became known as "other religions." It is difficult to exaggerate the impact of the voyages of discovery of the fifteenth and sixteenth centuries on European thinking. As the bewildering diversity of human cultures became increasingly evident, traditional ways of thinking were challenged. Explorers, diplomats, and missionaries sent back a steady stream of reports detailing the exotic habits of newly encountered peoples. The modern concepts of culture and religion developed in part out of attempts to explain the very different ways of thinking and living observed among the peoples of Asia, Africa, the Americas, and the islands of the Pacific.

Not only is the concept of religion as we understand it today a modern one, it is also ambiguous. Part of the problem is determining just what

---

existed in all ages and cultures. Religious activity has always been distinguished from nonreligious activity, religious specialists from other specialists, sacred places from profane places, and holy times from profane times.
Martin Riesebrodt, *The Promise of Salvation: A Theory of Religion*, trans. Steven Rendall (Chicago: University of Chicago Press, 2010), 1–2.

24. Especially helpful works on secularization include José Casanova, *Public Religions in the Modern World* (Chicago: University of Chicago Press, 1994); Rob Warner, *Secularization and Its Discontents* (New York: Continuum, 2010); Charles Taylor, *A Secular Age* (Cambridge, MA: Harvard University Press, 2007); Craig Calhoun, Mark Jeurgensmeyer, and Jonathan VanAntwerpen, eds., *Rethinking Secularism* (New York: Oxford University Press, 2011); Michael Warner, Jonathan VanAntwerpen, and Craig Calhoun, eds., *Varieties of Secularism in a Secular Age* (Cambridge, MA: Harvard University Press, 2010); and Peter Berger, *The Many Altars of Modernity: Toward a Paradigm for Religion in a Pluralist Age* (Berlin: de Gruyter, 2014).

should be included in or excluded from the concept. Must a religion include belief in God or gods? If so, then much of Buddhism, Jainism, and some Hindu traditions are excluded. But if belief in supernatural beings is not required, then should we not also include Marxism, Maoism, or secular humanism as religions? If, however, the meaning of "religion" is stretched so broadly as to include secular humanism, then the category of religion loses its classificatory value; it no longer distinguishes distinctively *religious* ways of thinking and living from other ways of thinking and living.

Some definitions of religion give priority to individual beliefs and practices over social and institutional aspects of religion. Philosopher and mathematician Alfred North Whitehead, for example, characterizes religion as "what the individual does with his own solitariness. . . . If you are never solitary, you are never religious."[25] In his enormously influential *The Varieties of Religious Experience*, William James famously defines religion as "the feelings, acts, and experiences of individual men in their solitude, so far as they apprehend themselves to stand in relation to whatever they may consider the divine."[26] James explicitly states that he is ignoring the social or institutional aspect of religion and is focusing on "personal religion pure and simple," since personal religion is the "primordial thing" from which emerge theological doctrines and ecclesiastical institutions.[27] This approach continues to exert influence and is reflected in Marianne Rankin's assertion that religious or spiritual experiences "are at the heart of the religious traditions, many of which can be traced back to life-changing moments of revelation and transformation."[28]

Although individual experience is important, this emphasis must be tempered by recognition of the significant role of social and institutional factors in religion. It is true that religions such as Judaism, Christianity, Islam, and Buddhism have grown out of the personal experiences of great leaders such as Moses, Jesus, Muhammad, and Gautama. But we should not exaggerate the role of the individual, since even these religious figures lived and taught within existing social, cultural, and religious contexts, and the social implications of their teachings quickly became institutionally established among their followers. Ever since the pioneering work of Émile

25. Alfred North Whitehead, *Religion in the Making* (New York: Macmillan, 1960), 16–17.
26. William James, *The Varieties of Religious Experience* (1902; repr., New York: Penguin Books, 1985), 31.
27. James, *Varieties*, 29.
28. Marianne Rankin, *An Introduction to Religious and Spiritual Experience* (New York: Continuum, 2008), 1.

Durkheim, one of the founders of the modern discipline of sociology, many scholars have understood religion primarily in social institutional terms. Regarding religious beliefs and rituals as symbolic expressions of social realities, Durkheim defined religion functionally as "a unified system of beliefs and practices relative to sacred things, that is to say, things set apart and forbidden—beliefs and practices which unite into one single moral community called a Church, all those who adhere to them."[29]

But if James can be criticized for ignoring the broader social and institutional aspects of religion, Durkheim is problematic for overemphasizing the social system. Although the individual cannot be separated from broader social patterns informing belief and practice, individual beliefs can be distinguished from the religious institutions of the society at large. Persons are responsible agents who develop particular beliefs and commitments, some of which may well be contrary to prevailing social norms. And some individuals have profound religious experiences that set them on a path quite different from what the institutional tradition expects and approves. Someone growing up in a Buddhist society, for example, can nevertheless find herself believing in the reality of a creator God just as a person living in an Islamic society can become convinced that there is no God. There is a delicate and complex relationship between a person's beliefs and experiences and her surrounding sociocultural influences.

Religions involve beliefs and ways of interpreting the world. Thus Keith Yandell helpfully defines a religious tradition as "a conceptual system that provides an interpretation of the world and the place of human beings in it, that builds on that interpretation an account of how life should be lived in that world, and that expresses this interpretation and life-style in a set of rituals, institutions, and practices."[30] Religions historically have offered particular ways of understanding the cosmos, humanity, and whatever it is that is said to transcend this world. Moreover, Yandell recognizes that most religions follow a general schema in which a deeply rooted problem is identified and then a solution proposed. "A religion proposes a *diagnosis* (an account of what it takes the basic problem facing human beings to be) and a *cure* (a way of permanently and desirably solving that problem): one basic problem shared by every human person and one fundamental solution that, however adapted to different cultures and cases, is essentially the

29. Émile Durkheim, "Definition of Religious Phenomena and of Religion," in *The Study of Religion: A Reader*, ed. John S. Harding and Hillary P. Rodrigues (London: Routledge, 2014), 100.

30. Keith Yandell, *The Epistemology of Religious Experience* (Cambridge: Cambridge University Press, 1993), 15.

same across the board. Religions differ insofar as their diagnoses and cures differ."[31] This description clearly fits major religions such as Christianity, Hinduism, Buddhism, and Islam, although the pattern is less apparent in other religions such as Shinto.

Religions also often include a belief in personal or impersonal powers or beings that are "superhuman" or "supernatural" in the sense that they transcend ordinary human capacities or forces of nature.

> A defining feature of many religions, which separates them from other deeply absorbing and meaningful activities, is their concern with powers or agents that are regarded as mostly existing beyond the grasp of the five senses or instrumental apparatus. These spirits, gods, or energies are thus "supernatural," in that they transcend or are beyond the natural world. They are not merely unseen physical energies, such as certain frequencies of light or electro-magnetism, as studied by physicists. The religious individual conceives of reality as somehow larger than what is normally perceived or conventionally studied by the sciences.[32]

In his seminal work *An Interpretation of Religion*, John Hick rejects the search for a clear definition of religion, opting instead to characterize religion in terms of the "family-resemblance" notion advanced by Ludwig Wittgenstein in his classic discussion of the meaning of the word "game."[33] Wittgenstein points out that there is no single feature shared by all games and no one definition that captures all the meanings of "game" in its many uses. Yet these diverse meanings do bear some resemblance to each other. There is a network of similarities among the many uses of "game," not unlike the physical resemblance among members of a natural family, so that we can recognize some relationships among the different meanings of "game" across various contexts. Similarly, although there may not be one characteristic shared by *all* religions, the similarities among them are sufficient for it to make sense to speak of, for example, Theravada Buddhism, Protestant Christianity, Mormonism, Vedanta Hinduism, and Shia Islam as religions. Instead of trying to come up with a tidy definition, focusing

---

31. Keith Yandell, *Philosophy of Religion: A Contemporary Introduction*, 2nd ed. (London: Routledge, 2016), 11. Emphasis in original. For a helpful guide to how the diagnosis and cure structure is reflected in Judaism, Christianity, Islam, Hinduism, and Buddhism, see Harold Coward, *Sin and Salvation in the World Religions* (Oxford: Oneworld, 2003).

32. Rodrigues and Harding, *Introduction to the Study of Religion*, 3.

33. John Hick, *An Interpretation of Religion*, 2nd ed. (New Haven, Yale University Press, 2004), 3–5; cf. Ludwig Wittgenstein, *Philosophical Investigations*, trans. G. E. M. Anscombe, 3rd ed. (New York: Macmillan, 1958), sec. 66.

on these patterns of similarity helps us to understand better what we mean by "religion."

This is the approach used by Ninian Smart, who identifies seven dimensions of religious phenomena characteristic of religious traditions. According to Smart, religions typically include a ritual or practical dimension, a mythological or narrative dimension, a doctrinal or philosophical dimension, an ethical dimension, a social or institutional dimension, an experiential dimension, and a material dimension.[34] Although our concern is primarily with the experiential dimension, it is important to see the multifaceted nature of religion and how religious experiences occur within a broader system of beliefs, institutions, and communal practices. Smart's multidimensional model reminds us that religion is not merely a private matter, for it has an inescapably social and communal aspect. Although it is individuals who have religious experiences, these experiences occur within broader social, cultural, and institutional contexts that give them meaning and significance.

Furthermore, when all seven of these dimensions are taken into consideration, it becomes clear that there can be significant overlap between the concepts of culture and religion. In some cases the distinction between the two is almost impossible to discern, so that it is difficult to know whether a practice is primarily religious or cultural.[35] The concepts of religion and culture, while distinct, are clearly related. This is evident in anthropologist Clifford Geertz's definition of culture as a "historically transmitted pattern of meanings embodied in symbols, a system of inherited conceptions expressed in symbolic forms by means of which men communicate, perpetuate, and develop their knowledge about and attitudes toward life."[36] Compare this with Roger Schmidt's understanding of religions as "systems of meaning embodied in a pattern of life, a community of faith, and a worldview that articulate a view of the sacred and of what ultimately matters."[37] Clearly there is considerable overlap between the concepts of culture and religion, and yet the concepts are distinct enough that the one cannot simply be reduced to or substituted for the other. This too has implications for how we think of religious experiences. Some experiences are clearly religious,

34. Ninian Smart, *Dimensions of the Sacred: An Anatomy of the World's Beliefs* (Berkeley: University of California Press, 1996).

35. For more on the relation between religion and culture, see Harold Netland, *Christianity and Religious Diversity* (Grand Rapids: Baker Academic, 2015), 24–39. Our understanding of culture today, like that of religion, is also a modern development. See Tomoko Masuzawa, "Culture," in M. Taylor, *Critical Terms for Religious Studies*, 70–93.

36. Clifford Geertz, *The Interpretation of Cultures* (New York: Random House, 1973), 89.

37. Roger Schmidt et al., *Patterns of Religion* (Belmont, CA: Wadsworth, 1999), 10.

while others are clearly not religious. But then there are those ambiguous experiences that *seem* religious in some ways but could also be interpreted in nonreligious ways.

Many people today prefer to speak of spirituality rather than religion, and of spiritual experience rather than religious experience. There certainly has been a major shift in public understanding of the connotations of the terms "religion" and "spirituality." Until well into the nineteenth century, within Christianity "spiritual" and "spirituality" generally referred to spiritual maturity or progress in sanctification and understanding of the great things of God. It was devout Christians, those adhering strictly to the path of discipleship enjoined by the Scriptures and the institutional church, who were labeled as spiritual. So long as the church remained faithful to its calling, spirituality was not in opposition to the church but rather was identified with those who followed its dictates. In this sense, spirituality could be understood as a particular aspect of institutionalized religion.

Today, however, spirituality is often contrasted with institutional religion. Religion, as we have seen, is a multifaceted reality that includes social institutions as well as doctrinal formulations. Many today reject the doctrinal and institutional aspects of religion while continuing to embrace its more personal, experiential components. The contemporary use of the term "spiritual" typically denotes this individualized experiential dimension.[38] Mary MacDonald observes that, "By the end of the twentieth century spirituality, long considered an integral part of religion, was increasingly regarded as a separate quest."[39] In this manner, spirituality has become contrasted with traditional forms of religion and increasingly identified as the preferred alternative to institutional religion. This recent reconceptualization of spirituality has often been associated with the so-called exotic spirituality of "the East," as expressed in popularized versions of Hinduism, Buddhism, and Daoism. However, this understanding of spirituality is also, at least partially, a modern construct.[40] Peter van der Veer states that there is no Sanskrit or Chinese equivalent to the English term "spirituality" and that "despite the ubiquitous reference to India and China (and indeed Asia) as

38. See Paul Heelas and Linda Woodhead, *The Spiritual Revolution: Why Religion Is Giving Way to Spirituality* (Oxford: Blackwell, 2005). The rejection of institutional religion for a highly personal and eclectic spirituality has deep roots in American history, going back to the early eighteenth century. See Leigh Eric Schmidt, *Restless Souls: The Making of American Spirituality*, 2nd ed. (Berkeley: University of California Press, 2012).

39. Mary MacDonald, "Spirituality," in Jones, *Encyclopedia of Religion*, 13:8718.

40. See Jane Naomi Iwamura, *Virtual Orientalism: Asian Religions and Popular Culture* (New York: Oxford University Press, 2011).

'spiritual,' spirituality is a modern, Western term." He brings together in insightful ways the concepts of spirituality and the secular in the modern era, arguing that "the spiritual and the secular are produced simultaneously as two connected alternatives to institutionalized religion in Euro-American modernity."[41]

Sociologists such as Robert Wuthnow have tracked the shift in American society away from institutional religion to a "spirituality of seeking." For Wuthnow, this shift reflects the fact that "people have been losing faith in a metaphysic that can make them feel at home in the universe and that they increasingly negotiate among competing glimpses of the sacred, seeking partial knowledge and practical wisdom." Instead of a spirituality of "dwelling" or "place," people now embrace a spirituality of "seeking" or "journey."[42] The term "religion" suggests rigid, authoritarian institutions; dogmatism and a lack of openness to alternative ways; and cold formalism. "Spirituality," by contrast, signifies flexibility and choice, tolerance and respect for alternative perspectives, room for doubt and searching, and the priority of personal experience. The increased percentage of those who identify as "nones"—that is, "people who answer 'none' when asked with what religious group they are a member or with which they identify"—is also related to this move toward a more personal and amorphous spirituality.[43] Many "nones" also characterize themselves as "spiritual but not religious" and have spiritual experiences. These experiences too must be taken into account when thinking about the range of religious experiences.

We will not make a sharp distinction between religious and spiritual experiences, since similar epistemological issues arise in both cases. Moreover, spiritual experiences often draw upon and incorporate the teachings and practices of institutional religions, although often in an eclectic and innovative manner. In what follows we will adopt Schmidt's definition of religion cited above as well as Smart's understanding of religions as complex multidimensional realities. Paradigm cases of religions, then, include Christianity, Islam, Buddhism, and Hinduism. But we will also use "religion" in a broader sense to include the beliefs and practices of those who reject institutional religion but practice some form of personal spirituality. When we

41. Peter van der Veer, *The Modern Spirit of Asia: The Spiritual and the Secular in China and India* (Princeton: Princeton University Press, 2014), 35.

42. Robert Wuthnow, *After Heaven: Spirituality in America since the 1950s* (Berkeley: University of California Press, 1998), 3.

43. Elizabeth Drescher, *Choosing Our Religion: The Spiritual Lives of America's Nones* (New York: Oxford University Press, 2016), 2. See also Linda Mercadante, *Belief without Borders: Inside the Minds of the Spiritual but Not Religious* (New York: Oxford University Press, 2014).

speak of religious experience, then, we are thinking primarily of experiences emerging within established institutional religious traditions, although much of what we say can also apply to those not identifying with any particular religion but practicing a more amorphous personal spirituality.

Religious Experience

Religious experiences are often contrasted with what are taken to be ordinary experiences of the world. Just as the concept of religion as a distinct domain of life became more popular with the rise of secularization, so too the idea of religious experience as a special kind of experience gained prominence in an increasingly secular world. "The conceptualization of 'religious experience' as something clearly separate from the rest of life only began to be tenable when religious interpretations of reality started to decline in power, and it became possible to imagine a range of human experiences that was *not* religious."[44]

This is perhaps most apparent when religious experiences include God, angels, or some other supernatural entity, as they do for many people. Thus Kai-Man Kwan speaks of a religious experience as "an experience that the subject takes to be an experience of God, or some supernatural being or state of affairs."[45] For Richard Swinburne a religious experience is "an experience that seems (epistemically) to the subject to be an experience of God (either of his just being there, or of his saying or bringing about something) or of some other supernatural thing."[46] Michael Peterson states, "*Religious experiences* differ, in part, from ordinary experiences in that what is experienced is taken by the person to be some supernatural being or presence (God either in himself or as manifest in some action), a being related to God (a manifestation of God or person such as the Virgin Mary), or some indescribable Ultimate Reality (such as the nondual Absolute [Brahman] or Nirvana)."[47] Many religious traditions accept the reality of an all-powerful creator God, or of spirits or demons of various kinds, so characterizing religious experience in this way makes sense.

But other religious traditions, such as Jainism, traditional Buddhism, and some forms of Hinduism, reject the existence of a creator God, and with

44. David Hay, *Religious Experience Today: Studying the Facts* (London: Mowbray, 1990), 10. Emphasis in original.
45. Kwan, *Rainbow of Experience*, 5.
46. Swinburne, *Existence of God*, 295.
47. Michael Peterson et al., *Reason and Religious Belief: An Introduction to the Philosophy of Religion*, 5th ed. (New York: Oxford University Press, 2013), 34. Emphasis in original.

Buddhism in particular the ontological status of supernatural beings or demons is likewise problematic. So unless we restrict religious experiences to theistic experiences, we should avoid defining them in terms of experiences of God or other divine beings. This makes the concept of a religious experience even more vague and difficult to define.

According to some, there must be something religiously significant about an experience that marks it as a *religious* experience. Thus, Keith Yandell maintains that a religious experience is "an experience doctrinally and soteriologically central to a religious tradition."[48] In other words, a religious experience includes a cognitive component and some connection between the subject's understanding of the experience and the broader doctrinal framework of the religious tradition of which the person is a part. This characterization works well for religious experiences within established religions but may be more problematic with those that go against what the relevant tradition teaches or with the experiences of those in the spiritual-but-not-religious category.

There are also much broader ways of thinking about religious experiences. Consider, for example, the definition offered in the *Stanford Encyclopedia of Philosophy*: "Religious experiences can be characterized generally as experiences that seem to the person having them to be of some objective reality and to have some religious import. That reality can be an individual, a state of affairs, a fact, or even an absence, depending on the religious tradition the experience is a part of."[49] This is indeed a broad understanding of religious experience, since a wide variety of things could be understood by the subject to have "some religious import." We will see in chapter 2 that, for some people, all of life is experienced religiously, so that their ordinary experiences of the world and events around them are interpreted in terms of God's presence and activity. This is taking religious experience in perhaps its broadest sense.

Sometimes religious experience is characterized in a particular way in order to highlight an especially significant aspect of such experiences. Thus, in *Understanding Religious Experience*, Paul Moser states, "A distinctive feature of religion consists in the role of *experienced religious meaning* as overarching existential meaning for a person's life."[50] Moser's concern is with religion's capacity to provide people with an understanding of life's

48. Yandell, *Epistemology of Religious Experience*, 15.

49. Mark Owen Webb, "Religious Experience," *Stanford Encyclopedia of Philosophy*, 1, http://plato.stanford.edu/entries/religious-experience/, accessed November 11, 2020.

50. Paul Moser, *Understanding Religious Experience: From Conviction to Life's Meaning* (Cambridge: Cambridge University Press, 2020), x. Emphasis in original.

overarching meaning, not only in the subjective or personal sense in which life has meaning for particular people but also in an objective sense of the actual meaning of human life, "what actually makes it *worthwhile* overall, that is, *worth our living* overall, despite its pain, frustration, and evil."[51] His proposal explains "how religious experiences and meanings are *integrative* for human selves, experiences, beliefs, practices and lives in a way that gives *overarching transformative meaning* to various human lives."[52] Moser provides a fascinating discussion of how such experiences were transformative for figures such as Leo Tolstoy, Gautama the Buddha, Confucius, Moses, and Paul. Obviously one can approach religious experience with this concern in view, and undoubtedly dramatic experiences do provide some individuals with an apprehension of life's overarching meaning that was nonexistent beforehand. But these are not the only possible kinds of religious experiences, nor is the provision of such transformative meaning necessarily their primary function.

For our purposes, it will be adequate to think of religious experiences broadly as experiences that seem to the subject, and perhaps also to other observers, to have religious or spiritual significance. Paradigm cases of religious experiences include what are taken to be visions of Jesus or Krishna, the experience of *samadhi* in Hindu meditation or *satori* in Zen, the biblical narrative of Moses hearing the voice of God while observing the burning bush, or perceiving an angel. Less dramatic cases might include experiencing God's presence while in prayer, experiencing peace while practicing *zazen* meditation, or having an overwhelming sense that God is directing one to take a certain course of action. What marks an experience as religious is that the subject or relevant observers regard it as religious. There is a bewildering variety of experiences across different religions that could fit this category, and obviously we cannot treat all kinds here. Our primary interest is with what are called theistic experiences, or experiences that are taken to be of God or some other supernatural being that acquires its meaning in relation to God. By "God" I mean an overwhelmingly powerful and benevolent being who is the creator of all that exists. Clearly this is not a theologically precise characterization of God as understood within Judaism, Christianity, or Islam, but it captures the heart of what many people mean by "God" when they say that they have experienced God. As we shall see in chapter 2, those with more doctrinally rich understandings of God will often have more highly ramified interpretations of experiences of God.

51. Moser, *Understanding Religious Experience*, 4. Emphasis in original.
52. Moser, *Understanding Religious Experience*, 24. Emphasis in original.

Perception and Religious Experience

Much of what we know about the world around us comes through our perception of things in the world. We look outside and see trees and houses. We take a walk and hear the birds singing and feel the pebbles on the path beneath our feet. In these examples we *perceive* things through the use of our senses of sight, hearing, and touch. The relation between perception and sense experience is so close that many philosophers identify perception only with sensory experiences. John Foster, for example, characterizes perception as "the sensory perception of items in the physical world by human subjects."[53] Many discussions on the epistemology of perception focus on sense perception, ignoring the possibility that there might be other forms of perception not dependent on any of the five senses.

But religious experience also often includes a form of perception. Many defenders of theistic experience draw an analogy between ordinary sensory experience and experience of God and argue that if ordinary sensory perception is accepted as a legitimate source of knowledge, then so too should theistic experience be accepted. Many religious experiences do involve one or more of the senses. Consider, for example, the report in the Gospel of Matthew of the experiences of the two women who visit the tomb after Jesus's crucifixion. They first see the empty tomb, then they see the "angel of the Lord," whose "appearance was like lightning and his clothing white as snow," and then they hear the angel speak to them (Matt. 28:2–7). Assuming the accuracy of the report, they had experiences in which sight and hearing played a significant part; they had perceptual experiences of the empty tomb and an angel appearing and speaking to them.

Other religious experiences, however, do not involve any of the five senses, and yet it can be argued that *something* is perceived in the experience. The philosopher and theologian John Hick, for example, speaks of an experience reported by his doctoral supervisor, Henry Price, Wykeham Professor of Logic at Oxford University. According to Hick, Price told him about a vivid experience he had in 1965, which Price described as "an experience of the sense of presence." Price wrote down a description of the experience and gave it to several friends, with strict instructions not to publish it while he was still alive. As reported by Hick, on a Sunday morning, after breakfast, Price was in an "unusually tranquil and peaceful frame of mind." He went into his drawing room, where he sat in his writing chair facing an empty fireplace. Hick recounts what happened next.

53. John Foster, *The Nature of Perception* (New York: Oxford University Press, 2000), 1.

Then in a gentle and gradual way it began to dawn on him that there was someone else in the room, located fairly precisely about two yards away to his right front. There was no kind of sensory hallucination, either visual or auditory, nothing seen or heard. He was not in the least alarmed, and the experience itself was so absorbing that he did not even feel any surprise at the time. It was just as if he had received a visit from someone he had never met before. They proceeded to have a conversation, though one conducted entirely by exchange of thoughts, about God's love for human beings, including himself. When God is said to love us this is not just some conventionally pious phrase but is to be taken literally. When we love someone we are fond of that person, or he is dear to us. In the same way, Henry was told, God was fond of him and he was dear to God.

Henry had a strong impression of the visitor's personality. He seemed to be very good and very wise, full of sympathetic understanding, and most kindly disposed towards him. He did not know how long the "conversation" lasted, guessing in retrospect about a quarter of an hour. But gradually he passed from exchanging thoughts with the visitor into a private meditation on what he had said, and after a while he became aware that the visitor was no longer there. The effects lasted for the whole of that day which, Henry said, was certainly the happiest day of his life. But it was something different from ordinary everyday happiness, more tranquil and also more profound, going down to the roots of his personality. He thought that "joy" was a better word for it.[54]

This account is fascinating for several reasons, but our main concern is with the fact that, assuming Hick's summary is accurate, Price clearly was aware of someone distinct from himself present in the room with him, although this person was not detectable through any of the five senses. Despite the lack of sensory input, Price's experience fits the structure of perceptual experience.

What is distinctive about perceptual experience is the structure of the experience. Perceptual experience is experience *of* an object or objects—that is, of something that is presented to one's consciousness. But the language of perception can be ambiguous. Keith Yandell illustrates the ambiguity with these sentences:

1. Kim seems less capable than she is. (Here, "seems" contrasts appearance with reality.)
2. It seems to Kim that she left the oven on. (Here, "seems" reports a shaky belief on Kim's part.)

54. John Hick, *John Hick: An Autobiography* (Oxford: Oneworld, 2002), 74–75.

3. There seems to Kim to be a chair in front of her. (Here, "seems" expresses how Kim is "appeared to"; whether there is a chair there or not, it remains true that if things are as they perceptually appear to Kim, a chair is in front of her.)[55]

These sentences indicate three distinct senses of *seems*—there is a contrastive sense in sentence 1, what Yandell calls an "opinionative or belief-expressive" sense in sentence 2, and an "experiential or perceptual" sense in sentence 3. This third sense is also often called the epistemic sense of "seems," and this is the sense of the term I will be using throughout this book. To use "seems" in its epistemic sense indicates what the subject is inclined to believe on the basis of perceptual experience. Adopting the epistemic sense of "seems," then, we can say that with perceptual experience "things and their properties seem *present* to you in a way they don't in nonperceptual thought."[56] When I perceive a tree in the yard I am "presented" with what seems (epistemically) to be, or appears to me as, a tree.

Consider the following experience that was reported to philosopher Phillip Wiebe. Although not particularly involved in religious matters, Sheila attended the United Church in Nelson, British Columbia, where the following event occurred.

As the congregation prayed during a communion service one morning, she saw Jesus walk out the door of the minister's office. He went to the center of the podium, looked at her and said, "Live by my commandments." The sandals on his feet made a noise as he walked, just as if he had been an ordinary person walking across the stage. She looked at her friends sitting on either side of her, wondering if they saw what she saw, but they gave no indication that they did. She wondered if she was hallucinating, so she looked again to where she had seen Jesus, and he was still standing there. This time he said to her, "I am here," which convinced her that her experience was real. She did not hesitate in making the identification.

Sheila was sitting about the fifth row from the front, twenty feet or so away from him, and saw his facial features very clearly. He appeared similarly to the image the tradition presents him in, but the color of the robe that he wore was quite unlike anything she had seen before. He was Mediterranean in appearance, and had dark hair. He was normal in size, and looked solid. The sense of beauty and love that emanated from him was overpowering. Sheila said that something extraordinary was present in the atmosphere of

---

55. Yandell, *Philosophy of Religion*, 159.
56. Alvin I. Goldman and Matthew McGrath, *Epistemology: A Contemporary Introduction* (New York: Oxford University Press, 2015), 131. Emphasis in original.

the church that she could not explain. . . . Sheila also said that she had the
sense of being confronted by God. . . . Sheila says that Jesus became very real
to her through this event, and that it solidified her faith.[57]

Sheila's remarkable experience clearly fits the structural pattern of perceptual
experience. Moreover, unlike Professor Price's experience, sensory experience is involved in Sheila's perception of Jesus: she sees him and hears his
voice. Yet more is at work than merely sense perception. Sheila experiences an
overpowering sense of beauty and love emanating from Jesus and feels that
she is being confronted by God. Such cognizance need not be any less genuine
merely because it is not reducible to deliverances from the five senses. But it
is also evident that some interpretation is involved in Sheila's experience.[58]
She recognizes the person as Jesus, identifies the love and beauty she experiences as coming from Jesus, and has a powerful sense of being confronted
by God. All of this involves judgments on Sheila's part. An experience of
perception often involves something being presented to one's consciousness in such a manner that he or she makes a judgment about the object of
perception.

Typically, especially with sense perception, there is a vividness or force
in what is presented that is absent in dreams or memory experiences. Paul
Gavrilyuk states, "In its basic form, perception entails an awareness of a
given object and is constrained by its object. As such, perception is different from imagination, memory, and reflection."[59] Perceptual experience
involves two basic components: there is "the given," or what is presented
to my consciousness, and then there is that part that I contribute to the
experience, a judgment of some kind that makes the experience intelligible.
Much of the debate over the epistemology of perception involves sorting
out how these two components function and relate to each other. Moreover, having a perception of an object does not guarantee that the object
actually exists apart from the perception or, if it does exist, that it is as it
is perceived to be. We are sometimes mistaken in beliefs we form on the
basis of perceptual experience. The weary traveler in the desert perceives
an oasis with trees in the distance, only to discover later that there is no
oasis. A man sees what he thinks is a fox only to discover that it is his
neighbor's dog. Thus the epistemology of perception is concerned with how

57. Phillip H. Wiebe, *Visions of Jesus: Direct Encounters from the New Testament to Today*
(New York: Oxford University Press, 1997), 62–63.
58. Interpretation in religious experience will be considered further in chapters 2 and 6.
59. Paul L. Gavrilyuk, "Encountering God: Spiritual Perception in the Bible, Tradition, and
Film," *International Journal of Orthodox Theology* 10, no. 1 (2019): 47.

we distinguish veridical perceptual experiences from illusory or misleading experiences.

But perception does not always involve judgments about the object of perception. I might perceive the dog on the side of the road but be so pre-occupied with something else that I hardly notice it, let alone make any judgment about it. One can perceive an object without thinking about it. Moreover, one can perceive an object without being aware of the identity or nature of the object. In the case of perceiving God, assuming this is possible, someone might perceive God without necessarily knowing that it is God that she is experiencing. As Jerome Gellman puts it, "A subject need not *take* the appearing object to be God in order to be said to be experiencing or perceiving God. God need only be presented to the subject in some way or other. To say that a person *perceives* God does not entail that he think about God or make a judgment about Him. And there are surely differing degrees of realization that it is God that one is perceiving."[60]

As we have seen, perceptual experiences are identified on the basis of their structure, not the phenomenal content of the experiences. The structure of perceptual experiences includes intentionality. In other words, perceptual experiences seem to point toward something beyond merely the subject undergoing the experience. Keith Yandell defines intentionality as follows: "An experience is *intentional regarding an object A* if and only if in order to give an accurate phenomenological description of the experience—to say how things at least appear to the experience's subject as she has the experience—one must use the concept of an *A*, where if *A* exists it is an object relative to the experience's subject."[61] An experience can have inten-tionality without being veridical. Take the experience of "seeing" an oasis in the desert; structurally, such an experience has intentionality. But the experience is veridical only if there actually is an oasis in the desert; it is nonveridical if there is not.[62]

Yandell also makes a helpful distinction between experiences that are *sub-ject/content* (s-c) in structure and those that are *subject/consciousness/object* (s-c-o) in structure.[63] Experiences that are s-c-o in structure appear to the subject to be experiences of something distinct from the subject. Perceptual experiences involving the senses are s-c-o in structure, such as when George

---

60. Jerome Gellman, *Experience of God and the Rationality of Theistic Belief* (Ithaca, NY: Cornell University Press, 1997), 15. Emphasis in original.

61. Yandell, *Epistemology of Religious Experience*, 34.

62. George Mavrodes, "Real v. Deceptive Mystical Experiences," in *Mysticism and Philo-sophical Analysis*, ed. Steven T. Katz (New York: Oxford University Press, 1978), 237.

63. Yandell, *Philosophy of Religion*, 26.

looks outside and sees a bird, or Mary hears a loud noise as the door slams shut. Yandell notes that s-c-o experiences can give rise to object claims, or claims that some object exists or has a particular quality. "An item O is an object relative to Mary if and only if 'Mary does not exist,' by itself or with any set of truths, *does not* entail 'O does not exist.'"[64] Object claims—the bird on the sidewalk has a broken wing—can be true or false, depending on whether the perceptual experiences giving rise to the claims are veridical or illusory. All religions make object claims of one sort or another, whether about God, Brahman, *nirvana*, angels, or whatever. Moreover, it is clear that some religious experiences do conform to the s-c-o structure. The example of the two women and the angels at the tomb of Jesus in Matthew 28 fits this pattern. Perceptual experiences involving one or more of the five senses are clearly s-c-o in structure. But can there also be perceptual experiences fitting this structure that do not involve any of the five senses? The account noted above concerning Henry Price's awareness of a person undetectable through the senses might well be a case in point.

Yandell argues that experiences that are simply subject/content in structure are not experiences of something distinct from the subject having the experience. These are experiences of an *aspect* of the subject. "An item *a* is an aspect relative to Mary if and only if 'Mary does not exist,' by itself or with some set of truths, *does* entail '*a* does not exist.'"[65] The following are examples of claims based on s-c experiences: I am full of an overwhelming sense of joy and peace; Tom is anxious; Susan has a headache. Subject/content experiences can give rise to aspect claims—that is, claims that some aspect of the subject exists or has some particular quality. But the aspect does not exist apart from the subject undergoing the s-c experience (pain does not exist apart from the subject experiencing pain).

Religious experiences can be of either the s-c-o structure or the s-c structure. The encounter with the risen Jesus, as recorded in Matthew 28, is an example of the s-c-o structure; someone who prays for God's special peace in the midst of a severe trial and then experiences an overwhelming sense of peace and comfort has had a religious experience of the s-c structure. In both cases, the question whether the experience is veridical is separate from that of the structure of the experience. Both kinds of experiences can have evidential value with respect to certain religious claims, although the kind of evidence provided will differ in each case. We will touch on this point again in chapter 7.

64. Yandell, "Religious Experience," 369.
65. Yandell, "Religious Experience," 370.

Types of Religious Experience

An astonishing variety of experiences fall under the category of religious experience. Theistic experiences, in which one seems to encounter God, are found not only in Christianity but also in other religions, including Judaism, Islam, Sikhism, and some forms of Hinduism. There are also reported experiences of angels or demons or spirits of one kind or another. Encounters with the spirits of one's ancestors are common in many religious traditions. There are enlightenment experiences in Jainism and Buddhism, although the nature of the experiences and what one becomes enlightened about differ in the two cases. There are claims to having experienced union with Brahman (Hinduism) or to having realized the reality of *sunyata*/emptiness (Buddhism). In many cultures and traditions, there are experiences of a vague sense of unity with nature or the cosmos. Religious experiences also differ phenomenologically. In some experiences, people hear audible voices; in others, they experience fits, catalepsy, convulsions, or falling over as though dead; other experiences include spontaneous vocalizations such as speaking in tongues or shouting; and in yet others, individuals undergo altered states of consciousness, including dreams, mesmeric trances, mediumistic trances, or possession. Religious experiences can be highly unusual, contrasting sharply with other ordinary experiences and available only to an elite group. Or they can be very much a part of normal life, without any unusual accompanying manifestations, such as when one simply is aware of God's presence or guidance in the mundane circumstances of ordinary living. How are we to make sense of such variety?

It is helpful to distinguish religious experience *tokens* from *types* of religious experience. A token is a single instance of a religious experience. When Sandra has a vision of the Virgin Mary, this is an experience token. When she has the same vision on three different occasions she has had three token experiences of the Virgin Mary. Religious experience tokens can be similar to each other or quite different. When a number of religious experience tokens are sufficiently similar in relevant respects, we can group them together under a religious experience type. When hundreds of people claim to have had visions of the Virgin Mary and the reported experiences are similar in relevant ways, then we have many examples of a religious type.

Kai-man Kwan states that the two primary criteria for inclusion within a religious type are the phenomenology and the ontology of the experience.[66]

66. Kwan, *Rainbow of Experiences*, 49.

The phenomenology of an experience is the "texture" of the experience, the kinds of sensations or feelings involved in the experience. When we speak of the ontology of an experience, we are referring to the kinds of things, processes, or properties that are included in the objects of the experience. Kwan argues that when determining a type of experience, the ontological criterion has priority over the phenomenological. He illustrates this by calling attention to sense experience, which is generally taken to be one type of experience. If, on the one hand, phenomenological factors are given priority, then it makes more sense not to regard sense experience as one type of experience but rather as five distinct types, since phenomenologically touch and sight are different. On the other hand, the five senses together enable us to experience a unified physical world despite the phenomenological differences in what the senses deliver, and thus it is reasonable to consider the senses as enabling a single type of experience—sense experience.

There are various ways in which we might classify types of religious experience, one of the most helpful classifications being that provided by Richard Swinburne.[67] One type of experience comprises "experiences that seem (epistemically) to the subject to be experiences of God or something supernatural, but where she seems to perceive the supernatural object in perceiving a perfectly ordinary non-religious object." An example might be someone looking at the night sky with all its stars and seeing this as the handiwork of God. Some interpretation is involved here, as someone else might observe the same object but not take it to be the handiwork of God.

In the second category are "the experiences that people have in perceiving very unusual public objects." The experiences of those who witnessed the post-resurrection appearances of Jesus would fit this category, although it is not necessary that what is publicly perceived constitute a miracle. Neither is it necessary that every person be able to perceive the unusual object. It could be that what is publicly perceived is available to some but not to others. It is also possible that the object of perception might be "experienced religiously" by some but not so by others.

While Swinburne's first two categories involve perception of public phenomena, the next three do not. The third category involves "cases where the subject has a religious experience in having certain sensations private to himself, sensations of a kind describable by the normal vocabulary used for describing the sensations that result from use of our five senses." Swinburne suggests that Joseph's dream of the angel in Matthew 1:20–21 might be

---

67. Swinburne, *Existence of God*, 298–300.

such an example. The experience was private for Joseph and not publicly available, but it seems that, if asked, Joseph could describe the appearance and speech of the angel in terms normally used for visual and auditory sensations.

A fourth category of experiences includes cases in which "the subject has a religious experience in having certain sensations private to himself, yet these are not of a kind describable by normal vocabulary." Although the content of the experience is such that some analogies to normal sensory experience might be possible, there is the feeling that words used in ordinary experience are inadequate and cannot capture the texture of the experience. Mystical experiences, which are typically held to be ineffable, might be examples of this category.

Finally, there are "religious experiences that the subject does not have by having sensations." In these experiences "it seems to the subject, perhaps very strongly, that he is aware of God or of some timeless reality or some such thing, and yet not because he is having certain sensations; it just so seems to him, but not through his having sensations—just as it may seem to me strongly that my hand behind my back is facing upward rather than downward, yet not because of any sensations."[68] Such experiences might fit the s-c-o schema noted earlier and be considered a kind of perception, as perhaps in the case of Professor Henry Price's experience noted earlier. But the more ordinary experiences of many Christians who have a sense of the presence of God at particular moments, although this awareness is not mediated through any of the five senses and does not fit the s-c-o schema, might also be included in this category. Experiences in which believers become convinced that God is "speaking" to them or "guiding" them, although this conviction is not brought about by any sensory experience, might fit as well.

Caroline Franks Davis lists six categories of religious experiences,[69] some of which clearly overlap with Swinburne's five categories. But she also adds an important new category, that of regenerative experiences. These are experiences that "tend to renew the subject's faith and improve his spiritual, moral, physical, or psychological well-being." Davis's inclusion of regenerative experiences is significant since these are "the most frequent type of religious experience among ordinary people—that is, people who are not mystics, ecstatics, prophets, or psychics."[70] This category includes the

68. Swinburne, *Existence of God*, 300.
69. C. F. Davis, *Evidential Force*, 32–64.
70. C. F. Davis, *Evidential Force*, 44.

conversion experiences of ordinary believers as well as of the great religious leaders, something any viable taxonomy of religious experiences must take into account. In the next chapter, we will examine several further types of religious experiences in which interpretation of the experience plays an especially significant role.

2

Religious Experience and Interpretation

Experiences often involve interpretive judgments as we try to make sense of what is presented to us. Whether it is our perception of dark and ominous clouds in the sky or an intense feeling of joy that overcomes us, we process our experiences by making judgments that enable us to act appropriately in light of what we encounter.[1] Doing so often involves some degree of interpretation. In this chapter we will examine various ways in which interpretation is involved in having or assessing religious experiences. In so doing, we will note the significance of background beliefs for interpreting experiences and also make some further distinctions in kinds of religious experiences.

Some judgments are immediate and clear: *That tea kettle is hot!* But others come more slowly and are more ambiguous: *That looks like a mountain lion on the rock above me, but it can't be because they don't live in this area.* The judgment about the tea kettle involves little interpretation, apart from the identification of the physical object as a tea kettle, whereas that about the mountain lion is more complex. That I see something on the rock above me is clear enough, but just what it is that I perceive is less obvious. The conclusion that it probably is not a mountain lion is an inference from the fact that they don't live in the area in question. We might say that

---

1. Not all experiences involve judgments. A person might, for example, see seagulls on the beach but be so preoccupied with other matters that this perception does not register—he simply is not consciously aware of the seagulls. Interpretation plays little, if any, role in this perception.

49

this conclusion reflects an interpretation of my experience of perceiving something on the rock above me. In this case an inference is involved, but interpretive judgments need not be the result of a conscious process of reasoning; they can be present in immediate observations.

Although interpretation is present in varying degrees with most experiences of the physical world, it plays a more significant role in experiences of nonphysical realities, such as emotional or moral experiences. Interpretation involves ascribing meaning and significance to something in light of what we already accept—that is, from our background beliefs and the wider social, cultural, and religious contexts in which we find ourselves. It is not surprising, then, that people from different cultures often understand or interpret experiences differently since they bring different assumptions and expectations to their experiences.

Religious experiences also involve interpretation, although the nature and extent of such interpretation are matters of controversy. Two extremes should be avoided. The first is the view that interpretation plays little if any part in religious experience, a perspective that fortunately is not widely held today. It is generally agreed that cultural, historical, and religious influences do affect the nature of our experiences, including religious experiences. More prevalent today, however, is a reductionistic tendency that regards religious experiences as little more than the products of social influences and background beliefs. Although shaped to some extent by our contexts, religious experiences cannot be *merely* the products of such influences.

Paul Moser helpfully observes that we must distinguish *the qualitative content* of an experience—what is presented to our consciousness—from *the interpretation* of that experience and that with interpretation comes the possibility of error in judgment.

> The interpretation of an alleged experience does not guarantee the reality of the experienced object, particularly *as interpreted*. It can miss the mark regarding the actual features and causes of an experience, and thus be misleading and mistaken regarding the experienced object. Interpreting an actual experience, in any case, is not creating that experience or its qualitative content. Interpretation can obscure the qualitative content of an actual experience for a person, but it does not constitute that content. So, there is room for error in such interpretation, given the independence of the content of an experience. . . . So, an experience can have a reality of its own, including in its qualitative content, apart from its being interpreted.[2]

2. Paul Moser, *Understanding Religious Experience: From Conviction to Life's Meaning* (Cambridge: Cambridge University Press, 2020), 46–47. Emphasis in original.

The possibility of being mistaken in judgments about an experience indicates that the experience cannot be *merely* the product of influences on the person having the experience.

In an influential 1965 essay on mysticism, Ninian Smart argues that some distinction must be made between experience and interpretation, but he argues that interpretations vary according to the degree of "ramification" they contain.[3] Smart uses the term "description" rather than "interpretation," and in what follows we will use these terms interchangeably. Consider the following descriptions of an experience: "I saw a dog" and "I saw a Yorkshire Terrier with beautiful black hair walking with a slight limp." The latter is more highly ramified than the former. Ramification refers to the extent to which a description of an experience involves terms or concepts that are theory-laden ("the Trinity," "glaciated landscape," "a meteor"), very specific ("golden retriever" rather than "dog"), or presuppose some specialized knowledge ("The professor's apology was made under duress"). More highly ramified descriptions commit the subject to more than what is immediately apparent in an experience. As Caroline Franks Davis puts it, "The more highly ramified a description is, the more it entails beyond what was actually observed."[4] Terms such as Holy Trinity, the Absolute, union, *bodhi* (awakening), or *nirvana* refer to concepts that gain their meanings through the doctrinal schemes governing their use within their relevant religious traditions and thus they have a high degree of ramification.

When a Christian uses "God" in a Christian context, part of the meaning of the term comes from the doctrinal statements that inform the Christian tradition, including "God created the universe," "God has acted through history," "God is loving and good," and "Jesus Christ is God." The concept of God within the Christian tradition is highly ramified since its meaning is determined by specific doctrinal claims. (It is, of course, possible for someone to use "God" in a less ramified sense, as meaning simply a supernatural being of some kind.) By contrast, when someone speaks of having the experience of being overwhelmed by peace and joy, the description is not highly

3. Ninian Smart, "Interpretation and Mystical Experience," *Religious Studies* 1 (1965); reprinted in Ninian Smart, *Concept and Empathy: Essays in the Study of Religion*, ed. Donald Wiebe (New York: New York University Press, 1986), 102. Citations are taken from the essay in *Concept and Empathy*. Keith Yandell makes a similar distinction between experiences that produce thin descriptions and those resulting in thick descriptions, depending on the phenomenological content of the experience itself as well as the degree to which the subject's understanding of the experience requires accepting other background beliefs. See Yandell, *Philosophy of Religion*, 2nd ed. (New York: Routledge, 2016), 160.

4. Caroline Franks Davis, *The Evidential Force of Religious Experience* (Oxford: Clarendon, 1989), 24.

ramified, since the concepts of peace and joy are readily understandable and fit easily within a variety of theoretically more tightly defined contexts.

Smart then distinguishes the mystic's interpretation of her own experience, which he calls *auto-description*, from an interpretation of the experience by someone else, or a *hetero-description*. Auto-descriptions can occur at the time of the experience or at a later time, as the subject reflects on her experience. Hetero-descriptions are interpretations of an experience by someone other than the person who has the experience. We have, then, the following kinds of descriptions or interpretations of religious experiences:

a. Low auto-description (auto-description with a low degree of ramification)

b. Low hetero-description (hetero-description with a low degree of ramification)

c. High auto-description (auto-description with a high degree of ramification)

d. High hetero-description (hetero-description with a high degree of ramification)[5]

Hetero-descriptions can come from someone within the same religious tradition as the subject or from someone outside that tradition, such as when a Christian or an atheist describes the experience of a Hindu. High hetero-descriptions by someone outside of the religious tradition of the subject can include sophisticated theoretical beliefs that serve as explanations, positive or negative, of the experience ("The vision Jim had could not have been from God since it called for immoral conduct" or "Sally's experience of peace and joy in the midst of loss was produced by the Holy Spirit").

The degree of ramification has implications for the ways in which an experience can provide epistemic justification for particular beliefs. The greater the ramification of an interpretation, the greater the need to defend its accompanying doctrinal commitments. That is, the justification of the relevant theoretical doctrinal beliefs does not arise simply from the experience itself. As Smart observes, "The higher the degree of ramification, the less is the description guaranteed by the experience itself. For where there is a high degree of ramification, some statements will be presupposed which have to be verified in other ways than by immediate mystical experience."[6]

5. N. Smart, "Interpretation and Mystical Experience," 104–5.
6. N. Smart, "Interpretation and Mystical Experience," 103.

Since people can be mistaken in their auto-interpretations, especially if they are highly ramified, "the criteria for judging mystical experience are partly exterior to the contemplative life."[7] This point applies more broadly than to just mystical experiences and it shows the importance of background beliefs for understanding and assessing experiences.

Background Beliefs

Our judgment about whether an experience is veridical or not does not flow merely from the experience itself but also from the relation between the experience and our other beliefs. Religious experiences do not occur in a cognitive vacuum; both the experiences and the interpretation or assessment of them take place within particular historical and social settings. When I see a car speeding down the highway, listen to a performance of a Mozart concerto, or sense what I take to be the guidance of the Holy Spirit, I bring to these experiences everything that goes into making me the person I am at that moment. Of course, what shapes me as a person includes much more than just my beliefs. So a comprehensive discussion of relevant background factors would include the impact of past experiences and what William Wainwright, following William James, calls "passional" factors in our reasoning.[8] But we will focus here on beliefs, especially the implicit or tacit beliefs that we take for granted.

Background beliefs can be divided into several categories. There are the "properly basic" beliefs we simply find ourselves accepting[9]—beliefs about the general reliability of memory, the reality of the external world, and so on. There is a certain constancy in such beliefs across historical and social contexts (it is not as if people in some cultures believe in the general reliability of memory but those in others do not). But there are also deeply engrained beliefs that have been shaped by our distinctive contexts, beliefs that most people in our particular context accept but that might not be accepted by others in different settings. Belief in reincarnation, for example, is deeply embedded in the belief structures of some cultures but not others. Then there are beliefs that are more particular to my own immediate context—beliefs I have that have been influenced by my family and friends or by political

7. N. Smart, "Interpretation and Mystical Experience," 1, 109.

8. William Wainwright, *Reason, Revelation, and Devotion: Inference and Argument in Religion* (Cambridge: Cambridge University Press, 2016), chap. 4.

9. Basic beliefs are beliefs that we accept but not on the basis of other beliefs. They are not inferred from other more fundamental beliefs. Properly basic beliefs are basic beliefs that are epistemically appropriate for us to accept. Properly basic beliefs are discussed further in chapter 5.

commitments I have because of my education. Finally, there are even more personal beliefs I have because of my past experiences—perhaps doubts about the trustworthiness of religious authority figures or even the reality of a God of love because of highly negative experiences I have had in the past. All of these beliefs help to shape how I understand my current experiences.

When someone has a religious experience or hears about someone else's experience, she does so within the context of an enormous set of prior beliefs that she already accepts. Let K stand for the set of relevant background beliefs that a person S has at the time of a particular experience. Most beliefs in K are not objects of S's explicit awareness; they are implicitly or tacitly accepted and only become objects of awareness when S focuses on them for some purpose.

Suppose that S has religious experience E. Whether it is reasonable for S to accept E as veridical is in part a function of E's relation to beliefs in K that S holds. Many of the beliefs in K will be true, or at least S will be justified in accepting them as true. But some beliefs in K will no doubt also be false or unjustified; nevertheless, S simply accepts them as part of her background beliefs. There is thus a sense in which the evidential force of E is relative to particular persons or groups depending on their respective background knowledge.[10] Whether it is reasonable for S to accept E as veridical depends in part on what S's background beliefs allow or lead her to expect. In this sense, one cannot simply state categorically whether accepting the veridicality of a religious experience is rational for everyone. Furthermore, justification operates at several levels, so that we need to ask not only about the justification of the claim that E is veridical but also about the justification of the relevant background beliefs in K that inform the judgment about E.

Imagine the following counterfactual scenario: Three modern individuals—Tom, Judy, and Ken—somehow find themselves back in Jerusalem at the time of the death of Jesus and each one has some understanding of Jesus's life prior to his crucifixion. Each is aware of the fact that Jesus was crucified and buried over a week ago. But each one now independently encounters what seems to be Jesus of Nazareth alive after his crucifixion. Each one now apparently sees him and hears him speaking. The man before them clearly looks like Jesus and identifies himself as Jesus. Let us call this experience EJ. Should they all accept what seems to be the case—Jesus was killed but now he is alive again? Is it reasonable for each to conclude that EJ is veridical?

10. On the person-relativity of evidence and arguments, see the fine discussion in W. Wainwright, *Reason, Revelation, and Devotion*, chap. 2.

Well, this depends in part on the background beliefs of each person. Let's assume that in addition to the properly basic beliefs typically found in K for most people, each one also holds certain background beliefs unique to him or her:

Tom's background beliefs (K^1):

1. There is a creator God who can and sometimes does reveal himself to humankind.
2. Miracles do occur.
3. There was something extraordinary about Jesus's teachings and actions prior to his death; God seems to have been active in Jesus's life in a very unusual manner.
4. Typically, dead people stay dead.
5. The physical senses can on occasion be misleading, producing false beliefs.
6. Extraordinary experiences require a higher degree of epistemic justification than ordinary experiences.

Judy's background beliefs (K^2):

7. There is no God or supernatural reality.
8. What is real is composed of physical properties and processes and is governed strictly by natural "laws."
9. Dead people stay dead.
10. The physical senses can on occasion be misleading, producing false beliefs.
11. The many reports of miracles are unreliable or, in many cases, simply fraudulent.
12. Extraordinary experiences require a higher degree of epistemic justification than ordinary experiences.

Ken's background beliefs (K^3):

13. There is a God, but God is so transcendent that human beings have no direct interaction with him.
14. Through certain mystical states one can discern some spiritual truths.
15. There is a supernatural realm inhabited by many spirits and demons that can produce highly unusual effects in our space-time world.

16. Typically, dead people stay dead, but there are some tantalizing reports of people coming back to life from the dead.

17. There are many reports of supernatural or paranormal events (healings, telekinesis, clairvoyance, levitation, etc.), and some are probably true.

18. Extraordinary experiences require a higher degree of epistemic justification than ordinary experiences, but reality is far more mysterious and complex than we think.

No doubt Tom, Judy, and Ken would each be somewhat confused and conflicted by EJ, but they would each respond to the experience differently based on their different background beliefs. Assuming that Tom is not aware of any factors that would undermine or defeat the veridicality of EJ and given his acceptance of 1, 2, and 3 in K^1, it would be reasonable for him to conclude that EJ is veridical.

But given 7, 8, and 9 in K^2, it would not be reasonable for Judy to assume that EJ is veridical. Undoubtedly, the experience of EJ could and probably should raise questions for her about some of her background beliefs, but as long as she accepts them, it would not be reasonable for her to accept EJ as veridical.

Assuming that Ken is not aware of any factors that would undermine or defeat the veridicality of EJ and given Ken's acceptance of 15, 16, 17, and 18, it would be reasonable for Ken to accept EJ as veridical, although his interpretation of the experience might well be different from Tom's.

In other words, given their respective sets of background beliefs, it can be rational for Tom, Judy, and Ken to draw different conclusions about the veridicality of EJ. And even if Tom and Ken both conclude EJ is veridical, they probably will have different interpretations of the experience and its significance. Tom, Judy, and Ken cannot all be correct in their interpretations and conclusions concerning EJ, but given a weak sense of rationality, they can each be reasonable in their conclusions. When background beliefs differ widely among observers of an event, a weaker sense of rationality can be appropriate as each makes judgments about the event. Thus two individuals who disagree over the veridicality of a particular religious experience, such as EJ, could both be (weakly) justified in their respective views.

Finally, while the question of whether an experience E can be accepted as veridical could be treated simply in terms of E and its relation to K for S, there is also a more fundamental sense in which the epistemic appropriateness of accepting the relevant background beliefs must also be addressed.

If we wish to move beyond the weaker, permissive sense of rationality to a stronger, normative notion of rationality, we will need to determine which relevant background beliefs in K should be accepted and which should be rejected. This involves assessing the truth or rationality of some fundamental background beliefs shaping S's understanding of reality. In the case of Tom, Judy, and Ken, this would mean determining the truth value of background beliefs such as 1 and 2 for Tom; 7, 8, and 9 for Judy; and 13, 15, and 16 for Ken.

Hard and Soft Religious Experiences

Interpretation is also involved in determining whether an experience is religious or not. Some experiences seem clearly to be religious, while others are more ambiguous. Consider the following experience reported to Canadian philosopher Philip Wiebe by Kenneth Logie, minister of a Pentecostal Holiness church in Oakland, California. The woman, Mrs. Lucero, was speaking in church about a previous vision she had had, when Jesus suddenly appeared in the church in front of the congregation.

> Kenneth reported another incident that took place in May 1959 in the same church. A woman in the congregation described a vision she said she had when she was in a hospital and was thought dead. Mrs. Lucero reported that Jesus appeared wearing the clerical robe of a Catholic priest. He told her to have faith in God. She explained that because she was of Catholic background, this apparel somehow assisted her in making the identification of the figure as Jesus.
>
> Kenneth says that when Mrs. Lucero got up to tell her story, she was wearing a black raincoat because the weather had been rainy that day. As she spoke she disappeared from view, and in her place stood a figure taken to be Jesus. He wore sandals, a glistening white robe, and had nail prints in his hands—hands that dripped with oil. Kenneth reports that this figure was seen by virtually everyone in the congregation, which he estimated at two hundred people. He also reports that the figure was filmed (in color) by a member of the church with the kind of eight millimeter movie camera popular at the time. Kenneth says that the photographer was so awestruck that he shook, and placed the camera on top of the organ in order to keep it steady. . . . Kenneth says that the effect upon the people in the church was electrifying. After several minutes Jesus disappeared and Mrs. Lucero was again visible.[11]

11. Phillip Wiebe, *Visions of Jesus: Direct Encounters from the New Testament to Today* (New York: Oxford University Press, 1997), 77–78.

This remarkable event raises many issues that we cannot pursue here. But whatever one concludes on other matters, it clearly is a report of a *religious* experience.

But other experiences are more ambiguous. Imagine Joe, a devout Christian, and Mike, an agnostic, camping out in the mountains. The night sky is unusually clear and filled with stars. As they marvel at the stunning beauty of the stars above and the peaceful stillness all around them, Joe is overcome by a sense of the awesome power and creativity of God. In a quiet and reverent voice he quotes from Psalm 19: "The heavens declare the glory of God; the skies proclaim the work of his hands." Mike looks at him and says, "Well, maybe. Or this could just be one of those unexplainable wonders of nature." Both Joe and Mike are looking at the same sky, but they experience it very differently. Does Joe have a "religious experience"—does he experience God the creator by observing the stars? One could certainly say so. But Mike, gazing at the same starry night sky, does not have a religious experience.

There is a measure of ambiguity in Joe's and Mike's experiences. Whether looking at the night sky is a religious experience depends on more than simply the phenomenology and content of the experience itself. In one sense, both Joe and Mike see the same thing. Yet their experiences are different. Joe takes the stars to be the handiwork of God the creator and he responds in worship. Mike simply sees the stars. Some experiences can be regarded as religious, but they can also plausibly be understood in a nonreligious manner, depending on one's background beliefs.

In considering the ambiguity of some religious experiences, it is helpful to adopt a distinction that is often made with respect to miracles, between hard and soft miracles. The notion of miracle is at least as controversial as that of religious experience, and although reports of the miraculous are found in other religions as well,[12] we will restrict our discussion to the idea of miracle in theistic traditions.

David Basinger observes that the word "'miracle' . . . is normally applied to unusual, remarkable events that it is assumed would not have occurred in the context in question if not for *the intentional activity of a supernatural being.*"[13] In the Christian context, for an unusual event to count as a miracle, God must be intentionally involved causally in bringing about that event. Other agents apart from God, such as angels or even human beings, can perform miracles, but theists hold that even in such cases, the source

---

12. See Kenneth L. Woodward, *The Book of Miracles: The Meaning of the Miracle Stories in Christianity, Judaism, Buddhism, Hinduism, and Islam* (New York: Touchstone, 2000).
13. David Basinger, "What Is a Miracle?," in *The Cambridge Companion to Miracles*, ed. Graham H. Twelftree (Cambridge: Cambridge University Press, 2011), 19. Emphasis in original.

of the miracle is ultimately the power and intentionality of God. We need not address the relation of God's causal activity to what are often called natural laws except to note that most Christian thinkers acknowledge that in some cases God can and does act directly to bring about a particular event, while in other instances he acts through intermediary causes. The notion of miracle is applicable in either case.

The idea of miracle includes both the event itself and its impact on those who become aware of the event. In one sense, of course, the event constitutes the miracle. Jesus of Nazareth being raised from the dead would be a miracle whether anyone ever knew about this or not. But built into the notion of miracle is the idea of a sign that communicates something. Miracles are highly unusual events that convey something about God's power and purpose, and it is the recognition of this divine activity that prompts us to identify something as miraculous. Part of what distinguishes a miracle from a random anomaly is the impact the event has on those who are aware of it. Our awareness of something as a miracle can be a kind of theistic experience, for in the miraculous event we encounter God acting in a certain manner.

But must a genuine miracle be something that cannot be explained in terms of strictly natural processes and causes? Some prefer a restrictive definition, defining miracles as exceptions and contrary to natural laws, whereas others adopt a much broader understanding of miracles. One way of accommodating both perspectives is to distinguish hard from soft miracles. The idea of a soft miracle, sometimes also called a coincidence miracle, comes from a 1965 article by R. F. Holland in which the following example is given:

> A child riding his toy motor-car strays on to an unguarded railway crossing near his house and a wheel of his car gets stuck down the side of one of the rails. An express train is due to pass with the signals in its favor and a curve in the track makes it impossible for the driver to stop the train in time to avoid any obstruction he might encounter on the crossing. The mother coming out of the house to look for her child sees him on the crossing and hears the train approaching. She runs forward shouting and waving. The little boy remains seated in his car, looking downward, engrossed in the task of pedaling it free. The brakes of the train are applied and it comes to rest a few feet from the child. The mother thanks God for the miracle; which she never ceases to think of as such, although as she in due course learns, there was nothing supernatural about the manner in which the brakes of the train came to be applied. The driver had fainted, for a reason which had nothing to do with the presence of the child on the line, and the brakes were applied automatically as his hand ceased to exert pressure on the control lever. He fainted on this

particular afternoon because his blood pressure had risen after an exception-
ally heavy lunch during which he had quarrelled with a colleague, and the
change in blood pressure caused a clot of blood to be dislodged and circulate.
He fainted at the time he did on the afternoon in question because this was
the time at which the coagulation in his blood stream reached the brain.[14]

This example illustrates the importance of background beliefs and interpretation in identifying something as a miracle. An atheistic naturalist, who
does not believe in God or other supernatural agents, after learning all the
relevant facts, would be entitled to conclude that this is a highly unusual
event that nevertheless has perfectly plausible natural causal explanations.
Nothing miraculous occurred. The mother, on the other hand, believing
in a God who can and does intervene in human affairs, is also reasonable
in regarding this as a case of divine intervention and thus a miracle. This
becomes even more plausible if we suppose that the mother was praying
specifically for God to save her child. Each perspective can be reasonable,
depending on the relevant background beliefs in light of which the event
is interpreted.

Adopting this distinction, then, soft religious experiences are experiences
that could plausibly be interpreted in strictly naturalistic terms but that,
given broader considerations, might also plausibly be understood religiously.
Whether one views the experience in naturalistic or religious terms depends
on the background beliefs one brings to the experience. An example of a
soft religious experience might be someone who, having spent considerable
time in prayer and fasting over an important decision she faces, claims to
have heard God's "voice" directing her to a particular course of action. In
the appropriate circumstances and with appropriate background beliefs, it
can be reasonable for her to believe that she has experienced God communicating with her. At the same time, it could also be reasonable for someone with a naturalistic worldview to regard this as yet another example of
wish-fulfillment, which has a perfectly reasonable naturalistic explanation.
Joe's experience, noted earlier, of seeing the starry night sky and worshiping
God the creator is also an example of a soft religious experience. With appropriate background beliefs, it makes good sense for Joe to treat this as an
encounter with God, although it can also be reasonable for Mike, with his
background beliefs, to understand the experience in strictly natural terms.

Hard religious experiences, by contrast, are experiences that cannot be
interpreted in strictly naturalistic terms; something about the experience—

14. R. F. Holland, "The Miraculous," *American Philosophical Quarterly* 2 (1965): 43.

the phenomenology or content of the experience or the broader context in which it occurs—makes it most reasonable to regard the experience as a real encounter with a divine being. The disciples of Jesus encountering the risen Christ after the resurrection—seeing him, hearing him speak, and touching him—would be a hard religious experience.

While soft religious experiences can provide some evidential value for the subject and for other observers, given the degree of interpretation involved in such experiences, their evidential force will be less than that of hard religious experiences. In general, the dispute over soft religious experiences is over not whether the experience is veridical but whether it is appropriate to ascribe religious significance to it. With hard religious experiences, by contrast, the dispute is not over the religious significance of the experience so much as over its veridicality.

Interpretation thus plays a significant role in soft religious experiences and affects how we assess them. Another way to put this is to say that judgment about the veridicality of an experience is related to the description or interpretation under which the experience falls. As Caroline Franks Davis puts it, "The veridicality of a perceptual experience is closely bound up with its auto-description, among other things. Perceptual experiences are veridical if the object was present, the event occurred, or the state of affairs obtained as it seemed to the subject (as described in his auto-description) and there was an 'appropriate' causal relation between the percept and the percipient." She observes that there is no single "right way" to describe a particular experience. "Which features are relevant and what degree of ramification and completeness appropriate depends largely on the context of utterance."[15] The context she speaks of includes one's background beliefs. Experiences that are not veridical under one description might be veridical under a less ramified description. Suppose, for example, that I see an Irish Setter, but I think it is a Golden Retriever. My experience would be veridical under description 1 below but not under description 2:

1. I see a dog.
2. I see a Golden Retriever.

An experience can be evidence for the truth of a more moderate claim, such as 1, even if it is not evidence for a more ramified or complex claim, as in 2. This too has implications for judgments about the veridicality of religious experiences.

15. C. F. Davis, *Evidential Force*, 25.

Cognitive Science of Religion

Interpretation can be relevant to religious experience in yet another way. There is a long history of critics attempting to debunk religion by providing naturalistic explanations for religious beliefs and practices.[16] For our purposes, *naturalistic explanations* are explanatory descriptions of a phenomenon that use only the empirical methodology of the natural and social sciences and exclude any supernatural entities as part of the explanation. Many assume that if a naturalistic explanation of religious belief or experience is available, then this somehow calls into question the truth of the belief or the veridicality of the experience. Naturalistic explanations are related to naturalism, although one can adopt a naturalistic theory about the origin of religion without necessarily embracing naturalism as a worldview. *Naturalism* is an ontological perspective about what exists and what kind of causal processes there are. That naturalism rejects the reality of God and other supernatural entities is clear enough, but beyond this there is surprisingly little consensus on what it entails.[17]

If naturalism is true, then there cannot be any veridical experience of God, since there is no God to experience. Thus whether veridical theistic experiences are possible depends in part on which perspective—naturalism or theism—is true. Setting this question aside, however, we can nevertheless consider whether naturalistic explanations of religion pose a problem for religious experience. We will look briefly at a new approach to the scientific study of religion—the cognitive science of religion (CSR)—that has produced results employed by both critics and defenders of theism. Our purpose here is not to explain CSR in any detail but merely to illustrate how its results can be interpreted in quite different ways.

Emerging in the 1990s, the cognitive science of religion is a growing interdisciplinary field of study involving psychologists, neuroscientists, anthropologists, linguists, and scholars of religion who apply the methodology and findings of the cognitive sciences to religious phenomena. Religious beliefs and practices have been common throughout history and remain so today in most societies worldwide. The main focus of CSR is to explain why belief in supernatural agents is "a near-ubiquitous feature of human

16. J. Samuel Preus, *Explaining Religion: Criticism and Theory from Bodin to Freud* (New Haven: Yale University Press, 1987). See Daniel L. Pals, *Eight Theories of Religion*, 2nd ed. (New York: Oxford University Press, 2006), for helpful introductions to the naturalistic theories of Karl Marx and Sigmund Freud.

17. Evan Fales, "Naturalism and Physicalism," in *The Cambridge Companion to Atheism*, ed. Michael Martin (Cambridge: Cambridge University Press, 2007), 118–28.

life."[18] Interestingly, in its concern with what is constant or universal among human beings, CSR goes against the influential tendency of twentieth-century anthropology to focus on differences among groups of people. CSR argues that the empirical evidence clearly shows that there are common cognitive features in humans that predispose them toward religious beliefs and practices. Justin Barrett and Roger Trigg state, "Primarily, CSR draws upon the cognitive sciences to explain how pan-cultural features of human minds, interacting with their natural and social environments, inform and constrain religious thought and action."[19]

Humans seem to have built-in natural tendencies to believe in supernatural entities such as God, gods, angels, or disembodied spirits. Based on his studies of children's beliefs about God, for example, Justin Barrett concludes,

> Children are prone to believe in supernatural beings such as spirits, ghosts, angels, devils, and gods during the first four years of life due to ordinary cognitive development in ordinary human environments. Indeed, evidence exists that children might find especially natural the idea of a nonhuman creator of the natural world, possessing superpower, superknowledge, and superperception, and being immortal and morally good. I call this type of supercreator god for short. That's right: children's minds are naturally tuned up to believe in gods generally, and perhaps God in particular.[20]

The findings of CSR support the idea that belief in superhuman agents such as God/gods is historically and cross-culturally common, and drawing upon theories of biological and social evolution, it provides explanations for this in terms of certain cognitive faculties or "tools" that have evolved because of their adaptive survival value. According to CSR, then, belief in supernatural entities such as gods and angels is a natural product or by-product of the evolutionary development of our cognitive faculties, and thus religious beliefs and practices are "natural."

Cognitive scientists of religion offer differing accounts of how these common cognitive mechanisms evolved, the details of which need not detain us

18. Jonathan A. Lanman, "Atheism and Cognitive Science," in *The Oxford Handbook of Atheism*, ed. Stephen Bullivant and Michael Ruse (New York: Oxford University Press, 2013), 489.

19. Justin L. Barrett and Roger Trigg, "Cognitive and Evolutionary Studies of Religion," in *The Roots of Religion: Exploring the Cognitive Science of Religion*, ed. Roger Trigg and Justin L. Barrett (London: Routledge, 2016), 4.

20. Justin L. Barrett, *Born Believers: The Science of Children's Religious Belief* (New York: Free Press, 2012), 3–4. Emphasis in original.

here. One of the more notable accounts, however, is what Kelly Clark and Justin Barrett call the Attribution Account. According to this explanation, "beliefs in supernatural agents, including ghosts, ancestor-spirits, and gods, have arisen in part because human beings are equipped with a functional cognitive unit—an agency detecting device—that identifies objects as intentional agents or events as caused by intentional agents, sometimes with only the slightest stimulation."[21] The cognitive mechanism responsible for attributing intentional agency to objects is called the hypersensitive agency detection device, or HADD. Michael Murray describes how HADD functions.

> HADD is triggered by various environmental stimuli including apparently purposeful motions (dots moving on a screen), configurations of matter (crop circles), or physical processes (dark clothes flapping in the breeze at twilight) with no apparent natural or agentive cause. When triggered, HADD spawns belief in unseen agents that are taken to be the causes of the motions, configurations, or processes. Evolutionary theorists hypothesize that such a mental tool would be adaptive since it would lead our ancestors to be especially sensitive to cues that might signal a predator. Furthermore, it would be adaptive for HADD to err on the side of excessive false positives since the cost of these would, for obvious reasons, be much greater than the cost of any false negatives. And indeed it does err in this way, thus explaining our tendency immediately to assume that bumps in the night are caused by some*one*.
>
> In light of the fact that HADD is hyperactive in this way, it generates many false positives and is thus unreliable. Of course, beliefs that are outputs of a mechanism known to be unreliable are unjustified, at least unless those beliefs have some sort of independent evidence supporting their truth. Thus, religious beliefs, spawned by HADD and not supported by independent evidence (and that covers the religious beliefs embraced by most folks) should be rejected as unreasonable or unjustified.[22]

In other words, belief in supernatural beings develops in part as a way of explaining natural phenomena that activate HADD. But while HADD has survival value—since the cost of being mistaken when there actually *is* a predator present is much greater than the cost of being mistaken when no predator is present—it results in many false positives, attributing intentional

21. Kelly James Clark and Justin L. Barrett, "Reformed Epistemology and the Cognitive Science of Religion," *Faith and Philosophy* 27, no. 2 (April 2010): 177.

22. Michael J. Murray, "Scientific Explanations of Religion and the Justification of Religious Belief," in *The Believing Primate: Scientific, Philosophical, and Theological Reflections on the Origin of Religion*, ed. Jeffrey Schloss and Michael J. Murray (New York: Oxford University Press, 2009), 170. Emphasis in original.

causal agency to beings that are not there. Thus, when it comes to supernatural entities, it is an unreliable belief-forming mechanism. CSR has relatively little to say about religious experiences themselves, as its focus is the origin of certain religious beliefs. But if it can be shown that the mechanism for forming beliefs about God and supernatural entities is unreliable, then one might naturally conclude that purported experiences of supernatural entities are also unreliable.[23]

Critics of religion sometimes use explanations from CSR to undermine the truth or rationality of religious beliefs.[24] Religious beliefs and practices are said to be, at best, the by-products of natural selection and are thus "accidental." Often the assumption is that if a plausible naturalistic explanation for religious belief can be produced, then this either refutes the truth of religious beliefs or undermines the grounds for the rationality of their acceptance. There are some important issues embedded in this assumption that we cannot pursue here. But let's assume that the basic account of CSR is acceptable, that there seems to be a natural in-built tendency on the part of people across cultures to believe in supernatural beings and processes, and that theories based on evolutionary adaptation can provide plausible explanations for this tendency. Several things should be noted about the implications of this for religious experiences.

First, since CSR addresses the origin of religious beliefs and practices, critics who rely on it must be careful to avoid the genetic fallacy. The ability to explain how beliefs came about says nothing about the truth of those beliefs. Speaking of naturalistic and evolutionary explanations of religious beliefs, Michael Murray and Andrew Goldberg note that even if they are plausible "such explanations don't explain religion away. After all, these accounts merely aim to explain the origins of religious beliefs and, as we all learned in our introduction to philosophy courses, an account of a belief's origin tells us nothing about its truth. . . . Nothing we say or discover

23. On the implications of CSR for religious experience, see Joshua C. Thurow, "Some Reflections on Cognitive Science, Doubt, and Religious Belief," in Trigg and Barrett, *Roots of Religion*, 189–207; and Hans Van Eyghen, *Arguing from Cognitive Science of Religion: Is Religious Belief Debunked?* (London: Bloomsbury Academic, 2020), 54–60.

24. See, e.g., Pascal Boyer, *Religion Explained: The Evolutionary Origins of Religious Thought* (New York: Basic Books, 2001); Scott Atran, *In Gods We Trust: The Evolutionary Landscape of Religion* (Oxford: Oxford University Press, 2002); and Daniel C. Dennett, *Breaking the Spell: Religion as a Natural Phenomenon* (New York: Viking, 2006). Helpful responses to such critiques include Murray, "Scientific Explanations"; Michael J. Murray and Andrew Goldberg, "Evolutionary Accounts of Religion: Explaining and Explaining Away," in Schloss and Murray, *Believing Primate*, 179–99; Charles Taliaferro, "Explaining Religious Experience," in Schloss and Murray, *Believing Primate*, 200–214; Thurow, "Some Reflections"; and Van Eyghen, *Arguing from Cognitive Science of Religion*.

about the origins of our religious beliefs is going to make any difference to our assessment of the truth of those beliefs."[25] Barrett and Trigg make a similar point.

> Some may immediately want to jump to the conclusion that if we can explain how we hold certain beliefs, and how they are interrelated with other features of human cognitive architecture, we are explaining such beliefs away. That, though, is far too quick. Many beliefs we naturally develop about the world around us are in fact true. They have to be if we are to function successfully in the world around us. For instance, babies very soon come to understand that objects should not be expected to go through solid walls. That they may have natural dispositions toward such beliefs surely does not count against their warrant.[26]

Furthermore, with respect to the assumption that HADD is unreliable in forming religious beliefs because it produces false positives, Murray points out that critics need to demonstrate "that HADD is unreliable specifically in the contexts in which religious beliefs are formed." After all, HADD is reliable in some contexts but not in others. "HADD might be unreliable when I hear creaking noises in the abandoned house down the block, but it might be quite reliable when I hear a whistled tune in the hall. Is HADD more like the former or the latter when it comes to religious belief?"[27] Answering *that* question will take one well beyond what cognitive science and the HADD hypothesis can deliver.

Many have pointed out that CSR cannot be used in a straightforward manner to either support or refute the truth of religious beliefs. That is, the findings of CSR can be interpreted in light of either theism or atheism. Barrett and Trigg state, "By itself, the science appears neutral with regard to whether or not religious (or non-religious) knowers are warranted in their beliefs. It appears to us that to either challenge or support religious beliefs by use of CSR, scholars must combine its insights with other philosophical commitments."[28] That is, if there are strong independent reasons for accepting atheistic naturalism, then the findings of CSR will be interpreted so that religious phenomena are given strictly naturalistic explanations. If, however, there are good reasons for embracing theism, then the same empirical data will be interpreted within a theistic framework.

25. Murray and Goldberg, "Evolutionary Accounts," 194–95.
26. Barrett and Trigg, "Cognitive and Evolutionary Studies," 8.
27. Murray, "Scientific Explanations," 171.
28. Barrett and Trigg, "Cognitive and Evolutionary Studies," 1.

Without getting into positive reasons for accepting Christian theism, it is worth observing that Christian teachings provide eminently plausible explanations for why people seem to have natural built-in tendencies to believe in God. Certain biblical and theological themes—such as that all humans are created in the image of God and that God has revealed himself in a general manner throughout the created order, including within the human conscience, so that all people have a rudimentary awareness of divine reality—make the findings of CSR unsurprising. This is what Christians might well expect.

> To those who believe in God, the origin and persistence of such beliefs may not be quite so strange. Theologians, such as Calvin, have often been prone to talk of a natural *sensus divinitatis*, a feeling of divinity, or a sense of the holy, in humans. We are not born with our minds as a *tabula rasa*, a blank slate, as was widely thought even a generation ago. Cognitive science now sees that the human mind is already inclined in certain directions, and the fact that our minds seem to naturally include some of the building blocks of religion may not be surprising from a scientific point of view. It certainly fits in with a theological understanding that God should perhaps want people to be able to have some rudimentary glimmerings of understanding, which would predispose them to religious belief.[29]

Barrett and Trigg refer to Calvin's notion of the *sensus divinitatis* within all persons, a God-given awareness of the divine, or as Paul Helm puts it, "a universal, immediate, intuitive conviction that God exists."[30] The *sensus divinitatis* can provide a theological explanation for what CSR has uncovered empirically. The relevant passage in Calvin's *Institutes of the Christian Religion* states,

> There is within the human mind, and indeed by natural instinct, an awareness of divinity. This we take to be beyond controversy. To prevent anyone from taking refuge in the pretense of ignorance, God himself has implanted in all men a certain understanding of his divine majesty. . . . If ignorance of God is to be looked for anywhere, surely one is most likely to find an example of it among the more backward folk and those more remote from civilization. Yet there is, as the eminent pagan [Cicero] says, no nation so barbarous, no people so savage, that they have not a deep-seated conviction that there is a God. . . . Therefore, since from the beginning of the world there has been no

29. Barrett and Trigg, "Cognitive and Evolutionary Studies," 9.
30. Paul Helm, *Faith and Understanding* (Grand Rapids: Eerdmans, 1997), 180.

region, no city, in short, no household, that could do without religion, there lies in this a tacit confession of a sense of deity inscribed in the hearts of all.[31]

It seems, then, that the findings of CSR actually provide empirical support for what Calvin is claiming. We should not assume that God could not work through a natural process, as suggested by CSR theories, in bringing about widespread awareness of God's reality. Perhaps something like HADD is the mechanism through which the *sensus divinitatis* Calvin speaks of is activated in persons. At the least, the empirical findings of CSR by themselves do not refute or even necessarily undermine the truth or rationality of belief in the reality of God. They can be interpreted in either naturalistic or theistic terms, and the question about which of these worldviews is rationally preferable must be settled on grounds other than simply the data provided by CSR.

Experiencing God through Natural Signs

So long as we think of experiences of God primarily as dramatic events such as Isaiah's vision of God in Isaiah 6, Saul's encounter with the risen Christ in Acts 9, or even more recent appearances of Jesus, it is easy to conclude that theistic experiences are rare. Most people do not have them. But many people do have more ordinary experiences in which God seems to be present.

Michael Rea encourages us to broaden our understanding of encounters with God so that God's presence and communication with people are experientially available to a much greater degree than generally thought. What Rea has in mind are "phenomenologically low grade sorts of encounters like sensing the majesty of God while watching waves crash on a beach or hiking down into the Grand Canyon, feeling awash in the love of God while singing hymns around the campfire, or feeling forgiven by God in the wake of confessing one's sins in prayer or hearing the Sunday morning liturgist declare, in the name of God, that the sins of the congregation are forgiven."[32] These are the kinds of ordinary experiences that anthropologist Tanya Luhrmann explores so effectively in *When God Talks Back*.[33] Luhrmann spent over two years observing and interviewing hundreds of

---

31. John Calvin, *Institutes of the Christian Religion*, ed. John T. McNeill, trans. Ford Lewis Battles (Philadelphia: Westminster, 1960), 1.3.1 (1:43–44). For the relation between the *sensus divinitatis* to the insights from the cognitive science of religion, see Clark and Barrett, "Reformed Epistemology," 174–89.

32. Michael C. Rea, *The Hiddenness of God* (New York: Oxford University Press, 2018), 91.

33. T. M. Luhrmann, *When God Talks Back: Understanding the American Evangelical Relationship with God* (New York: Knopf, 2012).

evangelicals associated with the Vineyard Christian Fellowship, probing their experiences of God. What is apparent from her study is that many people have experiences in which God is understood to be really present, speaking to them, guiding them, and loving and forgiving them. Yet God is not a physical being perceptible through our senses; when he "speaks" we do not (usually) hear an audible voice that anyone else might also hear. Luhrmann argues that experiencing God in this manner involves cultivating certain skills within the context of a worshiping community, so that one becomes able to discern God's presence and communication through what might otherwise be rather ordinary natural phenomena.

Many people do seem to experience God through experiences of quite ordinary features of our world. For example, many have a sense of the grandeur and creative power of God when they see the majestic beauty of the Grand Canyon. It is not simply that they intellectually accept the idea that God is a great creator; they have a feeling of awe and wonder at God's power, and they sense the Creator's presence as they look out at the rock formations. And yet many others, looking at the same formations, simply admire the beauty of nature without any awareness of God. It is not as if those who sense God's reality actually *see* God when looking at the Grand Canyon. When they perceive its many geological formations, they encounter the God who created these natural wonders. We might say that they experience the creative presence of God through perceiving the canyon. There is an element of interpretation at work in this experience, since others who see the same formations do not sense God.

C. Stephen Evans argues that in certain cases it can be helpful to think in terms of mediated experiences of God: by experiencing the Grand Canyon one might also be experiencing God. Evans observes that in mediated experiences "we experience one thing by means of an experience of another thing." Consider the following examples:

> An astronomer may examine the surface of the moon by looking through a reflective telescope. I may hear the voice of my son through a cell phone. In these cases the causal chain is more or less indirect. The light rays from the moon do not come directly to my eye but first impinge on the surface of a mirror, which the astronomer looks at. The sound waves from my son are not sent directly through the air to my ear, but first are converted into digital information, transmitted as electrical packets through various media, and are finally reconverted by my phone into sound waves.[34]

34. C. Stephen Evans, "Religious Experience and the Question of Whether Belief in God Requires Evidence," in *Evidence and Religious Belief*, ed. Kelly James Clark and Raymond J. VanArragon (New York: Oxford University Press, 2011), 41.

Even in cases where we think that we have direct, unmediated access to the object of experience (I hear music from the radio), there is a complex causal chain at work.

Similarly, there seem to be aspects of the world that, in appropriate circumstances, mediate experiences of God. In other words, in experiencing something in the world—the starry sky above or the Grand Canyon—one can also be made aware of some aspect of God's reality. Although he does not discuss religious experience as such, Evans provides an insightful proposal about mediated experiences of God through "natural signs" that can be applied to religious experiences. Evans develops the idea of natural signs of God in relation to the classical arguments for God's existence.

Why is it that although most philosophers conclude that the major theistic arguments fail as "proofs" for God's existence, there continues to be such interest in these arguments? Evans notes that even Immanuel Kant and David Hume, two of the strongest critics of the theistic arguments, could not quite dismiss the teleological argument. Both acknowledged that there is something in our makeup as human beings that keeps us coming back to the idea of design in the universe.[35] Evans builds on this by arguing that the theistic arguments are based on something that points to or mediates God's reality, even if it is difficult to take the insights at the heart of each and turn them into successful probative arguments. "Many of the classical arguments for God's existence, such as the cosmological, teleological, and moral arguments, are grounded in what I shall call 'natural signs' that point to God's reality."[36]

Evans adapts the notion of natural signs from the eighteenth-century philosopher Thomas Reid, who introduced the concept in reference to ordinary perceptual knowledge. A natural sign is "something that brings an object to our awareness and also produces a belief in the reality of that

---

35. C. Stephen Evans, *Natural Signs and Knowledge of God: A New Look at Theistic Arguments* (New York: Oxford University Press, 2010), 18–24. Hume's apparent openness to the idea of design is indicated by Philo's concluding comments in part 12 of *Dialogues concerning Natural Religion*, where Philo, generally taken as representing Hume, concludes "*that the cause or causes of order in the universe probably bear some remote analogy to human intelligence*" (David Hume, *Dialogues concerning Natural Religion and Other Writings*, ed. Dorothy Coleman [Cambridge: Cambridge University Press, 2007], 101; emphasis in original). Although Kant rejected the teleological argument as a formal proof of God's existence, he insisted that the argument "always deserves to be named with respect." Kant was fascinated by the attraction of the idea of design or purpose in nature, observing that this "increases the belief in a highest author to the point where it becomes an irresistible conviction." Immanuel Kant, *Critique of Pure Reason*, trans. and ed. Paul Guyer and Allen Wood (Cambridge: Cambridge University Press, 1998), B651–52, pp. 579–80.

36. Evans, *Natural Signs*, 2.

object."[37] Signs must not only be perceived; they must also be "read" or interpreted. Some natural signs are more ambiguous than others. "The natural signs that point to God's reality are signs that can be interpreted in more than one way and thus are sometimes misread and sometimes not even perceived as signs. They point to God but do not do so in a coercive manner. To function properly as pointers, they must be interpreted properly."[38]

Evans argues that if God exists, then there is good reason to think that some knowledge of God would be widely available and relatively easy to attain.[39] Awareness of God's reality would not be restricted to just a few individuals, nor would it require exceptional intelligence or the ability to follow complex arguments. But he also holds that knowledge of God would not be coercive and would be resistible.

> Though the knowledge of God is widely available, it is not forced on humans. Those who would not wish to love and serve God if they were aware of God's reality find it relatively easy to reject the idea that there is a God. To allow such people this option, it is necessary for God to make the evidence he provides for himself to be less than fully compelling. It might, for instance, be the kind of evidence that requires interpretation, and include enough ambiguity that it can be interpreted in more than one way.[40]

Natural signs pointing to God are both widely available and easily resistible. Theistic signs are a means, physical or mental, whereby a person becomes aware of God. They point to the reality of God rather than simply disposing us to form beliefs about God, and yet they are not coercive. The concept of a natural sign as evidence of the divine includes the idea that God is the cause of the sign, "that God created the sign to be a sign," and that there is a "natural propensity [in human beings] to form beliefs in God." Evans states, "If there are such theistic natural signs, we would then expect belief in God to be widespread, found in reasonably young children and across many cultures, and we would expect that those beliefs would be typically occasioned by the same types of experiences."[41] The idea of natural signs builds on the fact that human beings have a natural tendency to believe in God in certain circumstances, something that, as we have seen,

37. Evans, *Natural Signs*, 35.
38. Evans, *Natural Signs*, 2.
39. Evans, *Natural Signs*, 14.
40. Evans, *Natural Signs*, 15.
41. Evans, *Natural Signs*, 37–38.

is affirmed by the cognitive science of religion as well as the observations of Calvin. Natural signs could be one way in which this disposition or tendency for belief is activated.[42]

Although natural signs can be used as the basis for theistic arguments, formal arguments are not necessary for them to serve as evidence for God. "The signs can point to God's reality with no argument or conscious inference being part of the process."[43] The classical theistic arguments are each grounded in certain natural signs pointing to God's reality, and thus they provide a kind of mediated but noninferential evidence for God. Theistic arguments pick up on what is at the heart of the natural signs and develop these insights into formal arguments, but in so doing these arguments usually include at least one problematic premise. Nevertheless, even if a formal argument is inconclusive, the basic insight it builds on "may still point to God and make knowledge of God possible for those who have the ability and will to read the sign properly."[44] Evans also acknowledges that there is a sense in which perceiving natural signs can be understood as religious experiences.

> When a person comes to believe in God by way of a theistic natural sign, should this be construed as a direct experience of God? The analogy with Reidian natural signs suggests that the answer is yes. For Reid we experience physical objects by means of sensations. In a similar manner, if God has created the signs in order to make humans aware of his reality, and if there is a natural tendency to form a basic belief in God when one encounters the sign, then theistic natural signs could be seen as one of the means whereby humans come to perceive God.[45]

We will conclude this discussion by looking at the natural sign Evans suggests is at the heart of the cosmological argument.[46] The natural sign implicit in the cosmological argument is the experience of the world as "mysterious and puzzling," or the experience of "cosmic wonder" at the contingency of the universe; that is, it is entirely possible that nothing at all would exist, no universe of any kind. Of course, if that were the case, then

42. Evans, *Natural Signs*, 38–41.
43. Evans, *Natural Signs*, 45.
44. Evans, *Natural Signs*, 3.
45. Evans, *Natural Signs*, 182.
46. According to Evans (*Natural Signs*, 90, 132), teleological arguments are grounded in the natural sign of "beneficial order" and the moral argument is based on two signs: (1) our experience of ourselves as responsible and accountable moral beings and (2) our perception of the special value and dignity of human persons.

we would not be here to discuss natural signs. But here we are. Why then is there something rather than nothing? Since it is possible that nothing exists, why does *anything* at all exist?

> The perception of the world as contingent, as something that might never have been, is closely linked to the contrasting notion of something that lacks this character, something whose existence is in some way impervious to non-existence. . . . Implicit in our experience of cosmic wonder, in which we perceive the world as contingent, is a grasp of the idea that there could be a different manner of existing, a reality that has a deeper and firmer grip on existence than the things we see around us. . . . The experience of cosmic wonder, when we encounter objects in the universe or the universe as a whole and see this natural order as "contingent," might simply be a perception of the createdness of the natural world.[47]

In experiencing cosmic wonder, a person is engaging a natural sign through which they can become aware of the noncontingent creator God.

An example of how this can work is given by Paul Williams, a distinguished scholar of Buddhism who for twenty years was also a practicing Buddhist. Williams later converted to Roman Catholicism, and among the factors involved in his eventual rejection of Buddhism was his growing intellectual dissatisfaction with some central Buddhist metaphysical claims, including its inability to account for the contingency of the universe. It was Buddhism's failure to address satisfactorily the question "Why is there something instead of nothing?" that prompted Williams to look again at theism.

> I have come to believe that there is a gap in the Buddhist explanation of things which for me can only be filled by God. . . . Why is there something rather than nothing? Why is there anything at all? And why is there a world in which, among other things, the processes (causation, etc.) detected by the Buddha are the case? Why is it that this way of things *is* the way of things? . . . For me the question "Why is there something rather than nothing?" has become a bit like what Zen Buddhists call a *koan*. It is a constant niggling question that has worried and goaded me (often, I think, against my will) into a different level of understanding, a different vision, of the world and our place in it.[48]

47. Evans, *Natural Signs*, 62–63.
48. Paul Williams, *The Unexpected Way: On Converting from Buddhism to Catholicism* (Edinburgh: T&T Clark, 2002), 27–30. Emphasis in original. Evans refers to Williams's use of cosmic wonder in *Natural Signs*, 69–70.

In teasing out the implications of contingency—in turning the wonder of contingency into a Zen *koan*—Williams captures nicely what is at the heart of cosmological arguments and uses this as a window into God's noncontingent reality. The analogy to a Zen *koan* is especially intriguing, for just as the *koan* is used in Zen to stimulate a radically new perspective, so too a theistic natural sign can prompt one to become aware of a new reality—God.

Another example comes from the influential atheist J. J. C. Smart, who also sensed the force of the experience of contingency. In a 1955 essay Smart admits that although he thinks the cosmological argument itself is unsound, he is unable to dismiss the experience of contingency.

> However, now let us ask, "Why should anything exist at all?" Logic seems to tell us that the only answer which is not absurd is to say, "Why shouldn't it?" Nevertheless, though I know how any answer on the lines of the cosmological argument can be pulled to pieces by a correct logic, I still feel I want to go on asking the question. . . . That anything should exist at all does seem to me a matter for the deepest awe. But whether other people feel this sort of awe, and whether they or I ought to is another question. I think we ought to. If so, the question arises: If "Why should anything exist at all?" cannot be interpreted after the manner of the cosmological argument, that is, as an absurd request for the nonsensical postulation of a logically necessary being, what sort of question is it? What sort of question is this question, "Why should anything exist at all?" All I can say is, that I do not yet know.[49]

This haunting sense of cosmic wonder that Smart cannot get rid of can be seen as a natural sign pointing toward God.

Religious "Experiencing-As"

There is an influential tradition that looks at religious experience not so much in terms of individual episodic events but rather as a general way of experiencing life and the world. Religious experience in this sense is a religious way of interpreting life. There may be particular moments in which one is especially aware of God's presence, but these episodes are part of a more general pattern. This seems to fit the ordinary religious life of many believers, for whom sensing God's presence or having the conviction that God is guiding them or speaking to them is not a matter of having certain

---

49. J. J. C. Smart, "The Existence of God," in *New Essays in Philosophical Theology*, ed. Antony Flew and Alasdair MacIntyre (London: SCM, 1955), 46.

dramatic experiences but rather is an understanding of the broader flow of life. The totality of one's life, then, can be seen as a kind of extended way of experiencing God.

This perspective was developed in the 1960s by the theologian and philosopher John Hick. At a time when theology and philosophy of religion were still under assault from logical positivism, Hick's *Faith and Knowledge* (1966) marked a clear departure from previous approaches to religious epistemology. In this volume, Hick rejects the classical theistic arguments of natural theology as inconclusive at best and shifts the focus away from trying to demonstrate the truth of Christian theism, instead showing the rationality of Christians believing as they do.[50] Rather than attempting to show conclusively that God exists, Hick argues that it can be entirely rational for a Christian in appropriate circumstances to believe in God, and at the heart of this justification of belief are experiences of God.

Hick maintains that for most believers, it is not particular individual experiences but rather the believers' general experience of life that provides for them religious significance and meaning. "The primary locus of religious significance is the believer's experience as a whole."[51] For the typical believer, this is not a matter of inferring the reality of God from careful consideration of the evidence. "[The believer] professes, not to have inferred that there is a God, but that God as a living being has entered into his own experience. He claims to enjoy something which he describes as an experience of God."[52] In a 1971 essay Hick draws an analogy between religious experience and our experience of the physical world, a move that philosophers such as Richard Swinburne, Alvin Plantinga, and William Alston have also made. "The analogy I propose is that between the religious person's claim to be conscious of God and any man's claim to be conscious of the physical world as an environment, existing independently of himself, of which he must take account. In each instance a realm of putatively cognitive experience is taken

50. John Hick, *Faith and Knowledge*, 2nd ed. (Ithaca, NY: Cornell University Press, 1966). See also John Hick, *Arguments for the Existence of God* (New York: Herder & Herder, 1971). *Faith and Knowledge* helped to change the nature of the debate in religious epistemology. William Alston, whose *Perceiving God* will be considered in chapter 3, credits *Faith and Knowledge* with having shaped his own approach. "From the first edition, [*Faith and Knowledge*] made a profound impression on me, primarily for its insistence on the point that theistic faith, when live and fully formed, rests on the experience of the presence and activity of God in our lives." William P. Alston, "John Hick: Faith and Knowledge," in *God, Truth, and Reality: Essays in Honour of John Hick*, ed. Arvind Sharma (New York: St. Martin's Press, 1993), 25.
51. Hick, *Faith and Knowledge*, 113.
52. Hick, *Faith and Knowledge*, 95.

to be veridical and is acted on as such, even though its veridical character cannot be logically demonstrated."[53]

By experiencing the world as permeated with divine meaning, a believer is interpreting life in a very different way from a naturalist who sees everything in terms of strictly natural causes and events.

> This sense of "living in the divine presence" does not take the form of a direct vision of God, but of experiencing events in history and in our own personal life as the medium of God's dealings with us. Thus religious differs from non-religious experience, not as the awareness of a different world, but as a different way of experiencing the same world. Events which can be experienced as having a purely natural significance are experienced by the religious mind as having also and at the same time religious significance and as mediating the presence and activity of God.[54]

Interpretation is thus integral to a religious way of experiencing the world. But this is not unique to religious experience, since, according to Hick, *all* experience, including that of the secular naturalist, is inherently interpretive. Hick was influenced by Ludwig Wittgenstein's discussion of puzzle pictures—ambiguous pictures that can be interpreted in various ways—in his *Philosophical Investigations*. In this book Wittgenstein used the famous duck-rabbit drawing popularized by psychologist Joseph Jastrow to illustrate the interpretive element, what he called "seeing-as," involved in some cases of perception.[55] The duck-rabbit can be seen as either a rabbit's head facing to the right or a duck's head facing to the left. Either way of interpreting the drawing is possible. The lines on the page do not change, but what we see varies depending on whether we perceive a rabbit's head or a duck's head. Commenting on such puzzle pictures, Hick says, "We speak of seeing-as when that which is objectively there, in the sense of that which affects the retina, can be consciously perceived in two different ways as having two different characters or natures or meanings or significances."[56]

But whereas Wittgenstein regarded the seeing-as involved in puzzle pictures as unusual cases of perception, Hick claims that all of our conscious experiences include some interpretation, and he introduces the term

53. John Hick, "Rational Theistic Belief without Proofs," in *A John Hick Reader*, ed. Paul Badham (Philadelphia: Trinity Press International, 1990), 57.

54. Hick, "Rational Theistic Belief," 58–59.

55. Ludwig Wittgenstein, *Philosophical Investigations*, trans. G. E. M. Anscombe, 3rd ed. (New York: Macmillan, 1958), 194.

56. John Hick, "Religious Faith as Experiencing-As," in Badham, *John Hick Reader*, 36.

"experiencing-as" to convey this interpretive element. "All conscious experiencing involves recognition which goes beyond what is given to the senses and is thus a matter of experiencing-as."[57] One might object that in ordinary sense perception one simply *sees* the physical object and that it is only in cases of misperception that interpretation—or misinterpretation—enters into the experiential process. In looking at the ground, for example, one simply sees a tuft of grass. If we mistakenly think that the grass is a rabbit, then this is a case of faulty interpretation. But Hick insists that all conscious experience, including sense perception, occurs within an environment in which we attribute some kind of significance to what is presented in experience.[58] The interpretive element comes in even as we identify objects in ordinary sense experience—we recognize what is at our feet as a tuft of grass.

Experiencing-as occurs with differing degrees of interpretation. Our experiences of the world fall into three basic categories: physical, moral/aesthetic, and religious. The degree of epistemological ambiguity, and thus the need for greater interpretation, increases with each level. The most basic category of experiencing-as is that of the natural or physical world, followed by the moral/aesthetic level, with the religious category requiring the greatest amount of interpretation. "In the case of each of these realms, the natural, the human, and the divine, a basic act of interpretation is required which discloses to us the existence of the sphere in question, thus providing the ground for our multifarious detailed interpretations within that sphere."[59] To experience the world religiously is to attribute religious significance to it, and for the Christian, this is to experience all of life and history in light of God's presence and activity.

The religious dimension requires the greatest degree of interpretation because of the pervasive and irreducible religious ambiguity of the world. Having rejected the classical theistic arguments, Hick insists that we are left with inescapable ambiguity on religious questions.

> It seems, then, that the universe retains its inscrutable ambiguity. In some respects it invites whilst in others it repels a religious response. It permits both a religious and a naturalistic faith, but haunted in each case by a contrary possibility that can never be exorcised. Any realistic analysis of religious belief and experience, and any realistic defence of the rationality of religious conviction, must therefore start from this situation of systematic ambiguity.[60]

57. Hick, "Religious Faith as Experiencing-As," 39.
58. Hick, *Faith and Knowledge*, 96–97.
59. Hick, *Faith and Knowledge*, 107–8.
60. Hick, *An Interpretation of Religion*, 2nd ed. (New Haven: Yale University Press, 2004), 124.

The decisive factor that makes it reasonable for religious believers to believe as they do is religious experience. "It is as reasonable for those who experience their lives as being lived in the presence of God, to believe in the reality of God, as for all of us to form beliefs about our environment on the basis of our experience of it."[61]

Given the religious ambiguity of our world, we have a degree of "cognitive freedom" in religious matters. Although the physical environment can be ambiguous at times, interpretation generally plays a less significant role with physical objects than it does in the moral/aesthetic or religious dimensions. The physical environment is coercive in the sense that there is a narrow range of acceptable interpretations (if one fails to interpret fire appropriately, one gets burned). But there is greater cognitive freedom in the religious realm so that genuinely different interpretations of the world can be plausible. Christian thinkers often explain this ambiguity by saying that God desires a free and uncoerced relationship with his creatures, and thus an environment is necessary in which our behavior and beliefs are not compelled but can be somewhat freely developed. Although God has created us with a "religious bias" in our nature, religious belief and conduct are to be freely developed in our response to God. "In order to be cognitively free in relation to God we must possess an innate *tendency* to recognize his presence behind the phenomena of life, and yet a tendency which is not irresistible but which we may repress without doing violence to our nature."[62]

Cognitive freedom and religious ambiguity are related to Hick's understanding of faith. Faith is the interpretive element in religious experience, the "uncompelled subjective contribution to conscious experience which is responsible for its distinctively religious character."[63] Faith, as a way of interpreting the universe in light of God's presence and activity, is a "*total* interpretation, in which we assert that the world as a whole (as experienced by ourselves) is of this or that kind, that is to say, affects our plans and our policies in such and such ways." For Hick, "the primary religious perception, or basic act of religious interpretation" is "an apprehension of the divine presence within the believer's human experience."[64]

What are we to make of Hick's proposal? He is right to call attention to the role of interpretation in ordinary experience. How we understand particular experiences, as well as how we interpret the world in general, is

61. Hick, *Interpretation of Religion*, 210.
62. Hick, *Faith and Knowledge*, 139. Emphasis in original.
63. Hick, *Interpretation of Religion*, 160.
64. Hick, *Faith and Knowledge*, 114–15. Emphasis in original.

influenced by a wide variety of factors, including our background beliefs and commitments. The idea of a pure experience, untainted by any kind of interpretation, has been largely abandoned today, although, as we shall see in chapter 6, its possibility in mystical experience continues to be debated. Hick is also right in holding that many people do experience the totality of life and the world religiously. God is present and active throughout one's general experience of the world.

Furthermore, Hick correctly observes that there is greater epistemic ambiguity, and thus room for interpretation, in the moral and religious dimensions than there is on the physical level. The degree of epistemic ambiguity is indicated by the extent of disagreement among responsible persons within the three domains. There is little disagreement among those with normally functioning faculties over, for example, whether there is a chair in the room or whether the sound one hears is from a bird or a train. But there is increased disagreement on moral issues. This need not mean that moral relativism is correct. People can accept moral objectivity and thus agree, for example, that *the unjustified killing of any human being is morally wrong* but still disagree over what constitutes unjustified killing (e.g., capital punishment, abortion, killing an enemy in war). And there is certainly widespread disagreement among thoughtful and informed people over religious matters.

At the same time, however, Hick leaves us with important questions. For example, in emphasizing the totality of life as the arena in which religious experience occurs, he seems to ignore the significance of particular religious experiences. The two are not mutually exclusive, of course, and in his later work on religious pluralism, Hick does take into account the individual experiences of the leaders in the religions. However, his earlier discussions of "experiencing-as" minimize particular experiences in favor of a general way of interpreting the world.

Furthermore, Hick's work also fails to addresses exactly why someone should adopt a general religious interpretation of life in the first place. "Experiencing-as" can be a helpful way of speaking about the fact that some people seem to experience all of life in terms of the reality of God, but the question remains why some adopt this interpretation and others do not. Also, why do some people see the world as the handiwork of a creator God, while others, such as Buddhists, interpret life in terms of *karma* and dependent-origination? One answer, of course, is historical and sociological conditioning: those born into certain social and religious contexts simply find themselves interpreting life as Christians or Buddhists. But even allowing for the significance of such factors, social context is not automatically determinative. Not everyone in a Buddhist society interprets life in Buddhist ways, and the same applies to Christians. Conversion and deconversion are common realities as individuals discover new perspectives that they consider more plausible than what they previously held. Undoubtedly a variety of factors—one's background beliefs, influences from peers, and life circumstances and experiences as well as independent reasons one might have for religious commitments—come into play when explaining why a person adopts a particular religious interpretation of life.

Finally, Hick's notion of faith and experiencing-as in religion makes sense in a world that is highly ambiguous concerning religious matters. His comments on the "inscrutable ambiguity of the universe" suggest that rational considerations cannot indicate whether one worldview is more reasonable than others, that the reasons for and against Christian theism are roughly equivalent to those for atheistic naturalism or Vedanta Hinduism. But is this really the case? That there is widespread disagreement over such matters is clear, but it hardly follows from this that there is no correct position or that the available evidence does not favor one perspective more than others. In chapter 7, we will return to questions about the epistemic implications of religious disagreement and the place of natural theology in supporting the rationality of Christian theism. Although I acknowledge that there is some ambiguity in religious matters, I am also convinced that there are strong and persuasive reasons for preferring Christian theism over atheistic naturalism or nontheistic religious perspectives.

3

The Critical-Trust Approach

I f we never made mistakes about what we experience, then skepticism would not be such an attractive option. But we do err. What seems to be the case sometimes turns out to be otherwise. But if I can be mistaken on one occasion, how do I know that my other experiences are not also delusory? As the sixteenth-century skeptic Michel de Montaigne put it, "A wise man can be mistaken; a hundred men can; indeed, according to us, the whole human race has gone wrong for centuries at a time over this or that: so how can we be sure that human nature ever stops getting things wrong, and that she is not wrong now, in our own period?"[1] Skepticism about experience has a long history, going back to ancient Greece, India, and China.

There are two basic ways of responding to the fact that we are sometimes mistaken in our judgments. The first is to be skeptical of every belief unless we have indubitable grounds for accepting it. This was the path advocated by the seventeenth-century philosopher René Descartes, who was deeply troubled by the skepticism of thinkers like Montaigne. Descartes's infamous quest for absolute certainty must be understood within the broader context of widespread skepticism in early modern Europe.[2] During the middle of the eighteenth century, David Hume showed just how insidious

---

1. Michel de Montaigne, *An Apology for Raymond Sebond*, trans. M. A. Screech (London: Penguin Books, 1987), 156.
2. See, e.g., Richard Popkin, *The History of Skepticism: From Savonarola to Bayle*, rev. ed. (New York: Oxford University Press, 2003); Stephen Toulmin, *Cosmopolis: The Hidden Agenda of Modernity* (Chicago: University of Chicago Press, 1990); and Susan E. Schreiner, *Are You Alone Wise? The Search for Certainty in the Early Modern Era* (New York: Oxford University Press, 2011).

skepticism can be if one begins by questioning everything, including commonly accepted beliefs like causality. One lesson to be learned from the past four centuries is that if one follows Descartes, it is very difficult to escape pervasive skepticism.

The other approach, by contrast, begins by acknowledging that although we often are mistaken, in general we are justified in trusting our experiences unless we have good reasons not to do so. Thomas Reid, a contemporary of Hume, advocated this perspective in his refutation of Hume's skepticism. Taken up by later philosophers such as G. E. Moore, this approach affirms that we do know many things, that most of our experiences are veridical, and that we are justified in trusting our experiences unless we have good reasons not to do so. This, more or less, is the procedure we normally adopt in ordinary life. For example, with respect to sense experience and our awareness of the physical world, we generally *do* trust our sensory experiences unless there is reason not to do so. I believe that there is a computer on the desk in front of me because I have the experience of it visually seeming to be there in front of me. I believe that a dog is sleeping by the fire because I have the experience of it seeming to me that the dog is sleeping by the fire. In the absence of reasons not to trust these experiences it is reasonable to accept them as veridical. This applies not only to our perceptions of physical objects but also to our memory beliefs and intuitions.

In recent literature this approach has been known as phenomenal conservatism and is especially associated with Michael Huemer.[3] Chris Tucker states that phenomenal conservatism is the view that "if it seems to S that P, then in the absence of defeaters, S thereby has justification for believing P."[4] Unless one has good reason to conclude otherwise, what seems to be the case should be accepted as such. The notion of epistemic seeming, introduced in chapter 1, is crucial, and memory experiences, perceptual experiences, and a priori intuitions are understood as "kinds of seemings."[5] The term "seemings" refers to "a class of conscious mental states . . . that occur during the normal operation of perception, memory and intellectual reflection."[6] When I see the dog sleeping by the fire, I am having the experience of it *seeming to me that the dog is sleeping by the fire.* "Seems" is being used

3. See Michael Huemer, *Skepticism and the Veil of Perception* (New York: Rowman & Littlefield, 2001).

4. Chris Tucker, "Seemings and Justification: An Introduction," in *Seemings and Justification: New Essays on Dogmatism and Phenomenal Conservatism*, ed. Chris Tucker (New York: Oxford University Press, 2013), 1.

5. Tucker, "Seemings," 3.

6. Michael Huemer, "Phenomenal Conservatism über Alles," in Tucker, *Seemings and Justification*, 328.

here in an epistemic sense, as I form a belief about the dog on the basis of what appears to me to be the case. "Seemings," or experiences that present a particular state of affairs as obtaining, provide positive and noninferential reasons for beliefs about that state of affairs.[7]

Perceptual experiences, which typically involve an epistemic sense of seeming, generally have a forcefulness or vividness that is absent when one simply imagines an object. Consider, for example, the difference between imagining a tomato and perceiving a tomato.

> Even if you have a very vivid, very detailed imagination, or if you have very poor eyesight, you still would never confuse seeing a tomato with imagining one. The reason lies in what I call the "forcefulness" of perceptual experiences: perceptual experiences represent their contents as actualized; states of merely imagining do not. When you have a visual experience of a tomato, it thereby seems to you as if a tomato is actually present, then and there. When you merely imagine a tomato, it does not thereby seem to you as if a tomato actually is present.[8]

Huemer advocates what he calls the principle of phenomenal conservatism as stated above by Tucker.[9] A major reason for adopting the principle is the fact that without something very much like it, we cannot avoid the problem of regress in the justification of beliefs based on experience. As Huemer puts it, "If undefeated appearances are not a source of justified belief, then how is one to avoid skepticism about the external world, the past, values, abstract objects and so on? Unless this challenge can be met, we would be wise to place our trust in the appearances."[10] Phenomenal conservatism is a view about the justification of experiential beliefs— that is, the circumstances under which we are justified in accepting beliefs arising from experience. It maintains that "when something seems true to you, and you have no reason to think that this experience is misleading, then, from your perspective, it is sensible for you to believe it."[11] And this is certainly a reasonable approach to take with respect to experiences in general.

7. Logan Paul Gage and Blake McAllister, "Phenomenal Conservatism," in *Debating Christian Religious Epistemology*, ed. John M. DePoe and Tyler Dalton McNabb (New York: Bloomsbury Academic, 2020), 63.

8. Huemer, *Skepticism and the Veil of Perception*, 77.

9. Michael Huemer, "Compassionate Phenomenal Conservatism," *Philosophy and Phenomenological Research* 74, no. 1 (January 2007): 30.

10. Huemer, "Phenomenal Conservatism über Alles," 349. See also Huemer, *Skepticism and the Veil of Perception*, 175–78.

11. Gage and McAllister, "Phenomenal Conservatism," 65.

But should this approach also be used with religious experiences? Should religious experiences be presumed to be veridical unless there are good reasons to think otherwise? In a remarkable 1953 essay C. D. Broad, professor of philosophy at Cambridge University, defended a similar approach with religious experiences.

> When there is a nucleus of agreement between the experiences of men in different places, times, and traditions, and when they all tend to put much the same kind of interpretation on the cognitive content of these experiences, it is reasonable to ascribe this agreement to their all being in contact with a certain objective aspect of reality *unless* there be some positive reason to think otherwise. The practical postulate which we go upon everywhere else is to treat cognitive claims as veridical, unless there be some positive reason to think them delusive. This, after all, is our only guarantee for believing that ordinary sense-perception is veridical. We cannot *prove* that what people agree in perceiving really exists independently of them; but we do always assume that ordinary waking sense-perception is veridical unless we can produce some positive ground for thinking that it is delusive in any given case. I think it would be inconsistent to treat the experiences of religious mystics on different principles. So far as they agree they should be provisionally accepted as veridical unless there be some positive ground for thinking that they are not.[12]

Broad's comments are especially significant since, by his own admission, he was not a religious believer.[13] Furthermore, his comments were published at a time when Anglo-American philosophy, still heavily influenced by logical positivism, was hostile to religious claims, and thus any defense of the veridicality of religious experience was likely to be met with incredulity.

Broad's suggestion was later adopted by the Oxford philosopher Richard Swinburne in his influential *The Existence of God* (1979), where he defends what he calls the principle of credulity.[14] Since then, many philosophers have adopted something like this principle. We will consider several philosophers

---

12. C. D. Broad, "Arguments for the Existence of God," in *Religion, Philosophy, and Psychical Research: Selected Essays* (1953; repr., New York: Humanities, 1969), 197. Emphasis in original.

13. Broad, "Arguments for the Existence of God," 2.

14. More recently Swinburne has defended this approach in the context of discussions of phenomenal conservatism. See Richard Swinburne, "Phenomenal Conservatism and Religious Experience," in *Knowledge, Belief, and God: New Insights in Religious Epistemology*, ed. Matthew A. Benton, John Hawthorne, and Dani Rabinowitz (New York: Oxford University Press, 2018), 322–38.

who defend this approach to religious experiences, and except when discussing Swinburne's use of the principle, we will speak of this as the *critical-trust approach* to experiences, whether religious or not.

Swinburne's Principle of Credulity

Richard Swinburne's *The Existence of God* is arguably the most rigorous and influential work on natural theology in the twentieth century. Swinburne presents a complex inductive argument that appeals to a variety of evidential factors and argues that on balance it is more probable that God exists than that he does not. One of the phenomena Swinburne considers in this calculation is religious experience. Swinburne argues that a person who has an experience that he or she takes to be an experience of God has "good reason for believing that there is a God—other things being equal—especially if it is a forceful experience."[15] But he is not merely concerned with the evidential force of religious experience for the person having the experience; his interest is in the role that religious experience can play in a broader cumulative-case argument for God's existence. Thus religious experience is one factor among others demanding explanation, and Swinburne concludes that "the experience of so many people in their moments of religious vision corroborates what nature and history show to be quite likely—that there is a God who made and sustains man and the universe."[16]

Swinburne uses the term "perceive" in speaking about the awareness of God in theistic religious experiences, and he draws an analogy between awareness of objects through sense perception and apprehension of God. But, according to Swinburne, in perceiving God we are not using a distinctive "spiritual sense," something in addition to the five senses, that enables awareness of God.[17] Swinburne states, "'Perceive' is the general verb for awareness of something apart from oneself, which may be mediated by any of the ordinary senses—for example, it may be a matter of seeing or hearing or tasting—or by none of these." Swinburne accepts the causal theory of perception, so that "S perceives x . . . if and only if an experience of its seeming (epistemically) to S that x is present is caused by x's being present. So S has an experience of God if and only if its seeming to him that God is

15. Richard Swinburne, *The Existence of God*, 2nd ed. (New York: Oxford University Press, 2004), 325.

16. Swinburne, *Existence of God*, 342.

17. William J. Abraham, "Analytic Philosophers of Religion," in *The Spiritual Senses: Perceiving God in Western Christianity*, ed. Paul L. Gavrilyuk and Sarah Coakley (Cambridge: Cambridge University Press, 2012), 280.

present is in fact caused by God being present."[18] Perceptions can be public or private. Public perceptions are in principle available to anyone rightly situated with properly functioning faculties. In the case of private perceptions, however, not just anyone rightly situated with properly functioning faculties will perceive the object. Most religious experiences involve private, not public, perceptions.

Swinburne's principle of credulity can be stated simply: "It is a principle of rationality that (in the absence of special considerations) if it seems (epistemically) to a subject that x is present (and has some characteristic), then probably x is present (and has that characteristic); what one seems to perceive is probably so."[19] Or, as he put it in a later work, "It is basic to human knowledge of the world that we believe things are as they seem to be in the absence of positive evidence to the contrary."[20]

Most of what we believe about the world, we accept on the authority of others. Everything beyond what we can know through our own experience—including matters in geography, history, and science—we accept based on what others perceive and report. Thus Swinburne combines the principle of credulity with the principle of testimony: In the absence of special considerations, the experiences of others are (probably) as they report them. That is, "Those who do not have an experience of a certain type ought to believe any others when they say that they do—again, in the absence of evidence of deceit or delusion. . . . In the absence of counterevidence, we ought to believe that things are as they seem to be to other people; and we do, of course, normally so assume."[21] Although more attention is generally given to the principle of credulity, the principle of testimony has special significance for the epistemology of religious experience.[22] Unless I personally have religious experiences, my access to them comes through the reports of others who have had such experiences, in other words, through the testimony of others.

Whereas the principle of credulity applies to a person having a religious experience, the principle of testimony applies to those who learn about

18. Swinburne, *Existence of God*, 296.

19. Swinburne, *Existence of God*, 303.

20. Richard Swinburne, *Is There a God?*, rev. ed. (New York: Oxford University Press, 2010), 115–16. See also Richard Swinburne, *Epistemic Justification* (New York: Oxford University Press, 2001), 141–49.

21. Swinburne, *Is There a God?*, 116.

22. On the significance of testimony, see Jennifer Lackey, "The Epistemology of Testimony and Religious Belief," in *The Oxford Handbook of the Epistemology of Theology*, ed. William J. Abraham and Frederick D. Aquino (New York: Oxford University Press, 2017), 203–20; and Robert Audi, "The Place of Testimony in the Fabric of Knowledge and Justification," *American Philosophical Quarterly* 34 (1997): 405–22.

such experiences from others. In other words, the principle of testimony applies when one is at least one step removed from the religious experience itself. One might hear about the experience from the person who had it or hear about it from someone who directly heard the report from the subject, or one could read a report of the experience in a book. This introduces a complication in the case of the principle of testimony that is not present with the principle of credulity: the former principle deals not only with the veridicality of the original experience but also with the reliability of the transmission of testimony about the experience. The more links there are in the testimonial chain of transmission, the greater the possibility of error or misrepresentation in the reports of the experience. Whereas the principle of credulity concerns the veridicality of an experience, the principle of testimony also deals with the reliability of the reports of the experience—that is, whether the reports accurately reflect what the subject said about the experience. The principle of testimony states that we should accept the reliability of the reports unless we have good reason not to do so. But, of course, it is possible for the reports to accurately depict what the subject says he experienced and yet the experience itself not be veridical.

When the principle of credulity is applied to religious experience, it results in an initial presumption of veridicality: "In the absence of special considerations, all religious experiences ought to be taken by their subjects as genuine, and hence as substantial grounds for belief in the existence of their apparent object—God, or Mary, or Ultimate Reality, or Poseidon."[23] In other words, those who have a religious experience have prima-facie justification for accepting their experience as veridical, although this can be overturned by special considerations or new evidence that calls the experience into question. Similarly, the principle of testimony confers prima-facie justification for accepting the reports of others about their religious experiences, although Swinburne points out a special qualification in the case of testimony.

> Since (probably) others have the experiences that they report, and since (probably) things are as a subject's experience suggests that they are, then (with some degree of probability) things are as others report. However, the degree of probability is less in the conclusion than it is in either of the premises. If p is evidence for q, and q is evidence for r, then p is normally less evidence for r than it is for q. If the fingerprint is evidence of Jones's presence at the scene of the crime, and Jones's presence at the scene is evidence that he did the crime, the fingerprint is less evidence for Jones's having done the crime

23. Swinburne, *Existence of God*, 304.

than it is for his presence at the scene of the crime. Hence, if S reports that it seems (epistemically) to S that x is present, then that is reason for others also to believe that x is present, although not as good a reason as it is for S if in fact he is having the experience that he reports. However, clearly it is quite a good reason.[24]

Swinburne also notes that the evidential force of others' reports is enhanced to the degree that many other people report having similar experiences. "And of course, in so far as a number of others give similar reports, that greatly increases their credibility. There are large numbers of people, both today and in the past, who have had religious experiences apparently of the presence of God and that must make it significantly more probable that any one person's experience is veridical."[25]

What are the special considerations that might call into question the veridicality of a religious experience? Swinburne lists four kinds of considerations that could defeat experiential claims. First, if the apparent perception occurred under conditions that we have good reason to believe are unreliable, then there is good reason not to accept the experience as veridical. A highly unusual experience occurring while under the influence of alcohol or LSD, for example, should probably not be accepted as veridical. A second consideration is when "one may show that the perceptual claim was to have perceived an object of a certain kind in circumstances where similar perceptual claims have proved false."[26]

The third and fourth potential defeaters both arise from the fact that to perceive an object x is "to have one's experience of it seeming that x is present caused by x's being present." The claim to have perceived x can thus be challenged "either by showing that it is very, very probable that x was not present or by showing that, even if x was present, x's presence probably did not cause the experience of its seeming that x was present." So a third consideration that could defeat a claim to have experienced x would be showing that it is highly unlikely that x was present on the basis of other things that we know or have good reason to believe. And the fourth consideration involves showing that, even if x were present, x probably was not the cause of the apparent perception of x.[27]

The same factors will also apply to reports of religious experiences from others. But in the case of testimony, there are other special considerations

24. Swinburne, *Existence of God*, 323.
25. Swinburne, *Existence of God*, 323–24.
26. Swinburne, *Existence of God*, 311.
27. Swinburne, *Existence of God*, 314.

that might call into question the veracity of the reports of the experiences of others.[28] Is the report from the person who had the experience or has it been handed down from an oral tradition? How many persons are involved as links in the chain of transmission? What is known about the trustworthiness of each person transmitting the report? How much time has elapsed between the initial experience and the subsequent description of the event? Are there reasons to believe that either the person who had the experience or those reporting it might be motivated to embellish the report in significant ways?

Why should we accept the principles of credulity and testimony? Swinburne's answer is twofold: (1) we in fact *do* adopt these principles in ordinary life, and (2) failure to do so would result in the loss of the vast majority of what we think we know about the world.

> Without [the principle of credulity], there can be no knowledge at all. If you cannot suppose that things are as they seem to be unless some further evidence is brought forward—e.g., that in the past in certain respects things were as they seemed to be, the question will arise as to why you should suppose the latter evidence to be reliable. If "it seems to be" is good enough reason in the latter case, it ought to be good enough reason to start with. And if "it seems to be" is not good enough reason in the latter case, we are embarked on an infinite regress, and no claim to believe anything with justification will be correct. If the fact that something looks square is not good reason for supposing that it is square without it being shown that in the past things that looked square have usually proved to feel square, behave in a square-like way, etc., the question arises as to why we should believe that things were thus in the past, and the answer must be that it "seems" to us that we so remember. And if seeming is a good reason for believing in the latter case, then looking is a good reason for believing to start with. It is a slogan of science that we should rely on "the evidence of our senses," on "experience"; the principle of credulity crystallizes this slogan more precisely. . . . There is no avoiding ultimate reliance on the principle of credulity.[29]

In other words, something like the principle of credulity is presupposed in sense perception and our knowledge about the world as well as our memory beliefs and intuitions. But should the principle also be adopted in cases of

---

28. Phillip H. Wiebe, "Philosophy of Religion Approaches to the Study of Religious Experience," in *The Cambridge Companion to Religious Experience*, ed. Paul K. Moser and Chad Meister (Cambridge: Cambridge University Press, 2020), 62.

29. Richard Swinburne, *The Evolution of the Soul* (Oxford: Clarendon, 1986), 12. Similarly, Caroline Franks Davis says, "The principles of credulity and testimony are fundamental principles of rationality." Davis, *The Evidential Force of Religious Experience* (Oxford: Clarendon, 1989), 100.

religious experience? Swinburne insists that it is arbitrary to accept the principle with sense experience but not with religious experience unless there is good reason for excluding the latter, and he sees no good reason for doing so.

Other Formulations of the Principle

A number of other philosophers have adopted approaches similar to Swinburne's. John Hick's *Faith and Knowledge* (1966), which appeared over a decade earlier than Swinburne's *The Existence of God*, argues that the trust we normally place in our experiences of the physical world should also be applied to religious experiences.[30] In his later *An Interpretation of Religion* (1989), Hick states, "It is as reasonable for those who experience their lives as being lived in the presence of God, to believe in the reality of God, as for all of us to form beliefs about our environment on the basis of our experience of it."[31] Elsewhere he claims, "The basic principle that it is rational to base beliefs on our experience, except when we have positive reasons not to, applies impartially to all forms of putative cognitive experience, including religious experience. The debate about the rationality or otherwise of religious belief thus hinges upon possible reasons to distrust religious experience."[32]

Keith Yandell claims, "If one has an apparent experience of God under conditions in which there is no reason to think either that one would seem to experience God even were there no God or that one could not discover, if God does not exist, that this is so, then one has experiential evidence that God exists."[33] Yandell helpfully distinguishes what he calls the positive and negative ideas at work in experiential evidence. The positive idea is captured in the principle of credulity: "If someone seems to experience something, then that is reason to think that this thing exists." But there is also a negative component in our assessment of experiential evidence. "Since sometimes things seem to exist that do not exist after all (since experience is not always reliable), a type of experience can be evidence for the existence of something only if there is some way to tell whether or not experiences

30. John Hick, *Faith and Knowledge*, 2nd ed. (Ithaca, NY: Cornell University Press, 1966).

31. John Hick, *An Interpretation of Religion*, 2nd ed. (New Haven: Yale University Press, 2004), 210.

32. John Hick, *Dialogues in the Philosophy of Religion* (New York: Palgrave, 2001), 6. Similar statements are found in Charles Taliaferro and Chad Meister, *Contemporary Philosophical Theology* (London: Routledge, 2016), 79; and Jerome I. Gellmann, *Experience of God and the Rationality of Theistic Belief* (Ithaca, NY: Cornell University Press, 1997), 8–9.

33. Keith Yandell, *The Epistemology of Religious Experience* (Cambridge: Cambridge University Press, 1993), 17.

of that sort are deceptive."[34] An acceptable theory of experiential evidence "should recognize two fundamental points: that things experientially seem to be a certain way is evidence that things are as they seem, at least provided we do not have reason to think the experience in question unreliable; none the less, the experience may be unreliable."[35]

The question about the evidential force of religious experience is directly related to the notion of intentionality in experience, which is incorporated into Yandell's principle of experiential evidence.

> If S's experience E is intentional regarding X, then E is evidence that X exists unless (i) S would seem to experience X whether X was there to be experienced or not; (ii) were E not veridical, S could not discover this; (iii) E is of a type of experience that is systematically misleading; or (iv) no type of experience could count against X *exists*.[36]

In theistic or numinous experiences, God is the intentional object of the experience. Thus, "The simple ground behind the idea that numinous experience is evidence for the proposition *God exists* is that any experience that is intentional regarding an object provides evidence for the existence of that object, and that strong numinous experience is intentional regarding God, who is an object relative to the experience's subject."[37]

Kai-man Kwan adopts a similar principle, which he calls the principle of critical trust (PCT), but he distinguishes between weak and moderate versions of PCT.[38]

> Moderate PCT: If it seems (epistemically) to a subject S that p on the basis of a noetic experience E, then S has PFJ [prima-facie justification] for belief that p, which is sufficient for justified belief that p *simpliciter* in the absence of defeaters.
>
> Weak PCT: If it seems (epistemically) to a subject S that p on the basis of a noetic experience E, then S has *some* defeasible justification for his belief that p which is less than sufficient justification for justified belief that p *simpliciter*.[39]

34. Yandell, *Epistemology of Religious Experience*, 34.
35. Keith Yandell, "Religious Experience," in *A Companion to Philosophy of Religion*, ed. Philip L. Quinn and Charles Taliaferro (Oxford: Blackwell, 1997), 374.
36. Yandell, *Epistemology of Religious Experience*, 235.
37. Yandell, *Epistemology of Religious Experience*, 34.
38. Kai-man Kwan, "The Argument from Religious Experience," in *The Blackwell Companion to Natural Theology*, ed. William Lane Craig and J. P. Moreland (Oxford: Wiley-Blackwell, 2012), 498–552; see also Kwan, *The Rainbow of Experiences, Critical Trust, and God: A Defense of Holistic Empiricism* (New York: Bloomsbury Academic, 2011).
39. Kwan, "Argument from Religious Experience," 509. Emphasis in original.

Kwan observes that Swinburne's principle of credulity is a version of the moderate principle.

It is possible that the weak PCT might be applicable to a particular experience even if the moderate PCT is not. In such a case, there is still the possibility that "when a token [experience] coheres with many other tokens, that is, falls within a type of experience, then it can possess a degree of justification sufficient for PFJ [prima-facie justification]."[40] Thus, the PCT can be applied to a type of religious experience as well as to individual religious experiences. The principle applied to a type of experience results in

> Type PCT: If it seems (epistemically) to S that p on the basis of a noetic experience E, and E belongs to a well-established type of experience, then S has PFJ for belief that p, which is sufficient for justified belief that p *simpliciter* in the absence of defeaters.[41]

William Alston, Doxastic Practices, and Religious Experiences

William Alston's *Perceiving God* (1991) is an innovative and influential example of the critical-trust approach to religious experience.[42] Like Swinburne, Alston draws an analogy between sense perception and perception of God and argues that just as we are justified in adopting a critical-trust approach to sensory experience, so too the believer, in appropriate circumstances, can be justified in doing the same with what he or she takes to be experiences of God. But whereas Swinburne applied the principle of credulity to particular experiences, Alston uses the critical-trust approach in relation to what he calls "doxastic practices"—that is, practices that produce experiences and accompanying beliefs.

Alston accepts the "theory of appearing" account of perception, which holds that "perception just *is* the awareness of something's appearing to one *as such-and-such*, where this 'appearing' is a basic, unanalyzable relationship, not reducible to conceptualizing an object as such-and-such, or to judging or believing the object to be such-and-such."[43] In

---

40. Kwan, "Argument from Religious Experience," 510.
41. Kwan, "Argument from Religious Experience," 511. Emphasis in original.
42. William P. Alston, *Perceiving God: The Epistemology of Religious Experience* (Ithaca, NY: Cornell University Press, 1991), 195.
43. William P. Alston, "Précis of *Perceiving God*," *Philosophy and Phenomenological Research* 54, no. 4 (December 1994): 863. Emphasis in original.

perception the object is "*directly presented* or *immediately presented* to the subject."[44] That is, perception involves direct awareness of the object of perception.

> What I take to be definitive of perceptual consciousness is that something (or so it seems to the subject) *presents* itself to the subject's awareness as so-and-so—as red, round, loving, or whatever. When I stand before my desk with my eyes closed and open them, the most striking difference in my consciousness is that items that I was previously merely thinking about or remembering, if conscious of them in any way, are now *present* to me; they occupy space in my visual field. They are *given* to my awareness in a way that sharply contrasts with anything I can do by my own devices to conjure them up in imagination, memory, or abstract thought. . . . This phenomenon of apparent presentation of an object is what differentiates perceptual consciousness from other modes of consciousness.[45]

Given this understanding of perception, Alston insists that humans can perceive God, even though God is not a physical object.

Alston develops his proposal in terms of a reliabilist understanding of justification, which holds that "what makes a belief epistemically justified is the cognitive reliability of the causal process via which it was produced, that is, the fact that the process in question leads to a high proportion of true beliefs, with the degree of justification depending upon the degree of reliability."[46] Central to Alston's model are belief-forming mechanisms and processes, or doxastic practices. Alston states, "To be epistemically justified in believing that p is for that belief *to be based on an adequate ground*, which could either be experiences or other things one knows or justifiably believes. A ground is adequate provided it is a sufficiently reliable indication of the truth of the belief."[47]

A strength of Alston's approach is his acknowledgment of the importance of the broader social contexts within which beliefs are formed. Neither experiences nor beliefs appear in a social or cultural vacuum; religious experiences and beliefs arise in social contexts, often within institutional religious traditions, through socially established doxastic practices.[48] For Alston, a

44. Alston, *Perceiving God*, 21. Emphasis in original.
45. Alston, *Perceiving God*, 36–37. Emphasis in original.
46. Laurence Bonjour, "Internalism and Externalism," *The Oxford Handbook of Epistemology*, ed. Paul K. Moser (New York: Oxford University Press, 2002), 244.
47. Alston, "Précis of *Perceiving God*," 864. Emphasis in original.
48. See Mark Owen Webb, "Meaning and Social Value in Religious Experience," in Moser and Meister, *Cambridge Companion to Religious Experience*, 321–22.

doxastic practice is "a system or constellation of dispositions or habits, or to use the currently fashionable term, 'mechanisms,' each of which yields a belief as output that is related in a certain way to an 'input.'"[49] Sense experience involves a complex network of dispositions and practices that are socially reinforced and through which we form beliefs about the world, so that in appropriate circumstances, we make the judgment that, for example, there is a river in front of us.

So too, Alston argues, Christians typically operate within a complex social system that shapes experiences and beliefs so that in appropriate circumstances Christians form beliefs like *God loves me* or *God has forgiven me*. Many people have what they take to be direct, nonsensory experiences of God and form beliefs about God, at least in part, on this basis. Alston uses "mystical perceptual doxastic practice" or "mystical experiences" to designate practices and experiences that result in beliefs about God. The term "Christian mystical practice" (or CMP) refers to practices within the Christian tradition resulting in Christian beliefs about God. "I take mystical experiences to involve a *presentation, givenness,* or *appearance* of something to the subject, identified by the subject as God. It is this *presentational* character of the experiences that leads me to subsume them under a generic concept of perception, with this species termed mystical perception."[50] When a person has an experience produced by CMP, he or she is presented with what seems to be God, either God simply being present to the subject or God doing something, such as guiding, comforting, or convicting of sin. In recognizing that experiences and beliefs are embedded within socially established practices with their attendant assumptions, Alston is able to offer a much richer account of belief formation than models that focus on isolated individual experiences.

When a doxastic practice gains widespread acceptance over time, it becomes socially established, and the "outputs" of the practice—the beliefs formed on the basis of the practice—are generally accepted by the community. But, of course, we can be mistaken in beliefs formed through such practices, and thus well-established doxastic practices develop mechanisms for dealing with erroneous beliefs. We know from experience, for example, that our perception of physical objects can be distorted, and thus we learn not to accept uncritically what initially seems to be the case (e.g., the stick in the water is not actually bent). The doxastic practices of sense experience provide an initial justification of our beliefs formed through sensory

49. Alston, *Perceiving God*, 153.
50. Alston, "Précis of *Perceiving God*," 863. Emphasis in original.

perception, and if there are not sufficient reasons for rejecting a particular belief, then that belief can be regarded as having unqualified justification.

The question of the epistemic acceptability of CMP depends on whether the beliefs formed on the basis of CMP are prima facie justified. And, given reliabilism, this means that we are faced with the question of whether the usual ways of forming beliefs about God in CMP are sufficiently reliable.[51] How do we know that? At this point the analogy between doxastic practices producing sense perceptions and those producing perceptions of God is crucial, and Alston insists that both sense experience and some experiences of God are instances of perception. He rejects the common assumption that sense experience should be privileged over other forms of experience since sense experience is generally reliable and thus truth conducive to a much greater degree than other nonsensory forms of experience.

How do we know that sense perception is generally a reliable means of producing beliefs about the world? Despite a long history of attempts to demonstrate the reliability of sense perception in a non-question-begging manner, most philosophers conclude this has been unsuccessful.[52] Suppose, for example, that I am in a dark room, and I am unsure whether what is in front of me really is a table. I can reach out my hands to feel whether there is a table there. My sight, which is limited due to darkness, can thus be supplemented by touch. But notice that in this case, we are checking the reliability of one sense by using another sense. One cannot appeal to something independent of the five senses to confirm whether a table is really there. With respect to the general reliability of the senses, none of the attempts to justify sense perception by appealing to something external to sense experience escapes "epistemic circularity."[53] This does not mean that we are not justified in generally accepting beliefs formed on the basis of sense experience; there just is no noncircular way of demonstrating such justification. This has implications for experience of God. Alston states, "even if mystical perception cannot be shown, without epistemic circularity, to be reliable, it can't be judged epistemically inferior to sense perception on those grounds. To suppose it can, in the face of these results, is to apply a 'double standard.'"[54]

An element of circularity is inescapable even with sense perception. Although a doxastic practice such as sense perception has ways of determining

---

51. Alston, "Précis of *Perceiving God*," 865.

52. See chap. 3 of Alston, *Perceiving God*; and William P. Alston, *The Reliability of Sense Perception* (Ithaca, NY: Cornell University Press, 1993).

53. Similar problems affect attempts to justify introspection or memory beliefs.

54. Alston, "Précis of *Perceiving God*," 865.

what are and are not acceptable beliefs, "there is no appeal beyond the doxastic practices to which we find ourselves firmly committed."[55] But, he claims, this need not be a vicious circularity, for there are internal mechanisms of "significant self-support" within a doxastic practice system and the outputs, or beliefs, of particular practices can be assessed for consistency with those of other doxastic practices. It is here that the critical-trust approach of Alston's proposal becomes evident, for he maintains that it is rational to engage in any socially established doxastic practice that we do not have sufficient reasons for regarding as unreliable.

Sense perception and perception of God are thus similar in that in neither case can the doxastic practices producing the relevant beliefs be shown to be reliable in a strictly noncircular manner. Thus, to insist that beliefs formed on the basis of sense perception can be epistemically justified but those formed through Christian practices cannot is simply epistemic imperialism.[56] "I argue that it is rational to engage in any socially established doxastic practice that we do not have sufficient reasons for regarding as *unreliable.*"[57] Alston concludes, "*A firmly established doxastic practice is rationally engaged in unless the total output of all our firmly established doxastic practices sufficiently indicates its unreliability. In other terms, a firmly established doxastic practice is rationally engaged in provided it and its output cohere sufficiently with other firmly established doxastic practices and their output.*"[58] Beliefs formed through the relevant doxastic practices can be granted prima-facie justification, and if there are no sufficient overriders, then they can also be considered "unqualifiedly justified." Accordingly, a Christian can be justified in holding certain beliefs about God based on experiences of God arising from the doxastic practices of the Christian community.

> CMP [Christian mystical practice] is a functioning, socially established, perceptual doxastic practice with distinctive experiential inputs, distinctive input-output functions, a distinctive conceptual scheme, and a rich, inter-

---

55. Alston, *Perceiving God*, 177. Mark Owen Webb ("Meaning and Social Value in Religious Experience," 325) points out that, "We may not be able to show a source of beliefs to be reliable, in a non-circular way, but we can certainly show one to be unreliable. . . . Wishful thinking, astrology, taking auspices, and such don't have an impressive track record, so the epistemically careful have abandoned them as not reliable. . . . If we fail to show [a source of beliefs] to be unreliable, then it has passed a sort of minimal test, and so it may be rational to rely on it after all."

56. Alston, *Perceiving God*, 199.

57. Alston, "Précis of *Perceiving God*," 865–66. Emphasis in original.

58. Alston, *Perceiving God*, 175. Emphasis in original.

nally justified overrider system. As such, it possesses a prima facie title to being rationally engaged in, and its outputs are thereby prima facie justified, *provided we have no sufficient reason to regard it as unreliable or otherwise disqualified for rational acceptance.*[59]

Alston's proposal is carefully crafted and nuanced, and it provides a plausible way of thinking about perceptual experiences of God, although it has also been subjected to criticism.[60]

We have briefly looked at several philosophers who all share a basic commitment to the critical-trust approach to religious experiences. Swinburne, Yandell, and Alston frame the issues in terms of *perception* of God, with perception being understood as structurally similar to sense experience. Each of them insists that perception should not be limited to sensory experiences. Swinburne and Alston in particular appeal to an explicit analogy between sense experience and religious experience, arguing that since the critical-trust approach is justified in the former case, it also ought to be adopted in the latter.

Let's assume that the critical-trust approach is legitimate with sense experience as well as with memory, rational inference, and introspection. But what about religious experiences? Does the critical-trust approach also apply to what are taken to be experiences of God? Critics insist that even if it is appropriate with other kinds of experience, the critical-trust approach is not acceptable with religious experiences. The reasons typically given for this stem from the alleged differences between sense experience and religious experience. We will consider briefly four reasons why the critical-trust approach may be inappropriate for religious experiences, deferring until chapter 7 discussion of the most significant objection—namely, the problem of religious disagreement and diversity.

Nonsensory Perception?

Some religious experiences do involve use of one or more of the senses— for example, the report of the women seeing the angel at Jesus's tomb in Matthew 28:2–7—and thus it makes sense to think of these as perceptual experiences. But many religious experiences do not seem to involve any of the five senses. Christians claim to be aware of God's loving presence in

---

59. Alston, *Perceiving God*, 225. Emphasis in original.
60. A helpful overview of the critical issues can be seen in the symposium on *Perceiving God* in *Philosophy and Phenomenological Research* 54, no. 4 (December 1994).

the midst of suffering or of God communicating a message to them or of God forgiving them. Some, such as Professor Price mentioned in chapter 1, speak of being directly aware of a personal presence next to them, an apprehension of someone who clearly is distinct from them and yet not detectable through the five senses. Critics claim that although the critical-trust approach might be appropriate when one or more of the senses are involved, it cannot be extended to cases that involve *none* of them. Is it reasonable to speak of *perceiving* God when none of the senses are directly involved in the experience?

Richard Gale says no. He rejects the analogy between sense perception and perception of God because the latter supposedly lacks some of the salient features of the former. Gale asserts that for alleged experiences of God to count as perceptions of God, it is necessary that they have a structure such that God is the object of the experience.[61] But, he claims, religious experiences lack this structure. If we express it using Keith Yandell's categories introduced in chapter 1, Gale is saying that nonsensory religious experiences do not conform to a subject-content-object schema but rather to a subject-content schema. As such, they cannot be experiences *of something* that exists apart from the subject undergoing the experience.

Gale identifies certain "generic conditions" of perceptual experience that are derived from sensory experience, and he insists that these are necessary conditions for all cases of perception. Religious experiences are then examined to see whether they have the requisite qualities. If they "fail to satisfy one or more of these generic conditions, that will justify denying them perceptual status."[62] Gale then argues that experiences of God fail to meet one of the necessary conditions, that of the possibility of "individuating" the object of perception. In a perception of x, there must be some way of identifying and distinguishing x so that, in principle, x can be perceived by other subjects in appropriate circumstances (so that x can be the object of different perceptions by different subjects) and so that it is possible to distinguish between perceptions of x and perceptions of a different object y that is qualitatively similar to x.[63] Objects of sense perception, for example, have a certain spatial and temporal location so that they can be perceived "by different perceivers at the same time and the same perceiver at different

61. Richard Gale, "Why Alston's Mystical Doxastic Practice Is Subjective," *Philosophy and Phenomenological Research* 54, no. 4 (December 1994): 869–75. See also Richard M. Gale, "Swinburne's Argument from Religious Experience," in *Reason and the Christian Religion*, ed. Alan G. Padgett (Oxford: Clarendon, 1994), 56–63.
62. Gale, "Why Alston's Mystical Doxastic Practice Is Subjective," 871.
63. Gale, "Why Alston's Mystical Doxastic Practice Is Subjective," 872.

times."[64] Thus a ball can be perceived by different observers at the same time or by the same person on different occasions. But God is a spiritual being and not detectable through the senses or locatable within the space-time continuum. God also is not publicly accessible in the way that physical objects are; God can choose to have some people experience him but not others. Gale concludes that since we cannot properly individuate God in our experiences, we should reject the suggestion that theistic experiences are perceptions of God.

But why should we regard sense perception as providing the *necessary* conditions for all instances of perception? The distinguishing marks of perceptual experience have to do with the structure of the experience (subject-content-object), not the content nor even the medium through which the experience is conveyed. Alston correctly accuses Gale of engaging in epistemic imperialism—that is, taking the standards of one doxastic practice (sense perception) and making them normative for all.[65] Although Gale correctly points out that religious experiences do not necessarily share the kind of individuating features that we find in sense experience, he does not demonstrate why we must understand individuation in terms of sense experience or why we cannot individuate God in other nonsensory ways. Alston insists that religious communities, with their particular background beliefs and expectations, *do* provide appropriate criteria for identifying God in experience.[66]

George Pappas raises an interesting issue for Alston's notion of perception as a case of "appearing," where for S to perceive X is simply for X to appear to S as so-and-so.[67] Alston holds that although what "appears" or is "presented" to one's awareness might include some sensory content, it is not necessary that it do so to qualify as a perception. And thus we can have nonsensory perceptions of God. Pappas, however, argues that this is too permissive, since it allows for "unusually vivid cases of object or event memory" to count as perceptions. An acceptable theory of perception should enable us to distinguish between experiences in which we *actually do perceive* a mind-independent object, whether physical or not, and an experience of *remembering* an object. "One may remember one's childhood home, for example, and recall the shape and color of various rooms.

64. Gale, "Why Alston's Mystical Doxastic Practice Is Subjective," 871.

65. Alston, "Reply to Commentators," *Philosophy and Phenomenological Research* 54, no. 4 (December 1994): 893.

66. Alston, "Reply to Commentators," 892.

67. George Pappas, "Perception and Mystical Experience," *Philosophy and Phenomenological Research* 54, no. 4 (December 1994): 881.

This is not remembering that the rooms are of such-and-such character; it is object memory; what are recalled are the rooms. It seems clear that in this situation the rooms are presented to one's consciousness in a striking manner. Thus if being so presented is definitive of at least the generic notion of perception, then in so remembering one's childhood home one is also perceiving it."[68] In other words, a vivid memory can be "presented" to our awareness, and according to Pappas, when sensory characteristics are no longer regarded as definitive in perception, it then becomes difficult to distinguish a vivid memory from the actual perception of that object. By extending the notion of perception to include perceptions of God, Alston has made it too broad to be viable.

In response Alston argues that his account of perception does not need to admit such memory experiences as perceptions.

> The kind of presentation I take to constitute perceptual consciousness comes to the subject, first, with the "impression" that it is something *external*, something not part of the subject's mind or consciousness, that is being presented. This suffices to exclude introspection. Secondly, in perception the object is presented as *present*, both in the sense of being currently in some sort of dynamic relationship to the subject and as presently existing. This is what excludes memory, even of the object or event sort. In this connection I should stress that I take presentation to be necessary and sufficient for *perceptual consciousness* (experience). I don't claim it to be sufficient for *veridical perception*, i.e., for the subject's making a correct identification of the object perceived.[69]

Surely Alston is correct here. In ordinary experience, there is a qualitative difference between my memory—strong and vivid as it might be—of my childhood home and my actually standing in front of that home and seeing it. I see no reason for thinking that we cannot similarly make a distinction between one's *experience of God's presence* and *the memory of the experience of God's presence*.

In considering differences between sense perception and perception of God, it is worth noting the limitations of strictly sensory input with something as basic as our experience of other persons. For example, our senses enable us to see the shape of a body or facial expression or to hear a voice, and these sensory inputs are significant in our recognizing what is in front of us as a person. But identifying the object of such sensory awareness *as a*

---

68. Pappas, "Perception and Mystical Experience," 881.
69. Alston, "Reply to Commentators," 896. Emphasis in original.

person—to say nothing of identifying him as one's father or math teacher—involves much more than merely the deliverances of the five senses. Even in our ordinary experience of other people, much more than just the senses are necessary for perceptual experience. As Thomas Smythe observes, "There are parallels with this [nonsensory perception of God] in our perception of other people as being good, showing their power, expressing their love, complimenting others, or being domineering. Although we use sensory cues as a basis for our attributions in such cases, the experience is not reducible to sensory content or sensory qualities."[70]

Not Everyone Has Religious Experiences

All human beings with properly functioning faculties typically have sense experiences, but not all persons have religious experiences. Many perfectly normal people have no religious experiences. Part of the reason that we accept the critical-trust approach to sensory experience is the ubiquitous nature of such experiences. Some contend that, although it can be reasonable to apply the critical-trust approach to experiences that people in general share, we are not justified in doing so with a subset of experiences that only some people have.[71]

It is true that not everyone has religious experiences, at least as these are typically understood. But why should we expect that if any religious experiences are veridical, then everyone should have such experiences? Why suppose that certain experiences enjoyed by only part of the population are less likely to be veridical than those that are universally distributed? After all, some aspects of reality are accessible only to persons who satisfy certain conditions, so that some kinds of experience are restricted to particular groups. Not everyone, for example, can have the experience of understanding Gödel's incompleteness theorems or of conducting an orchestral performance of Beethoven's Ninth Symphony or of giving birth to a baby or of detecting cancerous cells in tissue. So there is nothing in itself in the lack of universality of religious experience that is necessarily problematic.

The lack of universality would be a problem if there were good reason to expect that if any such experiences are veridical, then all people would have these experiences. One might maintain, for example, that God desires for

70. Thomas W. Smythe, "Perceiving God," *Theology Today* 63 (2007): 460.
71. J. L. Schellenberg, *The Wisdom to Doubt: A Justification of Religious Skepticism* (Ithaca, NY: Cornell University Press, 2007), 174.

all people to come into a restored relationship with him and that all people having significant experiences of God is necessary for realizing this goal. But, in response, it might be argued that even if that is God's desire, there could nevertheless be good reasons why some people do not have religious experiences.[72] Perhaps a certain moral or spiritual disposition is necessary for such experiences, and thus sin or moral obtuseness makes them less likely for some people. Furthermore, theologians and philosophers have argued that God might have good reasons for maintaining a measure of religious ambiguity, with the result that not everyone automatically has religious experiences. As we saw in chapter 2, John Hick has argued that some religious ambiguity is necessary in order to preserve "cognitive freedom" in our response to God.[73] If everyone has clear and unmistakable experiences of God, as we typically do of the physical environment, then our responses to God would be coerced and not be genuinely free. Our purpose here is not to defend any of these suggestions but merely to note that so long as there is a plausible explanation for why not everyone has religious experiences, the disanalogy between sense experience and religious experience on this point need not be decisive.

But the restricted nature of religious experiences brings yet another objection. According to Michael Martin, if we are to treat experiences of God as good grounds for the existence of God, then "are not experiences of the absence of God good grounds for the nonexistence of God? After all, many people have tried to experience God and have failed." Martin picks up on the analogy between experiences of God and sensory experiences. "In ordinary life we suppose that the experience of a chair is a good ground for believing that the chair is present. But we also believe that the experience of the absence of a chair is a good ground for supposing that a chair is absent. If Swinburne is correct that the way things appear is good ground for the way they are, then surely the way things do not seem is good ground for the way they are not."[74] Martin argues that if the principle of credulity is acceptable, then there should also be a negative principle of credulity, which he formulates as follows:

NPC: If it seems (epistemically) to a subject S that x is absent, then probably x is absent.[75]

72. See Michael C. Rea, *The Hiddenness of God* (New York: Oxford University Press, 2018).
73. See Hick, *Faith and Knowledge*, 127–48.
74. Michael Martin, *Atheism: A Philosophical Justification* (Philadelphia: Temple University Press, 1990), 169–70.
75. M. Martin, *Atheism*, 170.

Strictly speaking, adoption of the NPC would not necessarily mean that we should reject the positive principle, but it would show that we can have conflicting evidence for the reality of God on the basis of experience. For some people, experience might provide prima-facie evidence for God; for others, it might provide prima-facie evidence against the reality of God.

Martin does have a point here. As Douglas Geivett observes, "negative seemings" often do have evidential force. It seeming to be the case that *x is not present* often is good evidence that *x* is not present.[76] He uses the example of it seeming to me that there is no elephant in the room with me as I write. That particular "negative seeming" provides a good ground for my believing that there is not an elephant in the room. Such negative seemings are especially significant when something that ought to be present under certain conditions seems not to be present under those conditions.[77] If I am expecting my mother to be in the kitchen cooking, then, upon my entering the kitchen, *it seeming that my mother is not in the kitchen* provides good ground for concluding that she is not in the kitchen.

But there are also good reasons for questioning the NPC in the case of experience of God. The NPC makes good sense when applied to inert physical objects such as chairs, especially when we would naturally expect it to seem that a chair is present if in fact a chair is present. But there are obvious differences between God and chairs. Chairs are inanimate physical objects that anyone with properly functioning sense faculties under normal conditions ought to be able to perceive. If there is a chair in the room, then anyone in the room should be able to see the chair; failure to see a chair supports the conclusion that there is no chair. But not only is God not a physical object, God is a personal agent and thus has something to do with whether or not he is perceived by humans. So the failure to experience God in and of itself does not necessarily provide evidence for the nonexistence of God.

It is also worth noting that there is a difference between *X seems to S to be absent* and *X does not seem present to S*, with the former being understood as a perception of X's absence. Can there be direct perceptions of the absence of God? Martin's argument is strengthened if it makes sense to think of *it seeming to S that God is absent* as an instance of perception. But can one actually *perceive* God's nonexistence? In a thoughtful discussion of

---

76. R. Douglas Geivett, "The Evidential Value of Religious Experience," in *The Rationality of Theism*, ed. Paul Copan and Paul K. Moser (London: Routledge, 2003), 189.

77. This is at the heart of the problem of divine hiddenness, which has received much recent attention. Michael Rea (*Hiddenness of God*, 18) thus speaks of the "experiential problem" of divine hiddenness—that is, what seems to be the "withdrawal of God's presence" or "the hiding of God's face."

the problem of evil, Jerome Gellman suggests that some people, in experiencing horrendous evils and suffering, do experience God's nonexistence.

> There is a type of experience in which a person experiences evil and right there in the evil perceives that God does not exist. . . . It seems to me, for example, implausible in the extreme to suppose that someone who endures the horrors of the Nazi Holocaust in the extermination camps of World War II, is *arguing*, either deductively or inductively, from the *fact* of those evils to the non-existence of God. Rather, what seems highly more plausible to say is that such a person has lost his or her faith because in experiencing those evils he or she has had an experience of God's non-existence. . . . What [such people] perceive in the evil is that the world is Godless, without a God. God's non-existence is made manifest to them.[78]

But while Gellman is surely correct in his portrayal of those who experience horrendous evil and, as a result, find themselves believing that God does not exist, it is not clear that *this experience* should be construed as a *perception* of God's nonexistence. Perception is intentional in that it is perception *of something*. It is difficult to see how one can literally perceive the *absence* of something. One can, of course, be aware of a state of affairs in which something that one might expect to be present is absent, but that is different from perceiving its nonexistence.

Critical Trust Only When Necessary

John Schellenberg points out another difference between religious experiences and the kinds of experiences to which we normally apply the critical-trust approach. He says that in order to minimize the possibility of being mistaken, we ought to be very reluctant to apply the "innocent until proven guilty" approach to our experiences. "If we really are would-be investigators, concerned for the truth and seeking understanding, then we will ascribe epistemic innocence—even an initial innocence—*only where we have to*: assuming that we have to pick certain belief-forming practices as innocent until proven guilty to get started, we will still pick only what we have to pick, in order to minimize the extent to which non-inquiry-based factors influence the direction of inquiry."[79]

---

78. Jerome Gellman, "A New Look at the Problem of Evil," *Faith and Philosophy* 2, no. 9 (April 1992): 213. I am grateful to Justin Mooney for drawing my attention to this distinction and essay.
79. Schellenberg, *Wisdom to Doubt*, 170. Emphasis in original.

Schellenberg acknowledges that we do accept something like the principle of credulity in sense experiences, introspective experiences, and memory experiences, but he insists that we do so only because there is no other option. If we are to make any sense of our world and to live successfully in it, we must adopt a critical-trust approach to experiences in these domains. Moreover, there is a coercive aspect to these experiences in that it is very difficult not to treat them as veridical unless we have good reason to question them in particular cases. But, he claims, religious experiences are not like this. We are not compelled to accept them as prima facie reliable as we are with sense experience. Although Swinburne is correct in claiming that denial of the principle of credulity with sense experience or memory results in skepticism, this is not the case with religious experience.[80] People can and do live flourishing lives and deepen their understanding of the world without accepting the reliability of religious experiences. Thus, Schellenberg concludes, the critical-trust approach should be restricted to "what is universal and unavoidable," such as experiences arising from "sensory, introspective, memorial, and (rationally) intuitive" practices.[81]

Clearly there are some important differences between religious experiences and sensory, memorial, introspective, and intuitive experiences. But why should we believe that a critical-trust approach is legitimate *only* where we have no other option? Very little by way of knowledge can be established by accepting only what is undeniable or *must* be presupposed in order to survive in our world. Indeed, Schellenberg omits testimony from his list of cases in which the critical-trust approach is appropriate, yet most of what we believe and act on is derived from the testimony of others. However, the impulse to trust the testimony of others is not undeniable or compelling in the way that sensory experience is, and we are often mistaken in beliefs based on testimony. Adopting Schellenberg's restriction would require us to dismiss as unwarranted much of what we normally accept as prima facie justified belief.

Religious Experiences and Checking Procedures

Another common critique is the claim that the critical-trust approach presupposes that we can distinguish nonveridical experiences from veridical ones, but in the case of religious experience, there are no acceptable criteria for making this distinction. Although there are agreed-on checking

---

80. Schellenberg, *Wisdom to Doubt*, 172.
81. Schellenberg, *Wisdom to Doubt*, 170.

procedures for assessing sense experiences, this is not the case with religious experiences.

C. B. Martin's *Religious Belief* (1959) appeared before Swinburne introduced the principle of credulity, but it rejects the analogy between religious experience and sense experience because of the lack of checking procedures with the former. Martin claims that, in contrast to sense experience, "there are no tests agreed upon to establish a genuine experience of God and to distinguish it decisively from the nongenuine."[82] The following quotation makes clear that Martin is looking for the kind of checking procedures associated with sense experience.

> Certainly, people have had special sorts of experience which incline them to claim with the greatest confidence that their experiences are of God. But whether the experiences are or are not of God is not to be decided by describing or having those experiences. For whether anything or nothing is apprehended by experiences is not to be read off from the experiences themselves. The presence of a piece of blue paper is not to be read off from my experience as of a piece of blue paper. Other things are relevant: What would a photograph reveal? Can I touch it? What do others see? It is only when I admit the relevance of such checking procedures that I can lay claim to apprehending the paper, and, indeed, the admission of the relevance of such procedures is what gives meaning to the assertion that I am apprehending the paper. *What I apprehend is the sort of thing that can be photographed, touched, and seen by others.* . . . It can be objected, "But God is different, and we never meant that our experiences of God should be checked by procedures relevant to physical objects." Of course not, but what *sort* of checks are there then, so that we are left with more than mere experiences whose existence even the atheist need not deny?[83]

This critique, in varying forms, has been pressed by a number of philosophers.[84]

Much could be said by way of response, and George Mavrodes's *Belief in God* (1970) provides a penetrating critique of Martin's objection. Mavrodes notes, for example, that even with sense experience, there are a variety of

82. C. B. Martin, *Religious Belief* (Ithaca, NY: Cornell University Press, 1959), 67. It is interesting that although Martin's book appeared six years after Broad's essay advocating the critical-trust approach to religious experiences, he makes no reference to it.

83. C. B. Martin, *Religious Belief*, 87–88. Emphasis in original.

84. See, e.g., Antony Flew, *God and Philosophy* (New York: Harcourt, Brace, & World, 1966), 124–39; Richard Gale, "Swinburne's Argument from Religious Experience," 39–63; Gale, *On the Nature and Existence of God* (Cambridge: Cambridge University Press, 1991), chap. 8; Louis P. Pojman, *Philosophy of Religion* (Mountain View, CA: Mayfield, 2001), 61–64; Michael Martin, *Atheism*, 158–62; Evan Fales, "Do Mystics See God?," in *Contemporary Debates in Philosophy of Religion*, ed. Michael L. Peterson and Raymond J. VanArragon (Oxford: Blackwell, 2004), 145–58.

checking procedures for different kinds of objects, some of which may be indirect and offer ambiguous results. Not all cases of perceiving physical objects are as clear-cut as the example of seeing a blue piece of paper. Nor does failure of others to perceive what I see necessarily mean that my experience is not veridical.

> I claim, for example, to see a timber wolf in Rocky Mountain National Park. My friend hurries to the same spot but sees no wolf. What significance has this failure? Notice that, unlike the paper, the wolf has some initiative in this affair. If the wolf does not want to be seen, then perhaps my friend will see him only if he is more clever than the wolf. . . . The world contains many things, and not all of them are as inert as a piece of paper. To demand that the corroboration of every experience should be equally as easy as substantiating the existence of the paper is simply to exhibit a foolish disregard for the relevant facts.[85]

Matters become even more complicated when the object of perception is a person, since persons have something to say about whether and how they are perceived by others. If this is the case with human persons, then it is even more so with God.

> It seems clear that if Christian theologians are correct then God will be experienced only when He chooses to reveal Himself. The wolf has a little initiative but he will sometimes be outwitted by the careful stalker. God, however, will not be outwitted or compelled. The failure, then, of one person to apprehend God has very little significance against someone else's positive claim. For it is quite possible that the failure stems from the fact that the man is in some way yet unready for the experience, or from the fact that God—for reasons which we may or may not guess—has not yet chosen to reveal Himself to him.[86]

So, failure to perceive God in a particular case is not the same thing as not perceiving a piece of blue paper.

85. George I. Mavrodes, *Belief in God: A Study in the Epistemology of Religion* (New York: Random House, 1970), 79.

86. Mavrodes, *Belief in God*, 79. Similarly, John Greco observes that "self-disclosure is not only selective, but also *intentional*." This "allows us to deny that experiential evidence of God must be available in the relevant sense—at all times available to all persons who are open to it. It is consistent with God's nature that, as other persons typically do, God has *good reasons* for selective self-disclosure." John Greco, "No-Fault Atheism," in *Hidden Divinity and Religious Belief: New Perspectives*, ed. Adam Green and Eleonore Stump (Cambridge: Cambridge University Press, 2015), 115. Emphasis in original.

William Rowe also argues that the principle of credulity should not be extended to religious experiences since we have no way of distinguishing veridical experiences of God from those that are not. He formulates what he takes to be an acceptable version of the principle of credulity as follows:

> When subjects have an experience which they take to be of x, and we know how to discover positive reasons for thinking their experiences delusive, if such reasons do exist, then it is rational to conclude that they really do experience x unless we have some positive reasons to think their experiences are delusive.[87]

Rowe's point is that if an experience E is to count as good evidence for the claim that x exists, then it must be, in principle, possible to tell that E is *not* veridical, if in fact E is not veridical. This is a reasonable expectation, and it is made explicit in Keith Yandell's formulation of the principle of experiential evidence.[88]

But why suppose that this requirement cannot be met with religious experience? To be sure, the criteria for distinguishing veridical from nonveridical experiences of God will not be identical to those applicable to the perception of physical objects. But, as Peter Losin observes, that experiences of God are not like sense experiences in this respect is significant only if it can be shown that there are no other means apart from sense experience by which veridical experiences of God can be distinguished from their nonveridical counterparts.[89] It is far from clear that this is the case.

Moreover, checking procedures often involve an element of circularity, and this is true even with checking procedures for sense experience. How do we distinguish a nonveridical perception from a veridical perception in sense experience? Losin points out that "identifying and dismissing a particular sensory experience as nonveridical often (if not always) involves assuming that another sensory experience is veridical."[90] I identify the perception of the bent stick in the water as nonveridical when I contrast that perception with my observation of the stick out of water or by feeling the stick itself with my hand. But a similar process of checking is also available to the theist.

87. William L. Rowe, "Religious Experience and the Principle of Credulity," *International Journal for Philosophy of Religion* 13 (1982): 91.

88. Yandell, *Epistemology of Religious Experience*, 233.

89. Peter Losin, "Experience of God and the Principle of Credulity: A Reply to Rowe," *Faith and Philosophy* 4, no. 1 (January 1987): 63.

90. Losin, "Experience of God," 63–64.

Suppose that by assuming that some experience of God or other is veridical we can identify and dismiss other experiences of God as non-veridical. This assumption, like its counterpart from sensory experience, need not be groundless or arbitrary. . . . I am suggesting it is open to the theist to claim that the kind of reasoning we typically engage in in checking particular sensory experience can perform a similar function in cases of experience of God. We can assume, if only provisionally, "for the sake of argument," that some experience of God or other is probably veridical; on this basis other experiences of God can be identified and dismissed as non-veridical.[91]

This is especially the case if we have independent grounds, such as an appeal to divine revelation, for expecting that veridical experiences of God would include certain characteristics or be consistent with particular teachings.

Mark Owen Webb provides two examples of experiences that illustrate the similarities in checking procedures between some religious experiences and sense experience.[92] Consider first the case of Anna.

Anna has committed some small wrong (say, petty theft) and feels bad about it. She consults her mother, who says, "You know God doesn't want you to do that. It's a sin. Your conscience is telling you that." Anna decides to pray to God and ask for forgiveness. While she is praying, she feels that God is forgiving her and comforting her, while at the same time giving her courage to confess to the person she has wronged, and make amends. When asked about her prayer experience, she says, "I felt God's presence, both convicting me of sin and forgiving me." The members of her church confirm and accept her report as true and genuine, because that is what they would expect to happen, given their tradition's interpretation of scripture, how it comports with their own experiences, and by the effect it has had on Anna's behavior.

A variety of beliefs and expectations on the part of Anna, her mother, and the broader religious community are embedded in this brief example, and these provide ways for Anna and others to check whether she really was experiencing God's presence convicting her of sin and forgiving her. "When she reports her experience, her coreligionists compare it with what they would expect, given their complex picture of God and His relations to the world, a picture developed over centuries. The social setting of Anna's experience provides checks and tests, all of which her experience passes."[93] Now compare Anna's experience with that of Bill.

91. Losin, "Experience of God," 64–65.
92. Webb, "Meaning and Social Value," 322–23.
93. Webb, "Meaning and Social Value," 322.

Bill is walking down the street in New York City and sees a man who looks like Ben Vereen. Being a big fan of musical theater, he recognizes him, and approaches him. The man confirms that he is indeed Ben Vereen, and after a brief chat about plays and movies, Ben autographs Bill's tourist map, and they part ways. When he gets back to Lubbock, Bill tells his theater friends about his encounter. They accept his story, saying, "Yes, Ben Vereen is known to be very friendly with fans, and he is in New York right now for the new production of *Cats*."

Bill's experience involves much more than merely the visual and auditory sensory input in the encounter. As Webb notes, "His sensory report is informed by knowledge he already has (what Ben Vereen looks like, plus his memories of Ben's various parts in plays and movies), checked by background facts that are known to his community (yes, Ben was in New York at the time, and the person's behavior comports with what is known about Ben's character), and supported by what they would expect to happen, based on what they know about New York and Ben Vereen." Even sense experience is subject to checks for coherence with background knowledge and the "socially supplied information" that we find with religious experience.[94]

As we conclude this chapter, we should distinguish two kinds of testing procedures for religious experiences—those that are tradition-dependent and those that are not. Criteria that are tradition-dependent are internal to a particular religious tradition; they are derived from the authority structure of that tradition, but they will not necessarily be accepted by those outside of that tradition. The Christian tradition, for example, has given considerable attention to the issue of discerning veridical from nonveridical experiences of God. Other religious traditions have their own internal criteria and mechanisms for identifying what are taken to be genuine experiences of the relevant spiritual reality. As we will see in the next chapter, identifying genuine experiences of the Holy Spirit was a central concern of Jonathan Edwards and John Wesley. In the following quotation, William Wainwright addresses disputes arising within the Christian mystical tradition, but his comments apply to ordinary Christians' experiences of God as well.

The Christian tradition employs a variety of tests to determine whether a mystic really is perceiving God. These include the consequences of the experience for the mystic and others. (Does it promote charity and humility? Is its effect peace and psychological integration or, on the contrary, psychic disintegration? Do the mystic's experiences build up the community?) The tests also include the depth, profundity, and spiritual "sweetness" of what the mystic says on the basis of his or her experience, its agreement or disagreement with known truths, and a comparison of the mystic's experiences with others generally acknowledged to be genuine.[95]

Consistency with the teachings of Scripture has been a basic criterion for Christians evaluating experiences.[96] So there are criteria from within the Christian tradition that can be used to distinguish genuine experiences of God from those that are not.

But there are also criteria that are not dependent on particular religious traditions. As we have seen, Richard Swinburne offers four kinds of "special considerations" that, in particular cases, can in principle override the prima-facie justification provided by the principle of credulity. We can summarize these considerations in a general principle:

> The claim to have perceived X in experience E can be called into question if (i) the perception of X is incompatible with what we know or have very strong reasons to believe to be true on other grounds; (ii) there are good reasons to believe that E occurred under conditions or to a subject or through a mechanism that is unreliable; or (iii) there are good reasons to believe that X is not the cause of E.

So there are criteria, both internal to the Christian tradition and more broadly acceptable, that can be used to distinguish genuine or veridical experiences of God from those that are not.

I conclude that it can be perfectly reasonable to apply the critical-trust approach—the principles of credulity and testimony—to religious experiences, including theistic experiences. What seems to the subject to be an experience of God can be accepted as an experience of God, provided there are no compelling reasons to question the veridicality of the experience. The experience can also be taken as evidence for the reality of God.[97] But several

---

95. William J. Wainwright, *Philosophy of Religion*, 2nd ed. (Belmont, CA: Wadsworth, 1999), 129.

96. Christians often disagree over whether a particular kind of experience is consistent with the teachings of Scripture, but disagreement over the application of a criterion in a particular case does not mean that there is not a consensus on the acceptability of the criterion itself. Indeed, disagreement over its application implicitly acknowledges the legitimacy of the criterion.

97. "An experience that is subject-consciousness-object in structure, where the apparent object, if the experience is reliable, exists distinct from, and independent of, the subject, is evidence for the existence of that object." Keith E. Yandell, *The Philosophy of Religion: A Contemporary Introduction*, 2nd ed. (London: Routledge, 2016), 160.

qualifications should be noted. First, both the principles of credulity and testimony provide prima-facie justification for accepting the experiences as veridical. This initial justification can be overridden by other considerations calling the experience into question.

Second, the critical-trust approach applies not only to Christians and their experiences but to all who have religious experiences. Christians, Buddhists, Muslims, Hindus, and Bahais can all be justified in regarding their respective experiences as veridical so long as there are not good reasons for them not to do so. This means not that all of their experiences are veridical but only that it can be rational for them to treat their experiences as veridical unless there is reason not to do so. This is a minimalist or weak sense of rationality that acknowledges that very different experiences entailing incompatible claims can be regarded as veridical. The implications of this with respect to religious diversity and disagreement are considered further in chapter 7.

Finally, it should be apparent that the critical-trust approach operates within a broader context of background beliefs, values, and expectations that help to shape one's views on what reality is like and what we should expect. One's background beliefs and expectations shape in significant ways what one regards as plausible, thus affecting judgments about the veridicality of particular experiences. Beliefs about religious matters—whether there is a God or gods, the purpose and meaning of life, sin and forgiveness, what happens after death, etc.—form a significant part of one's background beliefs. Thus ultimately judgments about the veridicality of particular religious experiences cannot be assessed apart from consideration of the truth of the background beliefs that influence such judgments. This highlights the significance of what is sometimes called worldview analysis or, with respect to the Christian tradition, natural theology. Implications of this will also be considered in chapter 7.

4

Edwards and Wesley on Experiencing God

Although personal experience of God has been central to the Christian faith throughout the centuries, it has also been controversial. Simeon Zahl observes, "Few themes are more important in Christian life, and few are more fraught in Christian theology, than 'experience.' . . . In fact, disagreement over the reliability and significance of Christian religious experience has been one of the most fundamental and enduring debates in Protestant theology from the 1520s to the present."[1] In this chapter we will examine how two major Christian leaders in the eighteenth century, Jonathan Edwards and John Wesley, addressed questions about experiences of God in the context of the revivals and awakenings in Great Britain and America. Their primary interest was in identifying "true religion," or genuine and appropriate experiential responses to God. But they were also well aware of growing skepticism about Christian claims, and they looked to personal experience of God through the Holy Spirit to provide confidence in the truth of what Edwards calls "the great things of the gospel." We will first sketch the broader social and religious context of the times and then consider some prominent themes from both theologians concerning experiences of God.

1. Simeon Zahl, *The Holy Spirit and Christian Experience* (Oxford: Oxford University Press, 2020), 10, 17.

It is common to look at the rise of Pentecostalism and the charismatic renewal in the twentieth century as marking a distinctive turn to personal experience in Christianity, but the roots of experientialism lie much earlier, in the transformations of early modernity. The sixteenth-century Reformation not only launched a theological revolution, it also initiated profound social and cultural changes throughout Europe. The proliferation of new Protestant sects resulted in religious competition and conflict, with each group claiming to represent the one true faith. Theological questions became entangled with political and social agendas, as Roman Catholics and Protestants were embroiled in political intrigue and bloody wars, culminating in the brutal devastation of the Thirty Years War (1618–48).

An unintended consequence of the Reformation challenge to Catholic authority was the raising of basic epistemological questions in a fresh way: Given the many competing claims to religious truth, how do we determine which authority to follow? How is one to distinguish legitimate from illegitimate religious claims? A crisis in religious authority was felt not only among intellectuals but also throughout society at large. Susan Schreiner states, "The age from 1400 to 1600 was a period when the 'crisis consciousness' becomes a widespread perception, a time when people sensed that those values and structures that had seemed fixed were now shifting, cracking, crumbling, and the inherited form of civilization was disintegrating." The sixteenth century in particular "was a time of 'clanging, clashing certitudes.'"[2]

Concurrent with the crisis in religious authority was a series of unusual religious revivals and awakenings on both sides of the Atlantic. In America, the Great Awakening, associated especially with the Congregationalist minister Jonathan Edwards and the itinerant Anglican George Whitefield, swept through New England in the 1730s and 1740s. Great Britain had the English, Welsh, and Scottish revivals, in which John and Charles Wesley, along with Whitefield, were prominent. Many were converted, lives were dramatically changed, and there emerged a new emphasis on holy living.

One response to the crisis of authority was to look to the work of the Holy Spirit within the believer for certainty about theological matters, so that "the Spirit became the agent of certainty."[3] The turn to personal experience of God through the Holy Spirit developed over time into a fresh expression of Christian commitment, what Ted Campbell calls the "religion of the heart."

2. Susan E. Schreiner, *Are You Alone Wise? The Search for Certainty in the Early Modern Era* (New York: Oxford University Press, 2011), 13, ix.
3. Schreiner, *Are You Alone Wise?*, ix.

Before and during the [seventeenth century] English Revolution, concerns for heartfelt religious experience arose not only among the Quakers and other sectarian groups, but also among the more conventional Puritans as well. Pietism, among Continental Protestants in the late seventeenth and eighteenth centuries, developed its own forms of affective devotion, as did the Evangelical Revival of eighteenth-century Britain and the First Great Awakening in the British colonies of North America.[4]

Diverse groups were united in their conviction that "the 'heart,' denoting the will and the affections (or 'dispositions'), is the central point of contact between God and humankind." What was perceived as the austere formalism and theological scholasticism of established Lutheran and Reformed churches needed reform rooted in a transforming experience of God. "Affective experience became the center of the religious life, so that sacraments, moral discipline, and meditative techniques were relegated to the status of means to a greater end, namely, the personal and affective experience of God."[5] Social and intellectual upheaval helped to create the conditions in which personal experience of God was so significant. Bruce Hindmarsh observes,

Material, economic, and political conditions in the eighteenth century led to an unprecedented level of *movement* of people, goods, and ideas. The most important implication of this for evangelical revival is that this sort of exchange dislocated people and exposed them to differences, and to new opportunities and threats, while also underlining their sense of insecurity in the modern world. Religious experience became, therefore, far more voluntary and self-conscious, and far less a matter of custom or givenness, as women and men were presented with alternatives.[6]

But while the revivals had salutary effects on the spirituality of many, they also produced eccentric and even bizarre behaviors. Strange visions, trances, fainting, uncontrollable bodily movements, claims to having received direct revelations from God—as well as reports of encounters with the devil—were also part of the mix. In this context, the question of how to distinguish genuine experiences of God from those that are not became especially urgent. A second issue also lurked in the background, although it

4. Ted A. Campbell, *The Religion of the Heart: A Study of European Religious Life in the Seventeenth and Eighteenth Centuries* (Columbia: University of South Carolina Press, 1991), 2.
5. Campbell, *Religion of the Heart*, 3.
6. D. Bruce Hindmarsh, *The Evangelical Conversion Narrative: Spiritual Autobiography in Early Modern England* (New York: Oxford University Press, 2005), 79. Emphasis in original.

was not given the attention it attracted later in the twentieth century: Can one's experience of God provide epistemic support for one's conviction about the truth of Christian claims?

Simeon Zahl points out that the new focus on personal experience of God was in part a response to two perceived threats to Christian devotion.

> The first was the threat of domination of religion by "reason" or "rationalism," represented by the forms of thought associated at the eve of the nineteenth century with the Enlightenment. The second was an ongoing decline in Europe and beyond that was seen to be taking place in the wake of a perceived diminishing of the practical salience and energy of mainstream Protestant Christianity since the Reformation. In both cases, appeals to "experience" served as powerful alternatives and counterarguments that responded to these new—or at any rate newly urgent—problems.[7]

What criteria are appropriate for identifying genuine experiences of God? Do what seem to be experiences of God provide evidential support for Christian beliefs, either for the experiencer or for others? These are controversial questions, and in addressing them Edwards and Wesley distinguish between what are sometimes called "internal" evidential factors (those available to the believer herself) and "external" factors (those that are in principle available also to others). In the former category are the internal witness of the Holy Spirit and the special spiritual "sense" or supernatural "light" that is available to the regenerate but not to the unregenerate or "natural" person. Chief among the external factors is the observable change in the regenerate believer's life brought about by the Holy Spirit as manifest through the "fruit of the Spirit."

Despite their differences on some theological points, Edwards and Wesley have a similar approach to questions about experiences of God.[8] Both lived at a time when dramatic, sometimes outlandish, religious experiences were a frequent occurrence, and both were careful and perceptive observers of these experiences. Both were alert to theological and epistemological issues raised

---

7. Simeon Zahl, "Experience," in *The Oxford Handbook of Nineteenth Century Christian Thought*, ed. Joel D. S. Rasmussen, Judith Wolfe, and Johannes Zachhuber (Oxford: Oxford University Press, 2017), 178–79.

8. Several studies compare Edwards and Wesley on religious experience. See Richard E. Brantley, "The Common Ground of Wesley and Edwards," *Harvard Theological Review* 83, no. 3 (July 1990): 271–303; Robert Doyle Smith, "John Wesley and Jonathan Edwards on Religious Experience: A Comparative Analysis," *Wesley Theological Journal* 25, no. 1 (Spring 1990): 130–46; and Richard B. Steele, *"Gracious Affection" and "True Virtue" according to Jonathan Edwards and John Wesley* (Metuchen, NJ: Scarecrow, 1994).

by religious experiences, and both defended in principle the veridicality of some of these experiences. Both were influenced by the Puritans and Pietists, and they were well aware of critiques of personal religious experience coming from Enlightenment skeptics as well as some established churchmen. Before examining Edwards and Wesley further, we will look briefly at some intellectual and religious influences on their times.

Puritans and Pietists

Puritanism began as a powerful reform movement within the Church of England during the sixteenth century. Some Puritans separated from the Church, traveled to America, and in 1620 established the Plymouth Colony in Massachusetts. A larger and less separatistic group arrived at Massachusetts Bay in 1630, where they tried to put into practice their ideal of a society completely devoted to the teachings of Scripture. But by the 1730s and 1740s the Puritan experiment in America was in decline, as the population of New England became more diverse and less interested in Puritan ideals.

Puritanism has had an enormous influence on subsequent Protestant Christianity, especially evangelicalism. It is the Puritan emphasis on personal experience of God through the special ministry of the Holy Spirit that is most significant for our purposes.[9] As "physicians of the soul," Puritan leaders "prescribed a demanding regime of personal devotions, including godly reading, psalm-singing, prayer, fasting, and spiritual meditation. . . . The sheer intensity of this spiritual praxis set the godly apart."[10] The spiritual disciplines and experiential stages of conversion are indicative of the turn toward a religion of the heart. Campbell remarks, "For the Puritans, the religious life had come to be centered on the changed 'heart'—the will and affections convicted, converted, and sanctified by the predestining grace of God."[11] The personal experience of conversion and the report of this transformative experience in personal testimony and spiritual autobiography were central to Puritan theology.[12] But the conversion experience was not an end in itself. Genuine conversion rooted in regeneration was expected to lead to appreciation of the sovereign majesty of God in all things and to holiness in living.

9. See George F. Nuttall, *The Holy Spirit in Puritan Faith and Experience* (Oxford: Blackwell, 1946).

10. John Coffey and Paul C. H. Lim, "Introduction," in *The Cambridge Companion to Puritanism*, ed. John Coffey and Paul C. H. Lim (Cambridge: Cambridge University Press, 2008), 4.

11. Campbell, *Religion of the Heart*, 53.

12. Hindmarsh, *Evangelical Conversion Narrative*, 25–60.

Concern with personal conversion and an experience of God resulting in the assurance of salvation also characterized Pietism, a seventeenth-century movement pioneered by Philip Spener and August Hermann Francke, which sought a deeper spirituality and holiness in living that was firmly grounded in the Bible. While there was diversity among the groups and not all of them rejected the institutional church, Pietists were distinguished from other Christians by their careful cultivation of the inner spiritual life. "Pietism," says Campbell, "stressed personal religious experience, especially repentance (the experience of one's own unworthiness before God and of one's own need for grace) and sanctification (the experience of personal growth in holiness, involving progress towards complete or perfect fulfillment of God's intention)."[13]

While a student at the University of Leipzig, Francke had a dramatic conversion experience. This experience—including an intense sense of sorrow for one's sin and fear of judgment, followed by relief and joy at being forgiven by God—became normative among Pietists. Hindmarsh observes that Francke's experience "was really a version of the Puritan morphology: conviction of sin under the law, despair and fear of divine judgment, the desire for redemption, struggle in prayer, and then a breakthrough to faith, followed by real sanctification and continued vigilance in self-examination. The crisis at the centre of all this became a distinctive feature of Pietist conversion."[14]

By the early eighteenth century, Pietistic beliefs and practices were spreading throughout Europe and the American colonies. Count Ludwig von Zinzendorf provided a place in Saxony for Pietist refugees who had been driven out of Bohemia and Moravia by Catholic authorities. Zinzendorf's estate, Herrnhut, became the home of the Moravians, who were among the earliest Protestant missionaries to the West Indies, North America, Asia, and Africa. Both Jonathan Edwards and John Wesley had contact with Pietists and were influenced by the movement.

The Problem of Enthusiasm

The new stress on personal experience of God came under withering attack from both established theologians and Enlightenment free-thinkers and deists. At the heart of the critique was the accusation of "enthusiasm," or what was understood as irrational religious extremism manifested by those

13. Campbell, *Religion of the Heart*, 71.
14. Hindmarsh, *Evangelical Conversion Narrative*, 58–59.

claiming a special relationship with God.[15] Following the Reformation, Protestants became enmeshed in controversies over authority and interpretation in religious disputes. Unlike Roman Catholics, Protestants lacked anything resembling the magisterial teaching office of the Catholic Church, and thus they looked to the Bible and spiritual discernment through the Holy Spirit for settling such disputes. "At first, in the early theology of Martin Luther, these two sources of authority were closely interwoven, but by the 1520s they had been teased apart, and the five centuries of Protestant debate over the value or otherwise of 'experience' had been set in motion."[16] By 1525 Luther was troubled by the more radically subjectivist and emotional experiences proliferating among Protestants, especially because in his view these expressions of "enthusiasm" (*Schwärmerei*) amounted to "a privileging of inner experience, interpreted as experience of God's Spirit, over the external instruments of the Bible and the biblically authorized sacraments."[17] Luther insisted on the priority of Scripture as the authoritative guide, and strong appeals to an inner experience of the Spirit, especially if they included claims to new spiritual insights, were problematic.

Criticism of emotionally charged experiences of God also came from those influenced by the Enlightenment movements of the time. For much of the twentieth century, it was customary to speak of "the Enlightenment" as a single homogenous intellectual movement in Europe obsessed with reason and explicitly committed to undermining traditional Christian institutions and commitments. The emergence of modern science, we were told, introduced new ways of understanding the natural world and human experience that made no reference to theological underpinnings. The institutional church and traditional theological beliefs were attacked as corrupt discredited vestiges of a bygone age, and biblical criticism undermined traditional confidence in the authority of the Bible as the divinely inspired Word of God. The Enlightenment, in the words of Peter Gay, was a form of "modern paganism" directly opposed to religion.[18]

While there is undoubtedly some truth in this characterization, more recent scholarship uncovers a more complex social and intellectual reality.[19]

---

15. David S. Lovejoy, *Religious Enthusiasm in the New World: Heresy to Revolution* (Cambridge: MA: Harvard University Press, 1985).

16. Zahl, *Holy Spirit and Christian Experience*, 18.

17. Zahl, *Holy Spirit and Christian Experience*, 18.

18. See Peter Gay, *The Rise of Modern Paganism*, vol. 1 of *The Enlightenment: An Interpretation* (New York: Norton, 1966).

19. See, e.g., S. J. Barnett, *The Enlightenment and Religion: The Myths of Modernity* (Manchester: Manchester University Press, 2003); David Sorkin, *The Religious Enlightenment: Protestants, Jews, and Catholics from London to Vienna* (Princeton: Princeton University Press,

There were multiple Enlightenment movements throughout Europe and North America with significant differences among them. Not all thinkers were anti-Christian; in fact, most Enlightenment figures retained some Christian commitments, and many Christian clergy, especially Protestants, were sympathetic to Enlightenment ideals.

The Enlightenment is often portrayed as a time of enormous confidence in the power of reason to solve all problems. It is true that many thinkers were remarkably optimistic about what reason could accomplish, and they were especially critical of what they regarded as ancient superstitions. Thus historian Louis Dupré identifies the emphasis on reason and emancipation from superstition as especially characteristic of Enlightenment thought.[20] But the emphasis on reason must be understood in light of the ongoing struggles with skepticism in the early modern period. The reintroduction of classical skepticism into Europe in the mid-sixteenth century, along with the growing awareness of religious and cultural diversity in the New World, encouraged pervasive skepticism and relativism.[21] The eighteenth-century Scottish philosopher David Hume, one of the most influential Enlightenment figures, was deeply skeptical about reason. "Reason," Hume famously declared, "is, and ought only to be, the slave of the passions, and can never pretend to any other office than to serve and obey them."[22] Peter Gay argues that the Enlightenment should not be construed as an age of reason so much as an age of criticism.[23] Hume's writings—especially his essay "Of Miracles" and his works *Dialogues concerning Natural Religion* and *The Natural History of Religion*—presented a sustained critique of traditional Christian claims about God.[24]

Despite this, most educated persons of the period continued to believe in some kind of deity and maintained that reason could provide support for

2008); and Jonathan Sheehan, "Enlightenment, Religion, and the Enigma of Secularization: A Review Essay," *American Historical Review* 108 (October 2003): 1061–80. A helpful guide to the vast literature on the Enlightenment can be found in Lynn Hunt, with Margaret Jacob, "Enlightenment Studies," in *Encyclopedia of the Enlightenment*, ed. Alan Charles Kors (New York: Oxford University Press, 2003), 1:418–30.

20. Louis Dupré, *The Enlightenment and the Intellectual Foundations of Modern Culture* (New Haven: Yale University Press, 2004), 7.

21. Julia Annas and Jonathan Barnes, *The Modes of Skepticism: Ancient Texts and Modern Interpretations* (Cambridge: Cambridge University Press, 1985), 5. See also Richard Popkin, *The History of Skepticism: From Savonarola to Bayle*, rev. ed. (New York: Oxford University Press, 2003).

22. David Hume, *A Treatise of Human Nature* (New York: Doubleday, 1961), 2.3.3, p. 375.

23. Gay, *Enlightenment*, 141.

24. For an analysis of Hume's views on religion, see Keith Yandell, *Hume's "Inexplicable Mystery": His Views on Religion* (Philadelphia: Temple University Press, 1990).

some beliefs about God. Explicit atheists, as we understand the term today, were relatively rare.[25] But skepticism about traditional Christian beliefs, combined with the influence of Newtonian physics, produced an attenuated form of theism known as deism. Deists typically accepted belief in a morally good Creator who rewards goodness and punishes wickedness, but they rejected the idea that God has revealed himself supernaturally through the Bible and that God intervenes in the natural order through miraculous events. Their alternative was a natural, nonsectarian, "reasonable" religion that could serve as the foundation of morality.[26]

The Protestant renewal movements, with their stress on the certainty available through personal experiences of God, can be seen as a kind of response to the skepticism of the day. As Campbell explains, "Although the religion of the heart movements have been portrayed as reactionary in clinging to older forms of belief and refusing to face the challenge of modern epistemologies, the fact is that these movements would themselves reflect much of the same passion for finding certitude as the philosophers of their age did. They could hardly see the critical nuance, but their own stress on the authority of the inward assurance reflected a shift towards experience as the basis of knowledge."[27]

Both Edwards and Wesley were well aware of Enlightenment thinkers and the challenges they presented to orthodox Christianity. Both, for example, were familiar with Hume's views. Edwards read Hume's *A Treatise on Human Nature* "with great interest" and in a 1755 letter he comments on Hume's writings: "I am glad of an opportunity to read such corrupt books; especially when written by men of considerable genius; that I may have an idea of the notions that prevail in our nation."[28] Similarly, in a 1769 letter Wesley states that he "read Dr. Campbell's excellent answer to David Hume's insolent book against miracles," and in a 1772 letter Wesley referred to Hume as "the most insolent despiser of truth and virtue that ever appeared in the world."[29] In a 1768 letter Wesley acknowledged the growing skepticism concerning the supernatural in England: "It is true, likewise,

25. See Alan Charles Kors, "The Age of Enlightenment," in *The Oxford Handbook of Atheism*, ed. Stephen Bullivant and Michael Ruse (New York: Oxford University Press, 2013), 195–211.

26. See Peter Harrison, *"Religion" and the Religions in the English Enlightenment* (Cambridge: Cambridge University Press, 1990).

27. Campbell, *Religion of the Heart*, 16–17.

28. As cited in George M. Marsden, *Jonathan Edwards: A Life* (New Haven: Yale University Press, 2003), 466–67.

29. John Wesley, *Journals and Diaries, 1765–75*, ed. Reginald Ward and Richard Heitzenrater, vol. 22 of *The Works of John Wesley* (Nashville: Abingdon, 1993), 172, 321. The letters are

that the English in general, and indeed most of the men of learning in Europe, have given up all accounts of witches and apparitions as mere old wives' fables." He saw this as a direct threat to belief in the miraculous as recorded in Scripture, since "giving up witchcraft [belief in the supernatural] is in effect giving up the Bible."[30] Wesley continues in the letter to include extensive reports of supernatural experiences and apparitions that he was personally aware of.

Yet neither Edwards nor Wesley rejected reason as an enemy of faith; to the contrary, both regarded a responsible use of reason as indispensable for sound theology. Wesley taught logic at Oxford and insisted that, properly construed, reason was essential for true religion. "It is a fundamental truth with us," he insisted, "that to renounce reason is to renounce religion, that religion and reason go hand in hand, and that all irrational religion is false religion."[31] Moreover, both Edwards and Wesley read with interest the work of John Locke, whose influence can be traced in the thought of each theologian.

Not everyone embraced the disenchanted world of mechanistic science and deism. Those involved in the spiritual awakenings of the period inhabited a world rich with miraculous signs and dramatic experiences of the supernatural. Many reported their lives transformed through an acute awareness of sin and, following repentance, the renewing experience of God's love and forgiveness. But in addition to these sober experiences, there were also many reports of strange experiences producing extreme behavior. What was taken by some to be a powerful movement of the Holy Spirit often included sensational and even freakish physical displays. Alleged experiences of God included fits, falling over as though dead, convulsions, shouting, speaking in tongues, trances, visions, hearing voices, clairvoyance, out-of-body experiences, nakedness in worship, dreams, trances, and alterations of consciousness.[32]

Not surprisingly, these spectacles were controversial, eliciting sharp criticism from established church leaders who dismissed them as "enthusiasm." Whereas Puritans and Pietists had been critical of *formalism* in the established church, critics of the awakenings and revivals complained of *enthusiasm*.

---

dated March 5, 1769, and May 5, 1772. I am grateful to Tom McCall for drawing my attention to these letters.

30. The letter is dated May 25, 1768, and is in *Journals and Diaries, 1765–75*, 135.

31. John Wesley, "A Letter to the Reverend Dr. Rutherforth, March 28, 1768," in *The Works of John Wesley* (London: Thomas Cordeux, 1812), 13:135.

32. Ann Taves, *Fits, Trances, and Visions: Experiencing Religion and Explaining Experience from Wesley to James* (Princeton: Princeton University Press, 1999), 3.

Both enthusiasm and formalism were epithets used to disparage what their beholders viewed as false forms of Christianity. . . . Thus, from the mid-seventeenth century at least, a "formalist" was understood as one who had the form of religion without the power, while an "enthusiast" was understood as one who falsely claimed to be inspired. Both terms came to the fore with the Puritan emphasis on "inward" or "heart" religion. Puritans used the word "experience" to talk about this dimension of inwardness. . . . Puritans disparaged the absence of experience as "formalism." Conversely, non-Puritans disparaged the "inward sense and feeling," that is the "experience," of the Puritans as "enthusiasm."[33]

It was above all the claim to have received a special, direct communication from God—a special revelation, inspiration, or "inner light" giving deeper understanding and certainty on spiritual matters than one would otherwise have—that made enthusiasts suspect in the eyes of the established church.[34] This was seen as a direct threat to the authority of Scripture and church teaching.

One of the sharpest critics of enthusiasm was John Locke, who devotes a chapter of the fourth edition of *An Essay concerning Human Understanding* to refuting its errors. Locke has often been criticized by theologians for stressing the role of reason in assessing claims to divine revelation, but his emphasis on reason must be understood in the context of the debates raging in his day over the authority of personal experience. For Locke, "enthusiasm" refers to an approach to spiritual matters that rejects reason and the authority of Scripture in favor of a direct appeal to personal inspiration or illumination from God. Enthusiasm, "though founded neither on reason, nor divine revelation, but rising from the conceits of a warmed or over-weening brain, works yet, where it once gets footing, more powerfully on the persuasions and actions of men than either of those two, or both together."[35] According to Locke, the experiences of enthusiasts produced a certitude that nothing could shake. "Reason is lost upon them, they are above it: they see the light infused into their understandings, and cannot be mistaken; 'tis clear and visible there; like the light of bright Sunshine, shows itself, and needs no other proof, but its own evidence: they feel the hand of GOD moving them within, and the impulses of the spirit, and cannot be mistaken in what they feel."[36] Locke pressed

33. Taves, *Fits, Trances, and Visions*, 16–17.
34. Michael Heyd, "Enthusiasm," in Kors, *Encyclopedia of the Enlightenment*, 2:1.
35. John Locke, *An Essay concerning Human Understanding*, ed. Roger Woolhouse (London: Penguin Books, 1997), IV.19, pp. 616–17.
36. Locke, *Essay concerning Human Understanding*, 617.

the epistemological question confronting enthusiasts: "The question then here is, how do I know that GOD is the revealer of this to me; that this impression is made upon my mind by his Holy Spirit; and that therefore I ought to obey it? If I know not this, how great soever the assurance is, that I am possessed with, it is groundless; whatever light I pretend to, it is but *enthusiasm.*"[37]

John Wesley and the early Methodists were especially vulnerable to charges of enthusiasm. Although he opposed enthusiasm, Wesley was more frequently identified with enthusiasts than most of the moderate revival leaders. The sentiment of established churchmen is exemplified in Anglican bishop Joseph Butler's words to Wesley: "Sir, the pretending to extraordinary revelations and gifts of the Holy Ghost is a horrid thing—a very horrid thing!"[38] So persistent were the attacks that Wesley devoted a 1747 sermon, "The Nature of Enthusiasm," to rebutting the charges.[39] As Ann Taves observes, Edwards and Wesley had a common response to the controversy over enthusiasm. "First, both Edwards and Wesley defined true religion in opposition to both formalism and enthusiasm. Second, they both equated true religion with vital or heart religion as manifest in conversion and a continuing process of sanctification. Third, they both defended the possibility of a direct or immediate experience of the Spirit of God and they both argued that authentic experience must be tried and tested in practice."[40]

Jonathan Edwards

Sometimes regarded as the greatest American evangelical theologian, Jonathan Edwards (1703–58) produced an impressive body of theological writings during a relatively short life. Although well acquainted with the broader intellectual currents of the day, Edwards's primary interest was in theology, in explicating the sovereign majesty of the triune God and defending Calvinist doctrines against attacks from deism and what he perceived as the errors

37. Locke, *Essay concerning Human Understanding*, 618. Emphasis in original. David Hume was another biting critic of enthusiasm, but whereas Locke criticized enthusiasm as a Christian, advocating a more reasonable and moderate form of Christianity, Hume used the excesses of enthusiasm to castigate Christianity. See David Hume, "Of Superstition and Enthusiasm," in *David Hume: Writings on Religion*, ed. Antony Flew (La Salle, IL: Open Court, 1992).

38. As quoted in Michael J. McClymond and Gerald R. McDermott, *The Theology of Jonathan Edwards* (New York: Oxford University Press, 2012), 152–53.

39. John Wesley, "The Nature of Enthusiasm," in *Sermons II, 34–70*, ed. Albert C. Outler, vol. 2 of *The Works of John Wesley* (Nashville: Abingdon, 1985), 46–60.

40. Taves, *Fits, Trances, and Visions*, 48.

of Arminianism. Edwards has had a substantial influence on American Protestant thought, especially on American evangelicalism.[41]

Edwards's father was a Congregationalist minister, and his maternal grandfather was Solomon Stoddard, pastor of the Northampton church in Massachusetts and one of the most influential church leaders in New England. After earning a bachelor's degree from Yale, Edwards ministered alongside his grandfather in Northampton, and upon the latter's death in 1729, he became the sole pastor of the church. Dismissed from his position in a dispute over conditions for church membership in 1750, Edwards moved to Stockbridge, Massachusetts, where he ministered to congregations of Native Americans as well as some whites. In 1757 he accepted the offer to become president of the College of New Jersey (later Princeton University), but he died from complications from a smallpox vaccine in 1758, only weeks after beginning his work as head of the College.

Edwards became well known for his astute observations about religious experience during the Great Awakening, from roughly 1735–43. His sensitivity to these issues stemmed in part from his own spiritual experiences.

> During his late teens, he underwent intense religious struggles and experiences that would shape the rest of his life. In his senior year, when he was still sixteen, he nearly died from a serious illness, and was terrified about the state of his soul, feeling that God "shook me over the pit of hell." During the next year he strenuously sought God and moral purity, but he did not find any resolution until the spring of his seventeenth year, when he began to have some remarkable experiences of a sense of joy in the beauty of God's goodness.[42]

In 1721, after reading Scripture, Edwards had what he called a "new sense" of God's glory. Shortly thereafter he had a pivotal experience as he "walked abroad in the pasture, and, looking around and at the sky, he perceived the simultaneous, paradoxical 'majestic meekness' and 'awful sweetness' of God."[43] Deeply moving experiences of God's grandeur and majesty became a pattern in Edwards's life. Marsden observes that "Edwards' spiritual labors, which were marked by intense devotional and personal disciplines, were punctuated by ecstatic experience as he went to the fields or the woods

41. See Douglas A. Sweeney, "Evangelical Tradition in America," in *The Cambridge Companion to Jonathan Edwards*, ed. Stephen J. Stein (New York: Cambridge University Press, 2007), 217–38.

42. George M. Marsden, "Biography," in Stein, *Cambridge Companion to Jonathan Edwards*, 21.

43. Kenneth P. Minkema, "Jonathan Edwards: A Theological Life," in *The Princeton Companion to Jonathan Edwards*, ed. Sang Hyun Lee (Princeton: Princeton University Press, 2005), 4.

for contemplation and prayer. He would be overwhelmed with a sense of God's glory, beauty, goodness, and love. He would be so overcome by a 'sweet delight in God and divine things' that he would break into ecstatic spiritual singing or chanting."[44]

In 1734 a spiritual awakening occurred among the congregation at Northampton, with similar revivals appearing throughout the Connecticut Valley the following year. "Nearly everyone seemed to be affected, experiencing God's grace, or at least awakened to their need for God's grace. Hundreds made very affecting professions of faith, and Edwards estimated that within a three-month period three hundred, or almost half the adult population, were savingly converted."[45] In 1737 Edwards published *A Faithful Narrative of a Surprising Work of God* based on these revivals. Eventually translated into several languages, the book established Edwards internationally as a thoughtful observer of revivalism and the experience of conversion.[46] Among those who read it were John and Charles Wesley. Later, when the Methodist movement was flourishing, John Wesley published his own abridgment of the work and made it standard reading in Methodist circles.[47]

But just as it was gaining international attention, the Northampton awakening began to subside. The event that effectively marked its end was the suicide of Edwards's uncle, Joseph Hawley, in 1735. Mentally unstable, suffering from depression and deeply troubled by the state of his own soul, Hawley slit his own throat.[48] This tragedy, along with the congregation's tendency to fall back into older habits, caused Edwards to think further about the nature of genuine encounters with God. The suicide was interpreted by Edwards as an example of the opposition launched by Satan against spiritual awakenings.

Edwards heard of the remarkable preaching of George Whitefield in England and the colonies, and he invited the evangelist to preach in Northampton. In October 1740, as Whitefield preached to packed audiences in Boston and Northampton, spiritual revival broke out, and the next two years were the apex of what came to be known as the Great Awakening. Lives were changed as sinners were dramatically converted, and many demonstrated a renewed passion for holiness and godly living. But the revivals also produced extravagant emotional displays and disturbing behavior, including strange visions, fainting, and claims of direct revelations from God.

44. Marsden, "Biography," 23.
45. Marsden, "Biography," 25.
46. Minkema, "Jonathan Edwards," 7.
47. Marsden, *Jonathan Edwards*, 173.
48. Marsden, *Jonathan Edwards*, 163–65.

The revivals prompted two sharply differing responses among the New England clergy. The "New Light" camp welcomed the movement as a genuine work of God, with real conversions and renewed spiritual vitality among nominal Christians. But the "Old Light" group was critical of what they regarded as the excesses of the revivals. New England was deeply divided, with the controversy especially acute at Yale, where Edwards gave the commencement address in 1741. Although he was well aware of the bizarre behavior of some, Edwards nevertheless defended the awakening as a profound movement of God's Spirit.

> While Edwards strongly warned against judging the condition of other people's souls, his sermon, soon published as a short treatise, *Distinguishing Marks of the Work of the Spirit of God* (1741), was a ringing endorsement of the awakening. Old Lights, who now included Yale's president, Thomas Clap, were discrediting the awakening on the grounds of its excesses and irregularities, especially the extreme emotional and physical responses of many who supposedly were savingly converted. Edwards explained that some indefensible irregularities were to be expected to be associated with any great work of God since Satan was working more intensely at such times trying to undermine true spiritual experiences by encouraging delusions. Intense emotional and physical responses to awakening preaching, Edwards argued, were neither proofs of the validity of the revivals nor proofs of their invalidity. The distinguishing marks of a true work of God were the same as they had always been: heart-felt love to God and conformity to the doctrines and practices revealed in God's Word.[49]

The Spiritual Sense and the Affections

There are reasons to believe that, although he died before he could complete it, Edwards was preparing an apologetic response to critiques of enthusiasm from both Enlightenment skeptics and establishment church leaders. Two questions in particular demanded attention: How can one be confident of the truth of the gospel? How can we distinguish genuine experiences of God from those which are spurious? Michael McClymond argues that in his response to deistic critics, Edwards was developing a novel approach that combined reasoned argument with the confidence that comes from inner experience.[50]

49. Marsden, "Biography," 28–29.
50. Michael J. McClymond, *Encounters with God: An Approach to the Theology of Jonathan Edwards* (New York: Oxford University Press, 1998), vi. See also Marsden, *Jonathan Edwards*, 110; and McClymond and McDermott, *Theology of Jonathan Edwards*, 149–66.

To what extent is it possible to establish truths about God through rational reflection and evidence from the world around us? Edwards acknowledges that evidential arguments can have some value even for the unregenerate. In *Religious Affections* he observes that arguments and evidence "may be greatly serviceable to awaken unbelievers, and bring them to serious consideration, and to confirm the faith of true saints."[51] In the *Miscellanies* he states, "Arguing for the being of God according to the natural powers from everything we are conversant with is short, easy, and what we naturally fall into."[52] Michael McClymond and Gerald McDermott point out that "the *Miscellanies* contain extensive presentations of Christian evidences, discussions of miracles, treatments of biblical history, and reconstruals of rational arguments for God's existence. . . . The classical arguments for God's existence—ontological, cosmological, teleological—all appear in the *Miscellanies*."[53] Thus Edwards follows the apologists of the day in appealing to miracles, the resurrection of Jesus Christ, and even the survival of the Jewish people as evidence for God's reality.

At the same time Edwards can be skeptical of reason's powers. Divine revelation and God's grace are required for the "natural man" to grasp what reason shows. According to William Wainwright, "Even though Edwards thinks that reason can prove God's existence, determine the nature of many of His attributes, discern our obligations to Him, and establish the credibility of scripture, he believes that grace is needed both to help 'the natural principles against those things that tend to stupefy it and to hinder its free exercise' (Misc. 626, T111) and to 'sanctify the reasoning faculty and assist it to see the clear evidence there is of the truth of religion in rational arguments' (Misc. 628, T251)."[54] Moreover, Edwards holds that although historical arguments and evidence can have a certain effect on the unregenerate so that they might agree that there is some probability of the truth of the gospel, this will be insufficient for the kind of confidence necessary for the believer to give up all for the sake of Christ. "'Tis unreasonable to suppose, that God has provided for his people, no more than probable evidences of the truth of the gospel."[55] Only "internal evidence" can provide the con-

---

51. Jonathan Edwards, *Religious Affections*, ed. John E. Smith, vol. 2 of *The Works of Jonathan Edwards* (New Haven: Yale University Press, 2009), 307.

52. Jonathan Edwards, *The "Miscellanies," a–500*, ed. Thomas A. Schafer, vol. 13 of *The Works of Jonathan Edwards* (New Haven: Yale University Press, 1994), misc. 268, p. 373.

53. McClymond and McDermott, *Theology of Jonathan Edwards*, 155, 158, 160.

54. William J. Wainwright, *Reason and the Heart: A Prolegomenon to a Critique of Passional Reason* (Ithaca, NY: Cornell University Press, 1995), 9.

55. Edwards, *Religious Affections*, 304.

fidence we require, and this is to be found in the "spiritual perception" or the "sense of the heart."

What is this special spiritual sense or perception through which believers apprehend divine realities? In "A Divine and Supernatural Light," Edwards claims, "There is such a thing, as a spiritual and divine light, immediately imparted to the soul by God, of a different nature from any that is obtained by natural means."[56] Or as he puts it in *Religious Affections*, those who are regenerated by the Holy Spirit are given "a new supernatural sense, that is as it were a certain divine spiritual taste, which is in its whole nature diverse from any former kinds of sensation of the mind."[57] This is "a true sense of the divine excellency of the things revealed in the Word of God, and a conviction of the truth and reality of them, thence arising."[58] The spiritual sense or divine light thus provides a spiritual apprehension of God's excellence and a conviction of the truth of what is revealed in Scripture.

Ever since Perry Miller's seminal 1948 essay "Jonathan Edwards on the Sense of the Heart,"[59] there has been general agreement on the importance of the notion of the "spiritual sense" or "sense of the heart" to Edwards's thought. But there is continuing debate over just how we should understand this. Is the spiritual sense something roughly analogous to the five traditional senses, so that it forms a kind of sixth sense in addition to the others? Or should we rather think of the term "spiritual sense" as a metaphor for awareness of divine truths that the Holy Spirit mysteriously brings about? Is the spiritual sense something that all people, unregenerate and regenerate alike, enjoy or is it restricted to the regenerate? The dispute over the first question hinges not only on rival interpretations of Edwards's writings but also on questions about the nature and degree of John Locke's influence on Edwards. Without trying to resolve the issues here, we will follow McClymond, who argues that since elements of Edwards's writings can be marshaled in support of either interpretation, the best course is to regard the spiritual sense as a complex reality encompassing both continuity and discontinuity with ordinary sensory experience.[60]

56. Jonathan Edwards, "A Divine and Supernatural Light," in *A Jonathan Edwards Reader*, ed. John E. Smith, Harry S. Stout, and Kenneth Minkema (New Haven: Yale University Press, 1995), 107.

57. Edwards, *Religious Affections*, 259. In using such language, Edwards attaches himself to a long tradition in Christian theology that speaks of a special spiritual sense for discerning spiritual realities. See Paul L. Gavrilyuk and Sarah Coakley, eds., *The Spiritual Senses: Perceiving God in Western Christianity* (Cambridge: Cambridge University Press, 2012).

58. Edwards, "Divine and Supernatural Light," 111.

59. Perry Miller, "Jonathan Edwards on the Sense of the Heart," *Harvard Theological Review* 41 (1948): 123–45.

60. McClymond, *Encounters with God*, 9–10.

The second issue raised above is less ambiguous, as Edwards is clear that the spiritual sense is only available to the believer through a special work of the Holy Spirit. The experience of conversion, resulting in regeneration, is crucial, so that "believers are able to perceive a holy beauty in God that is invisible to nonbelievers."[61] Edwards observes that the Holy Spirit "may indeed act upon the mind of a natural man; but he acts in the mind of a saint as an indwelling vital principle."[62] Thus, "there is a spiritual understanding of divine things, which all natural and unregenerate men are destitute of."[63] As McClymond explains, although the Holy Spirit is active among both believers and unbelievers, the work of the Spirit in the regenerate is distinctive.

> The regenerate and the unregenerate alike have mental notions or ideas of God, conveyed to them through the Word of God or by other means. Yet only the regenerate perceive the divine excellency, and the unregenerate remain wholly insensible to it. The regenerate and the unregenerate alike possess the natural faculty of reason, and both employ their reason with respect to spiritual things. Yet only the regenerate receive that divine and supernatural light that enables their natural reason to see God as God truly is. The regenerate and the unregenerate alike receive the influences of the Holy Spirit, for the Spirit does not act only on the elect. Yet only the regenerate have the Spirit communicated in such a way that the Spirit becomes united with them and acts in and through them as a "new vital principle." The regenerate and the unregenerate alike have affective sensibility, and both experience the "sense of the heart" with respect to those objects that engage them. Yet only the regenerate have that "spiritual sense" or "new sense" that consists in "delight" and in a "sweet sense" of God and spiritual things.[64]

The spiritual sense produces conviction of the truth of what is contained in Scripture. Edwards states, "There arises from this sense of divine excellency of things contained in the Word of God, a conviction of the truth and reality of them."[65] This is not simply an intellectual assent to the truth of certain doctrines; it is a deep, inner conviction as one *experientially senses*

---

61. McClymond and McDermott, *Theology of Jonathan Edwards,* 317. See also Paul Helm, "John Locke and Jonathan Edwards: A Reconstruction," *Journal of the History of Ideas* 7, no. 1 (1969): 54–58.

62. Edwards, "Divine and Supernatural Light," 108.

63. Jonathan Edwards, "A Spiritual Understanding of Divine Things Denied to the Unregenerate," in *Sermons and Discourses, 1723–1729,* ed. Kenneth P. Minkema, vol. 14 of *The Works of Jonathan Edwards* (New Haven: Yale University Press, 1997), 72.

64. McClymond, *Encounters with God,* 21.

65. Edwards, "Divine and Supernatural Light," 112.

God's beauty and excellence. "He that is spiritually enlightened truly apprehends and sees it, or has a sense of it. He don't merely rationally believe that God is glorious, but he has a sense of the gloriousness of God in his heart. There is not only a rational belief that God is holy, and that holiness is a good thing; but there is a sense of the loveliness of God's holiness."[66]

Moreover, the spiritual sense also helps one to grasp the truth of the claims of the gospel itself. Edwards states,

> A true sense of the divine excellency of the things of God's Word doth more directly and immediately convince of the truth of them; and that because the excellency of these things is so superlative. . . . When there is an actual and lively discovery of this beauty and excellency, it won't allow of any such thought as that it is an human work, or the fruit of men's invention. This evidence, that they, that are spiritually enlightened, have of the truth of the things of religion, is a kind of intuitive and immediate evidence. They believe the doctrines of God's word to be divine, because they see divinity in them, i.e., they see a divine, and transcendent, and most evidently distinguishing glory in them; such glory as, if clearly seen, don't leave room to doubt of their being of God, and not of men.[67]

In the above quote Edwards speaks of this apprehension of divine truth as "immediate" and "intuitive" and thus not the product of inferences. Elsewhere he says that this understanding "is without any long chain of arguments; the argument is but one, and the evidence direct; the mind ascends to the truth of the gospel but by one step, and that is its divine glory."[68] Edwards's point seems to be that through the spiritual sense we understand the statements expressed in Scripture as having an association with divinity because of their "excellence," and this experience provides noninferential justification for accepting their truth with conviction.

Contrary to the claims of some enthusiasts, Edwards makes clear that the divine light or spiritual sense does not involve the transmission of new truths not already contained in the Scriptures. "This spiritual light that I am speaking of, is quite a different thing from inspiration: it reveals no new doctrine; it suggests no new proposition to the mind, it teaches no new thing of God, or Christ, or another world, not taught in the Bible; but

66. Edwards, "Divine and Supernatural Light," 111–12.
67. Edwards, "Divine and Supernatural Light," 113–14. See William J. Wainwright, "Jonathan Edwards and His Puritan Predecessors," in Gavrilyuk and Coakley, *Spiritual Senses*, 232.
68. Edwards, *Religious Affections*, 298–99.

only gives a due apprehension of those things that are taught in the Word of God."[69]

A proper understanding of and response to God—"true religion"—involves the right disposition of the affections toward the excellence and beauty of divine things. "True religion, in great part, consists in holy affections."[70] If we think of the spiritual sense as something that the Holy Spirit provides the believer, enabling a penetrating understanding of the things of God, then the affections, or at least the holy and gracious affections, might be considered the appropriate human dispositional responses to the excellence and beauty of divine realities. Both the spiritual sense and the gracious or holy affections are possible only through God's special grace.

But what exactly are the affections? According to Edwards, "the affections are no other, than the more vigorous and sensible inclinations and will of the soul."[71] The affections reflect the core orientation of the person; or as John Smith puts it in his introduction to *Religious Affections*, they are "signposts indicating the *direction* of the soul, whether it is toward God in love or away from God and toward the world."[72] McClymond and McDermott explain that for Edwards, an individual person "was a bundle of affections that determine nearly everything that person feels, thinks, and does."[73] Affections involve desires or inclinations that are intimately related to the will, but not every action of the will or inclination is an affection. Although every act of the will involves a measure of like or dislike of the relevant object, only those that are sufficiently "vigorous" rise to the level of affections.

In speaking of the affections as involving inclinations and will, Edwards brings together *the understanding*, which perceives and judges, and *the will*, which moves a person either toward or away from an object in approving or rejecting, in loving or hating.[74] Smith explains Edwards's view as follows: "In every choice the soul likes or dislikes, and when these inclinations are 'vigorous' and 'lively,' they correspond to love and hatred. Affections are the *lively* inclinations which reveal the fundamental intent and direction of the heart."[75] There are, then, both cognitive and volitional components to affections, and Edwards resists any dichotomy between the heart and the mind.

---

69. Edwards, "Divine and Supernatural Light," 110.

70. Edwards, *Religious Affections*, 95.

71. Edwards, *Religious Affections*, 96.

72. John E. Smith, "Editor's Introduction," in Jonathan Edwards, *Religious Affections*, 12. Emphasis in original.

73. McClymond and McDermott, *Theology of Jonathan Edwards*, 311.

74. McClymond and McDermott, *Theology of Jonathan Edwards*, 312.

75. John E. Smith, "Religious Affections and the 'Sense of the Heart,'" in Lee, *Princeton Companion to Jonathan Edwards*, 104. Emphasis in original.

The object of the gracious affections and the spiritual sense is "the transcendently excellent and amiable nature of divine things, as they are in themselves" or "the beauty of holiness."[76] For Edwards, the primary affection is love. "The Scriptures do represent true religion, as being summarily comprehended in *love*, the chief of the affections, and fountain of all other affections."[77] The gracious affections, guided by the spiritual sense, are accompanied by an apprehension of the beauties of divine realities and a conviction of the truth of the claims of the gospel. "All those who are truly gracious persons have a solid, full, thorough and effectual conviction of the truth of the great things of the gospel."[78]

Genuine Experiences of God

How can we identify a genuine encounter with God? This issue was central to disputes over religious enthusiasm during the Great Awakening: Were the dramatic and emotional experiences undergone in the revivals an authentic work of the Holy Spirit or the product of an overly excited human imagination? Or, worse yet, were they the work of the devil? Edwards gave the question careful consideration, especially in *Distinguishing Marks of a Work of the Spirit of God* and in *A Treatise concerning Religious Affections*. While not uncritical of excessive displays, Edwards defended the authenticity of many of the experiences as real encounters with God. He believed that although we must always be careful in making judgments about another person's inner disposition, we can recognize the supernatural work of God in a life.

In order to identify a particular experience as a genuine encounter with God, we must be able to determine that the person having the experience exemplifies holy affections. In *Religious Affections*, Edwards proposes some principles that can be applied in determining whether persons give evidence of the holy affections at the heart of true religion. These can be difficult to apply, not least because of our tendency to self-deception and hypocrisy and what Edwards regarded as the ever-present danger of demonic counterfeits. But he thought that they could be useful guides for discriminating between genuinely gracious experiences of God and those deriving from other sources.

Edwards begins by listing twelve things that he thinks *cannot* be used as criteria for identifying God's gracious work. For example, the intensity

76. Edwards, *Religious Affections*, 240, 259–60.
77. Edwards, *Religious Affections*, 106. Emphasis in original.
78. Edwards, *Religious Affections*, 291.

of a religious affection (either the presence of intense emotion or the lack thereof) is no indication one way or another as to whether it is part of a genuine encounter with God. "Therefore they do greatly err, who condemn persons as enthusiasts, merely because their affections are very high. And on the other hand, 'tis no evidence that religious affections are of a spiritual and gracious nature, because they are great."[79] Similarly, the fact that the affections might produce dramatic physical displays is no indicator of true religion. Nor can we assume that what seems to be love associated with particular affections is the work of the Spirit. "'Tis no evidence that religious affections are saving, or that they are otherwise, that there is an appearance of love in them."[80] This is because of the reality of counterfeit experiences, including experiences of love: "There is sometimes great similitude between true and false experiences, in their appearances, and in what is expressed and related by subjects of them." Edwards notes that "there are perhaps no graces that have more counterfeits than love and humility."[81]

Having rejected some criteria that will not work, Edwards proposes twelve "signs" that *can* be used to identify genuinely gracious affections. These are not mechanical formulas to be applied as part of some kind of spiritual calculus. They are pointers or indicators, requiring wisdom and mature judgment in application, and in some cases it is not at all clear how one would apply them responsibly. But these signs reveal the kind of things Edwards thought should be part of genuine experiences of God. We can do no more here than mention a few of these signs.

For example, genuinely gracious affections are concerned with the excellence of divine things in themselves and not with any matters of self-interest that might accrue from consideration of the things of God. "The first objective ground of gracious affections, is the transcendently excellent and amiable nature of divine things, as they are in themselves; and not any conceived relation they bear to self, or self-interest." Or again, "Those affections that are truly holy, are primarily founded on the loveliness of the moral excellency of divine things. Or (to express it otherwise), a love to divine things for the beauty and sweetness of their moral excellency, is the first beginning and spring of all holy affections."[82]

The fifth sign Edwards discusses concerns the certainty or confidence in the believer produced by gracious affections. "Truly gracious affections are attended with a reasonable and spiritual conviction of the judgment,

79. Edwards, *Religious Affections*, 130.
80. Edwards, *Religious Affections*, 146.
81. Edwards, *Religious Affections*, 151, 146.
82. Edwards, *Religious Affections*, 240, 253–54.

of the reality and certainty of divine things." Edwards seems to be saying that those who genuinely encounter God through the gracious affections will have a high degree of confidence in the truth of basic Christian claims. "All those who are truly gracious persons have a solid, full, thorough and effectual conviction of the truth of the great things of the gospel. . . . The great doctrines of the gospel cease to be any longer doubtful things, or matters of opinion, which, though probable, are yet disputable."[83] And yet he tempers this confidence with the acknowledgment that a high degree of certitude by itself is not sufficient; confidence must be accompanied by "reasonable conviction." "But if the religious affections that persons have, do indeed arise from a strong persuasion of the truth of the Christian religion; their affections are not the better, unless their persuasion be a reasonable persuasion or conviction. By a reasonable conviction, I mean a conviction founded on real evidence, or upon that which is a good reason, or just ground of conviction."[84] Perhaps Edwards would include here the kind of evidences for the truth of Christianity he acknowledges elsewhere as having some value for unbelievers—evidence for the resurrection of Jesus Christ, the reliability of Scripture, and so on. But in the immediate context, the focus is on the evidential force of the glory and beauty of what is presented in the gospel. "A view of this divine glory directly, convinces the mind of the divinity of these things, as this glory is in itself a direct, clear, and all-conquering evidence of it; especially when clearly discovered, or when this supernatural sense is given in a good degree."[85]

Several of the signs Edwards presents have to do with an observable change in one's demeanor and character. Indeed, "If there be no great and remarkable, abiding change in persons, that think they have experienced a work of conversion, vain are all their imaginations and pretenses, however they have been affected."[86] Genuine conversion involves a transformation of the person, "turning him from sin to God." Truly gracious affections "naturally beget and promote such a spirit of love, meekness, quietness, forgiveness and mercy, as appeared in Christ."[87] Change in behavior as a sign of gracious affections finds its fullest expression in Edwards's twelfth sign.

> Gracious and holy affections . . . have that influence and power upon him who is the subject of 'em, that they cause that a practice, which is universally

83. Edwards, *Religious Affections*, 291.
84. Edwards, *Religious Affections*, 295.
85. Edwards, *Religious Affections*, 298.
86. Edwards, *Religious Affections*, 340–41.
87. Edwards, *Religious Affections*, 344–45.

conformed to, and directed by Christian rules, should be the practice and business of life.

This implies three things: (1) That his behavior or practice in the world, be universally conformed to, and directed by Christian rules. (2) That he makes a business of such a holy practice above all things; that it be a business which he is chiefly engaged in, and devoted to, and pursues with highest earnestness and diligence: so that he may be said to make this practice of religion eminently his work and business. And (3) That he persists in it to the end of life: so that it may be said, not only to be his business at certain seasons, the business of Sabbath days, or certain extraordinary times, or the business of a month, or a year, or of seven years, or his business under certain circumstances; but the business of his life; it being that business which he perseveres in through all changes, and under all trials, as long as he lives. The necessity of each of these, in all true Christians, is most clearly and fully taught in the Word of God.[88]

A holy life can be evidence both for the believer and for others. "It is manifest that Christian practice or a holy life is a great and distinguishing sign of true and saving grace. But I may go further, and assert, that it is the chief of all the signs of grace, both as an evidence of the sincerity of professors unto others, and also to their own consciences."[89]

John Wesley

Like Edwards, John Wesley (1703–91) gave careful attention to the place of personal experience of God in Christian faith. Wesley's father Samuel was a minister in the Church of England, and his mother Susanna instilled in young John the initial stirrings of a desire for wholehearted devotion to God. In 1725, while at Oxford University, Wesley had a profound spiritual experience, and from this point onward he strove to become the kind of Christian idealized in the Scriptures. But he lacked assurance that he was really accepted by God, and from 1725 to 1738, Wesley was on a quest for freedom from the power of sin and full confidence in his salvation.

Wesley was ordained a priest in the Church of England in 1728 and the following year he began lecturing at Oxford on classics, logic, and divinity.[90] While at Oxford, Wesley, together with his brother Charles, led a group of devoted young men—the Holy Club—in a rigorous and methodical study

---

88. Edwards, *Religious Affections*, 383–84.
89. Edwards, *Religious Affections*, 406.
90. Henry D. Rack, *Reasonable Enthusiast: John Wesley and the Rise of Methodism*, 2nd ed. (Nashville: Abingdon, 1992), 87.

of Scripture, regular prayer, and ministry to prisoners. In 1735 the Wesley brothers traveled to America as missionaries to the Indians and the colonists. When their ship ran into severe storms in the Atlantic, Wesley was deeply impressed by the calm faith of a group of German Moravians on board. The mission to America did not go well, and in 1738 he returned to England. Despite his intense devotion and discipline, Wesley continued to struggle with doubts about his relationship with God.

Back in England, Wesley met with the Moravian Peter Böhler, who urged him to place his faith in Christ alone for his salvation. Gradually, Wesley came to recognize that justification precedes sanctification and that justifying faith, not holy living, is what is necessary for salvation. He understood that justifying faith is given to the unjust sinner instantaneously by the Holy Spirit, and that "this faith implies a sense of forgiveness that one can feel tangibly, and that this faith brings with it the new birth, the power not to commit sin, and the witness of the Holy Spirit that one is now accepted as a son or a daughter of God."[91]

Then on May 24, 1738, while meeting with a group of Moravians on Aldersgate Street, John Wesley had a powerful conversion experience.

> In the evening, I went very unwillingly to a society in Aldersgate Street, where one was reading Luther's Preface to the Epistle to the Romans. About a quarter before nine, while he was describing the change which God works in the heart through faith in Christ, I felt my heart strangely warmed. I felt I did trust in Christ, Christ alone for my salvation; and an assurance was given me that he had taken away *my* sins, even *mine*, and saved *me* from the law of sin and death.[92]

This experience marked a decisive point in Wesley's own spiritual development, launching him into a remarkable ministry of evangelism and open-air preaching until his death.[93] An indefatigable evangelist, Wesley traveled some 250,000 miles throughout England, Scotland, Wales, and Ireland, preaching

91. John H. Tyson, "John Wesley's Conversion at Aldersgate," in *Conversion in the Wesleyan Tradition*, ed. Kenneth J. Collins and John H. Tyson (Nashville: Abingdon, 2001), 32.
92. *Works*, May 24, 1738, 18:249–50; quoted in Albert Outler, ed., *John Wesley* (New York: Oxford University Press, 1964), 66. Emphasis in original.
93. Albert Outler cautions against placing too much emphasis on this singular experience in Wesley's spiritual journey. Apart from his famous journal entry quoted here, Wesley apparently made only one other explicit reference to the Aldersgate event. Moreover, Outler notes that prior to Aldersgate, Wesley also had other experiences "of equal, or nearly equal, spiritual exaltation," and in the six months after Aldersgate, Wesley "reports numerous instances of acute spiritual depression, equal in severity to anything preceding." Outler, "The Aldersgate Experience," in *John Wesley*, 51.

about 40,000 sermons. Wesley and his associates organized those who responded positively to his preaching into tightly structured "societies" of "Methodists" that were committed to the cultivation of "scriptural holiness." By 1791 there were more than 70,000 identifiable Methodists in Britain and over 60,000 in North America.[94]

For Wesley, personal experience of God is central to both the believer's assurance of salvation and growth in holy living. Although Wesley's primary interest in such experience was theological, he was also sensitive to epistemological issues in religious experience. Wesley's writings touch on the two basic questions introduced earlier in this chapter: How are we to distinguish genuine experiences of God from those that are not? And, can experience of God provide evidence for or conviction about the truth of central Christian claims? As with Edwards, personal experience of God through the work of the Holy Spirit plays a central role in Wesley's answers to these questions.

In dealing with these issues, Wesley brings together the ideas of divine revelation, testimony, and perception of God, for it is in their interrelationship that we are to understand the special work of the Holy Spirit. As Douglas Koskela puts it,

> Wesley's epistemology of theology centered on the interplay between various forms of testimony and immediate perception of the divine, both of which can be seen as instances of divine revelation. In particular, scripture (and its various modes of mediation through the community of faith) provides the *content* of what is known about God and salvation, while perception of the divine provides the strongest and most important *evidence* that those claims are true. In both cases, Wesley understood the agency of God to be essential to the formation of a genuine knowledge of God—a factor that makes divine revelation an unavoidable category when coming to terms with Wesley's epistemology.[95]

Testimony is crucial for Wesley, and it functions on several levels. At a basic level, the written Scriptures are God's testimony to what God has done in history to make salvation possible—namely, the incarnation in Jesus Christ culminating in the cross and the resurrection. Human testimony also plays a subsidiary role in conveying what the Scriptures reveal, whether in the confessional statements from the early church, writings from the church

94. Geoffrey Wainwright, "Wesley, John and Charles," in *The Oxford Companion to Christian Thought*, ed. Adrian Hastings (New York: Oxford University Press, 2000), 750.

95. Douglas K. Koskela, "John Wesley," in *The Oxford Handbook of the Epistemology of Theology*, ed. William J. Abraham and Frederick D. Aquino (New York: Oxford University Press, 2017), 459. Emphasis in original.

fathers, the later sermons and writings of leaders such as Wesley himself, or the many experiences of believers. But such testimony is always subordinate to what God has revealed in Scripture. "The experience of Christians did not supply the content of robust Christian theism. It could, however, mediate the teachings of scripture on a different level from sermons, confessional statements, or the writings of Christian antiquity. . . . The claims of scripture mediated by the church are then tested in the lives of believers, the results serving to refine and confirm what has been received."[96]

On Knowing the Truth of the Gospel

How do we know that the content of the Christian faith, the gospel, is true? Given the growing skepticism emerging out of the eighteenth century, this was a natural and unavoidable question. In answering it, Wesley distinguishes between the external evidence and the internal evidence for the truth of Christian claims.

External evidence is available to both nonbelievers and believers alike. It is typically associated with natural theology, or the attempt to establish truths about God without appealing to premises derived solely from special revelation, the Bible. Natural theology has a long history in the Christian tradition, and in the eighteenth century it was exemplified by William Paley's formulation of the teleological argument and Samuel Clarke's version of the cosmological argument.[97] Wesley was well aware of the traditional arguments for Christian theism, but like Edwards, he regarded them as incapable of sustaining the kind of confidence in God's reality that we require.[98] Nevertheless, he did think that there is some publicly available evidence supporting claims about the reality of God and the divine inspiration of Scripture. For example, like many during this time, Wesley appealed to miracles and fulfilled prophecies as supporting the status of Scripture as divine revelation.

> There are four grand and powerful arguments which strongly induce us to believe that the Bible must be from God; viz., miracles, prophecies, the goodness of the doctrine, and the moral character of the penmen. All the miracles flow from divine power; all the prophecies, from divine understanding; the goodness of the doctrine, from divine goodness; and the moral character of

96. Koskela, "John Wesley," 464–65.

97. See Charles Taliaferro, *Evidence and Faith: Philosophy and Religion since the Seventeenth Century* (New York: Cambridge University Press, 2005).

98. See William J. Abraham, *Aldersgate and Athens: John Wesley and the Foundations of Christian Belief* (Waco: Baylor University Press, 2010), 4–5.

the penmen, from divine holiness. Thus Christianity is built upon four grand pillars: viz., the power, understanding, goodness, and holiness of God.[99]

Wesley's argument presupposes the accuracy and historical reliability of the Scriptures, something that even in his day was being questioned, and certainly for this to be persuasive today, considerable supporting argumentation is required. Our concern here, however, is not with the cogency of his argument but with the fact that Wesley did not hesitate to appeal to what he regarded as plausible external evidence in support of Christian claims. He also regarded supernatural phenomena, such as the apparently miraculous healings in the first centuries of the church, as evidence for the truth of the gospel.[100] But such external evidence was always less forceful and probative than the internal evidence of the Holy Spirit, which is immediately present to the believer. As Wesley put it,

> It is generally supposed, that the traditional [historical] evidence is weakened by length of time; as it must necessarily pass through so many hands, in a continued succession of ages. But no length of time can possibly affect the strength of this internal evidence. It is equally strong, equally new, through the course of seventeen hundred years. It passes now, even as it has done from the beginning, directly from God into the believing soul. . . . Traditional evidence is of an extremely complicated nature, necessarily including so many and so various considerations, that only men of a strong and clear understanding can be sensible to its full force. On the contrary, how plain and simple is this [internal evidence]; and how level to the lowest capacity! Is not this the sum: "One thing I know; I was blind, but now I see?" An argument so plain, that a peasant, a woman, a child, may feel its force.[101]

For Wesley, the strongest evidence—at least for the believer—for the truth of Christian claims is internal evidence—that is, the perception of God and conviction of the truth of the gospel brought about by the internal testimony of the Holy Spirit. "The internal evidence," says Koskela, "was not a source of new claims about God; rather, it was the perception of the mind and the heart beyond doubt that scripture's claims about God and salvation are true."[102] The internal testimony of the Spirit operates in conjunction

99. John Wesley, "A Clear and Concise Demonstration of the Divine Inspiration of the Holy Scriptures," in *The Works of John Wesley* (Grand Rapids: Zondervan, 1958), 11:484.

100. See John Wesley's "A Letter to the Reverend Doctor Conyers Middleton Occasioned by His Late 'Free Inquiry,'" in *Works of John Wesley*, 10:1–79.

101. Wesley, "Letter to the Reverend Doctor Conyers Middleton," 75–76.

102. Koskela, "John Wesley," 466.

with faith and God's special grace so that persons are enabled to apprehend spiritual matters. As William Abraham explains, "in prevenient grace God irresistibly and universally restores in us the initial capacity to perceive the truth. . . . This action of God simply provides the preparatory work for what we really need, namely, the more direct action of God by the Holy Spirit to enable us to become aware of and see for ourselves what God has done for us in Jesus Christ." What enables us to understand spiritual realities properly is the divine gift of "new spiritual senses," realized through faith. "Thus faith for Wesley is not just an act of trust on our part in response to the gospel; it is an act of trust generated by a God-given capacity to see and become aware of what God has done for us in the death of Jesus Christ."[103]

Romans 8:15–16 is a crucial text for Wesley: "The Spirit you received does not make you slaves, so that you live in fear again; rather, the Spirit you received brought about your adoption to sonship. And by him we cry, 'Abba, Father,' The Spirit himself testifies with our spirit that we are God's children." Wesley follows the theological tradition that links the testimony of the Spirit with a "spiritual sense," the faculty through which the believer apprehends God and spiritual truths.[104] Wesley draws an analogy between the spiritual perception of the divine brought about by the witness of the Spirit and our ordinary perception of the physical world through the five senses. For example, in his 1743 essay "Earnest Appeal to Men of Reason and Religion," Wesley states,

> Faith is that divine evidence whereby the spiritual man discerneth God, and the things of God. It is with regard to the spiritual world what sense is to the natural. It is the spiritual sensation of every soul that is born of God. . . . Faith, according to the scriptural account, is the eye of the new-born soul. Hereby, every true believer in God "seeth him who is invisible." Hereby (in a more particular manner, since life and immortality have been brought to light by the gospel) he "seeth the light of the glory of God in the face of Jesus Christ" and "beholdeth what manner of love it is which the Father hath bestowed upon us, that we (who are born of the Spirit) should be called the sons of God." It is the ear of the soul whereby a sinner "hears the voice of the Son of God and lives," even that voice which alone wakes the dead, saying, "Son, thy sins are forgiven thee." . . . It is the feeling of the soul whereby a believer perceives, through the "power of the highest overshadowing him," both the existence and the presence of him in whom "he lives, moves and has his being,"

103. Abraham, *Aldersgate and Athens*, 26.
104. Mark Mealey notes that in numerous places Wesley explicitly appealed to the spiritual senses idiom in patristic, medieval, Reformation, and early modern sources. Mark Mealey, "John Wesley," in Gavrilyuk and Coakley, *Spiritual Senses*, 241.

and indeed the whole invisible world, the entire system of things eternal. And hereby, in particular, he feels "the love of God shed abroad in his heart."[105]

Just as we grasp physical realities through the five senses, so too we need special "spiritual senses" through which we can perceive spiritual realities.

> Seeing our ideas are not innate, but must all originally come from our senses, it is certainly necessary that you have senses capable of discerning objects of this kind [viz., spiritual realities]—not those only which are called natural senses, which in this respect profit nothing, as being altogether incapable of discerning objects of a spiritual kind, but spiritual senses, exercised to discern spiritual good and evil. It is necessary that you have the *hearing ear* and the *seeing eye*, emphatically so called, that you have a new class of senses opened up in your soul, not depending on organs of flesh and blood to be *the evidence* of things not seen as your bodily senses are of visible things, to be the avenues to the invisible world, to discern spiritual objects, and to furnish you with ideas of what the outward "eye hath not seen, neither the ear heard." And till you have these "internal senses," till the eyes of your understanding are opened, you can have no *apprehension* of divine things, no idea of them at all. Nor, consequently, 'till then, can you either *judge truly*, or *reason justly* concerning them, seeing your reason has no ground whereon to stand, no materials to work with.[106]

But just what are the "internal senses"? Here we confront the same questions raised earlier about Edwards's reference to the spiritual sense. Is there one spiritual sense, or are there multiple spiritual senses analogous to the five physical senses? Or is the term "internal senses" simply a metaphorical way of speaking about the effect of the Spirit's work on the human intellect resulting in a fresh capacity to recognize spiritual truths? Although these issues are not resolved by Wesley, what he makes clear is that apart from the Spirit's special work, we cannot apprehend spiritual truths. Moreover, the witness of the Spirit through the spiritual senses seems to be direct and immediate. Mark Mealey observes that for Wesley, "Spiritual sensation is a direct, immediate experience of the spiritual object prior to any act of reason or affective response. . . . Just as for Wesley natural sensation is understood in a realistic manner as an 'immediate' and 'direct' contact with the visible world, and our only source of contact with the visible world, faith as spiritual sensation is an immediate and direct contact with the reality of God."[107]

105. John Wesley, "An Earnest Appeal to Men of Reason and Religion," in Outler, *John Wesley*, 386–87.
106. Wesley, "Earnest Appeal to Men of Reason," sec. 32–33, p. 395. Emphasis in original.
107. Mealey, "John Wesley," 247, 252.

Wesley treats the subject of the witness of the Spirit at some length in two sermons, the first published in 1746 and the second in 1767. In the earlier sermon, in reference to Romans 8:15–16, Wesley acknowledges the difficulty of understanding just *how* the witness of the Spirit works:

> How does [the Spirit] "bear witness with our spirit that we are children of God"? It is hard to find words in the language of men to explain "the deep things of God." Indeed, there are none that will adequately express what the children of God experience. But perhaps one might say (desiring any who are taught of God to correct, to soften, or strengthen the expression), the testimony of the Spirit is an inward impression on the soul, whereby the Spirit of God directly "witnesses to my spirit, that I am a child of God"; that Jesus Christ hath loved me, and given Himself for me; and that all my sins are blotted out, and I, even I, am reconciled to God.[108]

The comments about the Spirit directly acting to produce an "inward impression on the soul" fueled criticism of Wesley and the Methodists for being enthusiasts who claimed privileged access to God. Consequently, in his 1767 sermon Wesley responds by stating, "After twenty years' further consideration I see no cause to retract any part of this." He concludes the sermon without backing down: "The sum of all is this: the testimony of the Spirit is an inward impression on the souls of believers, whereby the Spirit of God directly testifies to their spirit, that they are children of God."[109] Although he was sensitive to the charge of excessive enthusiasm among those who have "mistaken the voice of their own imagination for this witness of the Spirit of God," Wesley was also wary of others who deny the work of the Spirit out of fear of enthusiasm. Accordingly, he advocated "a middle course— keep a sufficient distance from that spirit of error and enthusiasm, without denying the gift of God."[110]

On Discerning the Work of the Spirit

Is it possible to be mistaken about what we take to be the testimony of the Spirit? Clearly, this is possible, since Wesley himself acknowledges that some enthusiasts mistakenly attribute their unusual behavior to the Spirit's influence. But then how is one to identify a genuine work of the Spirit? The

108. John Wesley, "The Witness of the Spirit, I," in *Sermons I, 1–33*, ed. Albert C. Outler, vol. 1 of *The Works of John Wesley* (Nashville: Abingdon, 1984), 274.

109. John Wesley, "The Witness of the Spirit, II," in Outler, *Sermons I, 1–33*, 287, 296.

110. Wesley, "Witness of the Spirit, I," 269–70.

same issue that confronted Edwards also nagged at Wesley, who offers two responses. On the one hand, the believer should be able to perceive directly and with full confidence the testimony of the Spirit, much as we directly perceive the light from the sun above us.

> "But how may one who has the real witness in himself distinguish it from presumption?" How, I pray, do you distinguish day from night? How, do you distinguish light from darkness? Or the light of a star, or glimmering taper, from the light of the noonday sun? Is there not an inherent, obvious, essential difference between the one and the other? And do you not immediately and directly perceive that difference, provided your senses are rightly disposed? In like manner, there is an inherent, essential difference between spiritual light and spiritual darkness; and between the light wherewith the sun of righteousness shines upon our heart, and that glimmering light which arises only from "sparks of our own kindling." And this difference also is immediately and directly perceived, if our spiritual senses are rightly disposed.[111]

So long as one's spiritual senses are functioning properly, there is such an obviousness and clarity in the Spirit's witness that it no more makes sense to question it than it does to doubt the difference between physical light and darkness. At times Wesley seems to hold that the witness of the Spirit produces complete certainty about the believer's adoption by God. "The *manner* how the divine testimony is manifested to the heart I do not take upon me to explain. . . . But the fact we know; namely that the Spirit of God does give a believer such a testimony of his adoption that while it is present to the soul he can no more doubt the reality of his sonship than he can doubt of the shining of the sun while he stands in the full blaze of his beams."[112]

But this is a very strong claim regarding the witness of the Spirit. Wesley's language equates the certainty we have about the difference between the light of the sun and darkness with the certainty that accompanies the witness of the Spirit. The implication is that the Spirit's witness produces an immediate and complete confidence about spiritual matters just as sight immediately and clearly differentiates light from darkness. But even a cursory review of the spiritual reports from times of revivals, both in Wesley's day and since, shows that many believers lack this certainty and *do* wonder whether what they are experiencing really is the witness of the Holy Spirit.

Wesley assures us that when the spiritual senses are functioning properly they provide certainty. But how then does one know that one's spiritual

111. Wesley, "Witness of the Spirit, I," 282.
112. Wesley, "Witness of the Spirit, I," 276. Emphasis in original.

senses *are* functioning properly and that what one takes to be the witness of the Spirit really is as it seems? According to Wesley, this can be indirectly confirmed through the effects of the Spirit in one's life.

> "But how shall I know that my spiritual senses are rightly disposed?" This also is a question of vast importance; for if a man mistake in this he may run on in endless error and delusion. "And how am I assured that this is not my case; and that I do not mistake the voice of the Spirit?" Even by the "testimony of your own spirit"; by "the answer of a good conscience toward God." By the fruits which he hath wrought in your spirit you shall know the "testimony of the Spirit of God." Hereby you shall know that you are in no delusion; that you have not deceived your own soul. The immediate fruits of the Spirit ruling in the heart, are "love, joy, peace": "bowels of mercies, humbleness of mind, meekness, gentleness, long-suffering." And the outward fruits are the doing good to all men, the doing no evil to any, and the walking in the light—a zealous, uniform obedience to all the commandments of God.[113]

In other words, Wesley responds much like Edwards does: the reality of a transformed life, of the "fruit of the Spirit" (Gal. 5:22–23) in one's life, is confirming evidence that what one takes to be the inner witness of the Spirit is indeed the work of the Spirit. To seek something beyond this is to ask for the impossible. "To require a more minute and philosophical account of the *manner* whereby we distinguish these, and of the *criteria* or intrinsic marks whereby we know the voice of God, is to make a demand which can never be answered; no, not by one who has the deepest knowledge of God."[114]

There is much biblical wisdom in Wesley's discussion, but there is also something curious about his move to corroborate the claim to have experienced the witness of the Spirit by appealing to the external evidence of the fruit of the Spirit in one's life, especially because Wesley initially asserts that the kind of clarity and certainty that accompanies the witness of the Spirit is like perceiving the difference between light and darkness. If that analogy is sound, then the certainty available from the inner work of the Spirit is greater and more secure than what can be obtained from the external evidence of the fruit of the Spirit in one's life. So it seems a bit strange to appeal to the weaker, external evidence to support the stronger, internal witness.

---

113. Wesley, "Witness of the Spirit, I," 283. See also Wesley's sermon "The Marks of the New Birth (John 3:8)," in *The Sermons of John Wesley*, ed. Kenneth J. Collins and Jason E. Vickers (Nashville: Abingdon, 2013), 165–74.

114. Wesley, "Witness of the Spirit, I," 282. Emphasis in original.

Lingering Issues

Jonathan Edwards and John Wesley offer substantive, perceptive, and interesting discussions of a variety of issues concerning experiences of God. Although they were primarily theologians and pastors interested in how a correct understanding of experience can facilitate greater holiness in living and devotion to God, they were well aware of basic epistemological questions stemming from purported experiences of God. Both acknowledge the place of external evidences even for the unregenerate, although they give epistemic priority to the internal evidence provided by the special work of the Holy Spirit. Their treatment of the inner witness of the Spirit is theologically rich and reflects a major tradition within Protestant Christianity.[115] Surely any biblically faithful and theologically viable perspective on experiences of God will reflect the themes we find in Edwards and Wesley.

But questions remain: What does it mean to say that, following Edwards, the believer experientially *senses* God's beauty and excellence through gracious affections? What are the phenomenological "markers" of such an experience? Is this a momentary experience or an extended series of experiences? Are particular feelings (ecstasy, peace, joy) part of the experience? We are told that a distinguishing mark of gracious affections is the fact that they are caused by the Holy Spirit. But how does an individual (or others) know that they *are* caused by the Holy Spirit, especially when Edwards emphasizes that there are counterfeit experiences of even love? Is there something in the gracious affections themselves that identify the Spirit as the cause? Furthermore, despite Wesley's analogy with the light of the sun, becoming aware of the Holy Spirit's work is not like perceiving a beautiful sunset, where the sunset is both the object and a cause of perception. How then does one know, from the experience itself, that the Spirit *is* the cause of the affection?

We conclude this chapter by highlighting two significant issues emerging from our look at Edwards and Wesley. First, the claim that it is through the work of the Holy Spirit that we come to have confidence in the truth of the gospel needs some clarification. What is the question to which it is the answer? The Scriptures do teach that the special work of the Holy Spirit enables a person to recognize the truth of the gospel and have confidence in the gospel and in their acceptance by God (John 3:5–8; 16:8–15; Rom. 8:14–17; 1 Cor. 2:6–14; 2 Cor. 4:4; Gal. 4:6; 1 John 3:24). This teaching is typically referred to as the internal testimony of the Holy Spirit, which Stephen Davis defines as "that influence of the Holy Spirit on the minds

---

115. See Bernard Ramm, *The Witness of the Spirit: An Essay on the Contemporary Relevance of the Internal Witness of the Holy Spirit* (Grand Rapids: Eerdmans, 1959).

of believers that causes them to believe firmly that the Christian message, or some aspect of it, is true."[116] *That* the Holy Spirit produces confidence in the truth of the gospel is clear; *how* the Spirit does this is less clear, and the biblical teachings on the subject can be compatible with a variety of epistemic models.[117]

The claim that it is through the work of the Holy Spirit that we have confidence in the truth of the gospel can be understood in at least two ways. According to the first way, the statement could be regarded as an explanation, from within the Christian theological framework, of how people come to recognize and have confidence in the truth of the gospel. That is, given the truth of Scripture, an appeal to the witness of the Holy Spirit provides a theological explanation for how people are able to believe in the truth of the gospel and the teachings of Scripture. Not only is this a plausible way of understanding such language, but I think that something very much like this is an essential part of an acceptable Christian theological perspective. But, as noted above, this assertion can be compatible with various views of how the Holy Spirit brings about acknowledgment of the truth of the gospel. Furthermore, as a theological explanation, this statement about the witness of the Spirit depends on the teachings of Scripture, and thus the acceptability of the assertion is ultimately based on the logically more basic question of the acceptability of Scripture itself. The explanation may well be plausible to the believer who accepts the divine inspiration of Scripture, but it will be less persuasive to those who do not.

The second way in which the claim about the Holy Spirit's internal witness confirming the truth of the gospel can be understood is as an answer to a skeptic who wonders why one should accept the gospel as true in the first place. For the skeptic, the claim is less helpful or convincing.[118] Simply appealing to the witness of the Spirit, or spiritual perception, apart from independent justification of theism or the inspiration of Scripture is

---

116. Stephen T. Davis, "An Ontology of the Spirit," in *The Testimony of the Spirit: New Essays*, ed. R. Douglas Geivett and Paul K. Moser (New York: Oxford University Press, 2017), 59.

117. See William J. Abraham, "The Epistemological Significance of the Inner Witness of the Holy Spirit," *Faith and Philosophy* 7, no. 4 (October 1990): 434–50.

118. It is important to distinguish the question raised by a non-Christian skeptic about the truth of the teaching about the witness of the Holy Spirit from that of a believer who wonders whether a particular experience really is the witness of the Spirit. In the latter case, the believer can adopt the critical-trust approach and accept the veridicality of the experience unless she has reason, theological or otherwise, not do so. In appropriate circumstances, the deliverances of the "spiritual sense" can be accepted as veridical unless there are sufficient reasons for concluding otherwise. But an unbelieving skeptic, who does not share the believer's assumptions about the reality of God, will have reasons for questioning whether *any* experience can be a veridical experience of the witness of the Spirit.

a circular argument. What is needed first is a reason to believe that it is the Holy Spirit who produces this confidence or that the Scriptures, which teach about the witness of the Holy Spirit, are indeed true. Some form of natural theology might serve the purpose here. William Wainwright, for example, suggests that Edwards escapes vicious circularity in this respect by holding that theistic metaphysics can be supported by rational arguments and evidence.[119] The need for independent reasons, apart from personal experience, for accepting the truth of Christian theism is something we will encounter again in subsequent chapters.

Another lingering issue relates to Edwards's and Wesley's concern to distinguish genuine experiences of God from those that are not. Both theologians look to the moral disposition of one's life, understood in terms of the fruit of the Spirit, for identifying the presence and work of God. In other words, the external manifestations of the fruit of the Spirit provide evidence for the supernatural work of the Spirit in someone's life. Once again, this is an eminently biblical theme: Scripture does indicate that personal conduct provides evidence that a person is Christ's disciple (Matt. 5:43–48; 7:15–23; 22:34–40; John 13:34–35; 17:20–23; Rom. 12:9–21; Gal. 5:16–26; Col. 3:5–14; 1 John 2:5–6; 4:7–21). This point, widely accepted by ordinary Christians as well as theologians, is expressed clearly by Douglas Geivett and Paul Moser.

> The human cooperative reception of God's Spirit, as suggested, is no merely subjective matter, because it yields one's becoming loving and forgiving (to some discernible degree) as God is loving and forgiving. It yields salient fruit of God's Spirit, such as joy, peace, patience, kindness, goodness, faithfulness, humility, and self-control (see Gal. 5:22–23). These are not merely subjective phenomena. On the contrary, they are discernible by anyone attentive to them and open to the redemptive power of God. . . . *We can know the reality of the presence of God's Spirit by means of the fruits yielded by the Spirit.* God's Spirit makes one loving (to some discernible degree) as God is loving. This is the primary fruit of the Spirit, and it is identifiable and testable in a person's life. The presence of God's Spirit thus comes with salient evidence observable by any suitably receptive person.[120]

But how exactly are we to understand the evidential relation between the fruit of the Spirit and the veridicality of purported experiences of God, including the witness of the Spirit?

119. W. Wainwright, *Reason and the Heart*, 38–41.
120. R. Douglas Geivett and Paul Moser, "Introduction," in Geivett and Moser, *Testimony of the Spirit*, 15. Emphasis added.

Since Scripture teaches that those who are "in Christ" are "new creations" (2 Cor. 5:17) whose lives are to be characterized by the fruit of the Spirit, it makes sense to look for these qualities in the conduct of those who genuinely experience God. But this is a somewhat ambiguous criterion. If *all* who claim to be disciples of Jesus or to have experienced God unambiguously manifest the fruit of the Spirit, and if these qualities are found *only* among Christ's disciples, then the evidential force of this criterion would be quite strong. If all who claim to experience God—and only those who truly do so—lived lives marked by selfless love for others and joy and peace in difficult circumstances, then it would be plausible to regard the presence of these qualities as indicating the distinctive work of the Spirit. But the empirical realities are more ambiguous. Some claiming to experience God give strong evidence of the fruit of the Spirit in their lives, while others provide little such evidence, and still others have a rather mixed record. Moreover, many who do not profess to be Christians—secularists and followers of other religions—also seem to manifest love for others, peace, joy, humility, and so on.

This point was raised by William James, who refers explicitly to Edwards's appeal to the fruit of the Spirit.

> Were it true that a suddenly converted man as such is, as Edwards says, of an entirely different kind from a natural man, partaking as he does directly of Christ's substance, there surely ought to be some exquisite class-mark, some distinctive radiance attaching even to the lowliest specimen of this genus, to which no one of us could remain insensible, and which, so far as it went, would prove him more excellent than ever the most highly gifted among mere natural men. But notoriously there is no such radiance. Converted men as a class are indistinguishable from natural men; some natural men even excel some converted men in their fruits. . . . The real witness of the spirit to the second birth is to be found only in the disposition of the genuine child of God, the permanently patient heart, the love of self eradicated. And this, it has to be admitted, is also found in those who pass no crisis, and may even be found outside Christianity altogether.[121]

James's criticism has been pressed by many others as well, and we will return to this issue in chapter 7.

The plausibility of James's criticism does not refute the biblical teaching that there is an evidential relationship between the moral quality of one's

---

121. William James, *Varieties of Religious Experience* (1902; repr., New York: Penguin Books, 1985), 238–39.

life, as manifested in the fruit of the Spirit, and claims about the presence and work of the Spirit in one's life. But it does suggest that this is a "messy" criterion that cannot be applied in a strictly mechanical manner but rather requires discernment and must be used in conjunction with other appropriate theological measures.

5

Experiencing God, Basic Beliefs, and the Holy Spirit

For many believers, personal experience of God has a privileged status in the justification of one's beliefs. Philosophers might debate the soundness of theistic arguments, but the pious believer who experiences God simply *knows* that God exists. Within the Christian tradition, this experiential confidence in the reality of God is frequently identified with the witness or testimony of the Holy Spirit, and in chapter 4 we saw how Jonathan Edwards and John Wesley made use of this idea. For some believers, their experience of God somehow "stands on its own" apart from corroborating evidence, and confidence in its veridicality is said to come from the Holy Spirit. In this chapter, we will consider a sophisticated expression of this contention by Reformed epistemology, an influential movement inspired primarily by Alvin Plantinga. We will then look at some claims that William Lane Craig makes about the work of the Holy Spirit in bringing about confidence in the truth of the gospel. It is clear that the Holy Spirit is intimately involved in the process by which persons recognize and acknowledge the truth of the Christian message, but what is less perspicuous are the ways in which the Spirit accomplishes this.

Since the 1980s, the idea that in appropriate circumstances a believer can be entirely justified in his or her beliefs about God apart from any supporting evidence or argument has been central to Reformed epistemology. "Reformed epistemology," says John Greco, "is an approach to issues about faith and rationality organized around a central thesis: that beliefs about

God can be rational or reasonable even if they are not based on supporting evidence or reasons."[1] The term "Reformed epistemology" was coined because this claim was identified with the views of the Reformer John Calvin, but the assertion itself is epistemological and not necessarily tied to any one theological tradition. As Michael Bergmann observes, "Reformed epistemologists say that belief in God can be justified noninferentially, in the absence of theistic arguments (Reformed epistemology has nothing particularly to do with Protestantism or Calvinism other than the fact that Calvin's advocacy of the view inspired its name; there is no reason why Catholics or even Muslims, Jews, or Hindus could not endorse the view)."[2]

Reformed epistemologists maintain that in appropriate circumstances, belief in God can be for the believer a "properly basic" belief and thus epistemically acceptable apart from any corroborating argument or evidence. Although Plantinga has little to say about religious experience as such, this assertion is related to theistic experience, since having the right kind of experience is what grounds a believer's holding beliefs about God in a properly basic way. Caroline Franks Davis explains that "belief in God turns out to be properly basic only because it is generated by experiences— religious experiences—which there is no good reason to think delusive."[3] As such, the claims of Reformed epistemology can also be understood as an example of the critical-trust approach to theistic experiences. Moreover, the proper basicality of belief in God is linked to Christian theological beliefs about the work of the Holy Spirit, since it is the Spirit that is said to produce the believer's confidence in the truth of the Christian gospel (Rom. 8:15–16; 1 Cor. 2:14; 2 Cor. 4:4; Gal. 4:4–6; 1 Thess. 1:5; 1 John 4:13). Before considering whether belief in God can be properly basic, we should clarify what we mean by properly basic beliefs.

Can one be fully justified in his or her belief in God apart from any evidence or supporting arguments? This possibility might seem strange, since a dominant perspective during the past several centuries has insisted that belief in God is irrational or unreasonable unless theists can provide compelling evidence for the existence of God. Accepting this challenge, many Christian philosophers and theologians have argued that there is sufficient evidence to support reasonable belief in God.

1. John Greco, "Reformed Epistemology," in *The Routledge Companion to Philosophy of Religion*, ed. Chad Meister and Paul Copan (London: Routledge, 2007), 629.
2. Michael Bergmann, "Foundationalism," in *The Oxford Handbook of the Epistemology of Theology*, ed. William J. Abraham and Frederick D. Aquino (New York: Oxford University Press, 2017), 264.
3. Caroline Franks Davis, *The Evidential Force of Religious Experience* (Oxford: Clarendon, 1989), 87.

But Alvin Plantinga and Reformed epistemologists vigorously reject the "evidentialist" challenge to Christian faith. Beginning with *God and Other Minds* in 1967, Plantinga has provided a trenchant critique of the evidentialist stricture that belief in God is irrational unless supported by sufficient evidence or argument.[4] Although in his later writings Plantinga developed a sophisticated model of warrant and proper function and argued that the believer can be fully warranted in his or her Christian beliefs, the aspect of his work that has had the greatest impact on Christian philosophers and theologians is his contention that belief in God can be properly basic.[5] As Plantinga put it in a seminal essay in 1983, for the believer it can be "entirely right, rational, reasonable, and proper to believe in God without any evidence or argument at all."[6] Elsewhere he states, "Belief in God is perfectly proper and rational, perfectly justified and in order, even if it is not accepted on the basis of [theistic] arguments, even if the believer doesn't know of any such arguments, and even if in fact there *aren't* any such arguments."[7]

4. Alvin Plantinga, *God and Other Minds* (Ithaca, NY: Cornell University Press, 1967).

5. In his later work, Plantinga frames the issues in terms of whether Christian beliefs can be *warranted*, where warrant is understood as the property that, when combined with true belief, results in knowledge. Warrant is connected with the notion of proper function of one's cognitive faculties so that, in addition to its being true, "a belief has warrant just if it is produced by cognitive processes or faculties that are functioning properly, in a cognitive environment that is propitious for the exercise of cognitive powers, according to a design plan that is successfully aimed at the production of true belief." Alvin Plantinga, *Warranted Christian Belief* (New York: Oxford University Press, 2000), xi. In other words, a belief is warranted only if it is produced by our noetic structure and epistemic inclinations when they are functioning properly in accordance with their design plan in appropriate circumstances. Not surprisingly, Plantinga understands the design plan in accordance with Christian teaching about God and creation.

Plantinga's thesis takes the form of a conditional: *If* God, as Christians understand him, exists, and if a Christian's belief in God meets the other requirements for warrant stipulated above, then the Christian's belief is probably warranted and constitutes knowledge. But, of course, this presupposes the truth of Christian theism. "But *is* it true? This is the really important question. And here we pass beyond the competence of philosophy, whose main competence, in this area, is to clear away certain objections, impedances, and obstacles to Christian belief. Speaking for myself, and of course not in the name of philosophy, I can say only that it does, indeed, seem to me to be true, and to be the maximally important truth." Plantinga, *Warranted Christian Belief*, 456. Emphasis in original.

6. Alvin Plantinga, "Reason and Belief in God," in *Faith and Rationality: Reason and Belief in God*, ed. Alvin Plantinga and Nicholas Wolterstorff (Notre Dame: University of Notre Dame Press, 1983), 17. For a helpful overview of Plantinga's project, see James Beilby, "Plantinga's Model of Warranted Christian Belief," in *Alvin Plantinga*, ed. Deane-Peter Baker (Cambridge: Cambridge University Press, 2007), 125–65.

7. Alvin Plantinga, "Reformed Epistemology," in *A Companion to Philosophy of Religion*, ed. Philip L. Quinn and Charles Taliaferro (Oxford: Blackwell, 1997), 385. Emphasis in original.

Properly Basic Beliefs

In order to appreciate what Plantinga is proposing we must first grasp the notion of basic beliefs, which is often associated with foundationalist theories of knowledge. Foundationalism is a theory of epistemic justification that holds that the set of justified beliefs "consists of *basic beliefs*—beliefs that a subject is justified in holding even in the absence of any justifying reason for them—and [that] all other justified beliefs derive their justification at least in part from such basic beliefs."[8] In other words, beliefs that we are justified in holding fall into one of two classes: (1) beliefs that are epistemically appropriate apart from any supporting evidence or argument and (2) beliefs that are appropriately based on or derived from the former beliefs. Foundationalism has a long history and was defended in Aristotle's argument in the *Posterior Analytics* against an infinite regress in the justification of beliefs: if we are to have any justified beliefs at all, at least some beliefs must be such that their epistemic acceptability is not a result of their being justified in terms of yet other beliefs.[9]

Basic beliefs are beliefs that we accept but not on the basis of other beliefs; they are not inferred from other more fundamental beliefs that we hold. In appropriate circumstances, we simply find ourselves accepting them. They form the foundation or basis for other beliefs that we hold. The notion of a basic belief is descriptive: if belief P is foundational for Sam in the sense that it is not the product of inference from other beliefs, then P is a basic belief for Sam. Basic beliefs are to some extent person-relative. That is, P might be a basic belief for Sam but not for Rachel, who accepts P as a result of a compelling argument and evidence for P. Or Sam might accept P as a basic belief at one time but not at a later time. (Perhaps Sam comes to doubt P and then later accepts P as a result of examining evidence in support of P.)

But not all basic beliefs *ought* to be accepted. Some basic beliefs might in fact be false. *Properly basic beliefs* are basic beliefs that we ought to accept or that are epistemically appropriate for us to accept as basic. Obviously a key issue here is successfully distinguishing properly basic beliefs from basic beliefs that should be rejected and providing sound criteria for this

---

8. James van Cleve, "Why Coherence Is Not Enough: A Defense of Moderate Foundationalism," in *Contemporary Debates in Epistemology*, ed. Matthias Steup and Ernest Sosa (Oxford: Blackwell, 2005), 168. Emphasis in original. See also Laurence Bonjour, *The Structure of Empirical Knowledge* (Cambridge, MA: Harvard University Press, 1985), 26–28; and Noah Lemos, *An Introduction to the Theory of Knowledge* (New York: Cambridge University Press, 2007), chap. 3.

9. Bergmann, "Foundationalism," 255–57. See Aristotle, "Posterior Analytics," in *The Basic Works of Aristotle*, ed. Richard McKeon (New York: Random House, 1941), I.3, pp. 113–14.

distinction. Although there is debate over criteria for their identification, the following are among some widely acknowledged properly basic beliefs:

1. There is an external (extra-mental) world around me.
2. In general, memory is reliable.
3. In general, the five senses are reliable.
4. Other minds apart from my own exist.
5. The universe did not just "pop" into existence five seconds ago.
6. The same belief (statement, proposition) cannot be both true and false simultaneously.

Statements 1–6 express beliefs that are generally accepted as true. But no one has been able to demonstrate their truth in a non-question-begging manner or to show that there is sufficient evidence for accepting them. Attempts to justify them by appealing to other more basic beliefs are problematic at best. They are basic beliefs, and they are also usually regarded as properly basic for at least two reasons. First, they are so deeply entrenched in our cognitive structures and processes that it is almost impossible not to accept them. These beliefs are epistemically coercive in the sense that it is very difficult, if not impossible, genuinely to reject them and live successfully. Furthermore, as we accept them and base other beliefs on them, we are able to deepen our understanding of the world.

There are different kinds of foundationalism. Laurence Bonjour, for example, distinguishes three kinds of foundationalism. *Strong foundationalism* regards properly basic beliefs as infallible, certain, indubitable, or incorrigible. The outstanding advocate of strong foundationalism is the seventeenth-century philosopher René Descartes, who, in response to widespread skepticism at the time, sought complete certainty in our foundational beliefs.[10] *Moderate foundationalism* maintains that the noninferential justification possessed by properly basic beliefs need not amount to absolute certainty or indubitability, but "it must be sufficient by itself to satisfy the adequate-justification condition for knowledge." *Weak foundationalism* holds that basic beliefs possess only a very low degree of epistemic justification on their own, "a degree of justification insufficient to satisfy the adequate-justification condition for knowledge or to qualify them as acceptable justifying premises for further belief."[11] Moderate and weak

---

10. See René Descartes, *Discourse on Method and The Meditations* (London: Penguin Books, 1968).

11. Bonjour, *Structure of Empirical Knowledge*, 26, 28.

foundationalism are thus "fallibilist" in that they acknowledge that properly basic beliefs are not necessarily true and that, in appropriate circumstances, they can be modified or abandoned.

Belief in God as Properly Basic

Plantinga leveled a powerful critique of what he calls "classical foundational-ism," and because of this many theologians have assumed that foundation-alism itself has been refuted. But this is to misunderstand both the nature of foundationalism and Plantinga's critique.[12] Plantinga attacks what he calls the evidentialist challenge to Christian belief; that is, the view that "belief in God is irrational or unreasonable or not rationally acceptable or intellectually irresponsible or somehow noetically below par because, [the critics claim,] there is *insufficient evidence* for it."[13] Plantinga claims that the evidentialist challenge is based on classical foundationalism, a perspec-tive that he says has been dominant in Anglo-American philosophy in the modern era. He argues that classical foundationalism is untenable, and therefore the evidentialist challenge should be rejected.

Classical foundationalism as defined by Plantinga corresponds roughly to Bonjour's strong foundationalism noted above. It holds that a belief P is rational if and only if P is a properly basic belief or can be inferred from one or more properly basic beliefs. But it has a very restricted class of properly basic beliefs, so that *only* beliefs that are evident to the senses, self-evident, or incorrigible can be properly basic beliefs. Beliefs that are evident to the senses include beliefs constituting reports of sense experi-ence ("I hear a loud noise"). Self-evident beliefs are such that upon under-standing the meanings of the terms, one can see immediately the truth (or falsity) of the statement ("2 + 2 = 4" or "bachelors are unmarried males"). Incorrigible beliefs are those about which one cannot be wrong if uttered sincerely ("I feel pain"). Thus, according to classical foundationalism, a subject S is rational in believing P if and only if P is a belief that is evident to the senses, self-evident, or incorrigible, or P can be inferred from one or

---

12. As Bergmann ("Foundationalism," 253) observes, "Foundationalism is a much mis-understood position in epistemology. It is often criticized for certain excesses, despite the fact that these excesses are actually not a part of foundationalism itself but are, instead, un-necessary additions that have on occasion been combined with it. Although foundationalism takes an important and illuminating stand on the structure of knowledge and rationality, its essential ingredients are rather minimal. When properly understood, its main tenets are virtually undeniable."

13. Alvin Plantinga, "Reason and Belief in God," 17. Emphasis in original.

more such basic beliefs through proper inference procedures. Otherwise it is irrational for S to believe P.

Plantinga's critique of this view is twofold.[14] First, he points out that the statement of classical foundationalism itself is self-referentially incoherent since it does not meet the conditions that it stipulates for all rational belief. It is neither a properly basic belief nor can it be derived from such beliefs, as defined by the model. On its own terms, then, it should be rejected as irrational. Second, he demonstrates that classical foundationalism is far too restrictive in its criteria for properly basic beliefs, for it rules out many beliefs that we normally accept as perfectly reasonable. For example, basic beliefs 1 through 5 as listed above[15] would all need to be rejected, since they are neither properly basic on classical foundationalism's criteria nor has anyone shown how they can be inferred from such beliefs. Although Plantinga has shown the problematic nature of classical foundationalism, his critique should not be understood as refuting all forms of foundationalism.[16] As we have seen, there are other more moderate forms that are not susceptible to his criticisms.

The set of properly basic beliefs that classical foundationalism allows is far too restrictive, but how inclusive should we be? What are acceptable criteria for determining which beliefs can be properly basic? Acknowledging that there is no consensus on these questions, Plantinga asserts that for the Christian in appropriate circumstances, belief in God can also be properly basic and thus be epistemically appropriate apart from any supporting evidence. Plantinga distinguishes *having evidence for a belief* from *having grounds for the belief*. Evidence, for Plantinga, is propositional evidence—that is, evidence from other propositions that one believes and that comes in the form of arguments.[17] When one provides evidence for P, one is appealing

14. Plantinga, "Reason and Belief in God," 59–63; Plantinga, *Warranted Christian Belief*, 94–99.

15. Some might contend that belief 6 is self-evident.

16. Not everyone agrees that Plantinga has demonstrated the bankruptcy of classical foundationalism. See the exchange between Plantinga and Philip Quinn in the following series of articles: Philip Quinn, "In Search of the Foundations of Theism," *Faith and Philosophy* 2, no. 4 (1985): 469–86; Alvin Plantinga, "The Foundations of Theism: A Reply," *Faith and Philosophy* 3, no. 3 (1986): 298–313; and Philip Quinn, "The Foundations of Theism Again: A Rejoinder to Plantinga," in *Rational Faith: Catholic Responses to Reformed Epistemology*, ed. Linda Zagzebski (Notre Dame: University of Notre Dame Press, 1993), 14–47. A helpful assessment of the exchange is found in William Hasker, "The Foundations of Theism: Scoring the Quinn-Plantinga Debate," *Faith and Philosophy* 15, no. 1 (January 1998): 52–67. See also J. DePoe, "In Defense of Classical Foundationalism: A Critical Evaluation of Plantinga's Argument that Classical Foundationalism Is Self-Refuting," *South African Journal of Philosophy* (2013): 245–51.

17. Plantinga, *Warranted Christian Belief*, 70.

to other beliefs in support of P or relying on an argument in support of P. Properly basic beliefs do not require evidence, but they are not necessarily arbitrary since they are based on justifying grounds. As James Beilby observes,

> While a properly basic belief is not accepted on the evidential basis of other propositions, it is not groundless. There is a subtle but very important difference between "evidence" and "grounds." If I see a person displaying typical pain behavior, I form the belief that "she is in pain." I don't reason from their behavior to the belief or use their behavior as evidence for the belief. Rather the experience is the occasion for the belief, and my belief is grounded by the experience. Consequently, the grounds for accepting properly basic beliefs consist in the circumstances in which the belief is formed, circumstances which include the relevant "experience."[18]

In distinguishing evidence from grounds Plantinga draws attention to perceptual beliefs ("I see a tree"), memory beliefs ("I had breakfast this morning"), and beliefs that ascribe mental states to other persons ("That person is angry").

> Although beliefs of this sort are typically and properly taken as basic, it would be a mistake to describe them as *groundless*. Upon having experience of a certain sort, I believe that I am perceiving a tree. In the typical case I do not hold this belief on the basis of other beliefs; it is nonetheless not groundless. My having that characteristic sort of experience—to use Professor Chisholm's language, my being appeared treely to—plays a crucial role in the formation and justification of that belief. We might say this experience, together, perhaps, with other circumstances, is what *justifies* me in holding it; this is the *ground* of my justification, and, by extension, the ground of the belief itself.[19]

Similarly, memory beliefs and beliefs about other minds are grounded in certain experiences that we have; they are not the product of inference from premises in an argument. "In each of these cases, a belief is taken as basic, and in each case properly taken as basic. In each case there is some circumstance or condition that confers justification; there is a circumstance that serves as the *ground* of justification."[20] It is worth noting that Plantinga adopts a rather narrow understanding of evidence and that with a broader

18. James Beilby, *Epistemology as Theology: An Evaluation of Alvin Plantinga's Religious Epistemology* (Aldershot: Ashgate, 2006), 43–44.

19. Alvin Plantinga, "Belief in God as Properly Basic," in *The Philosophy of Religion Reader*, ed. Chad Meister (London: Routledge, 2008), 382. Emphasis in original.

20. Plantinga, "Belief in God as Properly Basic," 383. Emphasis in original.

notion of evidence, such as *whatever makes some truth evident to us*, the sharp distinction between grounds and evidence for belief collapses.[21]

Plantinga argues that although belief in God is properly basic, it nevertheless is not arbitrary since it has justifying grounds producing the belief. The grounds are the circumstances in which, when the noetic faculties are operating properly, belief in God arises. For many believers, it will be particular experiences—perhaps gazing at the majestic beauty of towering mountain peaks or holding a newborn infant in one's arms—that provide the grounds for belief in God the creator. Plantinga's language often suggests that our beliefs, both perceptual beliefs about the world and beliefs about God, are involuntary. For example, when I look out of my window and form the belief that there is a tree out there, it is not within my power to withhold that belief. In the appropriate circumstances, I simply find myself having the belief. "Beliefs of this sort," he says, "are not under our voluntary control." Similarly, in appropriate circumstances the believer simply finds herself forming beliefs about God. But in neither case is it a matter of one *deciding* to have the belief in question. "I am a theist; I believe that there is such a person as God; but I have never *decided* to hold this belief. It has always just seemed to me to be true. And it isn't as if I could rid myself of this belief just by an act of will."[22]

Plantinga understands epistemic justification "in a broadly deontological way, so that it includes being within one's epistemic rights and also includes being epistemically responsible with respect to belief formation."[23] For a person to be justified in believing P, he must be fulfilling his epistemic responsibilities—he cannot be "flouting any epistemic duties or obligations."[24] Plantinga does not spell out just what these epistemic responsibilities include, but the overall thrust is that justification is minimalist in the sense that so long as one is not violating clear rationality norms in believing P, one is epistemically permitted to believe P. The justifying conditions are to some extent person-relative, so that someone else in other circumstances might justifiably not believe P. But in each case, justification is understood

21. See C. Stephen Evans, "Religious Experience and the Question of Whether Belief in God Requires Evidence," in *Evidence and Religious Belief*, ed. Kelly James Clark and Raymond J. VanArragon (New York: Oxford University Press, 2011), 38–39. Moreover, there is some ambiguity in Plantinga's use of "grounds" and "evidence," particularly as these concepts are related to his views on natural theology. See Paul Helm, *Faith and Understanding* (Grand Rapids: Eerdmans, 1997), 188–89.

22. Alvin Plantinga, *Knowledge and Christian Belief* (Grand Rapids: Eerdmans, 2015), 16–17. Emphasis in original.

23. Plantinga, *Warranted Christian Belief*, 100.

24. Plantinga, *Knowledge and Christian Belief*, 36.

in terms of permission to believe or "being within one's intellectual rights" to believe.[25]

The proper basicality of belief is defeasible,[26] so that changing epistemic circumstances—including the introduction of new evidence or arguments—can result in a belief no longer being properly basic for someone. There can be potential defeaters for proper basicality so that objections to Christian belief cannot simply be ignored. If there are successful defeaters for a belief P, then P cannot be properly basic for that person. Thus, objections such as the problem of evil or the claims of biblical higher criticism or the theories of Freud and Feuerbach need to be shown to be untenable. But Plantinga argues that objections to the rationality or justification of Christian beliefs (what he calls the de jure question) are not independent of the question of the truth of core Christian claims (the de facto question), and thus "a successful atheological objection will have to be to the *truth* of theism, not to its rationality, justification, intellectual respectability, rational justification, or whatever."[27] The critic must somehow show that Christian theism is false, not simply argue that it is irrational or intellectually deficient in some manner. So long as Christian theism is not demonstrated to be false, a Christian can be fully justified in accepting some beliefs about God as properly basic.

Awareness of religious diversity and widespread disagreement over religious claims is often regarded as a potential defeater for the claim that belief in God is properly basic. Even if we grant that there are circumstances in which a Christian can be entitled to treat belief in God as properly basic (the argument goes), exposure to religious disagreement changes the relevant conditions, so that belief in God in these circumstances requires evidential support. Given the competing claims to exclusive truth among religions, anyone who insists that *his* religion is true should be expected to produce supporting evidence.

In answer to this argument, Plantinga maintains that even when confronted by radical religious disagreement, the Christian does not need to defend her beliefs by appealing to reasons or evidence.[28] He acknowledges that for some people, awareness of diversity does undermine confidence in

---

25. Plantinga, *Knowledge and Christian Belief*, 18–19.

26. To say that the status of a belief as properly basic is defeasible means that the introduction of new information or evidence calling the belief into question can remove the justification for holding that belief.

27. Plantinga, *Warranted Christian Belief*, 191.

28. See Alvin Plantinga, "Pluralism: A Defense of Religious Exclusivism," in *The Rationality of Belief and the Plurality of Faith*, ed. Thomas D. Senor (Ithaca, NY: Cornell University Press, 1995), 191–215; and Plantinga, *Warranted Christian Belief*, 422–57. For a critique of Plantinga's claims, see Anita Renusch, "Thank God It's the Right Religion!—Plantinga on

their beliefs.[29] But this is merely a sociological or psychological fact about how some people respond to diversity, with no significant implications for what is required in order to be rational in believing. Although having reasons for belief can be helpful for those whose confidence in Christian beliefs diminishes in the face of religious disagreement, this is not required in order to be rational in accepting core Christian claims.

Proper Basicality and the Holy Spirit

The Holy Spirit is given a prominent place in Plantinga's Reformed epistemology, especially as this is worked out in his Aquinas/Calvin model in *Warranted Christian Belief*. His discussion of the role of the Spirit is rich and insightful, but our concern here is not with his externalist model based on proper function but rather with the more limited issue of the role of the Holy Spirit in properly basic beliefs about God.

Plantinga appeals to John Calvin's notion of the *sensus divinitatis* (sense of the divine) to explain how it is that people come to have properly basic beliefs about God, and he directly links the *sensus* with the witness of the Holy Spirit. God has created us in such a way that in appropriate circumstances when our epistemic faculties are functioning as designed, the *sensus divinitatis* moves us to form certain beliefs about God. "Calvin's basic claim is that there is a sort of natural instinct, a natural human tendency, a disposition, a nisus to form beliefs about God under a variety of conditions and in a variety of situations."[30] Plantinga claims that the knowledge of God delivered through the *sensus divinitatis* is not the product of inference or argument.

> The deliverances of the *sensus divinitatis* are not quick inferences from the circumstances that trigger its operation. It isn't that one beholds the night sky, notes that it is grand, and concludes that there must be such a person as God: as an argument, this would be pretty weak. It isn't that one notices some feature of the Australian outback—that it is ancient and brooding, for example—and draws the conclusion that God exists. It is rather that upon the perception of the night sky or the mountain vista or the tiny flower these beliefs just arise within us. They *arise* in these circumstances; they are not conclusions from them. The heavens declare the glory of God and the skies

Religious Diversity," in *Plantinga's "Warranted Christian Belief": Critical Essays with a Reply by Alvin Plantinga*, ed. Dieter Schönecker (Berlin: de Gruyter, 2015), 147–68.

29. Plantinga, *Warranted Christian Belief*, 456.
30. Plantinga, *Warranted Christian Belief*, 171.

proclaim the work of his hands (Psalm 19): but not by way of serving as premises for an argument.[31]

According to Plantinga, "the *sensus divinitatis* resembles the faculties of perception, memory, and a priori knowledge."[32] Just as my perceptual belief that there is a tree in front of me is not an inference from premises in an argument but rather is directly produced through my seeing the tree, so too the natural awareness of God is produced immediately in the proper circumstances.

> These circumstances, we might say, trigger the disposition to form the beliefs in question; they form the occasion on which those beliefs arise. Under these circumstances, we develop or form theistic beliefs—or, rather, these beliefs are formed in us; in the typical case we don't consciously choose to have those beliefs. . . . The *sensus divinitatis* is a disposition or set of dispositions to form theistic beliefs in various circumstances, in response to the sorts of conditions or stimuli that trigger the working of this sense of divinity.[33]

Thus in appropriate circumstances, beliefs such as "This vast and intricate universe was created by God" can be properly basic for Christians, and since the existence of God is entailed by such a belief, we can say that belief in God's existence can thus be properly basic. "God has so created us that we have a tendency or disposition to see his hand in the world around us. More precisely, there is in us a disposition to believe propositions of the sort *this flower was created by God* or *this vast and intricate universe was created by God* when we contemplate the flower or behold the starry heavens or think about the vast reaches of the universe."[34]

But coming to have such beliefs is not the result merely of the natural operations of the noetic faculties as God created them. Sin has damaged but not obliterated the *sensus divinitatis*, so a special work of the Holy Spirit is necessary for conviction about the truth of Christian beliefs. Confidence in the truth of Christian teaching comes "by way of the work of the Holy Spirit, who gets us to accept, causes us to believe, these great truths of the gospel. These beliefs don't come just by way of the normal operation of our natural faculties; they are a supernatural gift."[35]

31. Plantinga, *Knowledge and Christian Belief*, 35. Emphasis in original.
32. Plantinga, *Knowledge and Christian Belief*, 35.
33. Plantinga, *Warranted Christian Belief*, 172–73.
34. Plantinga, "Belief in God as Properly Basic," 383.
35. Plantinga, *Warranted Christian Belief*, 245.

We face an issue here similar to what emerged in our discussion of Jonathan Edwards and John Wesley in chapter 4: Is the *sensus divinitatis* a special spiritual or noetic faculty beyond the normal faculties such as the senses, inference, introspection, and memory? Or does the term simply refer to the ways in which God works through the normal noetic faculties to bring about belief in Christian teachings? Plantinga is not entirely clear on this point, although he unambiguously affirms that it is through the work of the Holy Spirit that one believes the truths of Scripture. "These beliefs do not come to the Christian just by way of memory, perception, reason, testimony, the *sensus divinitatis*, or any other of the cognitive faculties with which we human beings were originally created; they come instead by way of the work of the Holy Spirit, who gets us to accept, causes us to believe, these great truths of the gospel. These beliefs don't come just by way of the normal operation of our natural faculties; they are a supernatural gift."[36] Some understand Plantinga to be speaking of the *sensus divinitatis* as a special cognitive faculty in addition to the ordinary faculties humans enjoy, and this would place him within the "spiritual senses" tradition.[37] But this, I think, is not required by his language. Regardless of Plantinga's own view, however, Blake McAllister and Trent Dougherty have argued persuasively that it is better to understand the *sensus divinitatis* not as a special spiritual cognitive faculty but rather as a cognitive mechanism operating through the standard faculties, under the influence of the Holy Spirit, through which one apprehends truths about God.[38]

According to Plantinga, the result of this special work of the Spirit through the *sensus divinitatis* is that we directly, noninferentially, apprehend the truth of Christian beliefs. "In the model, the beliefs constituting faith are typically taken as basic; that is, they are not accepted by way of argument from other propositions or on the evidential basis of other propositions in this way, though perhaps some believers do in fact reason this way."[39] Plantinga illustrates how this works.

> We read Scripture, or something representing scriptural teaching, or hear the gospel preached, or are told of it by our parents, or encounter a scriptural teaching as the conclusion of an argument (or conceivably even as an object

36. Plantinga, *Warranted Christian Belief*, 245.

37. William J. Abraham, "Analytic Philosophers of Religion," in *The Spiritual Senses: Perceiving God in Western Christianity*, ed. Paul L. Gavrilyuk and Sarah Coakley (Cambridge: Cambridge University Press, 2012), 285–87.

38. Blake McAllister and Trent Dougherty, "Reforming Reformed Epistemology: A New Take on the *Sensus Divinitatis*," *Religious Studies* 55 (2019): 537–57.

39. Plantinga, *Knowledge and Christian Belief*, 60.

of ridicule), or in some other way encounter a proclamation of the Word. What is said simply seems right; it seems compelling; one finds oneself saying "Yes, that's right, that's the truth of the matter; this is indeed the word of the Lord." I read, "God was in Christ, reconciling the world to himself"; I come to think: "Right, that's true; God really was in Christ, reconciling the world to himself!" And I may also think something a bit different, something *about* that proposition: that it is indeed a divine teaching or revelation, that, in Calvin's words, it is "from God." What one hears or reads seems clearly and obviously true, and (at any rate in paradigm cases) seems also to be something the Lord is intending to teach."[40]

Thus, while some believers might make use of arguments or reasons in favor of the Christian faith, the "typical believer" does not do so but simply finds herself, in the appropriate circumstances, accepting certain beliefs about God and the gospel.

Plantinga's discussion of the *sensus divinitatis* and the Holy Spirit is thoughtful and illuminating, although some have questioned his interpretation of John Calvin.[41] Paul Helm, for example, argues that in some ways the *sensus* serves a quite different function for Calvin than it does for Plantinga. For Calvin the *sensus* is not reflected in a particular kind of experience; on the contrary, Helm states that "the idea of an experience of God does not enter into any of the terminology Calvin uses to characterize the *sensus*." Furthermore, he holds that Calvin does not seem interested in the question of the rationality or justification of Christian beliefs as such.

> What we find in Calvin, I suggest, is little or no interest in the rationality of religious belief. . . . Rather, what Calvin emphasizes is not rationality but responsibility. His interest in the *sensus* is not due to an interest in the rational grounds for theistic belief, but to a concern to establish that since all men and women in fact have some knowledge of God, they are culpable when they do not form their lives in such a way that is appropriate to such knowledge. . . . It does not follow from Calvin's remarks about the seed of religion that

---

40. Plantinga, *Knowledge and Christian Belief*, 60–61. Emphasis in original.
41. See, e.g., Derek S. Jeffreys, "How Reformed Is Reformed Epistemology? Alvin Plantinga and Calvin's '*Sensus Divinitatis*,'" *Religious Studies* 33, no. 4 (December 1997): 419–31; Georg Plasger, "Does Calvin Teach a *Sensus Divinitatis*? Reflections on Alvin Plantinga's Interpretation of Calvin," in Schönecker, *Plantinga's "Warranted Christian Belief*, 169–89; and Paul Helm, "Review of *Warranted Christian Belief*," *Mind* 110, no. 440 (October 2001): 1110–15. For Calvin's notion of the *sensus divinitatis* and its relation to natural theology, see Paul Helm, *John Calvin's Ideas* (New York: Oxford University Press, 2004), chap. 8; and J. V. Fesko, *Reforming Apologetics: Retrieving the Classic Reformed Approach to Defending the Faith* (Grand Rapids: Baker Academic, 2019), chap. 3.

a person is entitled to believe in God reasonlessly, nor does Calvin say that it does. He does not say that it does nor does he deny that it does.[42]

These are important points. But our concern here is not with the proper interpretation of Calvin but rather with how Plantinga has developed within his own epistemological model what he takes to be insights from Calvin. Three prominent themes in Plantinga's proposal have special relevance for the subject of religious experience: (1) the claim that belief in God is properly basic for believers, (2) the causal role of the Holy Spirit in believers coming to apprehend truths about God, and (3) the independence of the work of the Spirit from evidence and reasons for belief. These themes also find expression in the writings of William Lane Craig, a prominent philosopher and apologist who has been significantly influenced by Plantinga.

Craig on the Holy Spirit, Belief, and Evidence

Although William Lane Craig is well known for his rigorous use of evidence and arguments in defense of the existence of God and the historicity of the resurrection of Jesus, he follows Plantinga in holding that belief in God is properly basic for believers. Like Plantinga, Craig brings together the properly basic nature of Christians' beliefs and the witness or testimony of the Holy Spirit. Craig states that Christian believers "*know* that our Christian beliefs are true because they are properly basic, warranted beliefs grounded in our veridical experience of the witness of the Holy Spirit in our hearts. Rational argument and evidence may confirm our Christian beliefs to us but cannot defeat them if we are walking in the fullness of the Spirit."[43]

Awareness of God's reality comes through our immediate experience of God. In his debate with philosopher Walter Sinnott-Armstrong, for example, Craig claims that "we can know that God exists wholly apart from arguments simply by immediately experiencing Him. . . . Belief in God is for those who seek Him a properly basic belief grounded in our experience of God, as we discern Him in nature, conscience, and other means."[44] From these statements, then, it is clear that what grounds the Christian's belief in God is a particular kind of experience, "our veridical experience of the

42. Helm, *Faith and Understanding*, 181, 198, 201.

43. William Lane Craig, "Classical Apologetics," in *Five Views on Apologetics*, ed. Steven B. Cowan (Grand Rapids: Zondervan, 2000), 54. Emphasis in original.

44. William Lane Craig and Walter Sinnott-Armstrong, *God? A Debate between a Christian and an Atheist* (New York: Oxford University Press, 2004), 26–27.

witness of the Holy Spirit in our hearts" or "our experience of God, as we discern Him in nature, conscience, and other means." We are not told whether this experience is a singular event, a series of particular experiences, or even a more general way of interpreting the world. Regardless, the important point is that what grounds our confidence in God's reality is an experience of God through the witness of the Spirit and not consideration of evidence or arguments supporting Christian claims.

Craig appeals to biblical passages such as John 14:26; Romans 8:15–16; Galatians 3:26, 4:6; and 1 John 2:20, 27; 3:24; 4:13 in support of the assertion that the believer's confidence in the truth of the gospel comes from the work of the Holy Spirit. Referring to John 14:26—"But the Advocate, the Holy Spirit, whom the Father will send in my name, will teach you all things and will remind you of everything I have said to you"—Craig states, "Now the truth that the Holy Spirit teaches us is not, I'm convinced, the subtleties of Christian doctrine. There are too many Spirit-filled Christians who differ doctrinally for that to be the case. What John is talking about is the inner assurance the Holy Spirit gives of the basic truths of the Christian faith, what Plantinga calls the great truths of the gospel. *This assurance does not come from human arguments but directly from the Holy Spirit himself.*"[45] Craig thus explicitly contrasts the assurance from the Spirit with an assurance "from human arguments."

Craig uses the term "self-authenticating" in speaking of the experience of the Spirit. "Although arguments and evidence may be used to support the believer's faith, they are never properly the basis of that faith. For the believer, God is not the conclusion of a syllogism; he is the living God of Abraham, Isaac, and Jacob dwelling within us. How then does the believer know that Christianity is true? He knows because of the self-authenticating witness of God's Spirit who lives within him."[46] In a remarkable passage Craig states,

> Fundamentally, the way we know Christianity to be true is by the self-authenticating witness of God's Holy Spirit. Now what do I mean by that? I mean that the experience of the Holy Spirit is veridical and unmistakable (though not necessarily irresistible or indubitable) for him who has it; that such a person does not need supplementary arguments or evidence in order to know and to know with confidence that he is in fact experiencing the Spirit of God; that such experience does not function in this case as a premise in any

45. William Lane Craig, *Reasonable Faith: Christian Truth and Apologetics*, 3rd ed. (Wheaton: Crossway Books, 2008), 44. Emphasis added.
46. Craig, *Reasonable Faith*, 46.

argument from religious experience to God, but rather is the immediate experiencing of God himself; that in certain contexts the experience of the Holy Spirit will imply the apprehension of certain truths of the Christian religion, such as "God exists," "I am condemned by God," "I am reconciled to God," "Christ lives in me," and so forth; that such an experience provides one not only with a subjective assurance of Christianity's truth, but with objective knowledge of that truth; and that arguments and evidence incompatible with that truth are overwhelmed by the experience of the Holy Spirit for him who attends fully to it.[47]

Many interesting questions are prompted by this paragraph: Can one be mistaken about what he or she takes to be the witness of the Spirit? If so, how does the believer know that the experience of what seems to be the witness of the Holy Spirit is indeed veridical? What does it mean to say that the experience is unmistakable but not indubitable? In what sense does the experience "overwhelm" arguments and evidence incompatible with Christian claims? Rather than address each of these questions, however, we will focus briefly on the notion of self-authentication.

The term "self-authenticating" is used in different ways, but in religious studies and philosophy it is typically used to designate a certain kind of experience that allegedly grants immediate and complete certainty to the subject of the experience. A self-authenticating experience is usually defined in terms of two conditions: (1) the experience is seen *immediately* (non-inferentially) to be veridical, and (2) the person undergoing the experience is said to have a special kind of certainty so that he or she *cannot* be mistaken about the veridicality of the experience or the claims based on it. As Keith Yandell puts it, "*Self-authentication* is a three-term relation; there is a person to whom an experience authenticates, an experience that does the authenticating, and a belief or proposition that is authenticated. Further, the idea is, the belief or proposition in question is evidenced or authenticated in a particularly strong way—in such a way, in fact, that the person cannot be mistaken in accepting that belief or in believing that proposition if they base accepting or believing on having had the experience."[48] This is a very strong claim to make for any experience, especially for a religious experience, and not surprisingly the notion of self-authentication is highly controversial. We will consider shortly whether this really is the best way to understand the biblical language of the witness of the Holy Spirit, but

47. Craig, *Reasonable Faith*, 43.

48. Keith Yandell, *Philosophy of Religion: A Contemporary Introduction*, 2nd ed. (New York: Routledge, 2016), 206; See also Yandell, *The Epistemology of Religious Experience* (Cambridge: Cambridge University Press, 1993), 163–82.

for now we simply observe that Craig makes a very strong claim about the nature of our experience of the Spirit.

Craig also suggests that it is only the believer who is walking "in the fullness of the Spirit" who can have complete confidence in the truth of Christian teaching. "Only as we walk in the fullness of the Spirit can we be guaranteed the assurance of which Paul speaks [in Rom. 8:15–16]. Thus, the witness of the Holy Spirit is a veridical experience that will be unmistakable for the person who attends to that witness; that is to say, the person who responds appropriately to the Spirit's witness cannot mistake that witness for anything other than what it is."[49] The apparent implication is that lack of complete confidence in the truth of the gospel on the part of a believer is due to his or her failure to walk in the fullness of the Spirit.

Craig acknowledges that there are defeaters to Christian beliefs that need to be addressed, but he claims that the Spirit's inner witness "overwhelms" such challenges: "The claim that the Spirit's witness is self-authenticating entails that belief grounded in the witness of the Holy Spirit is an intrinsic defeater of the defeaters brought against it; that is to say, it is a belief enjoying such a high degree of warrant that it simply overwhelms any putative defeater."[50] The meaning of "overwhelms" in the statement is ambiguous. On the one hand, it could be referring to psychological or subjective certitude; the believer has such a high degree of confidence in the truth of the gospel that she is simply unable to acknowledge the epistemic force of the defeater. As a state of subjective confidence, this could be the case for someone even if theism is false and there is no God (although in that case, of course, one's confidence would not be the result of the witness of the Holy Spirit). On the other hand, Craig could be using "overwhelms" in an epistemic sense of justified certainty, so that because of the witness of the Spirit, the believer justifiably concludes that any defeater must be false. Presumably Craig is using the term in the second sense.

Self-Authenticating Experiences?

Alvin Plantinga and William Lane Craig follow Jonathan Edwards and John Wesley and the mainstream Christian tradition in emphasizing that it is the Holy Spirit who produces confidence in the truth of the Christian gospel. As we noted earlier, this Christian theological explanation for how individuals come to believe the truth of the gospel should hold a prominent place in any

49. Craig, "Classical Apologetics," 31.
50. Craig, "Classical Apologetics," 34.

responsible Christian treatment of the issue. It is a central tenet of orthodox Christian theology that the Holy Spirit plays an essential role in a person coming to accept the Christian gospel and to have confidence in the teachings of Scripture, for without the Spirit there is no real knowledge of God (Rom. 8:14–17; 1 Cor. 2:6–14; 1 John 3:24). A special work of God's grace is necessary to remove the effects of sin so that unbelievers can understand and respond to the gospel (1 Cor. 2:14; 2 Cor. 4:4). Ultimately it is the Holy Spirit who brings unbelievers to saving faith in Christ (John 3:5–8; 16:8–15; Rom. 8:9; 1 Cor. 2:14; Titus 3:4–7), and it is the Holy Spirit who grants to believers their confidence in God's acceptance. Galatians 4:6 states that God sends the Spirit of his Son into the hearts of believers, crying "*Abba*, Father." Romans 8:15–16 indicates that when believers cry "*Abba*, Father," it is the Spirit himself who "testifies with our spirit that we are God's children." William Abraham remarks that this text in particular has "given birth to a claim about certainty and assurance which invokes the possibility of a direct, inward experience of the Holy Spirit."[51] Paul Moser, drawing upon Galatians 4:6 and Romans 8:15–16, says, "This filial language of Paul, in the wake of Jesus, indicates that the Spirit of God seeks to witness, in an epistemically important manner, not only to God's reality and faithfulness, but also to one's having become (or, at least, one's becoming) a cooperative child of God. This position is distinctive in giving God's Spirit a central role in epistemically confirming God's reality and work."[52] Thus, in appealing to the inner witness of the Holy Spirit, Plantinga and Craig are drawing upon a crucial theme in orthodox Christian teaching.

There is much in Plantinga's and Craig's discussions of the Holy Spirit and the formation of Christian belief that is both true and significant, and much of what they say echoes themes we saw earlier in the work of Edwards and Wesley. Nevertheless, I argue that some of their claims should be modified in important respects. We will consider first the issue of the self-authenticating nature of the witness of the Holy Spirit, then examine some limitations to the claim that belief in God is properly basic, and finally look at the relation between the work of the Holy Spirit and evidence.

Should we understand the inner witness of the Holy Spirit as a self-authenticating experience so that in having it one knows with complete certainty the truth of Christian claims? Is it necessarily the case that those who experience the Spirit's work know immediately and with complete

51. William Abraham, "The Epistemological Significance of the Inner Witness of the Holy Spirit," *Faith and Philosophy* 7, no. 4 (October 1990): 437.
52. Paul Moser, "The Inner Witness of the Spirit," in Abraham and Aquino, *Oxford Handbook of the Epistemology of Theology*, 114.

certainty the truth of Christian claims and that no amount of counterevidence or argumentation can overcome this confidence? I will argue that for at least three reasons, self-authentication is not the best way to think about the inner witness of the Holy Spirit.

First, it is important to acknowledge that there are appeals to self-authenticating experiences in various religions (especially among Hindus, Jains, and Buddhists), and both the nature of the experiences and the claims based on them are in conflict; not all such claims can be true. Thus, not every claim to self-authentication can be accepted as such; what *seems* to the subject to be self-authenticating may in fact not be so. In other words, some assessment of claims to self-authentication is required. Craig acknowledges that adherents of other religions can make claims similar to Christianity, but he dismisses this as irrelevant. "But how is the fact that other persons claim to experience a self-authenticating witness of God's Spirit relevant to *my* knowing the truth of Christianity via the Spirit's witness? The existence of an authentic and unique witness of the Spirit does not exclude the existence of false claims to such a witness."[53] True, the fact that there is a false claim to the self-authenticating witness of the Spirit does not necessarily mean that there cannot be a true claim to such an experience. But the fact of multiple competing claims to the self-authenticating witness of the Spirit does raise the question of how I can be sure that *my* experience, and not that of others, is genuinely self-authenticating. Mormons, for example, appeal to the testimony of the Holy Spirit for justification and certitude concerning Mormon claims. This shows that *merely* appealing to an allegedly self-authenticating experience grounded in the witness of the Holy Spirit is insufficient for determining *which* claim to the testimony of the Holy Spirit is really true.[54]

Moreover, the issue here is not that Hindus or Buddhists are claiming their own self-authenticating experiences of the Holy Spirit. Buddhists deny the reality of God so there is, for them, no Holy Spirit to experience. Rather, the issue is that Hindus, Buddhists, and Jains each claim self-authenticating experiences that (allegedly) guarantee the truth of some of the core claims of their respective religions. But the claims based on these allegedly self-authenticating experiences are mutually incompatible: Buddhists and Jains

53. Craig, *Reasonable Faith*, 49. Emphasis in original.

54. The Book of Mormon concludes with Moroni promising that the Holy Ghost will bring conviction of the truth of Mormon teaching: "And when ye shall receive these things, I would exhort you that ye would ask God, the Eternal Father, in the name of Christ, if these things are not true; and if ye shall ask with a sincere heart, with real intent, having faith in Christ, he will manifest the truth of it unto you, by the power of the Holy Ghost. And by the power of the Holy Ghost ye may know the truth of all things" (Moroni 10:4–5). *The Book of Mormon*, trans. Joseph Smith (Salt Lake City: Church of Jesus Christ of Latter Day Saints, 1982), 529.

deny the reality of God, whereas Christians and many Hindus affirm God's reality; Buddhists deny the reality of the soul, whereas Jains, Christians, and many Hindus affirm the reality of the soul in some form. It is not only Christians who claim certainty for their beliefs on the basis of self-authenticating experiences. But since the many claims allegedly grounded in self-authenticating experiences cannot all be true, not every experience purporting to be self-authenticating is veridical. Why then should the Christian believe that *his or her* experience is veridical (and thus self-authenticating) and that those of others are not? What is required are independent reasons for accepting Christian experiences as veridical, but once one appeals to reasons in support of the experience, it is no longer self-authenticating.

There is a second reason why appealing to self-authentication is not the best way to think about the inner witness of the Holy Spirit. Nothing in Scripture demands that we understand the work of the Holy Spirit in terms of self-authentication, as defined above. While Scripture makes it clear that ultimately it is the Spirit who brings about understanding of and confidence in the truth of the gospel, nowhere does it state that this confidence is a result of a self-authenticating experience of the Spirit. The Spirit's work might at times be direct and immediate, but there is nothing in Scripture ruling out the Spirit also working through other factors to bring about confidence in biblical truths. Nor do the biblical texts require that we understand this confidence in terms of the apodictic or indubitable certainty that self-authentication promises. The texts typically appealed to in this context are remarkably terse and their language, while compatible with self-authentication, does not demand it.

Third, it is important to pay close attention to the phenomenology of actual experiences of believers. To be sure, we should not base our interpretation of biblical texts merely on human experiences, but any interpretation of a text purporting to describe the experiences of believers that flies in the face of the lived realities of most believers is surely suspect, especially when that interpretation is not required by the text. The inner witness of the Holy Spirit is supposed to be something characteristic of believers in general, not an esoteric experience reserved for the spiritual elite. But many, if not most, Christians *do not* have experiences that fit the definition of self-authentication. For many believers, the inner witness of the Spirit seems to be something that works, often over a period of time, in conjunction with many other ancillary factors to produce conviction of the truth of the gospel, sustain faith, and grant assurance of salvation.

Moreover, asserting that believers who are genuinely walking with the Spirit will enjoy complete confidence in the truth of Christian claims, with the corollary that doubt and lack of confidence are due to sin or lack of submission to God, is at best misleading. To be sure, there is some truth to the assertion. For example, it is hardly surprising that a believer who lives with unconfessed sin and is unwilling to submit to God's authority will find himself having doubts and struggling with the claims of the Christian faith. But it is both false and unhelpful to say that lack of confidence in the truth of the gospel is always the product of sin.[55] Struggles with questions and doubt are not unusual among sincere believers who are trying to live in ways pleasing to God. It is both fascinating and ironic that many who avidly read books on apologetics and attend apologetics conferences are themselves already sincere and devoted believers who are seeking reasons and evidence to support what they already, in some measure, accept. Questions about the truth of one's beliefs can and do coexist with sincere acceptance of these beliefs. As Anthony Thiselton reminds us, "It is a practical disaster that in popular thought some view all doubt as a sign of weakness and lack of faith; while others, by contrast, extol doubt as always a sign of mature, sophisticated reflection. . . . Doubt, then, can function either negatively as a term that stands in contrast to trust, faith, or wholeheartedness; or positively as a term to denote self-criticism, humility, and careful reflection."[56]

In sum, construing the witness of the Spirit in terms of a self-authenticating experience is neither required by Scripture nor consistent with the lived realities of most believers. I suggest that a more helpful way to think about these matters is to apply the critical-trust approach to the witness of the Holy Spirit.[57] What seems to be an experience of the witness of the Holy Spirit should be taken as such unless there is good reason not to do so. This allows for a high degree of confidence in the truth of the gospel without appealing to the allegedly self-authenticating nature of the witness of the Spirit.

The Limits of Proper Basicality

It is difficult to exaggerate the impact of Plantinga's work on recent religious epistemology. *Warranted Christian Belief* is a rich, complex, and multifaceted treatise that deals with much more than simply the idea that

55. See Gary Habermas, "An Evidentialist's Response," in Cowan, *Five Views on Apologetics*, 65–66; Habermas, *The Thomas Factor: Using Doubt to Draw Closer to God* (Nashville: Broadman & Holman, 1999); Habermas, *Dealing with Doubt* (Chicago: Moody, 1990); and Os Guinness, *God in the Dark: The Assurance of Faith Beyond a Shadow of Doubt* (Wheaton: Crossway, 1996).
56. Anthony C. Thiselton, *Doubt, Faith and Certainty* (Grand Rapids: Eerdmans, 2017), 1, 3.
57. William Hasker, "The Epistemic Value of Religious Experience: Perceptual and Explanatory Models," in Senor, *Rationality of Belief and the Plurality of Faith*, 155–62.

in appropriate circumstances belief in God can be properly basic for believers.[58] But it is this claim that is most relevant to our concerns, and thus
we will examine it briefly. If Plantinga is correct, two consequences follow.
First, there is no general epistemic burden that the believer carries requiring supporting evidence or reasons for belief in God. Second, we should
think of religious experiences not as providing evidence for belief in God
but rather as the grounds from which particular beliefs about God arise. I
will argue that although there is a minimalist sense in which belief in God
can be properly basic for some believers in appropriate circumstances, this
is not the most helpful way to think about the rationality of belief in God
for most people.

Let's assume that some kind of foundationalist epistemological model is
correct and that, as Plantinga argues, any acceptable version of foundationalism will need to expand the class of properly basic beliefs beyond what
was permitted by classical foundationalism. Minimally, the six items listed
earlier in this chapter should be included as properly basic beliefs, but many
insist that other, more ordinary beliefs (e.g., "I had toast for breakfast this
morning") will also need to be included, although there is no consensus on
what kinds of beliefs qualify as properly basic. Nevertheless, as a corrective
to an excessively narrow form of foundationalism, Plantinga's proposal
makes an important contribution.

Is belief in God properly basic for Christians in the appropriate circumstances? Undoubtedly belief in God and other related beliefs can be properly
basic for some people. Plantinga rightly reminds us that not everyone should
be expected to provide sufficient evidence for belief in God in order for
such belief to be rational. Many ordinary Christians are unable to provide
significant evidence for their beliefs, but surely it would be implausible to
insist that they are all irrational if they cannot produce such evidence. One
thinks here not only of children and those with limited mental capacities but
also adults with little exposure to intellectual issues. My grandparents, for
example, had little formal education, lived much of their lives surrounded
by other Christians, and were active in church activities. It would be bizarre
to insist that they were irrational in believing as they did because they could
not provide sufficient evidence for their beliefs. Let's assume, then, that
Plantinga is correct in saying that it can be entirely reasonable for belief in

---

58. See the symposium discussion on *Warranted Christian Belief* by Douglas Geivett, Greg
Jesson, Richard Fumerton, Keith Yandell, and Paul Moser, along with a response by Plantinga
in *Philosophia Christi* 3, no. 2 (2001): 327–400. Deane-Peter Baker provides a summary of criticisms of Plantinga's proposal in "Plantinga's Reformed Epistemology: What's the Question?,"
International Journal for Philosophy of Religion 57 (Spring 2005): 77–103.

God to be properly basic for some people in appropriate circumstances. It does not follow, of course, that such belief is properly basic for all, or even for most, believers in typical circumstances.

It is helpful to distinguish descriptive, or empirical, factors from normative, or epistemic, issues. *Whether belief in God is a basic belief for someone* is a descriptive, or empirical, issue: Does she simply find herself believing in God apart from deriving this belief from other beliefs she holds? If so, it is for her a basic belief. But *whether belief in God derived in this way is properly basic* is a normative or epistemic question: Is it epistemically appropriate for her to hold this as a basic belief? Questions about belief in God as properly basic generally focus on the second question, but Plantinga also addresses the empirical issue, and he claims that the typical pattern for believers is to accept belief in God as a basic belief.

> Christian belief in the typical case is not the conclusion of an argument or accepted on the evidential basis of other beliefs, or accepted just because it constitutes a good explanation of phenomena of one kind or another. . . . Nor are [Christian beliefs] accepted as a result of historical research. Nor are they accepted as the conclusion of an argument from *religious experience.* . . . It isn't that the believer notes that she or someone else has a certain sort of experience, and somehow concludes that Christian belief must be true. It is rather that (as in the case of sense perception) the experience is the occasion for the formation of the beliefs in question. In the typical case, therefore, Christian belief is *immediate*; it is formed in the *basic* way.[59]

Although Plantinga concedes that some people might rely on arguments and reasons when they come to faith, this is not typical of most believers.

But is this really the case? Does the typical believer really simply find himself or herself accepting belief in God as a properly basic belief, so that it is the unusual person, the outlier, who seeks out evidence for Christian belief? Not only is such a claim not demanded by Scripture, but it goes against what we observe in the very diverse ways in which people do in fact come to believe in the gospel. As James Beilby observes, "The religious beliefs of the typical Christian are more likely based on a complex mixture of personal, social, and evidential factors in addition to pneumatological factors such as the internal instigation of the Holy Spirit."[60] Contrary to Plantinga's statement, it seems to me that for many people *some* consideration of the

---

59. Plantinga, *Knowledge and Christian Belief*, 64. Emphasis in original. See also Plantinga, *Warranted Christian Belief*, 259.
60. Beilby, "Plantinga's Model of Warranted Christian Belief," 148.

evidence or reasons for Christian teachings plays a significant role in their coming to faith. The process of coming to accept and maintain Christian commitments is, for many, complicated and messy, involving a wide variety of factors over a period of time.

Furthermore, many Christians do find that their confidence in Christian beliefs is shaken when they are confronted with challenges such as the problem of evil, the claims of science, radical biblical scholarship, or awareness of religious diversity and disagreement. Empirical research by social scientists indicates that sustained exposure to religious diversity and secularism, characteristic of late modernity, can have a profoundly destabilizing effect on one's own beliefs.[61] The awareness that other good and intelligent people we interact with hold quite different religious beliefs can be very disconcerting. Sociologist Peter Berger, for example, observes that under the conditions of modern pluralization "the management of doubt becomes a problem for every religious tradition."[62] Similarly, Charles Taylor argues that the transition to the modern world involves a massive shift that "consists, among other things, of a move from a society where belief in God is unchallenged and indeed unproblematic, to one in which it is understood to be one option among others, and frequently not the easiest to embrace." Modern Europe and North America have gone from a social context "in which it was virtually impossible not to believe in God, to one in which faith, even for the staunchest believer, is one human possibility among others. . . . Belief in God is no longer axiomatic. There are alternatives."[63] As an empirical matter, people respond to awareness of diversity and disagreement in different ways, with some deeply bothered by it and others not. A variety of factors are involved here, and we should avoid sweeping generalizations that ignore relevant complexities.

What about the normative issue? We have already noted that for some people in appropriate circumstances belief in God can be properly basic.

61. See Robert Wuthnow, *After Heaven: Spirituality in America since the 1950s* (Berkeley: University of California Press, 1998); Wuthnow, *America and the Challenges of Religious Diversity* (Princeton: Princeton University Press, 2005); Wade Clark Roof, *Spiritual Marketplace: Baby Boomers and the Remaking of American Religion* (Princeton: Princeton University Press, 2005); Elizabeth Drescher, *Choosing Our Religion: The Spiritual Lives of America's Nones* (New York: Oxford University Press, 2016); T. M. Luhrmann, *When God Talks Back: Understanding the American Evangelical Relationship with God* (New York: Knopf, 2012); Peter L. Berger, *The Many Altars of Modernity: Toward a Paradigm for Religion in a Pluralist Age* (Berlin: de Gruyter, 2014); and Peter L. Berger and Anton Zijderveld, *In Praise of Doubt: How to Have Convictions without Becoming a Fanatic* (New York: HarperOne, 2009).
62. Berger, *Many Altars of Modernity*, 32.
63. Charles Taylor, *A Secular Age* (Cambridge, MA: Harvard University Press, 2007), 3.

But is this the situation for most believers in today's world? The attraction of Plantinga's proposal is due in part to the analogy he draws between belief in God and the properly basic nature of beliefs about the reliability of memory and the reality of the external world and other minds. Virtually everyone accepts the latter beliefs as properly basic. Part of what it means to be a rational person is to accept the reality of the external world, the general reliability of memory and of the five senses, and the existence of other minds. In the proper circumstances we simply find ourselves holding these beliefs, and appropriately so. Why then should not believers also regard belief in God in a similar manner?

The analogy cannot be pressed too far, for there are important differences between beliefs about the reality of the external world or the general reliability of memory and belief in God. For example, it would be strange to question seriously the truth of the former beliefs, since normally functioning persons simply do not seriously doubt whether there really is an external world or whether in general memory is reliable. But many apparently normal people *do* question the existence of God.[64] Furthermore, belief in the reality of the external world is coercive or compelling in a way that belief in God, at least for many people, is not. It is very difficult genuinely to deny beliefs about the former, whereas for many people today it is not at all difficult to question the existence of God. So phenomenologically, there is a difference between how beliefs about the reality of the external world or the general reliability of memory function and how belief in God functions for many people. This alone suggests that one cannot make too strong an analogy between the two kinds of beliefs. If belief in God is properly basic, at least for some people in appropriate circumstances, then it is a different kind of properly basic belief than these others.

Properly basic beliefs face potential defeaters, such as the problem of evil or questions raised by religious disagreement. Consider, for example, the challenge posed by religious diversity. Does a believer's awareness of religious diversity and disagreement change the context enough that he should now reexamine his beliefs to see whether they are indeed supported by adequate

64. Some might object that those questioning the reality of God are *not* normal since it is the noetic effects of sin that causes people to reject God's reality. There is an important theological truth in this objection. Any biblically responsible perspective must acknowledge the significant effects of sin on our knowing processes and the fact that it is God's grace and the work of the Spirit that enables us to recognize truth about God. But my point here is not so much theological as it is a phenomenological observation about the different ways in which beliefs such as the general reliability of memory and the reality of God function among humankind at large. It is undeniable that large numbers of apparently normal people—people who live flourishing lives and function well, as far as we can tell—accept the former belief but question or reject the latter.

reasons? As noted above, Plantinga contends that even when aware of deep religious diversity, a believer can appropriately continue to accept belief in God as a properly basic belief. Although for some Christians awareness of religious diversity might raise questions and reduce confidence in their beliefs, this is an empirical or psychological fact; such awareness itself does not introduce new epistemic obligations.

But this response strikes many as irresponsible. Most people in today's diverse societies have an existential awareness of religious diversity and this, it seems to many, introduces some epistemic obligation to consider whether there are good reasons for continuing to hold one's own religious beliefs. The difference with other generally accepted properly basic beliefs is significant: Beliefs about the reality of the external world or the general reliability of memory are widely accepted as properly basic in part because there is little serious dispute about their truth. But this is not the case with belief in God. Many intelligent and morally respectable people sharply disagree about this question. As Gary Gutting puts it, "Isn't it just common sense to admit that, when there is widespread [disagreement] about a claim, with apparently competent judges on both sides, those who assert or deny the claim need to justify their positions?"[65]

The problem here concerns what James Beilby calls Plantinga's "minimalist approach to religious epistemology."[66] Plantinga's primary interest is in the question of how, given their metaphysical commitments, Christians should think about the epistemic status of their own beliefs and not in demonstrating the truth of Christian theism. His conclusion is actually fairly modest: it is possible for Christians in appropriate circumstances to maintain some of their Christian beliefs in a properly basic manner, and if the claims of Christian theism are true, then such beliefs can also be warranted, resulting in knowledge about God. But even if this is granted, Plantinga's discussion leaves many unsatisfied. In contexts of competing religious claims, people are looking for reasons for accepting *any* particular perspective—including Christian theism—as more likely to be true than other alternatives. Simply resorting to the assertion that in appropriate circumstances such belief can be properly basic is not very helpful.

Furthermore, the claim that one's core religious beliefs are properly basic is a move that is open to adherents of other religions as well. Buddhists or Muslims can also, in principle, defend the propriety of their respective

65. Gary Gutting, *Religious Belief and Religious Skepticism* (Notre Dame: University of Notre Dame Press, 1982), 83. I have substituted "disagreement" for "agreement" in the original text, as the latter is evidently a misprint.
66. Beilby, "Plantinga's Model of Warranted Christian Belief," 145.

beliefs in a manner parallel to Plantinga's defense of Christian beliefs. As Terence Penelhum observes,

> The views of thinkers such as Wolterstorff, Alston and Plantinga face a serious problem when the facts of religious pluralism are recognized. For if one maintains that some key religious beliefs of one's own tradition can be held without inference from independent foundations or are properly basic, one has to confront the fact that a parallel case can readily be made for key beliefs of other, incompatible religious traditions. If one supplements one's claim for the proper basicality of one's beliefs by saying they are occasioned by religious experiences, a parallel point can be made for the indigenous experiences of the other traditions also.[67]

Penelhum acknowledges that there is a sense in which one can maintain parity between beliefs based on sense perception and beliefs about God as properly basic. But this involves a weak notion of rationality that is insufficient for sustaining religious belief in the face of claims from contrasting religious traditions. "There is parity between commonsense beliefs and religious ones, but for religion, parity is not enough. If we content ourselves with the recognition that it is rational to hold our religious commitments (if we have them) as basic beliefs, we have to face living in a religiously Balkanized world. It is not clear to me that one can acquiesce in this Balkanization without relapsing into some form of the relativist conformism of the classical skeptic. This is not a garden path down which a person of faith can afford to wander."[68]

I think Penelhum is correct. It is difficult to see why belief in God can be properly basic for Christians but fundamental beliefs in other religions cannot also, in principle, be properly basic for their adherents.[69] For example, the central insights of Zen Buddhism—including the belief that ultimate reality is *sunyata*, or emptiness—are said to be perceived directly in the experience of enlightenment. They are not the product of rational argument, for evidence and argument are counterproductive in attaining enlightenment. Moreover, the experience of enlightenment grounds the rel-

67. Terence Penelhum, "Parity Is Not Enough," in *Faith, Reason, and Skepticism*, ed. Marcus Hester (Philadelphia: Temple University Press, 1992), 111.
68. Penelhum, "Parity Is Not Enough," 111.
69. My point concerns simply the claim about belief in God as properly basic and not whether adherents of other religions can also adopt Plantinga's model of warrant and proper function within their respective religious frameworks. For an interesting exploration of the latter issue, see Erik Baldwin and Tyler Dalton McNabb, *Plantingian Religious Epistemology and World Religions: Prospects and Problems* (New York: Lexington Books, 2019).

evant claims. Thus, belief in emptiness as the ultimate reality can be a basic belief for Zen Buddhists. Is it also properly basic for Buddhists? There is nothing in Reformed epistemology to show why this could not be the case. One should not take too much epistemic comfort from a position that not only allows the Christian believer to be "within her epistemic rights" in accepting certain Christian beliefs in a properly basic way but also can be used to support the rationality of central religious beliefs for adherents of other religious traditions.[70]

The Witness of the Spirit and Evidence

That it is the supernatural work of the Holy Spirit that enables us to recognize the truth of Christian teachings is, according to Scripture, clear enough, but *how* the Spirit does this is less obvious. Scripture nowhere spells out precisely how the Spirit does this, and the relevant biblical texts are compatible with various epistemological perspectives.

Both Plantinga and Craig assert that the Spirit generally works in believers in an immediate manner apart from the use of arguments or evidence for Christian claims. Plantinga's contention is related to his more general views on natural theology, which have changed over time. He certainly rejects the idea that believers are under some epistemic obligation to provide arguments or evidence in order to be justified in their beliefs. But are there good and cogent arguments for Christian theism? Here he is less clear. In his earlier work, such as *God and Other Minds* (1967), Plantinga dismisses theistic arguments as inconclusive at best.[71] But in an influential essay, "Two Dozen (or So) Theistic Arguments," Plantinga indicates that he does indeed think there are some strong theistic arguments.[72] The essay became the basis for a conference on the arguments suggested in Plantinga's paper, with the conference papers published as *Two Dozen (or So) Arguments for God: The Plantinga Project* (2018).[73] The volume includes a fascinating interview with Plantinga, in which he states that there are a number of strong theistic arguments that can be useful in engaging with unbelievers. "I think they're useful for helping people who don't believe in God to come to believe in God. I

---

70. The implications of religious diversity and disagreement are further considered in chap. 7.

71. Plantinga, *God and Other Minds*; Plantinga, "Reason and Belief in God"; Plantinga, "The Prospects for Natural Theology," in *Philosophical Perspectives*, vol. 5 of *Philosophy of Religion*, ed. James Tomberlin (Atascadero, CA: Ridgeview, 1991), 287–316.

72. The essay is available in D. Baker, *Alvin Plantinga*, 203–27.

73. Jerry L. Walls and Trent Dougherty, eds., *Two Dozen (or So) Arguments for God: The Plantinga Project* (New York: Oxford University Press, 2018).

think that they very often serve that purpose. And I think they're also useful when it comes to shoring up one's own belief." Moreover, he acknowledges that the Holy Spirit might also use evidence in bringing about belief. "It could also be that the Holy Spirit on some occasions works via argument. It could be that on a given occasion the Holy Spirit takes that as an occasion for inducing or increasing credence."[74] It is not clear how his comments in this interview relate to his earlier writings on theistic arguments and natural theology. The simplest answer is that his views on natural theology have changed over time.[75] Regardless, our concern is with the claim that the witness of the Holy Spirit is something that operates independently of evidence or reasons for accepting Christian claims, something that appears repeatedly in Plantinga's writings. Several things need to be said in response.

First, we should note that many people actually *do* come to accept the truth of the gospel through an extended process involving, among other things, careful consideration of the basis for accepting Christian claims.[76] For some, this might amount simply to listening to a talk about the historical evidence for the resurrection or reading a popular-level book on reasons for belief. For others it might include an extended investigation into the question of whether God really does exist or whether the New Testament really is reliable. The point is that many people do not simply accept core Christian claims in a properly basic way but rather engage in some process of reflection after which they conclude that the gospel really does "make sense" and ought to be accepted.

Interestingly, although Craig says that believers do not need evidence supporting their beliefs, he does acknowledge the importance of evidence and arguments for those who are not believers. "We can *show* that Christian theism is true by presenting arguments for theism and evidence for a specifically Christian theism, which go to show, when coupled with defensive

74. Trent Dougherty and Alvin Plantinga, "Trent Dougherty and Alvin Plantinga: An Interview on Faith and Reason," in Walls and Dougherty, *Two Dozen (or So) Arguments for God*, 448.

75. For a helpful discussion of Plantinga's understanding of natural theology, see Graham Oppy, "Natural Theology," in D. Baker, *Alvin Plantinga*, 15–47. Oppy's essay appeared before the interview with Plantinga cited above.

76. An especially interesting case is the conversion of Nabeel Qureshi, a Pakistani-American Muslim medical student who became a disciple of Jesus Christ. Through his friendship with David, a Christian, Qureshi was challenged to rethink his assumptions about the Qur'an and Islam as well as about Jesus and the New Testament. What is unmistakable in Qureshi's narration of his spiritual quest is the significant role that evidence and reason played in his questioning the reliability of traditional Islamic claims and coming to see the plausibility of Christian teachings on Scripture and Jesus. Nabeel Qureshi, *Seeking Allah, Finding Jesus: A Devout Muslim Encounters Christianity* (Grand Rapids: Zondervan, 2014). Contrary to popular stereotypes, appeals to evidence and reason often are a significant factor in the conversion of adherents of other religions to Jesus Christ.

apologetics, that Christian theism is the most plausible worldview a sufficiently informed, normal adult can adopt. The Holy Spirit will then use such arguments and evidence to draw unbelievers to a knowledge of God by removing their sinful resistance to the conclusion of our arguments."[77] Elsewhere Craig explicitly states that the Holy Spirit uses evidence and arguments with unbelievers to bring about faith. "The role of the Holy Spirit is to use our arguments to convince the unbeliever of the truth of Christianity. When one presents reasons for his faith, one is not working apart from or against the Holy Spirit. To return to a point mentioned earlier: it is unbalanced and unscriptural to simply preach the gospel if the unbeliever has questions or objections."[78] Whereas evidence and arguments are not necessary for believers, the Holy Spirit makes use of them in helping unbelievers come to recognize the truth of Christian claims.[79]

But there is something curious about maintaining that appeal to evidence and argument in support of one's beliefs is unnecessary or inappropriate for the believer but appropriate and helpful for the unbeliever. If the Holy Spirit can use reason, argument, and evidence to bring unbelievers to faith, why should we think that the Spirit cannot or does not work in a similar manner with believers? If in the case of unbelievers, presenting arguments and evidence need not be seen as working apart from the Holy Spirit, should we not acknowledge the same for believers? The comments of C. Stephen Evans are helpful:

> It seems to me to be a mistake to argue that the Holy Spirit could not operate by means of evidence. The Holy Spirit could be active in calling an individual's attention to the evidence, and in helping an individual properly to understand and interpret evidence, as well as in producing the conviction of sin that motivates the individual to receive the forgiveness that God offers. It seems quite possible, in fact, that the Holy Spirit could operate in an individual in such a manner that the individual's consciousness might be so focused on the evidence that the person would be unaware that it was in fact the Holy Spirit at work. . . . Though I see no reason to insist that the Holy Spirit must operate by way of evidence, I also see no reason to rule out such a case.[80]

77. Craig, "Classical Apologetics," 54. Emphasis in original.
78. Craig, *Reasonable Faith*, 56.
79. But it is interesting that Craig also speaks of the self-authenticating work of the Spirit in the unbeliever: "For the unbeliever as well as for the believer, it is the testimony of God's Spirit that ultimately assures him of the truth of Christianity. . . . *For the believer and unbeliever alike it is the self-authenticating work of the Holy Spirit that supplies knowledge of Christianity's truth.*" Craig, *Reasonable Faith*, 47. Emphasis added.
80. C. Stephen Evans, *The Historical Christ and the Jesus of Faith: The Incarnational Narrative as History* (Oxford: Clarendon, 1996), 286.

Evans reminds us of the variety of means, direct and indirect, through which God brings about desired effects in both believers and unbelievers. "Just as God may heal some people of physical illness directly, and others through the agency of a physician, so the Holy Spirit may produce a conviction of the truth of the Scriptures directly in some people as they read the Scriptures, and for others produce such a conviction by way of evidence."[81]

We need a much broader and more nuanced understanding of the many ways in which the Holy Spirit works in developing confidence in the truth of the gospel. Kevin Kinghorn and Jerry Walls encourage us to be attentive to the different ways in which the testimony of the Spirit operates. The Holy Spirit may "speak" in a "still, small voice" that a person recognizes as the voice of the God. This is not necessarily an audible voice, but "an inner voice that resembles an audible voice, that is almost as if one has heard a vocal utterance." Or "the Holy Spirit may causally influence a person's belief, without the person recognizing that the Holy Spirit has in any way communicated or otherwise acted."[82] When a person hears human testimony about God, the Spirit can directly incline the person to believe the testimony, or the Spirit might remove obstacles that would otherwise prevent one from believing. The Spirit might exert causal influence on a person's will, "by prompting the person to attend more closely to the human testimony."[83] Or the Spirit may cause the person to have a new desire for the gospel message to be true or may cause the person to see some truth in a new light. With respect to evidence and arguments, "the Holy Spirit may exert causal influence in helping a person attend to, and understand, the apologist's argument. Or the Holy Spirit may help a person overcome an unwillingness to admit that a certain conclusion does indeed follow from an argument."[84] There is always an element of mystery in how the Spirit influences someone's beliefs, will, desires, or emotions. "Yet, the mysterious nature of this causal story is no more mysterious than any other story about how an immaterial God can cause physical or mental events in our world."[85]

Theologian Graham Cole speaks of the Holy Spirit as "the great persuader," who uses diverse means to induce confidence in the gospel. "The Creator and Redeemer uses creaturely means—like proclamation, witness, and argument—to achieve his ends." Although the Spirit does use reason

---

81. Evans, *Historical Christ*, 289.

82. Kevin Kinghorn and Jerry L. Walls, "The Spirit and the Bride Say 'Come': Apologetics and the Witness of the Holy Spirit," in *The Testimony of the Spirit: New Essays*, ed. R. Douglas Geivett and Paul K. Moser (New York: Oxford University Press, 2017), 226.

83. Kinghorn and Walls, "Spirit and the Bride," 227.

84. Kinghorn and Walls, "Spirit and the Bride," 241.

85. Kinghorn and Walls, "Spirit and the Bride," 228.

and argument to bring about confidence in Christian teachings, we should not misunderstand this influence.

> [The Spirit's] ministry does not make our arguments any more logically certain. Logical certainty is about the way the steps in an argument validly hang together from premise to conclusion. It concerns the relationship of proposition to proposition. The Spirit, however, is the agent of certitude. Certitude, as John Henry Newman argued, has to do with the relationship between our minds and those propositions. Our attitude toward those arguments changes. Hostility becomes sympathy becomes embrace. We now have a confidence in those arguments, and they have a cogency for us that they did not have before.[86]

In other words, the Spirit does not take a fallacious argument and turn it into a sound one, but the Spirit might enable one to see the force of an argument or some evidence in a new way.

We conclude with a helpful word from William Abraham, who proposes that we think of the Spirit's role not simply with respect to particular individual beliefs but as functioning in a more complex manner within a broader systemic framework. Abraham challenges us to understand

> the appeal to the internal witness of the Holy Spirit as helping to render plausible a large scale, integrative system of belief. On this analysis one would construe the claim about the presence of the Holy Spirit in the believer's inner life as intimately related to a wider narrative of the activity of God in creation, in human experience generally, and in history, which in turn would be linked to a web of beliefs about the nature of God, other spiritual experiences, human nature, ethical commitment, life after death and the like.
>
> The specific experience of the Holy Spirit would not in itself underwrite the rationality of belief in the complex vision from which the very language of the inner witness of the Holy Spirit is derived and gains its meaning. Rather, taken with a host of other considerations, brought together as part of a cumulative case, and integrated into a judgment governed by tacit and largely implicit conventions of explanation, it would lend its own weight to the total evidence adduced.[87]

Once again, we see the importance of a broader context or system of beliefs for understanding and assessing the veridicality of particular experiences, in this case, that of the witness of the Holy Spirit.

86. G. A. Cole, "Holy Spirit in Apologetics," in *New Dictionary of Christian Apologetics*, ed. W. C. Campbell-Jack and Gavin McGrath (Downers Grove, IL: InterVarsity, 2006), 325–26.
87. Abraham, "Epistemological Significance," 447.

6

Mysticism

Mysticism has a special place in twentieth-century discussions of religious experience, since it promises a direct encounter with the religious ultimate and seems to be immune to the skeptical challenges plaguing ordinary experience. If one has a mystical experience, one simply *knows* that it is veridical, and no amount of counterevidence or argument can overcome this certitude. Consider, for example, the comments of Wayne Teasdale: "Mystical awareness confers an absolute *certitude* on the knower or the experiencer. . . . One cannot doubt the reality of the experience while in the midst of it. We all doubt all kinds of experiences we have in life—we doubt our fundamental subjectivity—but it is not possible to doubt mystical phenomena. The vividness, intensity, and immediacy are so profound, the magnitude of certainty so great, and the eternal so real, that the experiences are beyond doubt."[1]

If this is the case, then the critical-trust approach is unnecessary here since mystical experiences provide an impregnable certainty impervious to defeaters.

There are, however, good reasons for questioning the claims of self-authentication and absolute certainty said to flow from mystical experiences. I think that the critical-trust approach is applicable to mystical experiences just as it is to other religious experiences and that the

---

1. Wayne Teasdale, *The Mystic Heart: Discovering a Universal Spirituality in the World's Religions* (Novato, CA: New World Library, 1999), 24. Emphasis in original.

prima-facie justification they have can be overturned by challenges. But in this chapter our primary concern is not with these issues but rather with how the modern concept of mystical experience has advanced three inter-related themes that have become integral to common understandings of religious experience. These are the ideas that (1) mystical experience is at the heart of religious experience, (2) there is a common core to mystical experiences across religions and cultures, and (3) some forms of mysticism involve "pure consciousness events" that transcend all distinctions and categories. These are distinct claims, and not every defender of mysticism accepts all of them, but together they have influenced many religious studies scholars and theologians as well as more-popular perceptions of religious experience.

The roots of our current concept of mystical experience go back to the eighteenth century. There were, of course, experiences in premodern Hinduism, Buddhism, and Daoism, as well as in the ancient Greco-Roman world, that we would classify today as mystical. Even Christianity possesses a long and distinguished tradition of experiences of intimacy and union, in some sense, with God. The term "Christian mysticism" is used today to refer to the spirituality reflected in Christians as diverse as Origen, Gregory of Nyssa, Augustine of Hippo, Pseudo-Dionysius, Bernard of Clairvaux, Bonaventure, Meister Eckhart, Jan van Ruusbroec, Julian of Norwich, Teresa of Avila, John of the Cross, and Thomas Merton. Yet the term "mysticism" was not used to refer to this tradition of spirituality until the early modern period.[2]

According to Leigh Eric Schmidt, the word "mysticism" emerged only in the mid-eighteenth century as part of debates over "the place of ecstatic experiences in the Christian life, and its associations were initially more negative than positive."[3] Mystics were the "enthusiasts" of the Great Awakening and the Wesleyan revivals, and it was especially the claim to have direct communication with or revelation from God that distinguished mystics from more traditional Christian groups. But a fundamental shift in the discourse on mysticism took place in the 1840s and 1850s. The Transcendentalists, an eclectic group of New England literary and religious thinkers including Ralph Waldo Emerson and Henry David Thoreau, were fascinated

2. Louis Dupré, "General Introduction," in *Light from Light: An Anthology of Christian Mysticism*, ed. Louis Dupré and James A. Wiseman, 2nd ed. (New York: Paulist Press, 2001), 3–4. See also Amy Hollywood and Patricia Z. Beckman, eds., *The Cambridge Companion to Christian Mysticism* (New York: Cambridge University Press, 2012).

3. Leigh Eric Schmidt, *Restless Souls: The Making of American Spirituality*, 2nd ed. (Berkeley: University of California Press, 2012), 14.

with the religious and intellectual traditions from India and expanded and popularized the idea of mysticism.[4] Fascination with mystical experience was further fueled by the eighteenth-century Swedish Lutheran spiritualist Emanuel Swedenborg—"the most influential 'mystic' in the United States" in the 1840s[5]—who provided vivid descriptions of his spiritual experiences in writings that became best sellers. The concept of mystical experience continued to evolve into the early twentieth century. Ann Taves observes that "many modernizers in the West and elsewhere advanced the idea that a certain kind of experience, whether characterized as religious, mystical, or spiritual, constituted the essence of 'religion' and the common core of the world's 'religions.' This understanding of religion and the religions dominated the academic study of religion during the [twentieth] century."[6] This emphasis can be seen as an extension of the "religion of the heart" advocated by the earlier Puritans, Wesleyans, Quakers, and revivalists. But whereas these earlier movements were concerned with Christian spirituality, advocates of the new mysticism were eclectic and included spiritualists and adherents of other religions.

As Western scholars became more familiar with other religions, some began to emphasize similarities across the traditions and to speak of a common core shared by all religions. Not surprisingly, this common core was said to be found in religious experience, especially mystical experience. This idea was closely linked to the popular emphasis on interfaith dialogue and interreligious ecumenicity that emerged after the demise of colonialism and the destruction of World War II. Richard King notes that post-war interest in Asian religions and the conviction that mysticism constitutes the common core at the center of all religions provided a basis for the growing attraction of interfaith dialogue.[7] This new ecumenism coincided with a deepening sense of disillusionment among many in the West with traditional Christianity, so that belief in a common mystical core to the religions presented an attractive alternative to a discredited Christendom. During the 1960s and 1970s, the notion of "Eastern mysticism" (invariably singular) in the West became detached from the historical roots of Hindu, Buddhist, and Jainist teachings and practices, was demythologized for a

4. See Arthur Versluis, *American Transcendentalism and Asian Religions* (New York: Oxford University Press, 1993).

5. L. E. Schmidt, *Restless Souls*, 45.

6. Ann Taves, *Religious Experience Reconsidered* (Princeton: Princeton University Press, 2009), 3.

7. Richard King, "Mysticism and Spirituality," in *The Routledge Companion to the Study of Religion*, ed. John R. Hinnells (London: Routledge, 2005), 307.

secular Western market, and transformed into a therapeutic and spiritual commodity.[8]

William James

Few thinkers have had as great an impact on modern concepts of religious experience and mysticism as the American psychologist and philosopher William James (1842–1910). At a time when physicalism and naturalism were increasingly influential, James advocated an empirical and scientific approach to the study of religious phenomena without dismissing the possibility of there being an actual supernatural dimension to reality.

Born into a distinguished family (his father wrote on social and religious subjects, and his brother Henry went on to become a famous author), James completed his formal education in 1869 with an MD from Harvard. Deciding against medical practice, however, James began teaching anatomy and physiology at Harvard and explored psychology on his own. James's two volume *Principles of Psychology* (1890) established him as a dominant figure in the new discipline. James was invited to give the prestigious Gifford Lectures in 1901–2, which were subsequently published as *The Varieties of Religious Experience* (1902), a work that marks a transition in his interests from psychological to more explicitly philosophical issues. With the exception of *The Will to Believe* (1897), all his major philosophical works—*Pragmatism* (1907), *A Pluralistic Universe* (1909), *The Meaning of Truth* (1909), and the posthumous *Essays in Radical Empiricism* (1912)— came after his famous lectures. As a philosopher, James is remembered as one of the founders of radical empiricism and pragmatism in American philosophy.

James lived during a time of social and religious upheaval in the United States. Although Protestant Christianity remained the dominant religious force, significant fissures in the religious landscape were emerging. Unitarians and Universalists challenged Christian orthodoxy, and new movements such as the Transcendentalists, Shakers, Mormons, Millerites, Spiritualists, Theosophists, and Swedenborgians promised fresh ways of encountering the divine. The 1893 World's Parliament of Religions in Chicago provided unprecedented exposure to Asian religions and to impressive spiritual figures such as the Hindu Swami Vivekananda and Buddhists Dharmapala and Shaku Soen.

8. Sophia Rose Arjana, *Buying Buddha, Selling Rumi: Orientalism and the Mystical Marketplace* (Oxford: Oneworld Academic, 2020), 14.

In considering James's views on religious experience and mysticism we must begin by looking at his conception of religion. In *The Varieties of Religious Experience* James adopts a highly individualistic understanding of religion and religious experience. Ignoring the social and institutional dimensions of religion, James decides "to confine myself as far as I can to personal religion pure and simple." Accordingly, he famously defines religion as "the feelings, acts, and experiences of individual men in their solitude, so far as they apprehend themselves to stand in relation to whatever they may consider the divine."[9] We should note three things about this definition.

First, the divine is not restricted to the Christian understanding of God. Instead, James seeks to include nontheistic religions such as Buddhism, and thus he says that "we must interpret the term 'divine' very broadly, as denoting any object that is god*like*, whether it be a concrete deity or not."[10] He states further that if one were "to characterize the life of religion in the broadest and most general terms possible, one might say that it consists of the belief that there is an unseen order, and that our supreme good lies in harmoniously adjusting ourselves thereto."[11] James concludes *Varieties* with the rather enigmatic statement that the only thing that religious experience "unequivocally testifies to is that we can experience *something* larger than ourselves and in that union find our greatest peace." He does not identify this "something" with the God of classical Christian theism but rather is content to suggest that "beyond each man and in a fashion continuous with him there exists a larger power which is friendly to him and to his ideals."[12] But this "something" is deliberately left vague.

There is both a subjective and objective aspect to this "godlike" reality. On the one hand, this reality is defined in terms of what the subject *regards* as divine, and in this sense it is subjective. On the other hand, it is not *merely* a subjective conception, for as James makes clear at the end of *Varieties*, in religious experience the subject is presented with "something more" that transcends his or her consciousness.[13] This is the objective pole. But the relation between the subject's conceptualization of this "something more" and the actual nature of what is presented to the subject remains ambiguous.

9. William James, *The Varieties of Religious Experience* (New York: Penguin Books, 1985), 29, 31.

10. James, *Varieties*, 34. Emphasis in original.

11. James, *Varieties*, 53.

12. James, *Varieties*, 525. Emphasis in original.

13. James, *Varieties*, 507–15.

Second, James maintains that in religion, the personal experiences of individuals are what really matter, and religious beliefs, doctrines, institutions, and social conventions are secondary accretions that develop out of these experiences. Personal religion is "more fundamental than either theology or ecclesiasticism" because "churches, when once established, live at second-hand upon tradition." But "the founders of every church owed their power originally to the fact of their direct personal communion with the divine."[14] It is not that doctrines and institutions are unimportant, but James's main interest is in the effects of religious experience on believers, and this no doubt reflects his earlier interests in psychology.[15] In emphasizing the personal religious experience of individuals rather than institutional religion, James was reflecting a contemporary sentiment. Charles Taylor observes that James's focus on personal experience "is consonant with a major direction of change through the last several centuries in Latin Christendom. From the high Middle Ages, we can see a steadily increasing emphasis on a religion of personal commitment and devotion over forms centered on collective ritual."[16] James has been rightly criticized, however, for emphasizing personal experience at the neglect of the broader social and institutional contexts within which individual experiences occur and gain their significance.

Third, James not only thinks that religious experience is at the center of all religions but also that "personal religious experience has its root and centre in mystical states of consciousness."[17] Before we examine James's views on mysticism more closely, it will be helpful to consider some broader aspects of his approach to religious experience. Much of *Varieties* is descriptive, as James quotes from written autobiographical accounts of religious experiences. Most, but not all, of these accounts are by Europeans or North Americans who identify as Christian or who seem to fit within a broadly theistic perspective. James is especially interested in what he calls the religious "geniuses" or "pacesetters," as opposed to casual believers for whom religion is acquired "second-hand" and is "a dull habit."[18]

Additionally, James holds that human beings have an inherent capacity to apprehend realities inaccessible to the ordinary senses. "It is as if there

14. James, *Varieties*, 30.

15. See David C. Lamberth, *William James and the Metaphysics of Experience* (Cambridge: Cambridge University Press, 1999), 116.

16. Charles Taylor, *Varieties of Religion Today: William James Revisited* (Cambridge, MA: Harvard University Press, 2002), 9.

17. James, *Varieties*, 379.

18. James, *Varieties*, 6–7.

were in the human consciousness *a sense of reality, a feeling of objective presence, a perception* of what we may call '*something there*,' more deep and more general than any of the special and particular 'senses' by which the current psychology supposes existent realities to be originally revealed."[19] By taking the abovementioned experiential reports James endeavors "to prove the existence in our mental machinery of a sense of present reality more diffused and general than that which our special senses yield."[20] It is in the exercise of this special sense that James locates the feelings and awareness of the presence of the divine.

Throughout *Varieties* James also struggles to maintain a scientific perspective that explains religious phenomena through natural causes and yet is open to genuine experience of a transcendent reality that is not reducible to natural factors. Thus James offers an explanation of religious experience that includes the contribution of the subconscious, postulating what Lamberth calls "a subliminal or subconscious region of the mind in which cerebration (mental work) actually occurs, unbeknownst to the conscious mind."[21] In other words, one source of religious experience is the subconscious self, which James also refers to as the "subliminal region."[22]

But religious experiences for James are not *merely* the natural product of the subconscious self; they are also the result of interaction between the subconscious and a transcendent realm or "higher powers." James was open to the possibility that there might be external higher powers of some sort acting through the subconscious. "Just as our primary wide-awake consciousness throws open our senses to the touch of things material, so it is logically conceivable that *if there be* higher spiritual agencies that can directly touch us, the psychological condition of their doing so *might be* our possession of a subconscious region which alone should yield access to them. The hubbub of the waking life might close a door which in the dreamy Subliminal might remain ajar or open."[23] Religious experience, then, is the product of both what the individual contributes through the subconscious and what is given to it from "beyond."[24]

19. James, *Varieties*, 58. Emphasis in original.
20. James, *Varieties*, 63.
21. Lamberth, *William James*, 131. On late-nineteenth-century efforts to explain religion in terms of the subconscious, see Ann Taves, *Fits, Trances, and Visions: Experiencing Religion and Explaining Experience from Wesley to James* (Princeton: Princeton University Press, 1999), chaps. 7 and 8.
22. James, *Varieties*, 483–84.
23. James, *Varieties*, 242. Emphasis in original.
24. James, *Varieties*, 512–13.

We noted earlier that for James personal experience is at the heart of religion. He also regards mystical experience as central to religious experience. In a 1901 letter to Henry W. Rankin, James claims, "The mother sea and fountain-head of all religions lie in the mystical experiences of the individual, taking the word mystical in a very broad sense."[25] This perspective is emphasized in *Varieties*, for as Richard Niebuhr observes, the location of James's lectures on mysticism toward the end of the book "suggests that they are the *culmination* to which all of his previous inquiry leads."[26] But despite his interest in mystical experience, James claimed that he did not himself have such experiences. "My own constitution shuts me out from their enjoyment almost entirely, and I can speak of them only at second hand."[27]

In the two lectures on mysticism in *Varieties*, James brings together a number of rather disparate reports of experiences that are classified as mystical. These include fairly mundane experiences, such as the common experience of feeling that one has "been here before" or reliving a past experience, experiences in which a subject suddenly grasps the "full meaning" of life, experiences of a sense of unity within trance-like states, and experiences induced by intoxicants and alcohol. James also includes accounts by public figures such as Walt Whitman and the Hindu Vedantist Vivekananda, and he makes some vague references to Buddhist enlightenment experiences. He mentions the Muslim Sufi Al-Ghazzali and finishes with reports by Christian mystics such as St. John of the Cross and St. Theresa. Taken together, these reports are an eclectic and somewhat odd collection of quite diverse experiences.

James sets out "four marks" characterizing mystical experience, with the first two being the most significant. The first is *ineffability*. A mystical experience "defies expression" so that "no adequate report of its contents

---

25. As cited in Richard R. Niebuhr, "William James on Religious Experience," in *The Cambridge Companion to William James*, ed. Ruth Anna Putnam (Cambridge: Cambridge University Press, 2006), 230.

26. Niebuhr, "William James on Religious Experience," 230. Emphasis in original.

27. James, *Varieties*, 379. He did, however, have an experience that has many of the characteristics of mysticism in *Varieties*. In a letter to his wife, James speaks of an unusual and intense experience he had in July 1898 while hiking with some friends in the Adirondack Mountains. Unable to sleep that night, he walked outside in the woods, "where the streaming moonlight lit up things in a magical checkered play, and it seemed as if the gods of all nature-mythologies were holding an indescribable meeting in my breast with the moral gods of the inner life." Although unable to describe the experience or clarify its significance, James sensed that it was somehow very significant. James, as quoted in Robert D. Richardson, *William James: In the Maelstrom of American Modernism* (New York: Houghton Mifflin, 2006), 375. See also Henry Samuel Levinson, *The Religious Investigations of William James* (Chapel Hill: University of North Carolina Press, 1981), 101–2.

can be given in words." The "quality [of the experience] must be directly experienced; it cannot be imparted or transferred to others."[28] Whatever is encountered in mysticism eludes conceptual or linguistic categories and must be directly experienced by the subject. "This incommunicableness of the transport is the keynote to all mysticism."[29] Ineffability becomes a defining characteristic of mystical experience for later thinkers as well.

Second, although mystical experiences are "more like states of feeling than like states of intellect," they still have a *noetic quality*. "Although so similar to states of feeling, mystical states seem to those who experience them to be also states of knowledge. They are states of insight into depths of truth unplumbed by the discursive intellect."[30] James speaks of mystical experiences as "illuminations" or "revelations" since they are said to impart a deeper awareness or understanding of reality. These two qualities, held by James to be sufficient to identify an experience as mystical, are in tension; it is not obvious how an experience can be both ineffable and contain a noetic quality.

Two other qualities, although "less sharply marked," are nevertheless often present in mystical experience. One is *transiency*, as mystical states "cannot be sustained for long," and the other is *passivity*, since mystical experiences are not strictly within one's own control. James states, "Although the oncoming of mystical states may be facilitated by preliminary voluntary operations, as by fixing the attention, or going through certain bodily performances, or in other ways which manuals of mysticism prescribe; yet when the characteristic sort of consciousness once has set in, the mystic feels as if his own will were in abeyance, and indeed sometimes as if he were grasped and held by a superior power."[31]

Are mystical states essentially the same across religions and cultures, or are there fundamental differences among them? James is not entirely clear on this point. On the one hand, he admits that "the range of mystical experience is very wide."[32] Referring to contemporary attempts to define "religion" in terms of a common essence, James states, "The very fact that they are so many and so different from one another is enough to prove that the word 'religion' cannot stand for any single principle or essence, but is rather a collective name."[33] Here he seems to reject the idea of a common essence to religion and perhaps to mystical experiences as well.

28. James, *Varieties*, 380.
29. James, *Varieties*, 405.
30. James, *Varieties*, 380–81.
31. James, *Varieties*, 381.
32. James, *Varieties*, 382.
33. James, *Varieties*, 26.

On the other hand, James also speaks as if there is a common core to mystical experiences.

> This overcoming of all the usual barriers between the individual and the Absolute is the great mystic achievement. In mystic states we both become one with the Absolute and we become aware of our oneness. This is the everlasting and triumphant mystical tradition, hardly altered by differences of clime or creed. In Hinduism, in Neoplatonism, in Sufism, in Christian mysticism, in Whitmanism, we find the same recurring note, so that there is about mystical utterances an eternal unanimity which ought to make a critic stop and think, and which brings it about that the mystical classics have, as has been said, neither birthday nor native land. Perpetually telling of the unity of man with God, their speech antedates languages, and they do not grow old.[34]

In addition to his references to common themes in the experiences, James's use of "Absolute" to refer to what the mystics encounter also suggests a common object of mystical experiences. Not only are there common phenomenological characteristics to the experiences, but James seems to hold that such commonality across cultures and religions entitles us to conclude that they are encounters with the same religious reality—the Absolute.

Are mystical experiences veridical? How should we regard the claims made on the basis of mystical experience? James acknowledges that the question of truth is inescapable, but his response is modest and tentative. By their very nature, he says, mystical experiences are private, and thus the mystic enjoys a privileged status unavailable to the observer. The mystical experience carries with it a kind of self-certifying authority for the mystic. Mystics often have such a high degree of confidence in the veridicality of their experiences that nothing it seems can count against this or the claims based on these experiences.[35] But although mystical experience is authoritative for the mystic, James holds that this authority does not necessarily transfer to other observers lacking the original experience. "Mystical truth exists for the individual who has the transport, but for no one else."[36] In other words, although it can make sense for the mystic to treat his or her

34. James, *Varieties*, 419.
35. But this is not true of all mystics. Some struggle with questions about the veridicality of their experiences. See George Mavrodes, "Real v. Deceptive Mystical Experiences," in *Mysticism and Philosophical Analysis*, ed. Steven T. Katz (New York: Oxford University Press, 1978), 235–58.
36. James, *Varieties*, 405.

experience as self-certifying or fully authoritative, other observers cannot be expected to accept this judgment or the truth of claims based on the experience. The problem becomes especially acute when we take seriously the fact that mystics make differing, at times even incompatible, claims on the basis of their experiences.

We conclude our discussion of James's views on religious experience and mysticism with several observations. First, at a time when scientism and naturalism were in vogue, James presented a nuanced and sophisticated exploration of religious experience that opened up the possibility that we do have a kind of consciousness that is not limited by the five senses and that through this particular form of consciousness we can have access to spiritual realities. "Our normal waking consciousness, rational consciousness as we call it, is but one special type of consciousness, whilst all about it, parted from it by the filmiest of screens, there lie potential forms of consciousness entirely different."[37] This is no small achievement.

But James's discussion is also ambiguous at key points, and it is sometimes unclear whether he is making a psychological or a philosophical point. For example, in discussing the authority of mysticism, James seems to conflate the psychological state of *being fully confident in the truth of a belief* with the epistemic notion of *being justified or warranted in accepting that belief*. Having very strong confidence in the veridicality of an experience and in the truth of beliefs arising from that experience is one thing; being epistemically justified in making those judgments about the experience is something else.

There is another difficulty with James's treatment of mystical experience. The casual reader of *Varieties* might get the impression that James has done extensive empirical research in the major religions and that the reports he draws on provide a fair representation of experiences across cultures and religions. In fact, however, he had very limited knowledge of religions other than Christianity, and the accounts he includes are highly selective. As Levinson points out,

> James's acquaintance with different religions was limited by region, class, inheritance, and profession. . . . He could probably give brief characterizations of major Protestant denominations and great traditions like Christianity, Buddhism, and paganism. (Many educated persons sliced the religious world into these three pieces.) But the religions he observed firsthand were primarily religions that were active around the Boston area—especially

37. James, *Varieties*, 388.

those which attracted the attention of persons who were educated, and even more especially those which attracted the sons of heretical, desectarianized Christians like James's father, who read Swedenborg and had friends in the transcendentalists' inner circle.[38]

Moreover, "James, for all his attempts to receive new religions empathetically, failed to encounter old and alien ones." He had little use for Roman Catholicism, and he ignored Judaism. "It never occurred to him to visit the active Young Men's Buddhist Association in San Francisco when he visited there on several occasions, and the religions of Africa and Oceania were simply savage 'mumbo-jumbo.'"[39] James was hardly a dispassionate and curious investigator of the diverse religious traditions available to him. Nevertheless, his contributions to the empirical study of religious experience are significant, and his characterization of mystical experience influenced subsequent generations of religious studies scholars.

Rudolf Otto and "the Holy"

Rudolf Otto (1869–1937), professor of theology at the University of Marburg, exerted considerable influence on theologians and religious studies scholars through his book *Das Heilige* (1917), translated as *The Idea of the Holy*.[40] Otto also wrote *Mysticism East and West* (1926), an important comparative study of the Christian mystic Meister Eckhart and the Hindu theologian Shankara.[41] But Otto is known primarily for his notion of the

38. Levinson, *Religious Investigations of William James*, 10–11. James admits his ignorance of Buddhism in *Varieties*, 522.
39. Levinson, *Religious Investigations of William James*, 23–24.
40. Rudolf Otto, *The Idea of the Holy*, trans. John W. Harvey (1923; repr., New York: Oxford University Press, 1958).
41. Rudolf Otto, *Mysticism East and West: A Comparative Analysis of the Nature of Mysticism*, trans. Bertha L. Bracey and Richenda C. Payne (New York: Macmillan, 1932). Richard King calls this book "probably the most influential example of the association of Vedanta with Christian mysticism." Richard King, *Orientalism and Religion: Postcolonial Theory, India, and the "Mystic East"* (London: Routledge, 1999), 125. Otto argues that Shankara and Eckhart are mystics of the same type and share "a common theistic foundation." Otto, *Mysticism East and West*, 103–36. But King observes that more is at work in the comparison than merely dispassionate analysis. Otto's work "is a clear attempt to establish the superiority of the German mysticism of Eckhart over the Indian mysticism of Shankara." King, *Orientalism and Religion*, 125. Otto criticizes Shankara and Vedanta— "Eastern mysticism"—for being detached, amoral, world-denying, pantheistic, quietistic, and static, whereas Eckhart and "Christian mysticism" are alive and dynamic, moral and activist, grounded in God's grace, loving, and affirming of the world. In *Idea of the Holy* Otto claims that Christianity "is a more perfect religion and more perfectly religion than [other

numinous and his thesis that a sense of the numinous is at the heart of all religion.

Unlike William James, Otto traveled extensively throughout the Middle East and Asia, gaining rich personal experience of other religions. In 1911–12 and then again in 1927–28 he traveled throughout North Africa, Palestine, the Balkans, India, Burma, Ceylon, China, and Japan. His travels gave him a perspective lacking in most European and American scholars of the time. Philip Almond says these travels "gave Otto's subsequent writings a breadth and depth beyond that of virtually all of his contemporaries in the comparative study of religions."[42] Back in Germany, Otto took up an intensive study of Hinduism and Buddhism, learning Sanskrit well enough to translate the *Bhagavad Gita*.

Our main interest is in Otto's depiction of the experience of the numinous and his views on mystical experience. *The Idea of the Holy* includes a number of themes, including philosophical theses about knowledge of the divine, influenced by the works of Immanuel Kant and Jakob Fries; phenomenological theses that claim that all religions are grounded in religious experience, at the heart of which is the experience of a *mysterium tremendum fascinans et augustum* (the Holy); and theological theses that maintain that all religions are true to the extent that they base themselves on this experience, with Christianity having the highest expression of this experience.[43] Since it is the phenomenological claims about religious experience that are especially relevant for us, we will ignore the other two themes. But, as we shall see, Otto does not always distinguish the descriptive or phenomenological approach from his broader theological concerns.

According to Benjamin Schewel, Otto's central thesis is the idea

> that different religious traditions arise by variously schematizing a common core of religious experience, which he describes as the experience of *mysterium tremendum*. Otto suggests that this experience of *mysterium tremendum* arises from our encounter as finite beings with an infinite, loving, yet all-powerful spiritual reality. These encounters are schematized in different ways because of the different historical and cultural contexts in which they emerge. Otto observes that these schematizations evolve in a progressive

religions], in so far as what is potential in religion in general becomes in Christianity pure actuality" (56).

42. Philip C. Almond, *Rudolf Otto: An Introduction to His Philosophical Theology* (Chapel Hill: University of North Carolina Press, 1984), 18.

43. David Bastow, "Otto and Numinous Experience," *Religious Studies* 12 (1976): 160–61.

manner, whereby the "daemonic dread" that characterized early tribal religion is gradually transmuted into the loving encounter with divine grace that we see in modern Christianity.[44]

Otto embraced the assumption, widespread in his day, of an evolutionary development of religions from "primitive" traditions to theism, with Christianity being the apex of theism. But we can separate his claim about the experience of the *mysterium tremendum* as the common core of religion from his problematic views on the evolution of religions.

Otto coined the word "numinous" to refer to a sense of the presence of a numen (deity, supernatural being). The experience of the numinous includes a perception or apprehension of a *mysterium* (something mysterious) that is both *tremendum* (fearful or awesome) and *fascinans* (intriguing or attractive). For Otto, the numinous is an utterly unique category of experience that cannot be reduced to morality or anything else. He contends that religions include both rational and nonrational elements and that the Holy is both a rational and a nonrational object.[45] In Christianity, for example, various attributes are ascribed to God's nature, and since these attributes constitute "clear and definite *concepts*" and "can be grasped by the intellect" and "analysed by thought," the "object that can thus be thought conceptually may be termed *rational*."[46]

But such rational attributes do not exhaust the idea of deity; they actually suggest a "non-rational or supra-rational Subject of which they are the predicates."[47] There is a dimension of the Holy that is inaccessible to conceptual thought and can only be "felt." In ordinary experience, feeling can enable access to both rational and nonrational objects—that is, objects that can be conceptualized and those that cannot. But Almond explains that "when feeling is evoked by a nonrational object—that is, the nonrational side of the divine—it is qualitatively unique." The unique nature of nonrational feelings is due to their being grounded in a "sui generis nonrational object," the divine or the Holy.[48] The nonrational should not be confused with the irrational. Religion, for Otto, is not irrational, and he insists that there is an important place for rational analysis in religion. His point, however, is that religion is rooted in a qualitatively unique feeling or "emotional intuition"

44. Benjamin Schewel, *Seven Ways of Looking at Religion: The Major Narratives* (New Haven: Yale University Press, 2017), 136.
45. Almond, *Rudolf Otto*, 55–56.
46. Otto, *Idea of the Holy*, 1. Emphasis in original.
47. Otto, *Idea of the Holy*, 2.
48. Almond, *Rudolf Otto*, 57.

that includes a nonrational dimension and yet can be described as an apprehension of the numinous.[49]

It is engagement with this nonrational aspect of the numinous that constitutes the essential core of all religious experience. "There is no religion in which it does not live as the real innermost core, and without it no religion would be worthy of the name."[50] The numinous "is present in the richest faith in God as in the so different mystical experience of unity, and of the One in which all diversity of mundane being is immersed. . . . We call this element 'the numinous feeling.'"[51] Otto insists that the experience of the numinous "is a feature that recurs in all forms of mysticism everywhere."[52] This is a very strong claim indeed.

Two of the best-known illustrations of the sense of the numinous are Arjuna's vision of Krishna in the Hindu *Bhagavad Gita* and Isaiah's vision of the throne of God in the Old Testament.

> I behold Thee, infinite in form on all sides, with numberless arms, bellies, faces, and eyes, but I see not Thy end or Thy middle or Thy beginning, O Lord of the universe. O Form Universal. I behold Thee with Thy crown, mace and discus, glowing everywhere as a mass of light, hard to discern, (dazzling) on all sides with the radiance of the flaming fire and sun, incomparable. . . . This space between heaven and earth is pervaded by Thee alone, also all the quarters (directions of the sky) O Exalted One, when this wondrous, terrible form of Thine is seen, the three worlds tremble. . . . When I see Thee touching the sky, blazing with many hues, with the mouth opened wide, and large glowing eyes, my inmost soul trembles in fear and I find neither steadiness nor peace, O Vishnu! When I see Thy mouths terrible with their tusks, like Time's devouring flames, I lose sense of the directions and find no peace. Be gracious, O Lord of gods, Refuge of the worlds! (*Bhagavad Gita*, 11.16–17, 20, 24–25)[53]

> In the year that King Uzziah died, I saw the Lord, high and exalted, seated on a throne; and the train of his robe filled the temple. Above him were seraphim, each with six wings: With two wings they covered their faces, with two they covered their feet, and with two they were flying. And they were calling to one another:
>
>   "Holy, holy, holy is the LORD Almighty; the whole earth is full of his glory."

49. Daniel L. Pals, *Introducing Religion* (New York: Oxford University Press, 2009), 206.
50. Otto, *Idea of the Holy*, 6.
51. Otto, as quoted in Almond, *Rudolf Otto*, 58.
52. Otto, *Idea of the Holy*, 22.
53. *The Bhagavadgita*, trans. S. Radhakrishnan (New York: Harper & Row, 1948), 275–77.

At the sound of their voices the doorposts and thresholds shook and the temple was filled with smoke.

"Woe to me!" I cried. "I am ruined! For I am a man of unclean lips, and I live among a people of unclean lips, and my eyes have seen the King, the Lord Almighty." (Isa. 6:1–5)

Drawing on language from Immanuel Kant, Otto maintains that the human mind has a category of the Holy (*die Kategorie des Heiligen*), which "is a category of interpretation and valuation peculiar to the sphere of religion" and which attributes holiness to a divine object.[54] Although the concept of the Holy includes an ethical or moral component, the "morally good," it involves much more than this and cannot be reduced to moral values. This "something more" is what Otto calls the nonrational dimension of the Holy, and he uses "numinous" to refer to "this 'extra' in the meaning of 'holy' above and beyond the meaning of goodness."[55]

In the numinous experience a person is aware of the presence of an awe-inspiring reality distinct from oneself. "The numinous is thus felt as objective and outside the self."[56] A numinous experience, then, conforms to the subject-consciousness-object schema of perception that was introduced in chapter 1. In it one apprehends something mysterious and "wholly other," so that the subject has the feeling of being "in the presence of that which is a *mystery* inexpressible and above all creatures."[57] William Wainwright notes that "numinous experiences involve a 'sense of presence' and are thus noetic. They have the character of 'meetings' or 'encounters' with something or someone both terrifying and wonderful."[58] The Holy can be experienced through feelings, but it eludes conceptualization and cannot be described positively in language, although the *via negativa*, or way of negation, can clarify what it is not. Otto states, "The divine transcends not only time and place, not only measure and number, but all categories of reason as well. It leaves subsisting only that transcendent basic relationship which is not amenable to any category."[59] As Schewel remarks, "*Mysterium tremendum* thus refers to the mix of love and fear that arises from our experiential encounter with a spiritual reality that radically exceeds our powers of comprehension."[60]

54. Otto, *Idea of the Holy*, 5.
55. Otto, *Idea of the Holy*, 6.
56. Otto, *Idea of the Holy*, 11.
57. Otto, *Idea of the Holy*, 13. Emphasis in original.
58. William J. Wainwright, *Mysticism: A Study of Its Nature, Cognitive Value and Moral Implications* (Madison: University of Wisconsin Press, 1981), 4.
59. Otto, as quoted in Almond, *Rudolf Otto*, 69.
60. Schewel, *Seven Ways of Looking at Religion*, 137.

The numinous experience is not only mysterious and awe-inspiring; what is encountered "shows itself as something uniquely attractive and *fascinating.*"[61] Almond picks up on the paradoxical nature of the experience: "The *numen*, although wholly other, manifests itself nonetheless as having a bipolar character. On the one hand, it is an object which is *tremendum*, and thereby generates boundless awe and wonder in him who experiences it. On the other, it is an object which is *fascinans*, entrancing and captivating the individual. The moment of awe and terror is, as it were, balanced by a simultaneous moment of longing and desire."[62]

Otto's views, while highly influential, have been criticized on various counts. One problem Otto faces is the question about self-authenticating experiences that we noted earlier in chapter 5. Does the numinous experience provide its own epistemic justification? Is it self-authenticating? Almond notes that Otto tends to assume that the experience of the numinous is epistemically sufficient to warrant claims about the ontological reality of the numen. "At times he [Otto] writes as if he were arguing that the mere fact that the *numen* is felt *as* present is sufficient to guarantee the claim that it is present."[63] But if this is Otto's point, then his assertion is subject to the same criticisms of self-authenticating experiences that we noted in chapter 5.

Otto has also been criticized for blurring the distinction between descriptive phenomenology of religion and the normative task of theology of religions. It is one thing to say that the phenomenological evidence indicates that there is a common experience among the religions that can be descriptively characterized as *mysterium tremendum fascinans et augustum.* But it is something else to hold, as does Otto, that this common experience found among the religions is an experience of divine grace, which is a theological claim. Almond states, "The claimed objectivity of the numinous experience has a theological motif interwoven through it. Theologically expressed, the numinous experience is an experience of divine grace, a receiving of revelation."[64] Otto's tendency to pass from phenomenological description to theological assertion is also evident in his insistence that Christianity is the highest form of religion, a model toward which other religions are evolving. (Or perhaps we should say that Otto's claim is more a reflection of his contemporary cultural assumptions than a theological statement as such.)

61. Otto, *Idea of the Holy*, 31. Emphasis in original.
62. Almond, *Rudolf Otto*, 70.
63. Almond, *Rudolf Otto*, 82–83. Emphasis in original.
64. Almond, *Rudolf Otto*, 84.

But the strongest criticism of Otto concerns his insistence that the experience of the numinous is at the heart of all genuine religion. It is generally agreed that Otto has identified an important type of religious experience that is prominent not only in Christianity but in other theistic religions, including some theistic forms of Hinduism. But it simply is not accurate to say that numinous experiences are at the heart of *all* religions or even that all religions contain numinous experiences. Otto's thesis does not fit nontheistic religions. As Richard King observes,

> Despite Otto's great interest in the mystical systems of the East, his work remains fundamentally framed by his own liberal Protestantism. Consequently, Otto's account of the numinous experience fits rather well with the theistic experiences of the Judeo-Christian and Islamic traditions (and also one might argue with theistic elements within other religions such as Hinduism), but it does not work so well when applied to non-theistic traditions such as Buddhism, Jainism, and Taoism where experiences are not seen as an encounter between a creature and an overpoweringly majestic wholly other. Indeed, even within the Christian tradition, Otto's account is problematic when applied to figures such as Eckhart where theism appears to shade into monism.[65]

Ninian Smart agrees that the notion of numinous experience captures an important kind of religious experience, but he contrasts this with mystical experience, which for him is restricted to nontheistic contexts.[66] Numinous experiences are experiences of a being or divine reality presenting itself as other than the subject undergoing the experience. Mystical experiences, by contrast, are not an encounter with a "divine Other" but rather the attainment of a certain state, often involving a sense of union with what is religiously ultimate, or realization of a kind of understanding inaccessible to normal rational faculties. Smart rejects the idea that numinous experiences are even mystical experiences, to say nothing of the claim that they are at the heart of all religions.

> It is not easy to see the manifestation of a *mysterium tremendum et fascinans* as present in purely mystical experience, for instance in that of the Buddha attaining enlightenment. This seems a different phenomenon from the apprehension of a fearful Other such as one finds in the prophetic experience of Isaiah or Paul's vision on the Damascus Road. Putting the contrast rather

65. Richard King, "Mysticism and Spirituality," 314.
66. Ninian Smart, "Understanding Religious Experience," in Katz, *Mysticism and Philosophical Analysis*, 10–21.

crudely, the numinous experience as evocatively described by Otto is of an Other, while often mystical apprehension is delineated as non-dual, as if the subject-object duality disappears. The one is *tremendum*, to be shuddered at, and the other is supremely serene. Moreover, the one is often linked to the postulation of a creator, and the other need not be so at all.[67]

The idea of numinous experience is particularly problematic in Theravada Buddhism, where the ascent through the stages of meditation becomes increasingly subtle, "culminating in the realization of certain formulae such as 'There is nothing.' There is no creature-feeling, or sense of awe, or fascination with any phenomenological object."[68] Smart also criticizes Otto for misunderstanding the Buddhist teaching on *nirvana*, which is not experienced through a numinous experience. Since *nirvana* is the key concept of Theravada Buddhist doctrine and practice, "it is unsatisfactory to define religion by reference to the numinous or analogous notions."[69] Smart concludes that there are two main "poles of experience" in religion: "The first is precisely that depicted in Otto's famous *Das Heilige*—the numinous experience of the holy as a *mysterium tremendum et fascinans*, the Other. . . . The second is the contemplative or mystical experience which does not postulate an outside Other and which feels the disappearance of the subject-object distinction."[70]

King and Smart identify an important problem with Otto's thesis about the centrality of numinous experience to all religions. Although there are theistic experiences resembling numinous experience in many religious traditions, there are important traditions in which they are insignificant or absent entirely. Acknowledging this, however, does not diminish the significance of Otto's work in highlighting an important kind of theistic experience found in varying forms in many traditions. Furthermore, we can appreciate Smart's careful distinction between numinous and contemplative mystical experiences without agreeing that numinous experiences should be excluded from the category of mysticism. Most scholars adopt a broader understanding of mysticism than that presented by Smart. Many are more comfortable with R. C. Zaehner who, a generation before Smart, held that

67. Ninian Smart, *Dimensions of the Sacred: An Anatomy of the World's Beliefs* (Berkeley: University of California Press, 1996), 167.

68. N. Smart, *Dimensions of the Sacred*, 29.

69. Ninian Smart, "Numen, Nirvana, and the Definition of Religion," in *Concept and Empathy: Essays in the Study of Religion*, ed. Donald Wiebe (New York: New York University Press, 1986), 40. See also Donald S. Lopez Jr., "Approaching the Numinous: Rudolf Otto and Tibetan Tantra," *Philosophy East and West* 29, no. 4 (October, 1979): 467–76.

70. N. Smart, *Dimensions of the Sacred*, 167.

there is a specifically *theistic* form of mysticism that must be differentiated from monistic mysticism.[71] In what follows, we will use "mysticism" in a broader sense to include numinous or theistic mystical experiences.

When taken in this broader sense, it becomes more difficult to define "mysticism," as there is not such a sharp difference between mystical and other forms of religious experience. But Robert Ellwood offers a helpful definition: "Mystical experience is experience in a religious context that is immediately or subsequently *interpreted* by the experiencer as a direct, unmediated encounter with ultimate divine reality. This experience engenders a deep sense of unity and suggests that during the experience the experiencer was living on a level of being other than the ordinary."[72] Ellwood acknowledges that interpretation plays a role in mystical experience. Though this seems obvious to many, it is also controversial, as mystical experiences are often said to provide direct and unmediated access to the religious ultimate, thereby bypassing interpretation. We will consider some aspects of this debate below.

Ellwood's definition also characterizes mystical experience as an "encounter with ultimate divine reality." Mystical experience supposedly provides direct access to an ontological reality that is religiously ultimate. But this language is ambiguous, and Wayne Teasdale exploits this imprecision when he says, "Mysticism means direct, immediate experience of ultimate reality. For Christians, it is union and communion with God. For Buddhists, it is realization of enlightenment."[73] But what could this mean? Is it that *the same religious ultimate* is experienced by both the Christian and the Buddhist, but Christians experience it as God and Buddhists as enlightenment concerning *sunyata* (emptiness)? If so, then clearly interpretation is built into the experience itself, and it is difficult to see what Teasdale means by the claim to direct and immediate experience of ultimate reality. Or is it that the religious ultimate is a complex reality that can be directly apprehended, but different mystics simply grasp diverse aspects of this multifaceted reality? Ambiguity surrounding these and other questions is common in discussions of mysticism.

Perhaps this is a good place to comment also on a common misunderstanding of meditation and mystical experiences in Asian religions, especially Buddhism. During the twentieth century it became common

71. R. C. Zaehner, *Mysticism: Sacred and Profane* (London: Oxford University Press, 1961). See also R. C. Zaehner, *Concordant Discord* (Oxford: Clarendon, 1970), 150–71, 199–205.
72. Robert S. Ellwood, *Mysticism and Religion*, 2nd ed. (New York: Seven Bridges, 1999). Emphasis in original.
73. Teasdale, *Mystic Heart*, 20.

in the West to regard Buddhism as a religion centered on the practice of meditation, which culminates in the mystical experience of enlightenment. It was assumed that most, if not all, Buddhists meditate regularly and that many Buddhists experience enlightenment. But this is a modern Western perspective, cultivated in part by Buddhist apologists who wished to situate Buddhism in a privileged position in contrast to the more doctrinally focused monotheism of Western Christianity. Robert Sharf, for example, states that "the role of experience in the history of Buddhism has been greatly exaggerated in contemporary scholarship."[74] Although it is true that the Buddha's enlightenment (*bodhi*) experience is foundational for Buddhism and something Buddhists seek to replicate, enlightenment has traditionally been considered out of reach for most Buddhists.[75] David McMahan explains that in traditional Asian Buddhist cultures, meditation was not widely practiced by ordinary Buddhists; it was restricted to monastic communities and conducted under strict supervision. Few Buddhists attained enlightenment experiences. In traditional Tibetan Buddhism, for example,

> meditation is highly valued and considered necessary for the ultimate goal of the Buddhist path, but it is not an expectation and is undertaken by only a small minority of monks and even fewer laypeople. Meditation is considered a rigorous endeavor to be taken on by highly trained individuals who are willing to commit years of their lives to it. . . . In Asia, awakening [enlightenment] is considered a long-term project. In the West it is often assumed that meditation is the chief activity of the Buddhist monastic, but in fact it is mostly practiced by a minority of meditation specialists (as opposed to textual or ritual specialists).[76]

For many, especially in the West, Buddhist meditation and enlightenment, having become psychologized, democratized, and turned into a set of techniques leading to calmness and tranquility, are available to anyone.[77] But traditionally, the enlightenment experiences idealized in Buddhism were attained only by the elite and only after lengthy periods of training and

74. Robert H. Sharf, "Buddhist Modernism and the Rhetoric of Meditative Experience," *Numen* 42 (1995): 228.
75. David Burton, "Religious Experience in Buddhism," in *The Cambridge Companion to Religious Experience*, edited by Paul K. Moser and Chad Meister (Cambridge: Cambridge University Press, 2020), 187–89.
76. David L. McMahan, *The Making of Buddhist Modernism* (New York: Oxford University Press, 2008), 40.
77. McMahan, *Making of Buddhist Modernism*, 52–57, 183–88.

discipline. Robert Gimello argues that we should distinguish Buddhist meditation from mysticism and that not all Buddhist experience can be characterized as mystical. "Much that has been written in the west about Buddhist meditation has been written on the very assumption which we wish to challenge, viz. that Buddhist meditation is a form of mysticism or a means by which to attain mystical experiences."[78]

Perennialism

During the twentieth century, debates over the nature and degree of interpretation in mystical experience resulted in two broad positions, sometimes referred to as perennialism and constructivism. Perennialism is the view that, despite obvious differences between religions, there is a common core or essence that most religions share, and that they provide genuine encounters with or responses to the same divine reality.[79] Often the common core is identified with religious experience, and with mystical experience in particular. Variations on this theme abound in popular treatments of mysticism. In his popular 1970 anthology on mysticism, for example, F. C. Happold states, "Not only have mystics been found in all ages, in all parts of the world and in all religious systems, but also mysticism has manifested itself in similar or identical forms wherever the mystical consciousness has been present. Because of this it has sometimes been called the Perennial Philosophy."[80] Similarly, Wayne Teasdale claims, "This mystical tradition which underpins all genuine faith, is the living source of religion itself. . . . Each great religion has a similar origin: the spiritual awakening of its founders to God, the divine, the absolute, the spirit, Tao, boundless awareness. . . . Everything stems from mysticism, or primary religious experience, whether it be revelation or a personal mystical state of consciousness."[81]

The term itself gained currency with Aldous Huxley's popular book, *The Perennial Philosophy* (1945).[82] Huxley held that at the heart of the great religions is a profound wisdom rooted in a common mystical experience,

78. Robert Gimello, "Mysticism and Meditation," in Katz, *Mysticism and Philosophical Analysis*, 179.

79. Perennialism, as defined here, has significant affinities with religious pluralism, although the two are not identical. Religious pluralism maintains that all the major religions are culturally and historically conditioned human responses to the same religious ultimate, and thus they provide (roughly) equally effective paths to religious truth and salvation/liberation/enlightenment. Perennialists tend to be pluralists, but not all pluralists are perennialists.

80. F. C. Happold, *Mysticism: A Study and an Anthology* (London: Penguin Books, 1970), 20.

81. Teasdale, *Mystic Heart*, 11.

82. Aldous Huxley, *The Perennial Philosophy* (1945; repr., London: Grafton, 1985).

although the particular expression of this experience varies with traditions and cultures. The *philosophia perennis*, as he called this common wisdom, is "the metaphysic that recognizes a divine Reality substantial to the world of things and lives and minds; the psychology that finds in the soul something similar to, or even identical with, divine Reality; the ethic that places man's final end in the knowledge of the immanent and transcendent Ground of all being." Vestiges of the perennial philosophy "may be found among the traditionary lore of primitive peoples in every region of the world, and in its fully developed forms it has a place in every one of the higher religions."[83] But despite its popularity, Huxley's book is little more than a highly selective collection of quotations in English translation from the sacred texts of the religions, which are taken out of context and then interpreted so as to support his vision of the unity of religions.[84]

More sophisticated versions of perennialism can be found in scholars such as Huston Smith, Frithjof Schuon, and Seyyed Hossein Nasr.[85] Although not embracing the perennial philosophy as such, other influential scholars—including religious pluralists such as John Hick, Wilfred Cantwell Smith, Paul Knitter, and Perry Schmidt-Leukel—share with it a commitment to the view that the religions are diverse but legitimate human responses to a common religious ultimate.[86] Not surprisingly, mystical experience plays a significant role in each of their models of pluralism.

Walter Stace, a British professor of philosophy at Princeton University, is often identified as a perennialist because of his claims about a "universal common core" that exists in all mystical experiences across religions and

83. Huxley, *Perennial Philosophy*, 10.

84. See, e.g., King, *Orientalism and Religion*, 162–64; Keith Ward, *Religion in the Modern World: Celebrating Pluralism and Diversity* (Cambridge: Cambridge University Press, 2019), 3; and Schewel, *Seven Ways of Looking at Religion*, 123–25.

85. Huston Smith, *Forgotten Truth* (New York: Harper & Row, 1976); H. Smith, *Beyond the Post-Modern Mind* (New York: Crossroad, 1982); H. Smith, "Is There a Perennial Philosophy?," *Journal of the American Academy of Religion* 55, no. 3 (1987): 553–66; Frithjof Schuon, *The Transcendent Unity of Religions*, trans. Peter Townsend, rev. ed. (New York: Harper & Row, 1975); Seyyed Hossein Nasr, *Knowledge and the Sacred* (Albany: State University of New York Press, 1981); Nasr, "The *Philosophia Perennis* and the Study of Religion," in *The World's Religious Traditions: Current Perspectives in Religious Studies*, ed. Frank Whaling (New York: Crossroad, 1986), 181–200.

86. John Hick, *An Interpretation of Religion: Human Responses to the Transcendent*, 2nd ed. (New Haven: Yale University Press, 2004); Wilfred Cantwell Smith, *Towards a World Theology: Faith and the Comparative History of Religion* (Maryknoll, NY: Orbis, 1989); Paul Knitter, *No Other Name? A Critical Survey of Christian Attitudes toward the World Religions* (Maryknoll, NY: Orbis, 1985); Knitter, *Without Buddha I Could Not Be a Christian* (Oxford: Oneworld, 2009); and Perry Schmidt-Leukel, *Religious Pluralism and Interreligious Theology* (Maryknoll, NY: Orbis, 2017).

cultures. In *Mysticism and Philosophy* (1961) Stace argues that there are two universal mystical experiences: extrovertive mystical experiences and introvertive mystical experiences.

> The essential difference between them is that the extrovertive experience looks outward through the senses, while the introvertive looks inward into the Mind. Both culminate in the perception of an ultimate Unity—what Plotinus called the One—with which the perceiver realizes his own union or even identity. But the extrovertive mystic, using his physical senses, perceives the multiplicity of external material objects—the sea, the sky, the houses, the trees—mystically transfigured so that the One, or the Unity, shines through them. The introvertive mystic, on the contrary, seeks by deliberately shutting off the senses, by obliterating from consciousness the entire multiplicity of sensations, images, and thoughts, to plunge into the depths of his own ego. There, in that dark and silence, he alleges that he perceives the One—and is united with it—not as a Unity seen through multiplicity (as in the extrovertive experience), but as the wholly naked One devoid of plurality whatever.[87]

Despite their differences, both types "culminate in the perception of, and union with, a Unity or One, though this end is reached through different means in the two cases." Stace holds that "both types are universal in the sense that both exist and have existed alike in all times, ages, and cultures."[88]

According to Stace, Christian theistic mystical experiences are in the category of universal introvertive experiences. Introvertive mystical experiences are far more important than extrovertive experiences, and "there is no doubt that in essence they are the same all over the world in all cultures, religions, places, and ages."[89] Thus there is a basic similarity between Christian mystical experiences and those of Hindus. "The language of the Hindus on the one hand and the Christians on the other is so astonishingly similar that they give every appearance of describing identically the same experience."[90] Introvertive mystics from around the world claim that they have attained a state characterized as "a complete vacuum of particular mental contents," a state of "*pure* consciousness—'pure' in the sense that it is not consciousness *of* any empirical content. It has no content except itself."[91] Introvertive mysticism is characterized by a sense of unity understood as

---

87. W. T. Stace, *Mysticism and Philosophy* (Philadelphia: Lippincott, 1960), 61–62.
88. Stace, *Mysticism and Philosophy*, 62.
89. Stace, *Mysticism and Philosophy*, 62–63, 85.
90. Stace, *Mysticism and Philosophy*, 36.
91. Stace, *Mysticism and Philosophy*, 86. Emphasis in original.

the transcendence of all distinctions, including that between the mystic and the religious ultimate.

> In the introvertive mystical experience there is no multiplicity and no distinction. . . . And if that which is here experienced is perceived or interpreted to be the One, the Universal Self, the Absolute, or God, then it should follow that the individual self which has the experience must lose its individuality, cease to be a separate individual, and lose its identity because lost or merged in the One, the Absolute, or God.[92]

In support, Stace cites reports of experiences from mystics in Christianity, Judaism, Islamic Sufism, Vedanta Hinduism, and Zen Buddhism that all speak of apprehending a unified state transcending all distinctions and dualities. More recent scholars of mysticism have adopted the term "pure consciousness event" (PCE) to refer to such experiences.[93] A PCE is said to involve an "emptying out" by the subject of all experiential content and phenomenological qualities, including all concepts, thoughts, sense perceptions, and mental images.

But then how are we to understand the very different language and concepts often found in reports of mystical experience in the religions? Stace, like other perennialists, makes a basic distinction between the mystical experience itself and subsequent interpretation of the experience. "It is important as well as possible to make a distinction between a mystical experience itself and the conceptual interpretations which may be put upon it." He points to similarities between sense experience and mystical experience, arguing that, "It is probably impossible in both cases to isolate 'pure' experience." Nevertheless, although in neither case is the experience completely free of interpretation, we can still distinguish the experience itself from the interpretation of the experience. "It seems a safe position to say that there is an intelligible distinction between experience and interpretation, even if it be true that we can never come upon a quite uninterpreted experience."[94] Stace's thesis is that the introvertive experience itself is the same across cultures and traditions, and it is only the interpretations of the experience, shaped by cultures and religious traditions, that differ. Thus, for example, theistic mystics interpret their core introvertive experiences in terms of their

92. Stace, *Mysticism and Philosophy*, 111.

93. Jerome I. Gellman, "Mysticism and Religious Experience," in *The Oxford Handbook of Philosophy of Religion*, ed. William J. Wainwright (New York: Oxford University Press, 2005), 145.

94. Stace, *Mysticism and Philosophy*, 31–32.

particular traditions—Christians do so according to Christian categories, Sufi Muslims in terms of Islamic assumptions, Vedantin Hindus in line with Advaita Vedanta, and so on.

Stace's views were very influential and left a legacy concerning mystical experience that can be expressed in the following twofold claim: (1) it is possible to distinguish between the mystical experience itself, which is largely the same across cultures and religions, and the interpretations given this common experience; and (2) the core of introvertive mystical experience consists in a pure consciousness event devoid of phenomenological qualities, concepts, thoughts, and images. The state attained in the PCE is then identified by mystics as the Absolute, the One, the Void, Emptiness, or Brahman, depending on the particular mystic's broader interpretive tradition. But both of these claims came under withering attack beginning in the late 1970s.

Constructivism

The appearance in 1978 of *Mysticism and Philosophical Analysis*, a collection of essays by philosophers and religious studies scholars critical of perennialism, launched a vigorous debate over the nature and extent of interpretation in mystical experiences. The lead essay by Steven Katz, "Language, Epistemology, and Mysticism," was especially influential in its insistence that mystical experiences are largely shaped, if not actually determined, by the mystics' cultural, conceptual, and especially linguistic frameworks.[95] Constructivists—who emphasize social, religious, and linguistic factors shaping religious experiences—insist that, contrary to Stace and the perennialists, it is not possible to distinguish the core mystical experience from later interpretation, for interpretation is integral to the experience itself. Moreover, they reject the idea of a "common core" to mystical experiences across religious traditions and contend that there are no pure consciousness events. All experiences, including mystical experiences, necessarily are "mediated" through the mystics' social, cultural, and religious frameworks.

95. Steven T. Katz, "Language, Epistemology, and Mysticism," in Katz, *Mysticism and Philosophical Analysis*, 22–74. See also Steven T. Katz, ed. *Mysticism and Religious Traditions* (New York: Oxford University Press, 1983). Other influential constructivists include Wayne Proudfoot, *Religious Experience* (Berkeley: University of California Press, 1985); Matthew Bagger, *Religious Experience, Justification, and History* (Cambridge: Cambridge University Press, 1999); and Jess Byron Hollenback, *Mysticism: Experience, Response, and Empowerment* (University Park: Pennsylvania State University Press, 1996).

Katz's essay in turn stimulated equally vigorous rejoinders by scholars criticizing constructivists for inadequately supporting their claims and for being reductionistic in their treatment of mystical experience. *The Problem of Pure Consciousness* (1990), edited by Robert Forman, one of the most prominent defenders of pure consciousness events, provides a wide-ranging critique of Katz and other constructivists.[96] In his 2020 essay "Exploring the Nature of Mystical Experience," Katz replies to critics and provides a forceful and more nuanced defense of his thesis.[97] Although we cannot explore in depth the questions at the heart of this dispute, we will briefly highlight some central issues.

Constructivists are especially critical of the assertion that in mystical experience we can distinguish the pure experience from later interpretations of that experience. According to Katz, this is untenable because there are *no* unmediated or uninterpreted experiences.

> *There are NO pure (i.e. unmediated) experiences.* Neither mystical experience nor more ordinary forms of experience give any indication, or any grounds for believing, that they are unmediated. That is to say, *all* experience is processed through, organized by, and makes itself available to us in extremely complex epistemological ways. The notion of unmediated experience seems, if not self-contradictory, at best empty. This epistemological fact seems to me to be true, because of the sorts of beings we are, even with regard to the experiences of those ultimate objects of concern with which mystics have intercourse, e.g., God, Being, nirvana, etc.[98]

We cannot distinguish an initial mystical experience from the subsequent reports about the experience, treating the former as a pure experience common across religions and the reports as culturally or religiously conditioned

---

96. Robert K. C. Forman, ed. *The Problem of Pure Consciousness: Mysticism and Philosophy* (New York: Oxford University Press, 1990). See also Robert K. C. Forman, *Mysticism, Mind, Consciousness* (Albany: State University of New York: 1999); Jerome Gellman, *Mystical Experience of God: A Philosophical Enquiry* (London: Ashgate, 2001); Gregory Shushan, "Extraordinary Experiences and Religious Beliefs: Deconstructing Some Contemporary Philosophical Axioms," *Method and Theory in the Study of Religion* 26 (2014): 384–416; H. Smith, "Is There a Perennial Philosophy?"; and Larry Short, "Mysticism, Mediation, and the Non-linguistic," *Journal of the American Academy of Religion* 63, no. 4 (1995): 659–75.

97. Steven T. Katz, "Exploring the Nature of Mystical Experience," in *The Cambridge Companion to Mystical Experience*, ed. Paul K. Moser and Chad Meister (Cambridge: Cambridge University Press, 2020), 239–60.

98. Katz, "Language, Epistemology, and Mysticism," 26. Emphasis in original. In "Exploring the Nature of Mystical Experience" (243) Katz distinguishes between an experience being phenomenologically immediate and its being mediated. While a mystical experience can be immediate, and thus not involve inference, it is always mediated by concepts.

interpretations of that experience. To the contrary, "the experience itself as well as the form in which it is reported is shaped by concepts which the mystic brings to, and which shape, his experience." In other words, a Hindu does not have a pure experience of X which he then interprets and describes in the language and concepts of Hinduism; he has a "Hindu experience." The experience itself is the "at least partially, pre-formed anticipated Hindu experience of Brahman." The same can be said for the experience of the Christian mystic. Thus "the Hindu experience of Brahman and the Christian experience of God are not the same."[99] It is not just that the interpretations are different; the experiences themselves are fundamentally different.

How does Katz support this contention? He examines reports of Jewish, Christian, Hindu, and Buddhist mystics and argues that the mystics bring to their respective experiences certain linguistic, conceptual, and doctrinal influences that significantly shape what the mystics actually experience. Mystics are not after some generic pure mystical experience; they seek specific goals and adopt distinctive means to attain these goals as these are set out in their particular religious traditions.

> Thus, to take one example, the Buddhist "seeker" comes to his master (and the *Sangha*) and follows his prescribed meditations and yoga practices to reach that state in which suffering is annihilated and the erroneous notion of self, known as the doctrine of *anatmavada*, is completely overcome. Alternatively the Hindu "seeker" loyally adheres to his guru's instructions because he desires to affirm the ultimacy of his self and its relation to the universal self, known as *atmavada*. Again, the *Murid* is loyal to the rigorous discipline of his *Murshid* because he seeks to merge his soul with the personal God of Islam; while the Jewish Kabbalist practices his regimen of prayer and asceticism to find *devekuth* with God's extended-emanated being manifest in *Sefiroth*. The Buddhist *guru* does *not* teach what the Hindu *guru* teaches, though superficial association of the term confuses the unwary. . . . Decisive proof of this is found not only in a close examination of the respective "teachings" of the various teachers but also in the polemical spirit manifest by many, if not most, mystical masters. Shankara does not shrink from entering into heated polemics with his Buddhist opponents about the meaning of the ultimate experience, understood by him in a non-personal monistic way, or again with his more theistically minded Hindu colleagues—and of

99. Katz, "Language, Epistemology, and Mysticism," 26. Similarly, Wayne Proudfoot (*Religious Experience*, 123) states, "Any attempt to differentiate a core from its interpretations, then, results in the loss of the very experience one is trying to analyze. The interpretations are themselves constitutive of the experience."

saying that they are wrong! They do not understand! They do not have the ultimate experience!—only he and *his* students find the ultimate experience because only they are properly equipped to find it.[100]

Three points are especially significant. First, Katz highlights what he calls the "learned" aspect of mystical experience. "These are the many things that the mystical self has been taught in anticipation of—and as part of the search for—the mystical moment and that directly affect how that moment is experienced."[101] Mystics bring to their experiences particular ontologies that differ significantly for Christians, Hindus, and Buddhists. Mystics disagree not merely about whether there is a God but also about whether there is an enduring individual person and, if so, the relation of the individual to the religious ultimate. Mystical experiences usually take place within particular religious traditions, and each tradition typically has prescribed steps through which a mystic "learns to be a mystic."[102] For example, mystics generally work within particular religious communities under the influence of mentors, gurus, or guides. Mystics often learn a sacred language (Hebrew, Arabic, Sanskrit), which introduces them to certain sacred terms and concepts. Sacred scriptures play a role in shaping "the pre-experiential and then the experiential consciousness of the mystic." Katz observes that "Hindu mystical experience is incomprehensible apart from the *Veda* and the *Bhagavad Gita*, while the experience of kabbalists and Sufis is impenetrable without connecting it to the Torah and the Qur'an respectively. Likewise, Christian mystics grew up believing that the New Testament is the *Urgrund* for all theological inspiration and aspiration."[103] Given this, it is hardly surprising that mystics tend to find in their experiences what their respective traditions would lead them to expect. It is surely no accident that Christian mystics report experiences of Jesus or the Virgin Mary, not of the Dao or *nirvana*; that Zen Buddhists speak of experiencing *sunyata* (emptiness) but not Brahman; and that Vedantin Hindus claim identity with Brahman, not Allah. Experiences, including mystical experiences, do not occur in a social, religious, or intellectual vacuum.

Second, mystics have not historically regarded those in other religious traditions as experiencing the same reality but simply interpreting it differently. Given the very similar social and intellectual contexts of early

100. Katz, "Language, Epistemology, and Mysticism," 44–45. Emphasis in original. See also Katz, "Exploring the Nature of Mystical Experience," 250–53.
101. Katz, "Exploring the Nature of Mystical Experience," 253.
102. Katz, "Exploring the Nature of Mystical Experience," 256–58.
103. Katz, "Exploring the Nature of Mystical Experience," 258.

Buddhists and Hindus, for example, one might expect that they would acknowledge a shared experience of the same religious ultimate, albeit described differently. However, Buddhists and Hindus engage in vigorous polemics against each other, with each side convinced the other is in error and thus incapable of attaining the desired soteriological goal. Hindus and Buddhists typically do not regard the mystical experiences of the adherents of the other religion as simply alternative ways of accessing the same ontological ultimate.

Third, Katz also rightly points out the inadequacy of taking technical terms used by mystics to describe their experiences—whether in Sanskrit, Pali, Arabic, Hebrew, or Chinese—and assuming that because the same English word is used to translate these terms, they are all talking about the same thing. We cannot simply take English terms such as "union," "inexpressible," "paradoxical," "transcending all distinctions," or "undifferentiated" and assume that when used to translate key terms from other languages they necessarily refer to the same reality. "Choosing descriptions of mystical experience *out of their total context* does *not* provide grounds for their comparability but rather severs all grounds of their intelligibility for it empties the chosen phrases, terms, and descriptions of definite meaning."[104]

This can be illustrated with the English term "ineffable." In English translation, the Sufi calls Allah ineffable; for the Daoist, the Dao is ineffable; the Vedantin Hindu speaks of Nirguna Brahman as ineffable; the Buddhist refers to *nirvana* as ineffable; and the Christian mystic refers to the triune God as ineffable. It hardly follows from this, however, that "ineffable" means the same thing in each case, much less that the Sufi, Daoist, Hindu, Buddhist, and Christian are all experiencing the same "ineffable" ontological reality. In an early critique of John Hick's model of religious pluralism, Keith Ward makes a point that is relevant here. While it is true that many religious traditions—and, we might add, many mystics—speak of the religious ultimate as ineffable or indescribable, it does not necessarily follow that they all are referring to the same ontological reality.

> If X is indescribable by me, and Y is indescribable by me, it does not follow that X is identical with Y. On the contrary, there is no way in which X could be identified with Y, since there are no criteria of identity to apply. It is rather like saying, "I do not know what X is; and I do not know what Y is; therefore X must be the same as Y." If I do not know what either is, I *ipso facto* do not know whether they are the same or different. To assert

104. Katz, "Language, Epistemology, and Mysticism," 47. Emphasis in original.

identity is thus to commit the quantifier-shift-fallacy, or moving from "Many religions believe in an ineffable Real" to "There is an ineffable Real in which many religions believe."[105]

The fact that Christians, Muslims, Hindus, and Buddhists all describe their particular experiences as ineffable does not mean that their experiences are the same or that what they encounter in these experiences is the same reality. But neither does it mean that the experiences are *not* similar. If these experiences really are ineffable, then they cannot be characterized at all.[106]

Since ineffability plays such a significant role in accounts of mysticism, a brief comment on it is in order. Wayne Teasdale, following William James, asserts, "Mystical spirituality, at its peak moments, is *ineffable*. In its infinite presence, it is incomprehensible to the mystic, who has infinite potential but only finite ability as a human to experience, at least in this mode of experience. . . . When we know or experience the reality of the divine, we know it through its own modes of knowing, and hence it is ineffable. We have nothing to which to compare it. Essentially ungraspable and incomprehensible, the source eludes us."[107] And yet, again following James, Teasdale also insists that there is a cognitive component to mystical experience: "Mysticism is also supremely *noetic*. It grants us direct knowledge of the ultimate reality or the divine. Noetic means knowledge—actual, objectively real awareness of what is true through union with, or unmediated awareness of, what is ultimately real."[108] But how are these claims consistent?

A strong version of ineffability maintains that literally *no* concepts or linguistic terms can be applied to the experience or the object of the experience. Taken literally, then, strict silence about the experience is the only sensible option. Period. One is reminded of philosopher and mathematician Frank Ramsey's quip in response to the cryptic conclusion of Ludwig Wittgenstein's *Tractatus Logico-Philosophicus*: "What we cannot speak about we must pass over in silence." Ramsey's response: "What we can't say we can't say, and we can't whistle it either!"[109] Silence is then the only option.

105. Keith Ward, "Truth and the Diversity of Religions," *Religious Studies* 26, no. 1 (March 1990): 5.

106. Shushan, "Extraordinary Experiences and Religious Beliefs," 396.

107. Teasdale, *Mystic Heart*, 22–23. Emphasis in original.

108. Teasdale, *Mystic Heart*, 23. Emphasis in original.

109. Ludwig Wittgenstein, *Tractatus Logico-Philosophicus*, trans. D. F. Pears and B. F. McGuinness (London: Routledge & Kegan Paul, 1961), 151. Ramsey's citation is from Cora Diamond, "'We Can't Whistle It Either': Legend and Reality," *European Journal of Philosophy* 19, no. 3 (2010): 335.

The irony, of course, is that advocates of ineffability nevertheless have plenty to say about what is inexpressible.[110]

A weaker form of ineffability might acknowledge that some things can be said meaningfully about mystical experiences but that linguistic and conceptual categories are inadequate to fully capture what is conveyed in the experience. But this is no longer ineffability as such but simply another form of the age-old problem of how we should understand religious language. It does not follow from the fact that human language is inadequate to fully "capture" the divine that nothing meaningful or true can be said about God. Theologians and philosophers have given careful and responsible attention to these issues for centuries.[111]

Some Assessment

Constructivists have raised important criticisms of perennialism, and if there is a consensus on mysticism today among religious studies scholars, it leans toward constructivism. Part of the reason for the attraction toward Steven Katz's thesis is the broader shift within the humanities and social sciences in general during the past several decades toward constructivist perspectives.[112] The idea that all experience is inherently interpretive and shaped (determined?) by the subject's social, cultural, and linguistic context is virtually axiomatic in many circles. Katz has been accused of exaggerating the social influences on mysticism, but even as we acknowledge the danger of reductionism in his argument, we cannot dismiss his critique of perennialism so easily.

Much depends here on how strongly we are to understand the claims about social influence or construction. Jerome Gellman helpfully distinguishes *weak constructivism* from *hard constructivism*. The former is the view that "there is no mystical experience without concepts, concepts being what 'construct' an experience." Hard constructivism, by contrast, main-

110. For a defense of a strong form of ineffability, see John Hick, "Ineffability," *Religious Studies* 36 (2000): 35–46. Critiques of strong ineffability include Keith Yandell, *The Epistemology of Religious Experience* (Cambridge: Cambridge University Press, 1993), chaps. 3–5; and William Rowe, "Religious Pluralism," *Religious Studies* 35, no. 2 (1999): 139–50.
111. The literature on religious language is vast. See William Alston, "Two Cheers for Mystery!," in *God and the Ethics of Belief*, ed. Andrew Dole and Andrew Chignell (Cambridge: Cambridge University Press, 2005), 99–114; and Alston, "Religious Language," in W. Wainwright, *Oxford Handbook of Philosophy of Religion*, 220–44.
112. See Robert K. C. Forman, "Introduction: Mysticism, Constructivism, and Forgetting," in Forman, *Problem of Pure Consciousness*, 4; and Philip C. Almond, "Mysticism and Its Contexts," in Forman, *Problem of Pure Consciousness*, 212.

tains that "a mystic's specific cultural background massively constructs—determines, shapes, or influences—the nature of mystical experiences."[113] Hard constructivism denies two core tenets of perennialism—(1) that we can distinguish between the mystical experience itself, which is the same across religious traditions, and the interpretations given this experience and (2) that there is a common pure consciousness event devoid of phenomenological qualities, concepts, and images. Weak constructivism, however, could be compatible with the assertion that there is some core mystical experience that involves common concepts across religious and cultural traditions. It is not always clear whether constructivists are defending soft or hard constructivism, but their language often suggests that mystical experiences are *entirely* the product of social, religious, and especially linguistic influences.[114] In his 2020 essay Katz clarifies his position, stating that the social and religious conditions influencing the mystic's experience do not "cause" the experience and that the experience cannot be reduced to such influences.[115]

Gellman presents the main argument of hard constructivism as follows:[116]

> A: The conceptual scheme a mystic possesses massively determines, shapes, or influences the nature of the mystical experience.
>
> B: Mystics of different mystical traditions possess pervasively different conceptual schemes.
>
> Conclusion: Therefore, there cannot be a common experience across cultural traditions.

Both premises are controversial. Constructivists are correct in maintaining that mystical experiences are influenced by the cognitive and religious frameworks of the subjects. However, as Gregory Shushan points out, "Accepting that experience is culturally *mediated* is not the same as accepting that it is entirely culturally *fabricated*."[117] William Wainwright observes that Katz's examples "show that there is a strong correlation between the tradition to which a mystic belongs, and the type of experience that he will have. They do not show that the connection is necessary, and thus do not

113. Gellman, "Mysticism and Religious Experience," 148.
114. Torben Hammersholt provides a helpful overview of the various ways in which Katz's original essay has been interpreted: "Steven T. Katz's Philosophy of Mysticism Revisited," *Journal of the American Academy of Religion* 81, no. 2 (June 2013): 467–90.
115. Katz, "Exploring the Nature of Mystical Experience," 247–48.
116. Gellman, "Mysticism, and Religious Experience" 150.
117. Shushan, "Extraordinary Experiences and Religious Beliefs," 391. Emphasis in original.

show that the experience is *constituted* by the tradition with which it is correlated."[118] Constructivists often sound like they are claiming that mystical experience is entirely the product of the mystic's social, religious, and linguistic context, but this is untenable. Some distinction, however imprecise, should be made between *what is given to the subject* in the experience and the entire *experience as a whole*.

That the entire experience is not constructed by the subject is indicated by two factors. First, if a mystical experience were entirely a social and religious construct, then we would not expect mystics to have such difficulty finding language to describe what they experience. For constructivists, language plays a large role in shaping and interpreting experience, but if this is so, then the common appeal to ineffability among mystics seems strange. As Shushan puts it, "The inadequacy of language to express the experience suggests that the experience originated prior to the attempt to put it into language."[119] There must be *something* distinct from the religious and linguistic influences that is presented to the subject's consciousness and is said to be incapable of being expressed adequately.

Second, if contextual factors are so influential, then we would expect the mystical experiences to be fairly predictable, following the expectations of the relevant religious tradition. And, as Katz reminds us, this is often the case. But mystical experiences are not entirely predictable, as mystics sometimes experience something at odds with their broader cultural and religious framework. For example, those who are not particularly religious occasionally have visions of Jesus or experience a sense of union with the divine, Muslims have visions of Jesus, and Gautama the Buddha's enlightenment experience was significantly different from what his contemporaries experienced through similar meditation practices.

Constructivists have rightly challenged some of the more problematic aspects of perennialism and have called attention to the formative contextual factors at work in the experiences of mystics. But in correcting the errors of earlier perspectives, we need to be careful not to fall into an opposite extreme. In their critique of the common core thesis, constructivists sometimes give the impression that different cultures and religions are discrete, hermetically sealed social systems with little if anything in common with other systems. But this simply misunderstands the nature of culture, religion, and language and minimizes the commonalities among human beings. Larry Short reminds us that people in different religions and cultures "come with

118. W. Wainwright, *Mysticism*, 20.
119. Shushan, "Extraordinary Experiences and Religious Beliefs," 396.

given physical, perceptual, and neurological equipment" as well as with common experiences of time, space, and causality.[120] And Shushan notes that accepting sociocultural influences on experience is fully compatible with acknowledging basic commonalities across such contexts.

> The existence of cross-cultural similarities of discrete experience types indicates that they must *originate* in phenomena which are independent of culture. . . . Just as we can accept difference without denying similarity, we can acknowledge cultural-linguistic and environmental factors without rejecting the possibility of common non-cultural factors (whether neurophysiological, psychological, or supernatural is irrelevant here). The fact that experiences are culturally situated does not invalidate cross-cultural phenomenological consistency.[121]

What are we to make of claims about pure consciousness events? Can there be PCEs? The application of the critical-trust approach to mystical experiences suggests that we should initially be open to the possibility of such experiences. At least two critics of constructivism, Robert Forman and R. L. Franklin, claim to have had such experiences.[122] But there are also serious problems with such claims.

A PCE is said to be an experience lacking all phenomenological qualities, including concepts, thoughts, sense perceptions, and mental images. All distinctions and dualities are transcended, and yet this is also an experience of which the subject is aware and that supposedly has some religious significance. But does this make any sense? If *no* concepts or phenomenological qualities apply, how does the subject distinguish the PCE from other experiential events? What is the difference between having a PCE and simply being in a deep sleep or even comatose state? A PCE would seem to fit the s-c schema introduced in chapter 1, rather than the s-c-o schema. But if so, can it provide evidence for any truths beyond simply having the experience itself? How could a PCE provide epistemic grounds for any conclusions about a divine reality distinct from the experience? Even if there are PCEs, what significant epistemological or religious insight could be provided by such experiences? As William Wainwright puts it,

> If the experience has no object, can it have any cognitive value? Paradigm cases of cognitive experience, such as sense perception and memory, have objects.

120. Short, "Mysticism, Mediation, and the Non-linguistic," 664.
121. Shushan, "Extraordinary Experiences and Religious Beliefs," 392.
122. Forman, "Introduction: Mysticism, Constructivism, and Forgetting," 28; Forman, *Mysticism, Mind, Consciousness*, 138–46; Franklin, "Experience and Interpretation in Mysticism," in Forman, *Problem of Pure Consciousness*, 303n27.

Paradigm cases of non-cognitive experience, such as pains, headaches and feelings of depression, do not. It would appear that if monistic states have no object, they are more like paradigm cases of non-cognitive experience than like paradigm cases of cognitive experience. Furthermore, an objectless experience cannot be noetic, i.e. an experience *of* something which is believed to be real, and yet it is difficult to see how it could possibly be cognitive if it is not noetic. It would seem, then, that if monistic experiences have no object *of any kind*, they are not cognitive experiences.[123]

Given the nature of PCEs, it is difficult to see how the experience of PCEs across cultures and traditions, if indeed there are such, could support the idea of a *common object* of mystical experience or that there is a religiously significant reality accessible through the PCE.

We conclude this discussion of mysticism with a comment about the need for much more study of mystics within their own cultural and religious contexts, including, where possible, in-depth interviews with mystics still living. Grace Jantzen states,

> There is far too much philosophical (and theological) writing about mysticism that shows no evidence of having studied actual mystics in depth, either in terms of their writings or in terms of the social and intellectual contexts in which those writings must be understood. Even those like William James and W. T. Stace who pepper their books with quotations from mystical writings can be shown with very little effort to have taken quotations out of context and to have regularly distorted the meaning or at least given a substantially false impression of the mystics' overall intention, fitting their words into preconceived conceptual patterns. And many philosophers don't bother to quote them at all.[124]

Discussions of mystical experience would be enriched through more extensive and thorough research in several areas. As Jantzen notes, particular mystics need to be understood within their own linguistic, cultural, and religious contexts, and this requires competence in the languages and conceptual frameworks of the mystics themselves. Furthermore, attention should be given not only to the religious elite but also to ordinary believers, who often have experiences that can be classified as mystical. Ordinary believers typically do not publish reports about their experiences, so uncovering people willing to talk about their experiences is difficult, but the results

123. W. Wainwright, *Mysticism*, 120. Emphasis in original.
124. Grace M. Jantzen, "Could There Be a Mystical Core of Religion?," *Religious Studies* 26, no. 1 (1990): 68.

could be significant. In conducting this research, attention needs to be given to both phenomenological similarities and differences in the experiences as they appear within various cultural and religious contexts. The empirical data need to be allowed to speak for themselves and not be pressed into preconceived categories.

Finally, Jantzen also correctly points out that much of the discussion on mysticism within religious studies concentrates on "Eastern" mysticism (singular) and ignores the tradition of Christian mysticism.[125] Giving proper attention to the long tradition of mystics within Christianity, to their concerns and the ways in which they frame issues, could have an enriching effect on current debates over mysticism.

125. Jantzen, "Could There Be a Mystical Core?," 59.

7

Theistic Experiences and Religious Diversity

I
n chapter 3 I argued that it can be reasonable to adopt a critical-trust approach to religious experiences. What seems to be an experience of God can be accepted as such, provided there are no compelling reasons to conclude otherwise. Similarly, a report about an alleged experience of God can be accepted as an accurate depiction of that experience unless there are good reasons to reject the report's reliability. In other words, the principles of credulity and testimony can be used with religious experiences. The critical-trust approach offers prima-facie justification for accepting religious experiences as veridical, but this can be overridden by successful defeaters. As we have seen, challenges to the veridicality of an experience or the reliability of a report can come from within a religious tradition or from more general epistemological considerations independent of any particular religious system.

The acceptability of the critical-trust approach applies not only to Christians and their experiences but also in principle to followers of other religious traditions as well. It does not follow from this that all or even most religious experiences in the many religions *are* veridical, only that believers in the various religions *can regard their experiences as veridical* provided that they do not have good reasons for concluding otherwise. So this amounts to a weaker or more permissive sense of rationality.

The degree of confidence one should place in the veridicality of an experience, either on the part of the subject undergoing the experience or others hearing about it, varies according to the relevant circumstances and the background beliefs of those involved. What we regard as possible or likely, as well as how we interpret experiences, is influenced in significant ways by what we already believe. Thus judgments about experiences and their potential defeaters depend in part on the broader constellation of beliefs, values, and dispositions of the person making the judgment. This means that Christians, for example, cannot assess the veridicality of purported experiences of God without also addressing the logically prior issue of the truth of central beliefs of Christian theism. And dealing with *that* question takes one beyond experiences alone to consideration of other issues concerning the reality of God and God's relation with the world.

In our earlier discussion we responded to some common objections to the critical-trust approach to religious experience, but we put off consideration of what many regard as the most significant challenge to this approach— religious diversity and disagreement. In this chapter, after setting out the nature of this objection, we will look briefly at an important debate over the epistemic implications of religious disagreement. I will argue that although not everyone must reexamine their beliefs in light of religious disagreement, in many cases it is important for those of religious diversity to reassess in appropriate ways the reasons for their beliefs. Some form of natural theology can play a critical role in justifying the broader Christian theistic framework from within which judgments about particular experiences are made. We will then examine two arguments from theistic experience that might be used to support Christian claims. Variations of these arguments are sometimes found in popular defenses of Christian claims, although they have not received much attention from philosophers. Although the arguments are weak as formal arguments, I nevertheless suggest that the insights on which they are based can be reframed and used more effectively in an inference to the best-explanation argument for Christian theism.

The Problem of Religious Diversity

Many philosophers think that religious diversity and disagreement undermine the reliability of the critical-trust approach to religious experiences. After all, there is general uniformity in our sensory experience and a broad consensus concerning the physical environment that is lacking with religious experience. Not only is it a fact that, unlike sense experience, not everyone has religious experiences, but among those who do have such experiences, there is significant diversity in the nature of the experiences and disagreement concerning claims deriving from them. For many, this undermines the case for extending the critical-trust approach to religious experiences.[1]

Michael Martin, for example, raises the problem in terms of incompatible belief systems that are supported by diverse experiences.

> *Prima facie* there does seem to be a remarkable incompatibility between the concept of God in the Western [Judeo-Christian] tradition and the concept of Brahman, the Absolute, etc., in Eastern thought. . . . As in science, a religious belief is part of a system of beliefs. Thus support for a religious belief indirectly supports the system of beliefs of which it is part. If religious experiences provide support for beliefs about the existence of certain entities, they provide support for the system to which these beliefs belong. The problem is that they provide support for incompatible systems. Indirectly, then, the appeal to religious experience results in inductive inconsistency.[2]

Similarly, Antony Flew claims, "Religious experiences are enormously varied, ostensibly self-authenticating innumerable beliefs many of which are in contradiction with one another or even themselves."[3]

The problem can be seen clearly by looking again at William Alston's proposal in *Perceiving God*, which we considered at some length in chapter 3. Alston, it will be recalled, developed a model for understanding Christian perceptions of God produced by doxastic practices within the Christian tradition. Alston summarizes his approach by stating, "*A firmly established doxastic practice is rationally engaged in unless the total output of all our firmly established doxastic practices sufficiently indicates its unreliability.* In other terms, *a firmly established doxastic practice is rationally engaged in provided it and its output cohere sufficiently with other firmly established*

---

1. See J. L. Schellenberg, *The Wisdom to Doubt: A Justification of Religious Skepticism* (Ithaca, NY: Cornell University Press, 2007), 171–83; Michael Martin, *Atheism: A Philosophical Justification* (Philadelphia: Temple University Press, 1990), 177–81; Gary Gutting, *Religious Belief and Religious Skepticism* (Notre Dame: University of Notre Dame Press, 1982), 169–71; Stephen Grover, "Religious Experiences: Skepticism, Gullibility, or Credulity?," in *Faith and Theory in Practice*, ed. Elizabeth S. Radcliffe and Carol J. White (Chicago: Open Court, 1993), 103–15; Keith DeRose, "Delusions of Knowledge concerning God's Existence: A Skeptical Look at Religious Experience," in *Knowledge, Belief, and God: New Insights in Religious Epistemology*, ed. Matthew A. Benton, John Hawthorne, and Daniel Rabbinowitz (Oxford: Oxford University Press, 2018), 292–93; and Sanford C. Goldberg, "Does Externalist Epistemology Rationalize Religious Commitment?," in *Religious Faith and Intellectual Virtue*, ed. Laura Frances Callahan and Timothy O'Connor (Oxford: Oxford University Press, 2014), 279–98.

2. Michael Martin, "The Principle of Credulity and Religious Experience," *Religious Studies* 22, no. 1 (March 1986): 88–89.

3. Antony Flew, *God and Philosophy* (New York: Harcourt, Brace & World, 1966), 126.

doxastic practices and their output."[4] Beliefs formed through appropriate doxastic practices are prima facie justified, and if there are no successful defeaters for such practices, then they are to be considered "unqualifiedly justified" as well. Alston applies this to Christian beliefs based on experiences of God arising from practices within the Christian community.

> CMP [Christian mystical practice] is a functioning, socially established, perceptual doxastic practice with distinctive experiential inputs, distinctive input-output functions, a distinctive conceptual scheme, and a rich, internally justified overrider system. As such, it possesses a prima facie title to being rationally engaged in, and its outputs are thereby prima facie justified, *provided we have no sufficient reason to regard it as unreliable or otherwise disqualified for rational acceptance.*[5]

But Alston acknowledges that religious disagreement presents a problem for his thesis.[6] Although his argument supports the rationality of Christian beliefs based on Christian experiences and practices, it also in principle supports the rationality of the beliefs of adherents of other religions based on *their* respective experiences and practices. At best then, Alston's argument supports a weak notion of rationality in which, in principle, very different religious communities can all be reasonable in holding their respective beliefs even if some of these are in fact incompatible. Although this by itself does not entail that Alston's model should be rejected, it does show its limitations. In spite of this, however, Alston concludes that it still can be rational for the Christian to "sit tight with the practice of which I am a master and which serves me so well in guiding my activity in the world" and to continue holding Christian beliefs on the basis of experiences of God.[7]

But the problem is that religious diversity actually undermines Alston's thesis about the reliability of religious doxastic practices for belief formation. And this in turn calls into question the justification of any particular religious community for regarding its own practices as reliable. Even if there is a weaker sense of justification in which religious believers in different religions can all be rational in holding their respective beliefs, the fact remains that not all of their experiences are veridical, since they produce incompatible descriptions and claims. Thus at least some of the doxastic practices must be unreliable. But if that is the case, then how can one be

---

4. William P. Alston, *Perceiving God: The Epistemology of Religious Experience* (Ithaca, NY: Cornell University Press, 1991), 175. Emphasis in original.
5. Alston, *Perceiving God*, 225. Emphasis in original.
6. Alston, *Perceiving God*, 255–85.
7. Alston, *Perceiving God*, 274.

confident that the practices in which one participates actually produce ve-ridical experiences and true beliefs? As John Schellenberg puts it, "If so many experiential practices are unreliable, then why not *this* one? If powerful experiences full of apparent meaningfulness and illumination may come to persons of intelligence and virtue and yet be *completely delusive*, then what reason do you have to suppose that such is not the case *here?*"[8]

This point was pressed forcefully by John Hick in an extended exchange with Alston. Hick argues that if Christians are to believe that Christianity is uniquely true in the manner suggested by Alston, then it follows that Christians should conclude that most of the beliefs of adherents of other religions that are based on their own respective experiences are actually false. But if so, then it also follows that most of the religious beliefs based on religious experiences worldwide are in fact false. And thus, for one par-ticular religious community to assume that *its* doxastic practices are reliable and that *their* beliefs are justified, with the implication that those of all other religious communities are not, is simply arbitrary, unless this can be justified on independent grounds.[9]

This criticism extends well beyond just Alston's particular model of be-lief formation.[10] Why should we think that the critical-trust approach is applicable to religious experiences in general, when the experiences are so different and the claims based on them in some cases are incompatible? It could be that experiences within one particular tradition, or experiences of one type, are generally veridical, and others are not. But if so, that will need to be demonstrated on grounds other than simply an appeal to the experi-ences themselves. Some independent reasons are necessary for accepting the broader religious system within which the religious experiences occur, whether Christianity or Theravada Buddhism.

---

8. Schellenberg, *Wisdom to Doubt*, 175–76. Emphasis in original. See also Thomas D. Senor, "The Experiential Grounding of Religious Belief," in *The Oxford Handbook of the Episte-mology of Theology*, ed. William J. Abraham and Frederick D. Aquino (New York: Oxford University Press, 2017), 75.

9. John Hick, "The Epistemological Challenge of Religious Pluralism," *Faith and Philosophy* 14, no. 3 (July 1997): 278. Hick's original essay, along with the exchange with Alston, is in John Hick, *Dialogues in the Philosophy of Religion* (New York: Palgrave, 2001), 25–72.

10. The challenge can also be formulated with respect to the reliability of testimony concern-ing religious experiences. "That testimony is one of the principle bases on which many people hold their religious beliefs is hard to dispute. Equally hard to dispute is that our world contains an array of mutually incompatible religious traditions each of which has been transmitted down the centuries chiefly by way of testimony. In light of this latter it is quite natural to think that there is something defective about holding religious beliefs primarily or solely on the basis of testimony from a particular tradition." Max Baker-Hytch, "Testimony amidst Diversity," in Benton, Hawthorne, and Rabinowitz, *Knowledge, Belief, and God*, 183.

Epistemic Implications of Disagreement

We saw in chapter 5 that in appropriate circumstances belief in God can be properly basic for some believers. Alvin Plantinga maintains that it can be "entirely right, rational, reasonable, and proper to believe in God without any evidence or argument at all."[11] But awareness of religious disagreement is seen by many as providing a formidable defeater for the contention that belief in God is properly basic. Even if in some circumstances it can be perfectly appropriate for believers to accept the reality of God apart from supporting evidence or arguments, surely in our globalizing world today, where any educated person is aware of significant religious diversity and disagreement, the epistemic calculus changes, and justification for one's beliefs depends in part on having adequate reasons for accepting them rather than other alternatives. Plantinga rejects this, but others think there is something arbitrary about clinging to one's own convictions in such circumstances without reassessing their credentials.

Does awareness of disagreement require some reassessment of one's convictions? Not necessarily. Consider disputes over matters of preference or taste. The fact that Judy disagrees with Joe over whether chocolate ice cream is better than raspberry cheesecake does not mean that Joe needs to rethink his preferences. But things become more complex when issues of truth are involved. Yet even in such cases, not every disagreement calls into question one's own beliefs. Suppose that Jim and Satoshi disagree over the efficacy of a particular treatment for cancer. Jim does not think it is effective, but Satoshi does. Jim has no medical background and has not read any medical studies concerning the treatment, but Satoshi is a respected oncologist doing research on precisely that treatment. The fact that Jim disagrees with Satoshi does not mean that Satoshi should revise his views on the treatment. Given Satoshi's expertise in oncology, however, Jim ought to reconsider his own views, since Satoshi's opinion has credibility that Jim's lacks.

But there are also cases in which the epistemic implications of disagreement are less clear. These cases involve questions about which there is a true answer, and both disputants seem to have good evidence for their positions, to be equally familiar with the relevant issues, and to be equally competent and conscientious in their approaches. In other words, in these disputes, neither person seems to have an epistemic advantage over the other. Does disagreement in these cases mean that one should reassess or even modify

---

11. Alvin Plantinga, "Reason and Belief in God," in *Faith and Rationality: Reason and Belief in God*, ed. Alvin Plantinga and Nicholas Wolterstorff (Notre Dame: University of Notre Dame Press, 1983), 17.

one's own commitments? This has become the focus of a vigorous debate in the past several decades. Without delving into technical issues, we will briefly highlight two major approaches to the question and then make some general observations concerning religious disagreements.

The kind of disagreement that is relevant here is one among "epistemic peers." The term is used to refer to those meeting two conditions: "(1) they are equals with respect to their familiarity with the evidence and arguments which bear on that question; and (2) they are equals with respect to general epistemic virtues such as intelligence, thoughtfulness, and freedom from bias."[12] In other words, neither party has obvious reasons to question the credentials of the other. But the notion of an epistemic peer is not as clear-cut as it might seem. For example, what is to be included as relevant evidence on an issue? Disagreement on a controversial issue often includes disputes over just what is relevant and what counts as evidence. Moreover, assessment of the evidence is based on one's background beliefs—an enormous set of often implicit or tacit beliefs, some of which are shaped by experiences unique to each individual. Furthermore, for many people, a significant factor in judging someone to be an epistemic peer is the apparent moral quality of that person's life. Moral integrity is widely regarded as an important part of what makes someone wise and responsible in making judgments on religious or spiritual matters.[13] So in addition to having access to roughly the same evidence and having basically the same intellectual virtues, epistemic peerhood in religious matters also involves what seems to be parity in moral integrity and virtues.

What does it mean to say that the background beliefs of two individuals are equal with respect to how they affect judgments about the evidence? As Anita Renusch remarks, "If our concept of evidence incorporates experiences, intuitions as well as insights, and even background beliefs, two persons having the same evidence seems virtually impossible."[14] Are any two individuals ever truly equal when it comes to intelligence, thoughtfulness, and freedom from bias? How could we ever determine whether any individuals really are epistemic peers?

---

12. Thomas Kelly, "The Epistemic Significance of Disagreement," in *Oxford Studies in Epistemology*, ed. Tamar Szabó Gendler and John Hawthorne (Oxford: Oxford University Press, 2005), 1:174–75.

13. There is, of course, disagreement among thoughtful people over some moral issues. The point here is simply that the idea of an epistemic peer includes the conviction that the other party is not somehow morally deficient in a way that would affect responsible judgment on the issue in question.

14. Anita Renusch, "Thank God It's the Right Religion!—Plantinga on Religious Diversity," in *Plantinga's "Warranted Christian Belief": Critical Essays with a Reply by Alvin Plantinga*, ed. Dieter Schönecker (Berlin: de Gruyter, 2015), 155.

Despite these difficulties, however, we can work with a less precise, more impressionistic understanding of an epistemic peer.

> Whereas genuine peer disagreement (that is, disagreement in which both parties have *exactly* the same evidence) might be an ideal, disagreements in which people come close to that ideal without matching it are not without epistemic significance. We could also express that by saying that evidential equality and hence epistemic peerhood is not a matter of all-or-nothing but comes in degrees, its epistemic impact rising to the extent the conditions of peerhood are fulfilled. The more a person thinks that she has evidence in common with her dissenter, the more troubled she will and should be by the current disagreement she has with that person.[15]

It is this more informal sense of epistemic peerhood that is important for our purposes. Moreover, what is important is not the ability to determine conclusively whether two individuals really *are* epistemic peers but rather that one or both individuals *regards* the other as an epistemic peer.[16] So the crucial issue then is what the epistemic implications are for a Christian when she regards someone else who disagrees with her to be an epistemic peer. Should she change her views, reassess them in light of the evidence, or simply remain committed to her beliefs despite the disagreement?

Intuitively it seems that awareness of disagreement among epistemic peers should result in some reflection on the grounds for one's own beliefs. Thomas Kelly notes that "it is natural to suppose that persistent disagreement among epistemic peers should undermine the confidence of each of the parties in his or her own view."[17] On a descriptive level it seems clear that awareness of disagreement, when the other party is regarded as roughly equal in intelligence and epistemic virtue, does tend to undermine confidence in one's own position. Classical arguments for skepticism, from Sextus Empiricus to Montaigne, often appeal to disagreement on basic issues. But *should* awareness of disagreement over religious matters have this effect? This is the normative question, and two broad approaches have been offered in response.

Suppose that Sally and James disagree over the truth of P and they meet the conditions for epistemic peerhood. All of the evidence that bears directly on P is called first-order evidence, and both Sally and James are aware of the first-order evidence. Some philosophers hold that the fact of disagreement

---

15. Renusch, "Thank God!," 155. Emphasis in original.
16. Renusch, "Thank God!," 152.
17. Kelly, "Epistemic Significance of Disagreement," 168–69.

itself constitutes additional, higher-order evidence that provides both Sally and James with a defeater for their respective views. *Conciliationism* is the position that, given the circumstances of their disagreement, both James and Sally should either revise or abandon their perspectives on P, or at least be less confident in their perspectives, perhaps even suspending judgment about P. Some adjustment in perspective on the truth of P is required.

Others, however, reject conciliationism and insist that it can be perfectly reasonable for Sally and James to remain firm in their original perspectives on P despite awareness of epistemic peer disagreement. The *steadfastness* view maintains that disagreement by itself does not present a problem for belief in P (or -P); there can be more than one rational response to the evidence relevant to P.[18] It is best to think of conciliationism and steadfastness not as mutually exclusive categories but rather as two points at either end of a spectrum of possible views on disagreement. Not all disagreements are alike, and it is not difficult to construct hypothetical cases in which one or the other response might seem appropriate. Depending on the particulars of each case, one might accept a position closer to conciliationism in one instance while leaning toward steadfastness in others.

Plantinga adopts a version of steadfastness concerning religious disagreement: even when fully aware of deep disagreement, the Christian is not required to defend his beliefs by appealing to reasons or evidence; the believer can continue to treat belief in God as properly basic.[19] Plantinga acknowledges that for some people awareness of diversity does undermine confidence in their beliefs. But this is merely a sociological or psychological fact about some people, and it has no implications for what is necessary in order to be rational in believing.

One reason for Plantinga's conclusion is his rejection of the notion of genuine epistemic peerhood in cases of disagreement between Christians and others. According to Plantinga, the informed Christian will think that she has something that someone from another religion does not and thus that she actually is in an epistemically privileged position. Take the belief that an eternal creator God exists. A Christian believes this, but a Buddhist does not. The Christian might agree that both she and the Buddhist have

18. Helpful essays debating the merits of conciliationism and steadfastness can be found in David Christensen and Jennifer Lackey, eds., *The Epistemology of Disagreement: New Essays* (Oxford: Oxford University Press, 2013).

19. See Alvin Plantinga, "Pluralism: A Defense of Religious Exclusivism," in *The Rationality of Belief and the Plurality of Faith*, ed. Thomas D. Senor (Ithaca, NY: Cornell University Press, 1995), 191–215; and Alvin Plantinga, *Warranted Christian Belief* (New York: Oxford University Press, 2000), 422–57.

very similar "internal markers" (both are firmly convinced of the truth of their respective beliefs, both find the other's claim implausible, etc.) and that they both seem to be equally intelligent, sincere, thoughtful, and conscientious in their treatment of available relevant evidence. Still, according to Plantinga, the Christian will not really consider the Buddhist to be an epistemic peer. The Christian "must think that there is an important difference: she thinks that somehow the other person has made a mistake, or has a blind spot, or hasn't been wholly attentive, or hasn't received some grace that she has, or is blinded by ambition or pride or mother love or something else; she must think that she has access to a source of warranted belief the other lacks."[20]

If Christian teachings are true, what the believer has that the Buddhist does not is the testimony of the Holy Spirit, and this puts her in an epistemically advantageous position so that she and the Buddhist really are not epistemic peers. "She thinks she is in a better epistemic position with respect to [Christian claims] than those who do not share her convictions; for she believes she has the witness of the divinely guided church, or the internal testimony of the Holy Spirit, or perhaps another source for this knowledge."[21] Renusch summarizes Plantinga's position as follows: "Believing that due to the work of the *sensus divinitatis* and the Holy Spirit she got it right and the adherents of other religions got it wrong, sticking to her beliefs in the face of religious diversity is rational for the Christian believer. Christians—Plantinga lets us know—nonculpably believe that they are in a 'better epistemic position' than those holding beliefs incompatible with Christian belief."[22]

If Christian claims are true, then it does make sense to believe that the Christian and the Buddhist are not genuinely epistemic peers. But if what is at issue is the question *whether the Christian or the Buddhist is correct about the reality of God*, then simply appealing to the witness of the Holy Spirit as providing an epistemic advantage is circular. Moreover, this move is also available to followers of other religions, who naturally believe that *they* are in an epistemically privileged position compared with Christians. Buddhists appeal to insight gained through *bodhi* (awakening) and maintain that belief in a creator God is a sign of malfunctioning cognitive faculties; Hindus have the supreme experience of *samadhi* (union), in which all distinctions are transcended; Mormons rely on the witness of the Holy

20. Plantinga, *Warranted Christian Belief*, 453.
21. Plantinga, *Warranted Christian Belief*, 455.
22. Renusch, "Thank God!," 148.

Ghost; and so on. So rejecting the claim to genuine epistemic peerhood because one is in a privileged position is a move that not only Christians can make. The crucial question then becomes who, if anyone, *really* is in such a position. And this is just another way of asking which religious perspective is true. On a weak notion of rationality, religious believers from diverse traditions can each be reasonable in maintaining that their own positions are correct and that they are in a privileged position. But they cannot all be correct, even if they might all be reasonable in holding their respective positions.

Moreover, even if one feels that one's own position is correct and thus that one is epistemically privileged in some way, there is something about the realization that other intelligent and conscientious persons disagree that calls into question the appropriateness of one's own belief. At the least, it is not unreasonable to suppose that in many cases this indicates that one should review again the reasons for one's own position.

David Basinger, for example, maintains that in circumstances in which there are deep religious disagreements, Christians should be prepared to provide some positive reasons for their beliefs. He acknowledges the reality of epistemic peer conflict and also admits that it can be epistemically appropriate for a believer to remain within their "epistemic rights" and continue to believe without providing reasons for belief. But if a believer wants to maximize truth and minimize error, then she has an epistemic obligation to reexamine her own beliefs to see if there are good reasons for accepting them. What he calls "Basinger's Rule" stipulates that "if a religious exclusivist wants to maximize truth and avoid error, she is under a prima facie obligation to attempt to resolve significant epistemic peer conflict."[23] A Christian in this situation has an obligation to reassess her own beliefs, as well as the relevant beliefs of others, in an effort to determine whether "those beliefs that form the core of [her] exclusivity really are beliefs worthy of continued acceptance."[24] Insofar as she makes a responsible effort to do so and finds no compelling reasons to reject her views, she is justified in maintaining her beliefs.

What kind of reassessment is called for? It is not necessary to come up with compelling reasons that any rational person would accept, as this is an impossible ideal. Moreover, what is appropriate will depend on various contextual factors. Not every disagreement requires reevaluation, but clear

23. David Basinger, *Religious Diversity: A Philosophical Assessment* (Burlington, VT: Ashgate, 2002), 11.

24. Basinger, *Religious Diversity*, 27.

disagreement over beliefs fundamental to one's religious worldview should be taken seriously. Furthermore, the obligation to reassess the reasons for belief does not fall evenly on everyone. Investigating intellectual issues and providing responsible resources for those with questions is a responsibility that falls more directly on Christian leaders in positions of authority (pastors, denominational leaders, seminary educators, public intellectuals, etc.) than on individual lay believers. For most Christians, it will be sufficient if, after giving the relevant issues some basic thought, they are not aware of decisive reasons not to believe and they know that other Christians with greater expertise have examined the questions carefully and assure them that belief is justified. Others, however, with a deeper understanding of and interest in the relevant issues will need to probe the reasons for belief more deeply. What counts as sufficient critical reflection varies with the individual, the issue, and the relevant circumstances.

Natural Theology and Religious Experience

Our background beliefs affect judgments about our experiences. If, for example, my background beliefs include belief in the reality of a personal creator God who has revealed himself to humankind in the Bible and who desires a relationship with people, then I will approach what seems to be an experience of God open to the possibility that it is veridical. But if my background beliefs include the conviction that there is no God or supernatural reality and that everything that occurs can be explained adequately in terms of strictly natural processes and entities, then I will approach what seem to be experiences of a supernatural reality with skepticism, looking for strictly natural explanations.[25] Similarly, Buddhists, Hindus, and Muslims have their own background beliefs that shape how they regard particular experiences. In each case, whether it is reasonable to accept an experience as veridical depends in part on the truth of relevant background beliefs. If we wish to get beyond merely a weak sense of rationality that permits different communities to make incompatible judgments about religious experiences, we need to assess the truth or rationality of these broader background systems of belief. We will need to examine reasons for accepting the truth of

25. Charles Taliaferro states, "If a general naturalistic understanding of the world is held to be plausible or more credible than theism, numinous experiences will (in general) be discounted in terms of evidence. Only if we assume theism is a live option can numinous experiences come into play in providing support for theism." Charles Taliaferro, "In Defense of the Numinous," in *Philosophy and the Christian Worldview*, ed. David Werther and Mark D. Linville (New York: Continuum, 2012), 102.

the core beliefs at the heart of Christian theism, and this has traditionally been the task of natural theology.

Commenting on the challenge that religious diversity presents Alston's model, William Wainwright proposes that we look to natural theology to establish good reasons for accepting Christian theism in general, and then from within that framework we can apply the critical-trust approach to religious experiences.[26] He is right. But just what is natural theology? Within the Christian context, natural theology is the attempt to establish truths about God without drawing upon premises that presuppose the divine authority of Scripture.[27] We should not think that natural theology necessarily denies the authority of Scripture or rejects the idea of divine revelation. Indeed, according to Christian teachings, if we are able to know anything about God apart from relying on the written Scriptures, this is only because God has revealed himself in a general way through the created order.

Many people think of natural theology primarily in terms of the scholastic agenda and methodology of St. Thomas Aquinas. Scott MacDonald characterizes this tradition as "a kind of demonstrative science" consisting of "truths about God which are either (1) self-evident or evident to sense perception, or (2) derived by deductively valid proofs the (ultimate) premises of which are self-evident or evident to sense perception."[28] Natural theology in this sense involves conclusive, demonstrative arguments in which the premises are supposed to entail the conclusion. This ideal has been enormously attractive from the thirteenth century onward, but most philosophers (including many Christians) regard this project as problematic at best. Recent work has shown that "proving" truths about God deductively is a much more complicated endeavor than often thought, in part because of an inescapable "person-relativity" inherent in such arguments.[29]

26. William J. Wainwright, "Religious Language, Religious Experience, and Religious Pluralism," in Senor, *The Rationality of Belief and the Plurality of Faith*, 187. In *Perceiving God* (270) Alston also expresses openness to using theistic arguments to show the epistemic superiority of Christian theism over other alternatives. "The attempt to argue from neutral starting points for the truth of Christian beliefs deserves much more serious consideration than is commonly accorded it today in philosophical and (liberal) theological circles. I believe that much can be done to support a theistic metaphysics, and that something can be done by way of recommending the 'evidences' of Christianity."

27. Charles Taliaferro, "The Project of Natural Theology," in *The Blackwell Companion to Natural Theology*, ed. William Lane Craig and J. P. Moreland (Oxford: Blackwell, 2012), 1.

28. Scott MacDonald, "Natural Theology," in *Routledge Encyclopedia of Philosophy*, ed. Edward Craig (London: Routledge, 1998), 6:708.

29. See George I. Mavrodes, *Belief in God* (New York: Random House, 1970); Mavrodes, "On the Very Strongest Arguments," in Long, *Prospects for Natural Theology*, 81–91; William Wainwright, "Theistic Proofs, Person Relativity, and the Rationality of Religious Belief," in

But there is no reason to restrict natural theology to conclusive deductive arguments. In the early modern period, for example, John Locke, Joseph Butler, and William Paley advanced inductive and probabilistic arguments for Christian theism. In the twentieth century, Richard Swinburne developed a rigorous example of an inference to the best-explanation argument and Stephen Evans has proposed a noninferential model of natural theology based on Thomas Reid's notion of natural signs.[30] Natural theology takes many forms.

Although natural theology flourished until well into the eighteenth century, it came under vigorous attack from philosophers such as David Hume and Immanuel Kant. The influence of Kant in particular was so powerful that by the mid-twentieth century it became virtually axiomatic in many theological circles that natural theology had been thoroughly discredited.[31] But by the turn of the century, there was a remarkable resurgence of interest in natural theology—including classical theistic arguments—and it is today a flourishing field within philosophy of religion and analytic theology.

Theologians and philosophers who were influenced by Hume's and Kant's critique of natural theology but still interested in defending the rationality of Christian belief increasingly turned to personal experience of God for justification of belief. Yet, as early as 1960, Ninian Smart saw that reliance on personal experience alone was inadequate for this and that what was needed was a kind of natural theology that addressed questions such as "Why be a Christian rather than a Buddhist?"[32]

> Any appeal to religious experience (whether intuitive or otherwise) must inevitably lead to a consideration of the experience not merely of Christians but of Buddhists and others, and thereby to an examination of the way experience is linked to different sorts of doctrines. Through this investigation one is bound to ask what the criteria are for choosing between different formulations of religious belief. And from the apologetic point

---

Evidence and Religious Belief, ed. Kelly James Clark and Raymond J. VanArragon (New York: Oxford University Press, 2011), 77–94; and W. Wainwright, *Reason, Revelation, and Devotion: Inference and Argument in Religion* (Cambridge: Cambridge University Press, 2016).

30. Richard Swinburne, *The Existence of God*, 2nd ed. (New York: Oxford University Press, 2004); C. Stephen Evans, *Natural Signs and Knowledge of God: A New Look at Theistic Arguments* (New York: Oxford University Press, 2010).

31. See Charles Taliaferro, *Evidence and Faith: Philosophy and Religion since the Seventeenth Century* (New York: Cambridge University Press, 2005); and Andrew Chignell, "'As Kant Has Shown . . .': Analytic Theology and the Critical Philosophy," in *Analytic Theology: New Essays in the Philosophy of Theology*, ed. Oliver D. Crisp and Michael C. Rea (Oxford: Oxford University Press, 2009), 117–35.

32. Ninian Smart, *A Dialogue of Religions* (London: SCM, 1960), 11.

of view it is necessary to give reasons for accepting one's own faith rather than some other.[33]

Smart is correct. Natural theology is relevant to theistic experiences in at least two ways. First, the evidential force of theistic experiences, both for the subject and for others hearing about the experience, depends in part on the rationality of accepting the relevant background beliefs informing the experience. If one is justified in accepting Christian theism as true—or even if one thinks it might possibly be true—this will have implications for how one assesses the veridicality of theistic experiences.

Second, the fact that many people do have theistic experiences can itself be part of the evidence that is used in evaluating worldviews, especially in constructing an inference to the best-explanation argument for Christian theism. The significance of religious experience for cumulative-case arguments has been noted by Caroline Franks Davis, who states that "its most important place will be within a 'cumulative argument,' where it works in conjunction with evidence from a wide range of sources to support the belief systems of specific traditions."[34]

Cumulative-case arguments are widely used in decision-making in ordinary life, including in medical diagnoses, legal arguments in court, public policy debates, and in academic disciplines such as history and the physical sciences.[35] William Wainwright describes the nature of such arguments.

A type of reasoning is employed in diverse forms of human inquiry that is neither deductive nor inductive but an inference to the best explanation. Conclusions are drawn from a variety of independent considerations. None is itself sufficient to establish the conclusion. They can't always be fully articulated. Nor do they stand in deductive or inductive relations to the conclusion. Nevertheless, when taken together, they entitle us to infer that some hypothesis or interpretation makes more sense of a range of facts than its alternatives. There are general rules and guidelines for inferences of this kind. Their application, however, requires judgment. The quality of a person's judgment is affected by learning and experience, familiarity with the subject matter, and, in some cases, character or taste.[36]

33. Ninian Smart, "Revelation, Reason and Religions," in *Prospects for Metaphysics: Essays of Metaphysical Exploration*, ed. Ian Ramsey (London: Allen & Unwin, 1961), 92.

34. Caroline Franks Davis, *The Evidential Force of Religious Experience* (Oxford: Clarendon, 1989), 3.

35. See Peter Lipton, *Inference to the Best Explanation*, 2nd ed. (London: Routledge, 2004).

36. William J. Wainwright, *Philosophy of Religion*, 2nd ed. (Belmont, CA: Wadsworth, 1999), 182. On cumulative-case arguments for Christian theism, see Basil Mitchell, *The Justification*

In cumulative-case arguments, different pieces of evidence interact with each other, affecting the overall plausibility of the case. "Other types of evidence help us make sense of religious experiences and increase the likelihood that they are veridical; religious experiences help us make sense of other experiences and beliefs and increase the likelihood that certain beliefs are true; and all types of evidence work together to support a network of highly ramified beliefs."[37]

A cumulative-case argument for Christian theism maintains that a strong case for the truth of central Christian claims can be established through the careful accumulation and analysis of a wide variety of data from various dimensions of our experience and the world. The argument draws attention to significant features of our world from distinct domains that demand some explanation for their existing and having the characteristics they do. The argument claims that if Christian theism is false and there is no God, then these factors are difficult to account for or explain. Conversely, Christian theism, if true, provides a satisfactory explanation for these realities. Not only that, but if Christian theism is true, then some of these realities are precisely the kinds of phenomena we would expect to see in our world.

For example, one might appeal to certain characteristics of our world as things that are best explained if Christian theism is true, such as the structure of the universe itself (its contingency, the fine tuning of the universe, the evidence for a beginning to the universe), the presence of goodness and beauty in the world (the fact that there is goodness and beauty as well as our capacity as humans to apprehend and appreciate this), the human mind's ability to apprehend truth and to engage in critical self-reflection, the phenomena of moral awareness (the reality of moral truths as well as our ability to apprehend such truths), and the many highly unusual things about the historical Jesus of Nazareth (his remarkable teachings, apparent miracles, crucifixion, and reports of his resurrection appearances). While none of these phenomena, either individually or collectively, entails the truth of Christian claims, the argument insists that the truth of Christian teachings provides a more plausible explanation for these realities than do the alternatives.[38] There is of course an inescapable measure of personal judgment in

---

of Religious Belief (Oxford: Oxford University Press, 1981); W. Wainwright, *Philosophy of Religion*, 178–87; and William J. Abraham, "Cumulative Case Arguments for Christian Theism," in *The Rationality of Religious Belief: Essays in Honour of Basil Mitchell*, ed. William J. Abraham and Steven W. Holtzer (Oxford: Clarendon, 1989), 17–37.

37. C. F. Davis, *Evidential Force of Religious Experience*, 241.

38. A comprehensive cumulative-case argument will also consider the evidence against Christian theism presented by, for example, the problem of evil or the challenge from religious diversity. The overall argument, however, is that although such negative evidence provides some reason

such arguments, but this does not mean that such judgments are necessarily arbitrary. As William Abraham puts it, "Personal judgment simply means the ability to weigh evidence without using some sort of formal calculus."[39]

The fact of widespread theistic experiences can also be used as part of a cumulative-case argument for Christian theism. The fact that so many people claim to have experienced God requires some explanation, and Christian theism provides this. The plausibility of such an argument will be enhanced to the extent that theistic experiences can be shown to occur widely among diverse groups of people throughout history. The more widespread the experiences are—the more extensive their distribution across historical, cultural, ethnic, and religious contexts—the greater the need is for an explanation. In what follows, we will look briefly at two arguments based on what are taken to be experiences of God. Although the evidential force of each argument taken by itself is not particularly strong, the arguments can be adapted and used effectively as part of a cumulative-case argument for Christian theism.

The *Consensus Gentium* Argument

We have seen that religious disagreement can have significant epistemic implications, but what is not as widely recognized is that religious *agreement* also affects the rationality of belief. An ancient argument for the reality of God, the *consensus gentium* (common consent) argument, is based on perceived agreement about God's reality. The traditional argument concerned belief in God, but it can be adapted so that it deals with consensus concerning the veridicality of experiences of God. Variations of the argument go back to Plato and Cicero, with early modern advocates such as the Cambridge Platonists, Pierre Gassendi, and Hugo Grotius. John Calvin echoes the argument in the *Institutes* when he states, "There is within the human mind, and indeed by natural instinct, an awareness of divinity. . . . God himself has implanted in all men a certain understanding of his divine majesty." He then cites Cicero in support: "Yet there is, as the eminent pagan says, no nation so barbarous, no people so savage, that they have not a deep-seated conviction that there is a God."[40] The passage Calvin probably

---

not to accept Christian claims, there are significantly stronger reasons for accepting Christian theism than rejecting it.

39. Abraham, "Cumulative Case Arguments," 34.

40. John Calvin, *Institutes of the Christian Religion*, ed. John T. McNeill, trans. Ford Lewis Battles (Philadelphia: Westminster, 1960), 1.3.1 (1:43, 44).

has in mind is from Cicero's dialogue *Nature of the Gods*, which has the Epicurean Velleius state the following regarding the gods:

> For [Epicurus] alone perceived, first, that the gods exist, because nature herself has imprinted a conception of them on the minds of all mankind. For what nation or what tribe of men is there but possesses untaught some "preconception" of the gods? . . . For the belief in the gods has not been established by authority, custom, or law, but rests on the unanimous and abiding consensus of mankind; their existence is therefore a necessary inference, since we possess an instinctive or rather an innate concept of them; but a belief which all men by nature share must necessarily be true; therefore it must be admitted that the gods exist.[41]

The common-consent argument was critically discussed by John Locke, David Hume, and John Stuart Mill, but it has been largely ignored during the past century. One of the reasons for its demise was the growing awareness of the diversity of religious beliefs worldwide; it became more difficult to claim a clear consensus on belief in a monotheistic God.

The traditional argument proceeds from the observation that the great majority of humankind believes in God (or the gods) to the conclusion that God exists. But there is an ambiguity in the way the argument is expressed. Cicero referred to belief in the gods (plural) whereas Calvin spoke of an awareness of "divinity." For the argument to be cogent with respect to Christian theism, it is important that the belief in question be about the one creator God. In what follows, we will assume that "God" refers to the God of monotheism.

The form of the argument summarized by Cicero is certainly not sound. The reality of God hardly follows from the mere observation, even if accurate, that almost everybody believes that God exists. But a more modest and promising version contends that *the prevalence of belief in God's existence provides some positive evidence for the truth of that belief*. That is, the fact that large numbers of people throughout history in diverse cultures have believed in God's reality can be taken as some evidence for God's existence. Both Linda Zagzebski and Thomas Kelly defend versions of this form of the argument.[42] We will briefly look at their reformulation of the argument from

---

41. Cicero, *Nature of the Gods*, trans. H. Rackham (Cambridge, MA: Harvard University Press, 1951), 1.xvi–xvii, pp. 45–46.

42. See Linda Zagzebski, "Epistemic Self-Trust and the *Consensus Gentium* Argument," in Clark and VanArragon, *Evidence and Religious Belief*, 22–36; and Thomas Kelly, "*Consensus Gentium*: Reflections on the 'Common Consent' Argument for the Existence of God," in Clark and VanArragon, *Evidence and Religious Belief*, 136–56.

common consent and then suggest how this approach could be adapted to theistic experiences. The claim would then be that *the fact that large numbers of people throughout history in diverse cultures and religious traditions report having had experiences of God provides some positive evidence for the conclusion that some theistic experiences are veridical.*[43]

Zagzebski's interest in the argument flows from her broader concerns with epistemic self-trust—that is, the natural tendency we all have to trust in our own cognitive faculties, the relation between our faculties and our surrounding environment, and our trust in the faculties of other people.[44] Self-trust is another way of expressing the critical-trust approach we normally adopt with respect to the deliverances of our cognitive faculties. She argues that we have a natural desire to attain truth and a natural belief that this desire can be satisfied by using our natural faculties and cognitive processes such as perception, memory, and inference. This belief is pre-reflective and is presupposed in any act of critical reflection. "Before we reflect upon the justification of our beliefs or the reliability of our faculties, we already trust ourselves and our environment, including other people. Trust is the condition of the pre-reflective self."[45] Epistemic trust in one's own faculties is inescapable and cannot be justified on the basis of more basic reasons. Any attempt to justify the reasoning process or perception of an object presupposes that I *can* trust my memory or an act of inference or that there really is a relation between the act of perception and the world around me. But although self-trust is inescapable, it is also defeasible. I can be shown that my initial inclination to trust a particular inference, for example, was unjustified. But even that correction operates within a general context of self-trust in inference as generally truth-conducive. We manifest "epistemic conscientiousness" when we use appropriate critically reflective processes to "get at the truth."[46]

Zagzebski argues that the same factors at work in our own epistemic self-trust are also present in our response to others. There is an initial

43. Does it matter whether the reported theistic experiences are perceptions of God that follow the subject-consciousness-object structure introduced in chapter 1 or the subject-content structure? If, as seems likely, the evidential force of s-c-o experiences is greater than that of s-c experiences, then the common-consent argument will be stronger if the reported experiences are all of the s-c-o structure. But, as we will see in the next argument to be examined below, experiences of the s-c structure ("I have peace and contentment in the midst of suffering") can also provide some evidence for the truth of certain Christian claims.

44. See Linda Zagzebski, *Epistemic Authority: A Theory of Trust, Authority, and Autonomy in Belief* (New York: Oxford University Press, 2012).

45. Zagzebski, "Epistemic Self-Trust," 25.

46. Zagzebski, "Epistemic Self-Trust," 26.

presumption of the trustworthiness of others. "I am rationally committed to not only thinking of others as trustworthy, but to actually trusting them on the same grounds as I trust myself. I must have the same attitude of general defeasible trust in all others that I have towards myself, and I must acknowledge that the level of trust that I have in myself when I am conscientious applies to many other people."[47] This does not mean that we should accept everything others tell us; trust of others is also defeasible. But critical analysis of the views of others takes place within a general presumption of the trustworthiness of others. Thus "general trust in myself commits me to the position that there is a defeasible presumption in favor of the beliefs of any other person, absent any particular reason I have for trusting or not trusting the person, and absent any reason I may have in advance for believing or disbelieving the proposition he believes."[48]

How does this relate to God's reality? "Other things being equal," Zagzebski says, "a belief independently acquired by large numbers of people is more trustworthy than the belief of one or a few. . . . It is common to treat widespread agreement as a defeasible reason to adopt or maintain a belief, so there is common consent that common consent gives a reason for belief."[49] A belief is independently acquired if its acceptance by two or more individuals is not due to their deriving the belief from a common source. Large numbers of people throughout history, in different locations and cultures, have professed belief in God.

> There are many millions of beliefs in God that *are* independently acquired. I think we should conclude that the epistemic presumption is in favor of the belief. The fact that another person believes in God gives each of us a defeasible reason to believe. The fact that many millions believe increases the reason, and the fact that many of those millions acquired their belief independently increases the reason further. It is an implication of self-trust that the fact that so many people all over the world at all times have believed in a deity gives each of us a *prima facie* reason to believe in a deity ourselves, a reason that exceeds the reason we would have for believing in God if we were aware of only one or a few believers.[50]

47. Zagzebski, "Epistemic Self-Trust," 29, 31.
48. Zagzebski, "Epistemic Self-Trust," 31.
49. Zagzebski, "Epistemic Self-Trust," 32. Similarly, Thomas Kelly ("*Consensus Gentium*," 138) says, "It is clear that, at least outside of the philosophy seminar room, we regularly treat the beliefs of others as evidence for the truth of what they believe, revising our own views in the light of what they think, and that (often enough) it is reasonable for us to do so."
50. Zagzebski, "Epistemic Self-Trust," 33. Emphasis in original.

Zagzebski formalizes her argument as follows:

1. Every person must have a general attitude of self-trust in her epistemic faculties as a whole. This trust is both natural and shown to be inescapable by philosophical reflection.

2. The general attitude of epistemic self-trust commits us to a general attitude of epistemic trust in the faculties of all other human beings.

3. So the fact that someone else has a belief gives me a prima-facie reason to believe it myself.

4. Other things being equal, the fact that many people have a certain belief increases my prima-facie reason to believe it, and my reason is stronger when the beliefs are acquired independently.

5. The fact that other people believe in God is a prima-facie reason to believe that God exists, and the fact that many millions of people constituting a strong supermajority believe (or have believed in prior ages) that God exists increases my prima-facie reason to believe in God myself. Discounting for dependence, there are still many millions of people who independently believe or have believed in past ages in the existence of God.[51]

The evidence provided by common consent is prima-facie evidence and is defeasible. Closer examination might well produce relevant factors calling the conclusion into question. Moreover, Zagzebski acknowledges that a parallel argument can be made for atheism from the fact that there are many people who disbelieve in God.[52]

Even if we grant the conclusion, however, the force of the evidence should not be exaggerated. The point is not that the fact that large numbers of people believe in God by itself renders such belief true or even reasonable. Rather, it is that widespread belief in God is a significant piece of evidence in favor of the truth of that belief. But it is not simply the widespread distribution of such beliefs that matters. It is the *persistence* of such beliefs over time, including in societies that have undergone high degrees of modernization and secularization, that makes this worthy of note.[53]

Zagzebski and Kelly construct the argument from common consent in terms of belief in God, but it can easily be adjusted so that *belief in God* is replaced by *belief that some people have had veridical experiences of God.*

51. Zagzebski, "Epistemic Self-Trust," 34.
52. Zagzebski, "Epistemic Self-Trust," 33–34.
53. Kelly, "*Consensus Gentium*," 144.

The initial premises in Zagzebski's argument above would remain the same, but the conclusion would be:

> The fact that other people believe that they have had veridical experiences of God is a prima-facie reason to believe that they have had such experiences, and the fact that many millions of people believe (or have believed in prior ages) that they have experienced God increases my prima-facie reason to believe that they have had such experiences. Discounting for dependence, there are still many millions of people who independently believe or have believed in past ages that they have experienced God.

The conclusion of the *consensus gentium* argument, then, is that there is prima-facie evidence for believing that at least some people have genuine experiences of God. I have eliminated "constituting a strong supermajority" from Zagzebski's conclusion because, although it does make sense to think of those throughout history who have believed in God as constituting a strong supermajority, it is less plausible to claim this about those actually reporting experiences of God. Nevertheless, it is not unreasonable to hold that many millions of people have had what they take to be experiences of God. Whether this argument really is cogent is a question for another time. But I will briefly note two points that might suggest fruitful ways in which an important insight embedded in this argument can be developed further.

First, an argument based *only* on common consent about what are taken to be veridical experiences of God will offer, at best, modest and defeasible evidence for the truth of this belief. But the fact of such common consent, if indeed it is a fact, can be used effectively as part of an inference to the best-explanation argument for Christian theism. If it can be shown that large numbers of people across cultures, historical eras, and religious traditions claim to have had experiences of God, then this phenomenon should be included among the things requiring an explanation. Speaking of the original argument, Thomas Kelly observes that if indeed belief in God is the dominant position of humankind, then there is a plausible inference from this fact to the conclusion that God probably exists.

> How should we understand the inference from "The dominant opinion in the group is p" to "p is true" or "p is probably true"? I suggest that we construe the inference as an inference to the best explanation. In general, I am justified in concluding that p is the case on the basis of the fact that p is the dominant opinion in the group only if the truth of p is part of the best explanation of the fact that p is the dominant opinion in the group. That p is the case and

most of the group has managed to pick up on this is one among many *po-tential* explanations of the fact that p is the dominant opinion: roughly, it is the kind of thing that would *actually* explain why p is the dominant opinion *if it were true*. To say that it is the *best* potential explanation is to say that it scores higher than any other, rival potential explanation when evaluated by the usual criteria of plausibility, fit with background knowledge, explanatory power, simplicity, and so forth.[54]

I think this is also a helpful way to think of the evidential force of the fact that many people believe that they have experienced God. Christian theism, if true, provides a plausible explanation for why it is that so many people in many diverse societies throughout history believe that they have experienced God.

But is it really the case that large numbers of people believe that they have experienced God? How widespread are such experiences? The number of those who say they have experienced God is undoubtedly smaller than that of those professing to believe in God, since not all who identify as theists have religious experiences. Even so, there is still good reason to maintain that a significant number of people worldwide have had what they take to be experiences of God and that this can be an important component in a cumulative-case argument.

In assessing the extent of experiences of God, much depends on how we understand the term "God." Christians, of course, are trinitarian and understand God as a triunity of Father, Son, and Holy Spirit. Other theistic traditions believe in an all-powerful and eternal creator, but reject the Christian teaching on the Trinity. Is it only those who explicitly accept a trinitarian understanding of God who can be said to have genuinely experienced God? This is unnecessarily restrictive. To be sure, any genuine experience of God, wherever it occurs, is due to the triune God's willingness to be experienced and to the initiative of God's grace enabling one to have the experience. But we need to distinguish between the ontological reality of God (what God is actually like) and the phenomenological nature of the experiences people have of God. One can have an authentic experience of the triune God without necessarily knowing that God is the Trinity of Father, Son, and Holy Spirit. Even Christians, who insist on the

---

54. Kelly, "*Consensus Gentium*," 142–43. Emphasis in original. Calling something the best explanation does not mean that one has literally examined every possible explanation and ruled all others out. The judgment is made on the basis of one's background knowledge and awareness of other serious potential explanations. It is to conclude that on the basis of what we already know, the available evidence, and potential rival explanations, this is the best explanation for the phenomenon in question.

trinitarian nature of God, generally do not claim to experience the Holy Trinity as such but rather to have experiences in which they are aware of *God*. Or perhaps they have a vision of Jesus or they experience the extraordinary peace of God, which is then attributed to the Holy Spirit.[55] In other words, the experiences themselves are usually less theologically ramified than the doctrine. Furthermore, as we have seen, experiences of God can take many forms, including anything from Rudolf Otto's numinous experiences to a strong sense of God's comforting presence in the midst of suffering or an awareness of God's creative power as one contemplates stars in the night sky. Or consider the examples given by Charles Taliaferro.

> Imagine, for the sake of argument, that theism is true and God exists. More specifically, let's imagine Christian theism is true and you attend a Eucharistic service. Imagine you are an agnostic but you experience beautiful music and listen to a liturgy on caring for others. If Christian theism is true, it seems you actually had an experience of God, for the service would have been a participation in the grace of God and sustained by God. Consider a more terrestrial example. Imagine your beloved baked you a cake with the wonderful words "I love you" on it. She is not around and you do not know she baked the cake or that the message was intended for you. Did you actually experience her loving attention when you ate the cake? We think that you did, even if you did not realize it.[56]

Taliaferro reminds us that experiences of God can come in very different configurations. If we include these latter cases as well as the more dramatic perceptual experiences, then it is plausible to hold that many have had what they take to be experiences of God.

It is difficult to know how widespread theistic experiences are. Our access to the religious experiences of others comes through reports of their experiences; we simply do not know how many theistic experiences have gone unreported, especially among ordinary believers, many of whom are illiterate and leave no records. It is not unreasonable to assume that the reports represent only a fraction of all theistic experiences people have had. In order to assess how widespread theistic experiences are today across cultures and societies, we need much more by way of careful empirical

---

55. Tom McCall correctly reminds me that there are those, such as Julian of Norwich in the fourteenth century, who do claim to have experienced the Holy Trinity. See Julian of Norwich, "Showings," in *Light from Light: An Anthology of Christian Mysticism*, ed. Louis Dupré and James A. Wiseman, 2nd ed. (New York: Paulist Press, 2001), 234–45.

56. Taliaferro, "In Defense of the Numinous," 105.

studies of the actual beliefs and practices of ordinary people, whether they are explicitly religious or not.

Nevertheless, there is some evidence that many people around the world have experiences of God. For example, beginning in the late twentieth century and continuing to the present there has been a remarkable movement worldwide as many Muslims have become followers of Jesus, often after having had visions or dreams of Jesus. A study out of Fuller Theological Seminary looked at 750 Muslims from 30 countries and 50 ethnic groups who became followers of Jesus Christ and found that dreams and visions played a significant role in their spiritual journeys. "More than one in four respondents, 27 percent, noted dreams and visions before their decision for Christ, 40 percent at the time of conversion, and 45 percent afterward."[57] A different study based on interviews with 322 Muslims from east Africa who decided to follow Jesus found that "some supernatural experience" such as a vision, dream, or healing was reported by 41 percent of the respondents.[58] These are among the cases that we know of; there may well be many other similar examples we have not heard about.

But it is not only Muslims who have visions of Jesus.[59] There have of course been many reports of appearances of Jesus throughout history, but there is a surprising number of accounts of perceptions of Jesus by ordinary people today in the West. Phillip Wiebe, a Canadian philosopher, spent several decades studying reports in which people claimed that Jesus appeared to them. He conducted in-depth interviews with over thirty people (including some non-Christians) who said that they were awake at the time of Jesus's appearance to them, that their eyes were open, and that it clearly was Jesus who was present.[60] Wiebe observes, "The claim that visions of Jesus still occur is not in doubt. What these visions signify, however, is a matter of

57. J. Dudley Woodberry, Russell G. Shubin, and G. Marks, "Why Muslims Follow Jesus," *Christianity Today* (October 2007): 3. https://www.christianitytoday.com/ct/2007/october/42.80.html.

58. Ben Naja, "A Jesus Movement among Muslims: Research from Eastern Africa," *International Journal of Frontier Missiology* 30, no. 1 (Spring 2013): 28. See also Tom Doyle, *Dreams and Visions: Is Jesus Awakening the Muslim World?* (Nashville: Nelson, 2012). Dreams also played an important part in the conversion of the Pakistani-American Muslim Nabeel Qureshi to Jesus. See Nabeel Qureshi, *Seeking Allah, Finding Jesus: A Devout Muslim Encounters Christianity* (Grand Rapids: Zondervan, 2014).

59. For further reports as well as extensive bibliography, see Craig S. Keener, *Miracles: The Credibility of the New Testament Accounts*, 2 vols. (Grand Rapids: Baker Academic, 2011), 2:870–84, "Appendix E: Visions and Dreams."

60. Phillip H. Wiebe, *Visions of Jesus: Direct Encounters from the New Testament to Today* (New York: Oxford University Press, 1997); Wiebe, *Visions and Appearances of Jesus* (Abilene, TX: Leafwood, 2014).

dispute. That such visions are significant—not least for those who experience them—is undeniable."[61] Perceptual encounters with Jesus seem to be far more common than is typically assumed. In addition, if we also include among theistic experiences the many reports of miraculous healings today, then the number of purported experiences of God increases dramatically. Summarizing the data from a 2006 report based on a survey conducted in ten countries in the Americas, Asia, and Africa by the Pew Forum, Craig Keener states that about two hundred million people report having "witnessed divine healings." More than one-third of Christians worldwide who do not identify themselves as Pentecostal or charismatic claim to have witnessed divine healings.[62] It does not follow from this that all or even most of these actually were miraculous healings, but it does show how widespread experiences of what seem to be miraculous events are.

Argument from Fulfilled Promises

There is another argument from theistic experiences worth examining. We saw in chapter 4 that John Wesley often treats the witness of the Holy Spirit as a direct and immediate work on the believer's life resulting in confidence in one's acceptance by God or in the truth of Christian claims. But William Abraham contends that implicit in Wesley's discussion is also another argument for God's reality that appeals to "the evidence drawn from the fulfillment of divine promises."[63] Scripture indicates that if certain conditions are met, then we can expect to realize certain things in our lives, and the fulfillment of these expectations can provide evidence for the truth of the gospel. This can be illustrated by Wesley's own conversion experience.

Abraham points to passages in Wesley's *Journal* leading up to the famous Aldersgate experience indicating his close attention to the promises of Scripture. In the June 4th entry, for example, Wesley states, "And I saw more than ever, that the gospel is in truth but one great promise, from the beginning of it to the end."[64] What exactly is the Scriptural promise that Wesley considered fulfilled in the Aldersgate experience? Abraham explains, "From the context I think that the promise was something like this: Those who give up the quest for God on the basis of their own righ-

61. Wiebe, *Visions and Appearances of Jesus*, 16.

62. Keener, *Miracles*, 1:237–38.

63. William J. Abraham, *Aldersgate and Athens: John Wesley and the Foundations of Christian Belief* (Waco: Baylor University Press, 2010), 6.

64. Wesley, *Journals and Diaries, 1735–38*, ed. W. Reginald Ward and Richard P. Heitzenrater, vol. 18 of *The Works of John Wesley* (Nashville: Abingdon, 1988), 254.

teousness or merit and trust entirely in God's work in Christ will come to experience a sense of pardon for all past sins."[65] This is not so much a promise based on one particular biblical text as it is an expectation drawn from a variety of texts and biblical themes. But it was the fulfillment of this expectation in his experience that evening that, in part, provided Wesley with assurance and confidence in the gospel. It is not as if Wesley constructed a formal argument for the conclusion that the scriptural promise had been fulfilled. Rather, there was for Wesley a certain expectation that was met, and the realization of this fact—which probably came as a noninferential, immediate judgment—provided him with confirmation of the truth of the gospel.

Although Wesley's judgment might have been quick and informal, Abraham makes explicit the reasoning underlying it.

> If many people have satisfied to a significant extent the conditions laid down for a sense of pardon from the guilt and power of sin, and if they, or a large proportion of them, then receive such a sense of pardon and power, this provides us with evidence for the truth of the claim that this promise was indeed made by a being with the wherewithal and the will to make good on that promise. Wesley puts the argument with exemplary succinctness into two sentences: "What the Scripture promises, I enjoy. Come and see what Christianity has done here; and acknowledge it is of God."[66]

Wesley's experience is a familiar one for many Christians. As people repent of their sin and cast themselves on God's mercy, seeking his forgiveness and pardon, they generally do experience God's forgiveness and deliverance from the power of sin. This in turn is often taken by believers as some evidence for the truth of the gospel and that God has indeed accepted them. Abraham summarizes the main point as follows: "God has promised that if we give up seeking salvation by works and seek the face of God in the appointed means of grace, then we will come to experience a sense of pardon and deliverance from sin. [Wesley] met the conditions and the fulfillment happened. Consequently he was entitled to take the fulfillment as evidence of the reality of God as an agent who fulfilled the promises of the gospel."[67] Many Christians can give similar testimonies.

65. Abraham, *Aldersgate and Athens*, 7.
66. Abraham, *Aldersgate and Athens*, 8. Justin Mooney correctly points out that implicit in this argument is that fulfillment of the promises in question is at least somewhat less probable on the negation of the hypothesis that Abraham claims this evidence confirms.
67. Abraham, *Aldersgate and Athens*, 16.

Abraham articulates this argument in terms of the experience of first sensing guilt for sin and then, upon repentance, realizing God's forgiveness, but we could broaden this to include other expectations raised by Scripture. For example, Scripture promises God's peace in difficult circumstances. Philippians 4:6–8 raises the expectation that when believers are anxious about something, as they present their requests to God in prayer with thanksgiving, "the peace of God, which transcends all understanding, will guard your hearts and your minds in Christ Jesus." Or the argument could be expressed in terms of expectations about the moral transformation of believers that is exemplified in a life manifesting the fruit of the Spirit (Gal. 5). Many Christian thinkers point to the presence of the fruit of the Spirit in one's life—love, joy, peace, forbearance, kindness, goodness, faithfulness, gentleness, self-control—as evidence that a person is indeed a child of God. This echoes the teachings of Jesus, who states that false prophets can be distinguished from the real thing "by their fruit" and that genuine disciples who enter the kingdom of heaven are those who do the will of the Father in heaven (Matt. 7:15–23). "No good tree bears bad fruit, nor does a bad tree bear good fruit. . . . A good man brings good things out of the good stored up in his heart, and an evil man brings evil things out of the evil stored up in his heart" (Luke 6:43–45). One's moral disposition and conduct are indicative of the transforming work of God's grace in one's life. As we saw in chapter 4, Jonathan Edwards and John Wesley both applied this criterion to what were said to be experiences of God: the moral qualities associated with the fruit of the Spirit in the life of a person were regarded as evidence that what seem to be experiences of God are indeed veridical.

Philosophers Gary Gutting and William Alston propose versions of an argument that appeals to the cultivation of moral qualities in the life of the believer. Speaking about experiences of God, Gutting states, "Given the veridicality of the typical experience of a very good and very powerful being concerned about us, we would, for example, expect that: (1) those who have had such experiences once would be likely to have them again; (2) other individuals will be found to have had similar experiences; (3) those having such experiences will find themselves aided in their endeavors to lead morally better lives."[68] Given Christian teachings, these are not unreasonable expectations. Furthermore, claims Gutting, with respect to some theistic experiences, "all these expectations are fulfilled to a very high degree." That is, "(1) Many people have numerous 'of-God' experiences and some even find themselves having a continual sense of the divine presence. (2) 'Of-God'

68. Gutting, *Religious Belief*, 152.

experiences are reported from almost every human culture, and the institutional traditions (e.g., churches) they sustain have been among the most enduring in human history. (3) In very many cases, those having 'of-God' experiences undergo major moral transformations and find a purpose and strength of will they previously lacked." Gutting concludes that the experiences themselves provide prima-facie warrant for the claim that God exists, and "the fulfillment of the expectations induced by the assumption that the experiences are veridical provides the further support needed for ultimate warrant."[69]

William Alston also develops an argument in terms of the expectation of "the moral and spiritual development of the individual" and "the individual's relation with God and with fellow creatures."

> The fulfillment of (alleged) divine promises of spiritual development by a large number of persons provides us with a significant reason for accepting the Christian belief system that involves the claim that such promises have been made. More specifically, if many people have satisfied, to a significant extent, the conditions laid down for the availability of the fruits of the Spirit, and if they, or a large proportion of them, then receive those fruits to a significant extent, this provides us with evidence for the truth of the claim that those promises were indeed made by a being with the wherewithal and the will to make good on them. Hence, it provides one with evidence for the truth of the religious belief system within which the claim of those promises was generated.[70]

Although the language in Galatians 5:22 about the fruit of the Spirit does not contain an explicit promise, there is an expectation that believers who live under the power of the Spirit will manifest the qualities listed. Thus life in accordance with the Spirit is contrasted with life according to the flesh, with the latter characterized by sexual immorality, impurity, idolatry, selfish ambition, and so on (5:19–21). Believers are not to live according to the flesh but rather to "walk by the Spirit" and to be "led by the Spirit" (5:16, 18). As we "live by the Spirit" and "keep in step with the Spirit" (5:25), our lives should manifest the fruit of the Spirit (5:22–23). These qualities of a life in tune with the Spirit are mentioned throughout the Scriptures as character traits that are to be found in Christ's disciples (Matt. 5–7; 22:34–40; Luke

69. Gutting, *Religious Belief*, 152–53.

70. William P. Alston, "The Fulfillment of Promises as Evidence for Religious Belief," in *Faith in Theory and Practice*, ed. Elizabeth S. Radcliffe and Carol J. White (Chicago: Open Court, 1993), 3, 7.

6:27–36; 10:25–37; Rom. 12:9–21; Eph. 4:17–5:7; 1 John 2:3–11; 3:16–18). J. I. Packer links the fruit of the Spirit to the life of holiness that is expected of every believer. "The holiness of a holy man, we may say, is the distinctive quality of his living, viewed both as the expression of his being set apart for God and as the outworking of his inward renewal by God's grace. . . . Holiness, thus viewed, is the fruit of the Spirit, displayed as the Christian walks by the Spirit (Gal. 5:16, 22, 25)."[71]

In other words, the language of "promise" used by Alston might be a bit misleading. It is not as though there is an explicit statement that mechanically guarantees that "if conditions A, B, and C are met, then D necessarily follows." The idea is more that of raising certain expectations about what ought to be present in genuine disciples of Jesus Christ who "live by the Spirit." When the word "promise" is used, we must understand it loosely, not as an ironclad guarantee that can easily be verified or falsified but as a way of emphasizing expectations about what should be evident among genuine believers who are living under the power of the Spirit.

There is something significant in these arguments from fulfilled expectations. Given that Scripture does raise expectations about certain realities on the part of those who meet appropriate conditions, it is legitimate to look to these realities in one's life as confirming, to some extent, God's presence or the veridicality of certain experiences. But just how strong is the evidence from fulfilled expectations?

We should distinguish the evidential force of the experience of fulfilled expectations for the subject himself from the strength of such evidence for others. For Wesley, the experience of having these expectations fulfilled was very significant indeed. And given appropriate background beliefs about Scripture and God's work in salvation, it is not unreasonable for believers who have experiences similar to Wesley's to regard them as confirming the truth of the gospel. But if all we had was Wesley's own personal experience to go on, then the evidential force of this for others who hear about it is not very strong. However, similar testimonies abound, including from Christians in many diverse traditions in many cultures across the centuries. To the extent that we find this pattern of fulfillment of expectations raised by Scripture to be present in many people across time and cultures, this provides some positive evidence for the truth of Christian claims. Just how extensive is this testimony? This is not the kind of thing lending itself to precise measurement, so any conclusions tend to be anecdotal and impressionistic. But Alston's comments are appropriate.

71. J. I. Packer, *Keep in Step with the Spirit* (Grand Rapids: Revell, 1984), 96.

To be sure, the fulfillment of alleged divine promises provides us with positive evidence for Christian belief only if those promises have been fulfilled significantly often. I am not going to try to show that this is the case. I believe that Christian autobiographical literature through the centuries, plus my own experience and the testimony of others, gives me an adequate basis for this assumption. Obviously, the literary records, plus oral testimony available to me, cover only a tiny proportion of Christian believers. However, it seems reasonable to assume that here, as in other matters, the persons who communicate certain occurrences in writing, or who orally report them to a given observer, constitute a very small proportion of those who undergo such occurrences.[72]

Let's assume that Alston is correct and that there are large numbers of Christians worldwide who could give testimony to having experienced the fulfillment of expectations raised by the Scriptures concerning the fruit of the Spirit. There are still a number of issues that need clarification if this is to be a cogent argument.

First, just what is it that the fulfillment of expectations is evidence *for*? There are at least four possibilities: (1) the truth of Christian theism or the gospel, (2) whether one really is a genuine believer and therefore saved, (3) whether a believer really is "walking in step" with the Holy Spirit, or (4) whether a particular experience is a veridical experience of God. It is, of course, possible that fulfilled expectations could be part of an answer with each issue, but the manner in which it serves as evidence differs somewhat in each case. For the sake of simplicity, in what follows we will take it that the fulfillment of expectations is supposed to provide evidence for the truth of the Christian gospel.

Second, it is difficult to know how to determine what counts as evidence of fulfilled expectations. Let's focus on the expectations concerning moral transformation or the fruit of the Spirit in the lives of believers. Just how much joy, peace, love, generosity, and self-control are to be present in the believer's life for this to be evidentially significant? How clear should the evidence be? What would count as the absence of such qualities—momentary lapses or sustained periods without the requisite qualities? One of the characteristics mentioned in Galatians 5:22 is love. In characterizing how his disciples are to live, Jesus both emphasizes the importance of love for others and sets a very high standard for what he expects: his followers are to love their neighbors as they love themselves (Matt. 22:34–40) and to love even their enemies (Matt. 5:44). In Galatians 5, prior to listing the fruit of the Spirit, Paul repeats the command to love one's neighbor: "For the entire

72. Alston, "Fulfillment of Promises," 8.

law is fulfilled in keeping this one command: 'Love your neighbor as your-self'" (Gal. 5:14). What the Scriptures have in mind is clearly not simply a general concern for the well-being of others. At what point are we able to say that the kind of love called for by Jesus and Paul is evident in one's life? This seems to be more of an ideal toward which believers are to strive, as we progressively walk in step with the enabling power of the Holy Spirit, rather than a quality that is either simply present or absent. If so, at what point can we conclude that the expectation is fulfilled?

Furthermore, it is unclear whether the fruit of the Spirit is present *only* in the lives of believers or whether these qualities can also be found among those who make no profession to be followers of Christ. If, for example, the expectation from Scripture is that *all* genuine believers will manifest clear evidence of the fruit of the Spirit in their lives and that these qualities will be found *only* among the regenerate, then the evidential calculus is set up in a certain way: the unambiguous presence of these qualities in believers along with their conspicuous absence among unbelievers would constitute evidence that what Christian teaching leads us to expect is indeed realized. This would then provide some confirming evidence of the truth of the gospel. But the matter is less clear if either (1) not all believers do give evidence of the fruit of the Spirit in their lives or (2) these qualities are also found in significant measure among those who are not believers. If either of these conditions obtains, then, unless there are plausible reasons that account for this, the evidential force of the argument from fulfilled expectations is diminished.

Let's consider the first case. If it is obvious that the lives of all, or almost all, professing Christians are characterized by the fruit of the Spirit—love, joy, peace, forbearance, kindness, goodness, faithfulness, gentleness, and self-control—then this would be a distinguishing trait of believers. But of course not all who claim to be Christian consistently manifest these qualities in their lives. Many Christians lack joy or peace, do not act in loving ways toward others, or do not seem to be kind and gentle. The lives of some Christians seem to be characterized much more by the "desires of the flesh" Paul describes in Galatians 5 than by the fruit of the Spirit. Indeed, Paul's point to believers is precisely that they *should* "walk by the Spirit" so that they do not "gratify the desires of the flesh" (Gal. 5:16). To be sure, there are good theological explanations for the fact that some believers do not manifest the fruit of the Spirit—sanctification is a process that takes time, even the regenerate continue to struggle with sin—and we should bear in mind that not everyone who claims to be a Christian is a genuine disciple of Jesus. After all, Jesus himself says, "Not everyone who says to me 'Lord,

Lord' will enter the kingdom of heaven, but only the one who does the will of my Father who is in heaven" (Matt. 7:21). But to the extent that there is ambiguity over the presence of these qualities in the lives of believers, this reduces the evidential force of the argument from fulfilled expectations.

Another potential difficulty comes from the fact that it is possible to point to many non-Christians who seem to manifest in their lives the qualities identified with the fruit of the Spirit. Reflecting on his own experience with people from many religions, for example, John Hick states, "I have not found that the people of the world religions are, in general, on a different moral or spiritual level from Christians. They seem on average to be neither better nor worse than are Christians." But, he asks, is this what we would expect "if Christians have a more complete and direct access to God than anyone else and live in a closer relationship to him, being indwelt by the Holy Spirit? Should not the fruit of the Spirit, which according to Paul is 'love, joy, peace, patience, kindness, goodness, faithfulness, gentleness, self-control' (Gal. 5:22–23), be more evident in Christian than in non-Christian lives?" Hick acknowledges that it is not realistic to expect that any particular Christian should be morally superior to any other particular non-Christian. "But surely the *average* level of these virtues should be noticeably higher among Christians than among non-Christians. Yet it does not seem to me that in fact Christians are on average noticeably morally superior to Jews, Muslims, Hindus, Sikhs, or Buddhists."[73]

Is Hick correct? His conclusion is based on his own experiences with Christians and followers of other religions; others, reflecting on their own experiences, might have quite different perspectives. I, for example, would like to think that on balance these moral qualities *are* evident in the lives of Christians to a greater degree than in others. But this would be an extremely difficult thing to demonstrate empirically, and I readily acknowledge that many who are not Christian manifest these qualities, sometimes to a much greater extent than many Christians. The significant point for our purposes, however, is that so long as Hick's claim is plausible for many people—as it surely is—this reduces the evidential force of an argument from fulfilled expectations concerning the fruit of the Spirit for the distinctive truth of the Christian gospel.

There are, of course, possible responses to Hick that could help to explain the apparent parity between followers of Christ and adherents of other

73. John Hick, "A Pluralist View," in *Four Views on Salvation in a Pluralistic World*, ed. Dennis L. Okholm and Timothy R. Phillips (Grand Rapids: Zondervan, 1996), 39, 41. Emphasis in original. As we saw in chapter 4, this point was also made by William James in his critique of Jonathan Edwards.

religions. As noted earlier, not everyone claiming to be a Christian is a genuine disciple of Jesus. For the comparison to really work, we would need to
know who the *real* disciples of Jesus are—a determination best left to God.
Others might argue that what *seems* to be joy, peace, love, or goodness in
the lives of non-Christians is not the real thing; what we observe in them is
merely an imitation of real joy and peace, which, by definition, are restricted
to the regenerate. Perhaps this is so, but such a claim strikes many as an ad
hoc response not demanded by Scripture and hard to square with what we
actually encounter among religious others. What we mean by "goodness" or
"peace" in the lives of Christians seems to be much the same as what these
terms designate when used of the lives of non-Christians. And so long as
this is the case, it is difficult to appeal to such qualities as providing evidence
for the distinctive truth of the gospel.

Another possible response is to acknowledge that the moral qualities identified with the fruit of the Spirit *are* present among followers of
other faiths and that this is due to the work of the Holy Spirit among
all people, regardless of religious affiliation. Amos Yong has developed a
pneumatological theology of religions that acknowledges a dynamic role
for the Holy Spirit among all peoples and within other religions.[74] The
acceptability of his proposal depends on the kind of support it has from
Scripture and central theological affirmations, matters that we cannot
pursue here.[75] But the relevant point is that if Yong's proposal is accepted,
then it becomes more difficult to appeal to the distinctive presence of the
fruit of the Spirit in the lives of believers as evidence for the truth of the
gospel.

Where does this leave the argument from fulfilled expectations? There
clearly is an important truth that the argument is trying to capture: the
realization in one's own life of what one is led to expect from the gospel
does provide some evidential support for the truth of the gospel. This, it
seems to me, is fully consistent with the biblical witness and the experiences
of many people. The difficulty lies in trying to formalize the nature of this
evidential relationship between what Scripture leads us to expect and what
is experienced in the lives of believers. Moreover, the evidential force of this
is greater for the individual who experiences the fulfillment than for other

---

74. See Amos Yong, *Beyond the Impasse: Toward a Pneumatological Theology of Religions*
(Grand Rapids: Baker Academic, 2003); and Yong, "The Holy Spirit and the World Religions:
On the Christian Discernment of Spirit(s) 'after' Buddhism," *Buddhist-Christian Studies* 24
(2004): 191–207.

75. See Gerald R. McDermott and Harold A. Netland, *A Trinitarian Theology of Religions:
An Evangelical Proposal* (New York: Oxford University Press, 2014), 54–57, 72–76.

observers. Although we have noted difficulties in the argument, I do believe that there is an evidential relation here that is significant.

However, the evidence produced by this kind of argument is modest and somewhat ambiguous. In referring to Wesley's use of the argument, Abraham observes, "The claim is a modest one. It provides some evidence for the truth of the gospel: it does not provide any kind of deductive proof or conclusive evidence."[76] And Alston remarks, "I claim only that the occurrence of promised outcomes in a considerable number of cases provides *a certain amount of evidence* for the truth of the Christian belief system. . . . I will not attempt to assess the strength of the evidence even in crude qualitative terms, except to say that it provides a *significant* amount of evidence, that it raises the probability of the system sufficiently to be worthy of notice."[77] This seems correct.

As we conclude this discussion, I suggest that it is best not to treat the argument from fulfilled expectations as something that stands on its own but rather to adopt the insight that the argument is based on and to use it as one element in a broader inference to the best-explanation argument for Christian theism. Abraham notes that "the evidence [from fulfilled expectations] generally works with other evidence, even though it adds its own weight to the total evidence available." Thus it is best seen as working within a network of evidence that persuades the believer of the truth of the gospel; it is part of an informal, cumulative-case argument.[78]

Although taken by itself this kind of evidence is not particularly strong, it can be significant when combined with other factors. In other words, we can appeal to the fact that many people do experience in their own lives the fulfillment of what Scripture leads us to expect—they do experience forgiveness of sin when they repent, they do find the fruit of the Spirit manifest in their lives as they live in obedience to God and submission to the Spirit, and so on. Although the presence of these things in the lives of believers might be less clear and pronounced than we would like, and in spite of the fact that the qualities associated with the fruit of the Spirit can also be present in the lives of nonbelievers, the point is that these expectations *are* realized in the lives of believers, and this is precisely what we would expect if Christian theism were true. This then can be part of the set of factors brought together in a cumulative-case argument for Christian theism. The evidential strength of this contribution to the broader argument depends in part on

76. Abraham, *Aldersgate and Athens*, 11.
77. Alston, "Fulfillment of Promises," 12. Emphasis in original.
78. Abraham, *Aldersgate and Athens*, 11.

the plausibility of theological explanations for the somewhat ambiguous record of these qualities in the lives of believers as well as the presence of these qualities among nonbelievers. But if there are other strong reasons for accepting Christian theism, then the realization of certain expectations put forward by the Christian gospel can serve as modestly confirming evidence of the truth of the gospel.

Conclusion

Many people have experiences that they take to be experiences of God. These take many different forms, but perceptual experiences are especially significant when considering the evidential force of theistic experience. Other kinds of theistic experience—being overwhelmed by the greatness of the Creator through observing the Milky Way in the night sky or sensing God's special peace and comfort during times of trial—are also significant, although they tend to be more ambiguous than perceptual experiences. Interpretation plays an important role in religious experience, especially in more ambiguous cases. Even mystical experiences—which are often held up as a privileged kind of experience not subject to normal epistemological strictures—involve some interpretation.

Throughout these chapters we have encountered a variety of issues in the epistemology of religious experience, most of which revolve around two basic questions: First, can one be justified in accepting a particular religious experience as veridical? Should one take what seems to be an experience of God as a genuine experience of God? Second, do religious experiences provide evidential support for particular religious beliefs or commitments? If so, how? These questions, although related, are distinct.

With respect to the first question, I have defended the critical-trust approach to religious, and especially theistic, experiences. In other words, what seems to be an experience of God can be accepted as such, so long as there are no compelling reasons for concluding otherwise. This applies both to the person having a religious experience and to those who hear about someone else's experience. So there is an initial presumption favoring the veridicality of theistic experiences. This presumption, however, is defeasible and can be overruled by factors that call into question the veridicality

259

of an experience or the reliability of a report of the experience. Some of these factors are internal to a particular religious tradition, while others are not tradition-specific but apply generally. For Christians, for example, consistency with the teachings of Scripture is a criterion that could call into question a particular experience. More generally, if an experience occurs under conditions that are known to produce delusory experiences, then this calls into question the veridicality of the experience.

Concerning the second question, I have argued that theistic experiences can provide some epistemic support for certain beliefs, both for the subject of the experience and for others. But the degree of evidential support will vary with the nature of the experience and the background beliefs of those assessing the experience. Given the critical-trust approach and provided there are no successful defeaters, theistic experiences can provide some evidence for some beliefs about God. For example, having an experience in which it seems epistemically that I perceive God's presence or that I sense God's forgiveness provides some evidential support for my believing that God is present or that God has forgiven me. In some cases, the evidential force is direct and noninferential, as with our perception of other persons. In other cases, the evidence may come through inference and an argument.

But the critical-trust approach applies not only to Christians and their experiences but also to adherents of other religions, and this raises questions about the implications of religious diversity and disagreement for the critical-trust approach. Although some see religious disagreement as ruling out the use of the critical-trust approach with religious experiences, I have argued that this is not necessarily the case. On a weaker notion of rationality, it can be reasonable for adherents of different religions to accept experiences within their respective traditions as veridical even if the claims based on these experiences cannot all be true. If, however, we desire a stronger notion of rationality for assessing religious experiences, then we will need independent reasons for accepting some experiences as veridical but not others.

It is here that assessment of the broader systems of belief within which particular experiences occur becomes significant. In applying the critical-trust approach, a person relies on a set of background beliefs, values, and expectations that influences their judgment on what can reasonably be accepted. What is regarded as veridical depends in part on the prior beliefs and commitments one brings to the experience. On the one hand, if I already accept the basic teachings of Christian theism as true, for example, then it can be eminently reasonable for me to accept as veridical any experiences that are consistent with Christian teachings. On the other hand, if I am convinced that there is no God or supernatural reality, then it can be reasonable for me to be skeptical of what seems to be an experience of God. In other words, ultimately, the veridicality of theistic experiences cannot be determined apart from addressing the question of the truth of core tenets within one's set of background beliefs. And thus epistemological questions about theistic experience cannot be separated from consideration of the truth of central Christian claims, a task typically identified with natural theology.

Within the Christian tradition, the Holy Spirit has a special role in experiences of God. For it is the Holy Spirit who enables us to acknowledge the truth of the gospel and who gives us confidence that we are indeed children of God. Our experiences of God's presence and guidance, of God's peace as well as conviction of sin, come through the work of the Holy Spirit in our lives. We saw how Jonathan Edwards and John Wesley appeal to the work of the Spirit in producing confidence in the truth of the gospel and how they distinguished between a genuine work of the Spirit and what is spurious. The idea of the inner witness of the Holy Spirit is central to their perspectives. It is also an important element in the Reformed epistemology of Alvin Plantinga, who links the witness of the Spirit to the claim that belief in God is properly basic. I argued that although there are circumstances in which belief in God can be properly basic for some people, this is not necessarily the case for most believers today. Moreover, we should not understand the inner witness of the Holy Spirit as being "self-authenticating" or indubitable, or something that necessarily operates apart from evidence and reasons for faith. The biblical teaching on the witness of the Spirit can be compatible with a variety of epistemological perspectives.

Finally, we examined two arguments that can be formulated from aspects of theistic experience: (1) the argument from *consensus gentium*, or common consent, about experiences of God, and (2) the argument from fulfilled expectations. Although each argument taken by itself is not particularly impressive, both contain insights that can be adapted and used in a different form in a cumulative-case argument for Christian theism. For example, the fact that many people throughout history and in many cultures have had what they take to be experiences of God is something of significance that needs to be explained. Similarly, many Christians claim to have experienced the fulfillment of certain expectations raised by Scripture and Christian teaching. This too is an important feature of human life in many cultures throughout history, and it requires some explanation. These characteristics of theistic experiences can be included, along with many other things, in a cumulative-case argument for Christian theism.

Theological and philosophical analysis of religious experiences depends in part on there being a rich and accurate accumulation of reports of the experiences of many people in diverse contexts, and for this we need much more by way of careful empirical research. We also need further probing and analysis of many issues by theologians and philosophers. So the conversation about theistic experiences must continue. But I am convinced that, with appropriate caveats noted throughout these chapters, it can be fully rational for one to maintain that he or she has had a veridical experience of God and to accept that someone else has experienced God. Although the evidential relationship is notoriously difficult to articulate precisely, theistic experiences can provide some evidence for certain beliefs about God, both for the one having the experience and for other observers.

Bibliography

Abraham, William J. *Aldersgate and Athens: John Wesley and the Foundations of Christian Belief.* Waco: Baylor University Press, 2010.

———. "Analytic Philosophers of Religion." In Gavrilyuk and Coakley, *Spiritual Senses,* 275–90.

———. "Cumulative Case Arguments for Christian Theism." In *The Rationality of Religious Belief: Essays in Honour of Basil Mitchell,* edited by William J. Abraham and Steven W. Holtzer, 17–37. Oxford: Clarendon, 1989.

———. "The Epistemological Significance of the Inner Witness of the Holy Spirit." *Faith and Philosophy* 7, no. 4 (October 1990): 434–50.

———. "The Epistemology of Conversion: Is There Something New?" In *Conversion in the Wesleyan Tradition,* edited by Kenneth J. Collins and John H. Tyson, 175–91. Nashville: Abingdon, 2001.

Abraham, William J., and Frederick D. Aquino, eds. *The Oxford Handbook of the Epistemology of Theology.* New York: Oxford University Press, 2017.

Adams, Marilyn McCord. "The Indwelling of the Holy Spirit: Some Alternative Models." In *The Philosophy of Human Nature in Christian Perspective,* edited by Peter Weigel and Joseph G. Prud'homme, 83–99. New York: Peter Lang, 2016.

Almond, Philip C. "Mysticism and Its Contexts." In Forman, *Problem of Pure Consciousness: Mysticism and Philosophy,* 211–19.

———. *Rudolf Otto: An Introduction to His Philosophical Theology.* Chapel Hill: University of North Carolina Press, 1984.

Alston, William P. "Christian Experience and Christian Belief." In Plantinga and Wolterstorff, *Faith and Rationality,* 103–34.

———. "The Fulfillment of Promises as Evidence for Religious Belief." In *Faith in Theory and Practice,* edited by Elizabeth S. Radcliffe and Carol J. White, 1–34. Chicago: Open Court, 1993.

———. "The Indwelling of the Holy Spirit." In *Divine Nature and Human Language,* 223–52. Ithaca, NY: Cornell University Press, 1989.

———. "John Hick: Faith and Knowledge." In *God, Truth, and Reality: Essays in Honour of John Hick,* edited by Arvind Sharma, 24–31. New York: St. Martin's Press, 1993.

———. *Perceiving God: The Epistemology of Religious Experience*. Ithaca, NY: Cornell University Press, 1991.

———. "Précis of *Perceiving God*." *Philosophy and Phenomenological Research* 54, no. 4 (December 1994): 863–68.

———. *A Realist Conception of Truth*. Ithaca, NY: Cornell University Press, 1996.

———. *The Reliability of Sense Perception*. Ithaca, NY: Cornell University Press, 1993.

———. "Religious Experience." In *Routledge Encyclopedia of Philosophy*, edited by Edward Craig, 8:250–55. New York: Routledge, 1998.

———. "Religious Language." In W. Wainwright, *Oxford Handbook of Philosophy of Religion*, 220–44.

———. "Reply to Commentators." *Philosophy and Phenomenological Research* 54, no. 4 (December 1994): 891–99.

———. "Two Cheers for Mystery!" In Dole and Chignell, *God and the Ethics of Belief*, 99–114.

Annas, Julia, and Jonathan Barnes. *The Modes of Skepticism: Ancient Texts and Modern Interpretations*. Cambridge: Cambridge University Press, 1985.

Aristotle. "Posterior Analytics." In *The Basic Works of Aristotle*, edited by Richard McKeon, I.3, pp. 113–14. New York: Random House, 1941.

Arjana, Sophia Rose. *Buying Buddha, Selling Rumi: Orientalism and the Mystical Marketplace*. Oxford: Oneworld Academic, 2020.

Asad, Talal. *Genealogies of Religion: Discipline and Reasons of Power in Christianity and Islam*. Baltimore: Johns Hopkins University Press, 1993.

Atran, Scott. *In Gods We Trust: The Evolutionary Landscape of Religion*. Oxford: Oxford University Press, 2002.

Audi, Robert. "The Epistemic Authority of Testimony and the Ethics of Belief." In Dole and Chignell, *God and the Ethics of Belief*, 177–201.

———. "The Place of Testimony in the Fabric of Knowledge and Justification." *American Philosophical Quarterly* 34 (1997): 405–22.

Badham, Paul, ed. *A John Hick Reader*. 1971. Reprint, Philadelphia: Trinity Press International, 1990.

Bagger, Matthew. *Religious Experience, Justification, and History*. Cambridge: Cambridge University Press, 1999.

Baker, Deane-Peter, ed. *Alvin Plantinga*. Cambridge: Cambridge University Press, 2007.

———. "Plantinga's Reformed Epistemology: What's the Question?" *International Journal for Philosophy of Religion* 57 (Spring 2005): 77–103.

Baker-Hytch, Max. "Testimony amidst Diversity." In Benton, Hawthorne, and Rabinowitz, *Knowledge, Belief, and God*, 183–202.

Baldwin, Erik, and Tyler Dalton McNabb. *Plantingian Religious Epistemology and World Religions: Prospects and Problems*. New York: Lexington Books, 2019.

Barnett, S. J. *The Enlightenment and Religion: The Myths of Modernity*. Manchester: Manchester University Press, 2003.

Barrett, Justin L. *Born Believers: The Science of Children's Religious Beliefs*. New York: Free Press, 2012.

———. "Cognitive Science, Religion, and Theology." In Schloss and Murray, *Believing Primate*, 76–99.

Barrett, Justin L., and Roger Trigg. "Cognitive and Evolutionary Studies of Religion." In Trigg and Barrett, *Roots of Religion*, 1–15.

Basinger, David. *Religious Diversity: A Philosophical Assessment*. Burlington, VT: Ashgate, 2002.

———. "What Is a Miracle?" In *The Cambridge Companion to Miracles*, edited by Graham H. Twelftree, 19–35. Cambridge: Cambridge University Press, 2011.

Bastow, David. "Otto and Numinous Experience." *Religious Studies* 12 (1976): 159–76.

Beilby, James. *Epistemology as Theology: An Evaluation of Alvin Plantinga's Religious Epistemology*. Aldershot: Ashgate, 2006.

———. "Plantinga's Model of Warranted Christian Belief." In Baker, *Alvin Plantinga*, 125–65.

Benton, Matthew A., John Hawthorne, and Dani Rabinowitz, eds. *Knowledge, Belief, and God: New Insights in Religious Epistemology*. New York: Oxford University Press, 2018.

Berger, Peter L. *The Many Altars of Modernity: Toward a Paradigm for Religion in a Pluralist Age*. Berlin: de Gruyter, 2014.

Berger, Peter L., and Anton Zijderveld. *In Praise of Doubt: How to Have Convictions without Becoming a Fanatic*. New York: HarperOne, 2009.

Bergmann, Michael. "Foundationalism." In Abraham and Aquino, *Oxford Handbook of the Epistemology of Theology*, 253–73.

Bonjour, Laurence. "Internalism and Externalism." In *The Oxford Handbook of Epistemology*, edited by Paul K. Moser, 234–63. New York: Oxford University Press, 2002.

———. *The Structure of Empirical Knowledge*. Cambridge, MA: Harvard University Press, 1985.

Bowie, Fiona. "Miraculous and Extraordinary Events as Religious Experience." In Moser and Meister, *Cambridge Companion to Religious Experience*, 261–83.

Boyer, Pascal. *Religion Explained: The Evolutionary Origins of Religious Thought*. New York: Basic Books, 2001.

Brainard, F. Samuel. "Defining 'Mystical Experience.'" *Journal of the American Academy of Religion* 64, no. 2 (1996): 359–93.

Brantley, Richard E. "The Common Ground of Wesley and Edwards." *Harvard Theological Review* 83, no. 3 (July 1990): 271–303.

Broad, C. D. "Arguments for the Existence of God." In *Religion, Philosophy, and Psychical Research: Selected Essays*, 175–201. 1953. Reprint, New York: Humanities, 1969.

Burton, David. "Religious Experience in Buddhism." In Moser and Meister, *Cambridge Companion to Religious Experience*, 187–207.

Bush, Stephen S. *Visions of Religion: Experience, Meaning, and Power*. New York: Oxford University Press, 2014.

Calhoun, Craig, Mark Jeurgensmeyer, and Jonathan VanAntwerpen, eds. *Rethinking Secularism*. New York: Oxford University Press, 2011.

Calvin, John. *Institutes of the Christian Religion*. Edited by John T. McNeill. Translated by Ford Lewis Battles. Philadelphia: Westminster, 1960.

Campbell, Ted A. *The Religion of the Heart: A Study of European Religious Life in the Seventeenth and Eighteenth Centuries.* Columbia: University of South Carolina Press, 1991.

Casanova, José. *Public Religions in the Modern World.* Chicago: University of Chicago Press, 1994.

Chignell, Andrew. "'As Kant Has Shown . . .': Analytic Theology and the Critical Philosophy." In *Analytic Theology: New Essays in the Philosophy of Religion*, edited by Oliver D. Crisp and Michael Rea, 117–35. Oxford: Oxford University Press, 2009.

Christensen, David, and Jennifer Lackey, eds. *The Epistemology of Disagreement: New Essays.* Oxford: Oxford University Press, 2013.

Cicero. *Nature of the Gods.* Translated by H. Rackham. Cambridge, MA: Harvard University Press, 1951.

Clark, Kelly James, and Justin L. Barrett, "Reformed Epistemology and the Cognitive Science of Religion." *Faith and Philosophy* 27, no. 2 (April 2010): 174–89.

Clark, Kelly James, and Raymond J. VanArragon. *Evidence and Religious Belief.* New York: Oxford University Press, 2011.

Coffey, John, and Paul C. H. Lim. "Introduction." In *The Cambridge Companion to Puritanism*, edited by John Coffey and Paul C. H. Lim, 1–18. Cambridge: Cambridge University Press, 2008.

Cole, G. A. "Holy Spirit in Apologetics." In *New Dictionary of Christian Apologetics*, edited by W. C. Campbell-Jack and Gavin McGrath, 324–27. Downers Grove, IL: InterVarsity, 2006.

Collins, Kenneth J., and John H. Tyson, eds. *Conversion in the Wesleyan Tradition.* Nashville: Abingdon, 2001.

Cowan, Steven B., ed. *Five Views on Apologetics.* Grand Rapids: Zondervan, 2000.

Coward, Harold. *Sin and Salvation in the World Religions.* Oxford: Oneworld, 2003.

Craig, William Lane. "Classical Apologetics." In Cowan, *Five Views on Apologetics*, 25–89.

———. *Reasonable Faith: Christian Truth and Apologetics.* 3rd ed. Wheaton: Crossway, 2008.

Craig, William Lane, and J. P. Moreland, eds. *The Blackwell Companion to Natural Theology.* Oxford: Wiley-Blackwell, 2012.

Craig, William Lane, and Walter Sinnott-Armstrong. *God? A Debate between a Christian and an Atheist.* New York: Oxford University Press, 2004.

Crisp, Oliver. "Faith and Experience." In *The Oxford Handbook of Evangelical Theology*, edited by Gerald R. McDermott, 68–80. New York: Oxford University Press, 2010.

Davis, Caroline Franks. *The Evidential Force of Religious Experience.* Oxford: Clarendon, 1989.

Davis, Stephen T. "An Ontology of the Spirit." In Geivett and Moser, *Testimony of the Spirit*, 54–65.

De Cruz, Helen. *Religious Disagreement.* Cambridge: Cambridge University Press, 2019.

Dennett, Daniel C. *Breaking the Spell: Religion as a Natural Phenomenon.* New York: Viking, 2006.

DePoe, J. "In Defense of Classical Foundationalism: A Critical Evaluation of Plantinga's Argument That Classical Foundationalism Is Self-Refuting." *South African Journal of Philosophy* (2013): 245–51.

DeRose, Keith. "Delusions of Knowledge Concerning God's Existence: A Skeptical Look at Religious Experience." In Benton, Hawthorne, and Rabinowitz, *Knowledge, Belief, and God*, 288–301.

Descartes, René. *Discourse on Method and The Meditations.* London: Penguin Books, 1968.

Diamond, Cora. "'We Can't Whistle It Either': Legend and Reality." *European Journal of Philosophy* 19, no. 3 (2010): 335–56.

Dole, Andrew, and Andrew Chignell, eds. *God and the Ethics of Belief: New Essays in Philosophy of Religion.* Cambridge: Cambridge University Press, 2005.

Dougherty, Trent, and Alvin Plantinga. "Trent Dougherty and Alvin Plantinga: An Interview on Faith and Reason." In Walls and Dougherty, *Two Dozen (or So) Arguments for God*, 446–59.

Doyle, Tom. *Dreams and Visions: Is Jesus Awakening the Muslim World?* Nashville: Nelson, 2012.

Drescher, Elizabeth. *Choosing Our Religion: The Spiritual Lives of America's Nones.* New York: Oxford University Press, 2016.

Dupré, Louis. *The Enlightenment and the Intellectual Foundations of Modern Culture.* New Haven: Yale University Press, 2004.

———. "General Introduction." In Dupré and Wiseman, *Light from Light*, 3–14.

Dupré, Louis, and James A. Wiseman, eds. *Light from Light: An Anthology of Christian Mysticism.* 2nd ed. New York: Paulist Press, 2001.

Durkheim, Émile. "Definition of Religious Phenomena and Religion." In *The Study of Religion: A Reader*, edited by John S. Harding and Hillary P. Rodrigues, 94–100. London: Routledge, 2014.

Edwards, Jonathan. "A Divine and Supernatural Light." In *A Jonathan Edwards Reader*, edited by John E. Smith, Harry S. Stout, and Kenneth Minkema, 105–23. New Haven: Yale University Press, 1995.

———. *The "Miscellanies," a–500.* Edited by Thomas A. Schafer. Vol. 13 of *The Works of Jonathan Edwards.* New Haven: Yale University Press, 1994.

———. *Religious Affections.* Edited by John E. Smith. Vol. 2 of *The Works of Jonathan Edwards.* New Haven: Yale University Press, 2009.

———. "A Spiritual Understanding of Divine Things Denied to the Unregenerate." In *Sermons and Discourses, 1723–1729*, edited by Kenneth P. Minkema, 67–96. Vol. 14 of *The Works of Jonathan Edwards.* New Haven: Yale University Press, 1997.

Ellwood, Robert S. *Mysticism and Religion.* 2nd ed. New York: Seven Bridges, 1999.

Evans, C. Stephen. *The Historical Christ and the Jesus of Faith: The Incarnational Narrative as History.* Oxford: Clarendon, 1996.

———. *Natural Signs and Knowledge of God: A New Look at Theistic Arguments.* New York: Oxford University Press, 2010.

———. "Religious Experience and the Question of Whether Belief in God Requires Evidence." In Clark and VanArragon, *Evidence and Religious Belief*, 37–51.

Fales, Evan. "Do Mystics See God?" In *Contemporary Debates in Philosophy of Religion*, edited by Michael L. Peterson and Raymond J. VanArragon, 145–58. Oxford: Blackwell, 2004.

———. "Naturalism and Physicalism." In *The Cambridge Companion to Atheism*, edited by Michael Martin, 118–34. Cambridge: Cambridge University Press, 2007.

Fesko, J. V. *Reforming Apologetics: Retrieving the Classic Reformed Approach to Defending the Faith*. Grand Rapids: Baker Academic, 2019.

Flew, Antony. *God and Philosophy*. New York: Harcourt, Brace, & World, 1966.

Forman, Robert K. C. "Introduction: Mysticism, Constructivism, and Forgetting." In Forman, *Problem of Pure Consciousness*, 3–49.

———. *Mysticism, Mind, Consciousness*. Albany: State University of New York Press, 1999.

———, ed. *The Problem of Pure Consciousness: Mysticism and Philosophy*. New York: Oxford University Press, 1990.

Foster, John. *The Nature of Perception*. New York: Oxford University Press, 2000.

Franklin, R. L. "Experience and Interpretation in Mysticism." In Forman, *Problem of Pure Consciousness*, 288–304.

Gage, Logan Paul, and Blake McAllister. "Phenomenal Conservatism." In *Debating Christian Religious Epistemology*, edited by John M. DePoe and Tyler Dalton McNabb, 61–106. New York: Bloomsbury Academic, 2020.

Gale, Richard. *On the Nature and Existence of God*. Cambridge: Cambridge University Press, 1991.

———. "Swinburne's Argument from Religious Experience." In *Reason and the Christian Religion*, edited by Alan G. Padgett, 39–63. Oxford: Clarendon, 1994.

———. "Why Alston's Mystical Doxastic Practice Is Subjective." *Philosophy and Phenomenological Research* 54, no. 4 (December 1994): 869–75.

Gavrilyuk, Paul L. "Encountering God: Spiritual Perception in the Bible, Tradition, and Film." *International Journal of Orthodox Theology* 10, no. 1 (2019): 41–61.

Gavrilyuk, Paul L., and Sarah Coakley, eds. *The Spiritual Senses: Perceiving God in Western Christianity*. Cambridge: Cambridge University Press, 2012.

Gay, Peter. *The Enlightenment: An Interpretation*. Vol. 1, *The Rise of Modern Paganism*. New York: Norton, 1966.

Geertz, Clifford. *The Interpretation of Cultures*. New York: Random House, 1973.

Geivett, R. Douglas. "The Evidential Value of Religious Experience." In *The Rationality of Theism*, edited by Paul Copan and Paul K. Moser, 175–203. London: Routledge, 2003.

Geivett, R. Douglas, and Paul K. Moser. "Introduction." In Geivett and Moser, *Testimony of the Spirit*, 1–31.

———, eds. *The Testimony of the Spirit: New Essays*. New York: Oxford University Press, 2017.

Gellman, Jerome. *Experience of God and the Rationality of Theistic Belief*. Ithaca, NY: Cornell University Press, 1997.

———. *Mystical Experience of God: A Philosophical Enquiry*. London: Ashgate, 2001.

———. "Mysticism and Religious Experience." In W. Wainwright, *Oxford Handbook of Philosophy of Religion*, 138–67.

————. "A New Look at the Problem of Evil." *Faith and Philosophy* 2, no. 9 (April 1992): 210–16.

Gimello, Robert M. "Mysticism and Meditation." In Katz, *Mysticism and Philosophical Analysis*, 170–99.

Goldberg, Sanford C. "Does Externalist Epistemology Rationalize Religious Commitment?" In *Religious Faith and Intellectual Virtue*, edited by Laura Frances Callahan and Timothy O'Connor, 279–98. Oxford: Oxford University Press, 2014.

Goldman, Alvin I., and Matthew McGrath. *Epistemology: A Contemporary Introduction.* New York: Oxford University Press, 2015.

Greco, John. "No-Fault Atheism." In *Hidden Divinity and Religious Belief: New Perspectives*, edited by Adam Green and Eleonore Stump, 109–25. Cambridge: Cambridge University Press, 2015.

————. "Reformed Epistemology." In *The Routledge Companion to Philosophy of Religion*, edited by Chad Meister and Paul Copan, 629–39. London: Routledge, 2007.

Griffioen, Amber L. "'Signs for a People Who Reason': Religious Experience and Natural Theology." *European Journal for Philosophy of Religion* 9, no. 2 (2017): 139–63.

Griffith-Dickson, Gwen. *Human and Divine: An Introduction to the Philosophy of Religious Experience.* London: Gerald Duckworth, 2000.

Grover, Stephen. "Religious Experiences: Skepticism, Gullibility, or Credulity?" In *Faith and Theory in Practice*, edited by Elizabeth S. Radcliffe and Carol J. White, 103–15. Chicago: Open Court, 1993.

Guinness, Os. *God in the Dark: The Assurance of Faith Beyond a Shadow of Doubt.* Wheaton: Crossway, 1996.

Gutting, Gary. *Religious Belief and Religious Skepticism.* Notre Dame: University of Notre Dame Press, 1982.

Habermas, Gary. *Dealing with Doubt.* Chicago: Moody, 1990.

————. "An Evidentialist's Response." In Cowan, *Five Views on Apologetics*, 56–66.

————. *The Thomas Factor: Using Doubt to Draw Closer to God.* Nashville: Broadman & Holman, 1999.

Hammersholt, Torben. "Steven T. Katz's Philosophy of Mysticism Revisited." *Journal of the American Academy of Religion* 81, no. 2 (June 2013): 467–90.

Happold, F. C. *Mysticism: A Study and an Anthology.* London: Penguin Books, 1970.

Harrison, Peter. *"Religion" and the Religions in the English Enlightenment.* Cambridge: Cambridge University Press, 1990.

Hasker, William. "The Epistemic Value of Religious Experience: Perceptual and Explanatory Models." In Senor, *Rationality of Belief and the Plurality of Faith*, 150–69.

————. "The Foundations of Theism: Scoring the Quinn-Plantinga Debate." *Faith and Philosophy* 15, no. 1 (January 1998): 52–67.

Hay, David. *Religious Experience Today: Studying the Facts.* London: Mowbray, 1990.

Heelas, Paul, and Linda Woodhead. *The Spiritual Revolution: Why Religion Is Giving Way to Spirituality.* Oxford: Blackwell, 2005.

Helm, Paul. *Faith and Understanding.* Grand Rapids: Eerdmans, 1997.

————. *John Calvin's Ideas.* New York: Oxford University Press, 2004.

————. "John Locke and Jonathan Edwards: A Reconstruction." *Journal of the History of Ideas* 7, no. 1 (1969): 51–61.

————. "Review of *Warranted Christian Belief.*" *Mind* 110, no. 440 (October 2001): 1110–15.

Heyd, Michael. "Enthusiasm." In *Encyclopedia of the Enlightenment*, edited by Alan Charles Kors, 2:1–7. Oxford: Oxford University Press, 2003.

Hick, John. *Arguments for the Existence of God.* New York: Herder & Herder, 1971.

————. *Dialogues in the Philosophy of Religion.* New York: Palgrave, 2001.

————. "The Epistemological Challenge of Religious Pluralism." *Faith and Philosophy* 14, no. 3 (July 1997): 277–86.

————. *Faith and Knowledge.* 2nd ed. Ithaca, NY: Cornell University Press, 1966.

————. *God and the Universe of Faiths: Essays in the Philosophy of Religion.* New York: St. Martin's Press, 1973.

————. "Ineffability." *Religious Studies* 36 (2000): 35–46.

————. *An Interpretation of Religion.* 2nd ed. New Haven: Yale University Press, 2004.

————. *John Hick: An Autobiography.* Oxford: Oneworld, 2002.

————. "A Pluralist View." In *Four Views on Salvation in a Pluralistic World*, edited by Dennis L. Okholm and Timothy R. Phillips, 27–59. Grand Rapids: Zondervan, 1996.

————. "Rational Theistic Belief without Proofs." In Badham, *John Hick Reader*, 49–67.

————. "Religious Faith as Experiencing-As." In Badham, *John Hick Reader*, 34–48.

Hindmarsh, D. Bruce. *The Evangelical Conversion Narrative: Spiritual Autobiography in Early Modern England.* New York: Oxford University Press, 2005.

Holland, R. F. "The Miraculous." *American Philosophical Quarterly* 2, no. 1 (January 1965): 43–51.

Hollenback, Jess Byron. *Mysticism: Experience, Response, and Empowerment.* University Park: Pennsylvania State University Press, 1996.

Hollywood, Amy, and Patricia Z. Beckman, eds., *The Cambridge Companion to Christian Mysticism.* New York: Cambridge University Press, 2012.

Huemer, Michael. "Compassionate Phenomenal Conservatism." *Philosophy and Phenomenological Research* 74, no. 1 (January 2007): 30–55.

————. "Phenomenal Conservatism über Alles." In Tucker, *Seemings and Justification*, 328–50.

————. *Skepticism and the Veil of Perception.* New York: Rowman & Littlefield, 2001.

Hume, David. *Dialogues concerning Natural Religion and Other Writings.* Edited by Dorothy Coleman. Cambridge: Cambridge University Press, 2007.

————. "Of Superstition and Enthusiasm." In *David Hume: Writings on Religion*, edited by Antony Flew, 3–9. La Salle, IL: Open Court, 1992.

————. *A Treatise of Human Nature.* New York: Doubleday, 1961.

Hunt, Lynn, and Margaret Jacob. "Enlightenment Studies." In Kors, *Encyclopedia of the Enlightenment*, 1:418–30.

Huxley, Aldous. *The Perennial Philosophy.* 1945. Reprint, London: Grafton, 1985.

Iwamura, Jane Naomi. *Virtual Orientalism: Asian Religions and Popular Culture*. New York: Oxford University Press, 2011.

James, William. *The Varieties of Religious Experience*. 1902. Reprint, New York: Penguin Books, 1985.

Jantzen, Grace M. "Could There Be a Mystical Core of Religion?" *Religious Studies* 26, no. 1 (1990): 59–71.

Jeffreys, Derek A. "How Reformed Is Reformed Epistemology? Alvin Plantinga and Calvin's *Sensus Divinitatis*." *Religious Studies* 33, no. 4 (December 1997): 419–31.

Jensen, Debra. "Experience." In *The Brill Dictionary of Religion*, edited by Kocku von Stuckrad, 2:697–701. Leiden: Brill, 2006.

Jones, Lindsay, ed. *Encyclopedia of Religion*. 2nd ed. Detroit: Gale, 2005.

Julian of Norwich. "Showings." In Dupré and Wiseman, *Light from Light*, 234–45.

Kant, Immanuel. *Critique of Pure Reason*. Translated and edited by Paul Guyer and Allen Wood. Cambridge: Cambridge University Press, 1998.

Katz, Steven T. "Exploring the Nature of Mystical Experience." In Moser and Meister, *Cambridge Companion to Religious Experience*, 239–60.

———. "Language, Epistemology, and Mysticism." In Katz, *Mysticism and Philosophical Analysis*, 22–74.

———, ed. *Mysticism and Philosophical Analysis*. New York: Oxford University Press, 1978.

———, ed. *Mysticism and Religious Traditions*. New York: Oxford University Press, 1983.

Keener, Craig S. *Miracles: The Credibility of the New Testament Accounts*. 2 vols. Grand Rapids: Baker Academic, 2011.

Kelly, Thomas. "*Consensus Gentium*: Reflections on the 'Common Consent' Argument for the Existence of God." In Clark and VanArragon, *Evidence and Religious Belief*, 135–56.

———. "The Epistemic Significance of Disagreement." In *Oxford Studies in Epistemology*, edited by Tamar Szabó Gendler and John Hawthorne, 1:167–96. Oxford: Oxford University Press, 2005.

King, Richard. "Mysticism and Spirituality." In *The Routledge Companion to the Study of Religion*, edited by John R. Hinnells, 306–22. London: Routledge, 2005.

———. *Orientalism and Religion: Postcolonial Theory, India, and "The Mystic East."* London: Routledge, 1999.

Kinghorn, Kevin, and Jerry L. Walls. "The Spirit and the Bride Say 'Come': Apologetics and the Witness of the Holy Spirit." In Geivett and Moser, *Testimony of the Spirit*, 223–43.

Knitter, Paul. *No Other Name? A Critical Survey of Christian Attitudes toward the World Religions*. Maryknoll, NY: Orbis, 1985.

———. *Without Buddha I Could Not Be a Christian*. Oxford: Oneworld, 2009.

Kors, Alan Charles. "The Age of Enlightenment." In *The Oxford Handbook of Atheism*, edited by Stephen Bullivant and Michael Ruse, 195–211. New York: Oxford University Press, 2013.

———, ed. *Encyclopedia of the Enlightenment*. New York: Oxford University Press, 2003.

Koskela, Douglas K. "John Wesley." In Abraham and Aquino, *Oxford Handbook of the Epistemology of Theology*, 459–70.

Kwan, Kai-Man. "The Argument from Religious Experience." In Craig and Moreland, *Blackwell Companion to Natural Theology*, 498–552.

———. *The Rainbow of Experiences, Critical Trust, and God: A Defense of Holistic Empiricism*. New York: Bloomsbury Academic, 2011.

Lackey, Jennifer. "The Epistemology of Testimony and Religious Belief." In Abraham and Aquino, *Oxford Handbook of the Epistemology of Theology*, 203–20.

Lamberth, David C. *William James and the Metaphysics of Experience*. Cambridge: Cambridge University Press, 1999.

Lanman, Jonathan A. "Atheism and Cognitive Science." In *The Oxford Handbook of Atheism*, edited by Stephen Bullivant and Michael Ruse, 483–96. New York: Oxford University Press, 2013.

Lee, Sang Hyun, ed. *The Princeton Companion to Jonathan Edwards*. Princeton: Princeton University Press, 2005.

Lemos, Noah. *An Introduction to the Theory of Knowledge*. New York: Cambridge University Press, 2007.

Levinson, Henry Samuel. *The Religious Investigations of William James*. Chapel Hill: University of North Carolina Press, 1981.

Lipton, Peter. *Inference to the Best Explanation*. 2nd ed. London: Routledge, 2004.

Locke, John. *An Essay concerning Human Understanding*. Edited by Roger Woolhouse. London: Penguin Books, 1997.

Long, Eugene Thomas. "Experience and Natural Theology." In Long, *Prospects for Natural Theology*, 207–20.

———, ed. *Prospects for Natural Theology*. Washington, DC: Catholic University of America Press, 1992.

Lopez, Donald S., Jr. "Approaching the Numinous: Rudolf Otto and Tibetan Tantra." *Philosophy East and West* 29, no. 4 (October 1979): 467–76.

Losin, Peter. "Experience of God and the Principle of Credulity: A Reply to Rowe." *Faith and Philosophy* 4, no. 1 (January 1987): 59–70.

Lovejoy, David S. *Religious Enthusiasm in the New World: Heresy to Revolution*. Cambridge, MA: Harvard University Press, 1985.

Luhrmann, T. M. *When God Talks Back: Understanding the American Evangelical Relationship with God*. New York: Knopf, 2012.

MacDonald, Mary. "Spirituality." In Jones, *Encyclopedia of Religion*, 13:8718–21.

MacDonald, Scott. "Natural Theology." In *Routledge Encyclopedia of Philosophy*, edited by Edward Craig, 6:707–13. London: Routledge, 1998.

MacKenzie, Vickie. *Why Buddhism? Westerners in Search of Wisdom*. London: Element, 2002.

Marsden, George M. "Biography." In Stein, *Cambridge Companion to Jonathan Edwards*, 19–37.

———. *Jonathan Edwards: A Life*. New Haven: Yale University Press, 2003.

Martin, C. B. *Religious Belief*. Ithaca, NY: Cornell University Press, 1959.

Martin, Michael. *Atheism: A Philosophical Justification*. Philadelphia: Temple University Press, 1990.

———. "The Principle of Credulity and Religious Experience." *Religious Studies* 22, no. 1 (March 1986): 79–93.

Masuzawa, Tomoko. "Culture." In M. Taylor, *Critical Terms for Religious Studies*, 70–93.

———. *The Invention of World Religions: Or, How European Universalism Was Preserved in the Language of Pluralism.* Chicago: University of Chicago Press, 2005.

———. "World Religions." In Jones, *Encyclopedia of Religion*, 14:9800–9804.

Mavrodes, George I. *Belief in God: A Study in the Epistemology of Religion.* New York: Random House, 1970.

———. "On the Very Strongest Arguments." In Long, *Prospects for Natural Theology*, 81–91.

———. "Real v. Deceptive Mystical Experiences." In Katz, *Mysticism and Philosophical Analysis*, 235–58.

McAllister, Blake, and Trent Dougherty. "Reforming Reformed Epistemology: A New Take on the *Sensus Divinitatis.*" *Religious Studies* 55 (2019): 537–57.

McClymond, Michael J. *Encounters with God: An Approach to the Theology of Jonathan Edwards.* New York: Oxford University Press, 1998.

McClymond, Michael J., and Gerald R. McDermott. *The Theology of Jonathan Edwards.* New York: Oxford University Press, 2012.

McDermott, Gerald R., and Harold A. Netland. *A Trinitarian Theology of Religions: An Evangelical Proposal.* New York: Oxford University Press, 2014.

McMahan, David L. *The Making of Buddhist Modernism.* New York: Oxford University Press, 2008.

Mealey, Mark. "John Wesley." In Gavrilyuk and Coakley, *Spiritual Senses*, 241–56.

Mercadante, Linda. *Belief without Borders: Inside the Minds of the Spiritual but Not Religious.* New York: Oxford University Press, 2014.

Miller, Perry. "Jonathan Edwards on the Sense of the Heart." *Harvard Theological Review* 41 (1948): 123–45.

Minkema, Kenneth P. "Jonathan Edwards: A Theological Life." In *The Princeton Companion to Jonathan Edwards*, edited by Sang Hyun Lee, 1–15. Princeton: Princeton University Press, 2005.

Mitchell, Basil. *The Justification of Religious Belief.* Oxford: Oxford University Press, 1981.

Montaigne, Michel de. *An Apology for Raymond Sebond.* Translated by M. A. Screech. London: Penguin Books, 1987.

Moser, Paul K. "The Inner Witness of the Spirit." In Abraham and Aquino, *Oxford Handbook of the Epistemology of Theology*, 111–25.

———. *Understanding Religious Experience: From Conviction to Life's Meaning.* Cambridge: Cambridge University Press, 2020.

Moser, Paul K., and Chad Meister, eds. *The Cambridge Companion to Religious Experience.* Cambridge: Cambridge University Press, 2020.

Moser, Paul K., Dwayne H. Mulder, and J. D. Trout. *The Theory of Knowledge: A Thematic Introduction.* New York: Oxford University Press, 1998.

Murray, Michael J. "Scientific Explanations of Religion and the Justification of Religious Belief." In Schloss and Murray, *Believing Primate*, 168–78.

Murray, Michael J., and Andrew Goldberg. "Evolutionary Accounts of Religion: Explaining and Explaining Away." In Schloss and Murray, *Believing Primate*, 179–99.

Naja, Ben. "A Jesus Movement among Muslims: Research from Eastern Africa." *International Journal of Frontier Missiology* 30, no. 1 (Spring 2013): 27–29.

Nasr, Seyyed Hossein. *Knowledge and the Sacred*. Albany: State University of New York Press, 1981.

———. "The *Philosophia Perennis* and the Study of Religion." In *The World's Religious Traditions: Current Perspectives in Religious Studies*, edited by Frank Whaling, 181–200. New York: Crossroad, 1986.

Netland, Harold. *Christianity and Religious Diversity*. Grand Rapids: Baker Academic, 2015.

Niebuhr, Richard R. "William James on Religious Experience." In *The Cambridge Companion to William James*, edited by Ruth Anna Putnam, 214–36. Cambridge: Cambridge University Press, 2006.

Nongbri, Brent. *Before Religion: A History of a Modern Concept*. New Haven: Yale University Press, 2013.

Nuttall, George F. *The Holy Spirit in Puritan Faith and Experience*. Oxford: Blackwell, 1946.

Oppy, Graham. "Natural Theology." In D. Baker, *Alvin Plantinga*, 15–47.

Otto, Rudolf. *The Idea of the Holy*. Translated by John W. Harvey. 1923. Reprint, New York: Oxford University Press, 1950.

———. *Mysticism East and West: A Comparative Analysis of the Nature of Mysticism*. Translated by Bertha L. Bracey and Richenda C. Payne. New York: Macmillan, 1932.

Outler, Albert, ed. *John Wesley*. New York: Oxford University Press, 1964.

Packer, J. I. *Keep in Step with the Spirit*. Grand Rapids: Revell, 1984.

Pals, Daniel L. *Eight Theories of Religion*. 2nd ed. New York: Oxford University Press, 2006.

———. *Introducing Religion*. New York: Oxford University Press, 2009.

Pappas, George. "Perception and Mystical Experience." *Philosophy and Phenomenological Research* 54, no. 4 (December 1994): 877–83.

Penelhum, Terence. "Parity Is Not Enough." In *Faith, Reason, and Skepticism*, edited by Marcus Hester, 98–120. Philadelphia: Temple University Press, 1992.

Perceiving God symposium. *Philosophy and Phenomenological Research* 54, no. 4 (December 1994): 863–99.

Peterson, Michael, William Hasker, Bruce Reichenbach, and David Basinger. *Reason and Religious Belief: An Introduction to the Philosophy of Religion*. 5th ed. New York: Oxford University Press, 2013.

Plantinga, Alvin. "Belief in God as Properly Basic." In *The Philosophy of Religion Reader*, edited by Chad Meister, 379–88. London: Routledge, 2008.

———. "The Foundations of Theism: A Reply." *Faith and Philosophy* 3, no. 3 (July 1986): 298–313.

———. *God and Other Minds*. Ithaca, NY: Cornell University Press, 1967.

———. *Knowledge and Christian Belief*. Grand Rapids: Eerdmans, 2015.

————. "Pluralism: A Defense of Religious Exclusivism." In Senor, *Rationality of Belief and the Plurality of Faith*, 191–215.

————. "The Prospects for Natural Theology." In *Philosophical Perspectives*. Vol. 5 of *Philosophy of Religion*, edited by James E. Tomberlin, 287–316. Atascadero, CA: Ridgeview, 1991.

————. "Reason and Belief in God." In Plantinga and Wolterstorff, *Faith and Rationality*, 16–93.

————. "Reformed Epistemology." In *A Companion to Philosophy of Religion*, edited by Philip L. Quinn and Charles Taliaferro, 383–89. Oxford: Blackwell, 1997.

————. "Two Dozen (or So) Theistic Arguments." In Baker, *Alvin Plantinga*, 203–27.

————. *Warranted Christian Belief*. New York: Oxford University Press, 2000.

Plantinga, Alvin, and Nicholas Wolterstorff, eds. *Faith and Rationality: Reason and Belief in God*. Notre Dame: University of Notre Dame Press, 1983.

Plasger, Georg. "Does Calvin Teach a *Sensus Divinitatis*? Reflections on Alvin Plantinga's Interpretation of Calvin." In Schönecker, *Plantinga's "Warranted Christian Belief,"* 169–89.

Pojman, Louis P. *Philosophy of Religion*. Mountain View, CA: Mayfield, 2001.

Popkin, Richard. *The History of Skepticism: From Savonarola to Bayle*. Rev. ed. New York: Oxford University Press, 2003.

Preus, J. Samuel. *Explaining Religion: Criticism and Theory from Bodin to Freud*. New Haven: Yale University Press, 1987.

Proudfoot, Wayne. *Religious Experience*. Berkeley: University of California Press, 1985.

Quinn, Philip L. "The Foundations of Theism Again: A Rejoinder to Plantinga." In *Rational Faith: Catholic Responses to Reformed Epistemology*, edited by Linda Zagzebski, 14–47. Notre Dame: University of Notre Dame Press, 1993.

————. "In Search of the Foundations of Theism." *Faith and Philosophy* 2, no. 4 (1985): 469–86.

Quinn, Philip L., and Charles Taliaferro, eds. *A Companion to Philosophy of Religion*. Oxford: Blackwell, 1997.

Qureshi, Nabeel. *Seeking Allah, Finding Jesus: A Devout Muslim Encounters Christianity*. Grand Rapids: Zondervan, 2014.

Rack, Henry D. *Reasonable Enthusiast: John Wesley and the Rise of Methodism*. Nashville: Abingdon, 1992.

Radhakrishnan, S., trans. *The Bhagavadgita*. New York: Harper & Row, 1948.

Ramm, Bernard. *The Witness of the Spirit: An Essay on the Contemporary Relevance of the Internal Witness of the Holy Spirit*. Grand Rapids: Eerdmans, 1959.

Rankin, Marianne. *An Introduction to Religious and Spiritual Experience*. New York: Continuum, 2008.

Rea, Michael C. *The Hiddenness of God*. New York: Oxford University Press, 2018.

Renusch, Anita. "Thank God It's the Right Religion!—Plantinga on Religious Diversity." In Schönecker, *Plantinga's "Warranted Christian Belief,"* 147–68.

Richardson, Robert D. *William James: In the Maelstrom of American Modernism*. New York: Houghton Mifflin, 2006.

Riesebrodt, Martin. *The Promise of Salvation: A Theory of Religion*. Translated by Steven Rendall. Chicago: University of Chicago Press, 2010.

Rodrigues, Hillary P., and John S. Harding. *Introduction to the Study of Religion*. New York: Routledge, 2009.

Roof, Wade Clark. *Spiritual Marketplace: Baby Boomers and the Remaking of American Religion*. Princeton: Princeton University Press, 2005.

Rothberg, Donald. "Contemporary Epistemology and the Study of Mysticism." In Forman, *Problem of Pure Consciousness*, 163–210.

Rowe, William L. "Religious Experience and the Principle of Credulity." *International Journal for Philosophy of Religion* 13 (1982): 85–92.

———. "Religious Pluralism." *Religious Studies* 35, no. 2 (1999): 139–50.

Schellenberg, J. L. *The Wisdom to Doubt: A Justification of Religious Skepticism*. Ithaca, NY: Cornell University Press, 2007.

Schewel, Benjamin. *Seven Ways of Looking at Religion: The Major Narratives*. New Haven: Yale University Press, 2017.

Schilbrack, Kevin. *Philosophy and the Study of Religions: A Manifesto*. Malden, MA: Wiley Blackwell, 2014.

———. "Religions: Are There Any?" *Journal of the American Academy of Religion* 78, no. 4 (December 2010): 1112–38.

Schloss, Jeffrey, and Michael J. Murray, eds. *The Believing Primate: Scientific, Philosophical, and Theological Reflections on the Origin of Religion*. New York: Oxford University Press, 2009.

Schmidt, Leigh Eric. "The Making of Modern 'Mysticism.'" *Journal of the American Academy of Religion* 71, no. 2 (June 2003): 273–302.

———. *Restless Souls: The Making of American Spirituality*. 2nd ed. Berkeley: University of California Press, 2012.

Schmidt, Roger, Gene C. Sager, Gerald T. Carney, Julius J. Jackson, Albert Charles Muller, and Kenneth J. Zanga. *Patterns of Religion*. Belmont, CA: Wadsworth, 1999.

Schmidt-Leukel, Perry. *Religious Pluralism and Interreligious Theology*. Maryknoll, NY: Orbis, 2017.

Schönecker, Dieter, ed. *Plantinga's "Warranted Christian Belief": Critical Essays with a Reply by Alvin Plantinga*. Berlin: de Gruyter, 2015.

Schreiner, Susan E. *Are You Alone Wise? The Search for Certainty in the Early Modern Era*. New York: Oxford University Press, 2011.

Schuon, Frithjof. *The Transcendent Unity of Religions*. Translated by Peter Townsend. Rev. ed. New York: Harper & Row, 1975.

Senor, Thomas D. "The Experiential Grounding of Religious Belief." In Abraham and Aquino, *Oxford Handbook of the Epistemology of Theology*, 64–78.

———, ed. *The Rationality of Belief and the Plurality of Faith*. Ithaca, NY: Cornell University Press, 1995.

Sharf, Robert H. "Buddhist Modernism and the Rhetoric of Meditative Experience." *Numen* 42 (1995): 228–83.

———. "Experience." In M. Taylor, *Critical Terms for Religious Studies*, 94–116.

Sheehan, Jonathan. "Enlightenment, Religion, and the Enigma of Secularization: A Review Essay." *American Historical Review* 108 (October 2003): 1061–80.

Short, Larry. "Mysticism, Mediation, and the Non-linguistic." *Journal of the American Academy of Religion* 63, no. 4 (1995): 659–75.

Shushan, Gregory. "Extraordinary Experiences and Religious Beliefs: Deconstructing Some Contemporary Philosophical Axioms." *Method and Theory in the Study of Religion* 26 (2014): 384–416.

———. *Near-Death Experiences in Indigenous Religions*. New York: Oxford University Press, 2018.

Smart, J. J. C. "The Existence of God." In *New Essays in Philosophical Theology*, edited by Antony Flew and Alasdair MacIntyre, 28–46. London: SCM, 1955.

Smart, Ninian. *Concept and Empathy: Essays in the Study of Religion*. Edited by Donald Wiebe. New York: New York University Press, 1986.

———. *A Dialogue of Religions*. London: SCM, 1960.

———. *Dimensions of the Sacred: An Anatomy of the World's Beliefs*. Berkeley: University of California Press 1996.

———. "Interpretation and Mystical Experience." *Religious Studies* 1 (1965): 75–87.

———. "Numen, Nirvana, and the Definition of Religion." In *Concept and Empathy: Essays in the Study of Religion*, edited by Donald Wiebe, 40–49. New York: New York University Press, 1986.

———. *The Religious Experience*. 5th ed. New York: Cambridge University Press, 1996.

———. "Revelation, Reason and Religions." In *Prospects for Metaphysics: Essays of Metaphysical Exploration*, edited by Ian Ramsey, 80–92. London: Allen & Unwin, 1961.

———. "Soft Natural Theology." In Long, *Prospects for Natural Theology*, 198–206.

———. "Understanding Religious Experience." In Katz, *Mysticism and Philosophical Analysis*, 10–21.

Smith, Christian. *Religion: What It Is, How It Works, and Why It Matters*. Princeton: Princeton University Press, 2017.

Smith, Huston. *Beyond the Post-Modern Mind*. New York: Crossroad, 1982.

———. *Forgotten Truth*. New York: Harper & Row, 1976.

———. "Is There a Perennial Philosophy?" *Journal of the American Academy of Religion* 55, no. 3 (1987): 553–66.

Smith, John E. "Editor's Introduction." In Jonathan Edwards, *Religious Affections*, edited by John E. Smith, 1–83. Vol. 2 of *The Works of Jonathan Edwards*. New Haven: Yale University Press, 2009.

———. "Religious Affections and the 'Sense of the Heart.'" In *The Princeton Companion to Jonathan Edwards*, edited by Sang Hyun Lee, 103–14. Princeton: Princeton University Press, 2005.

Smith, Joseph, trans. *The Book of Mormon*. Salt Lake City: Church of Jesus Christ of Latter Day Saints, 1982.

Smith, Robert Doyle. "John Wesley and Jonathan Edwards on Religious Experience: A Comparative Analysis." *Wesley Theological Journal* 25, no. 1 (Spring 1990): 130–46.

Smith, Wilfred Cantwell. *Towards a World Theology: Faith and the Comparative History of Religion.* Maryknoll, NY: Orbis, 1989.

Smythe, Thomas W. "Perceiving God." *Theology Today* 63 (2007): 459–68.

Sorkin, David. *The Religious Enlightenment: Protestants, Jews, and Catholics from London to Vienna.* Princeton: Princeton University Press, 2008.

Stace, W. T. *Mysticism and Philosophy.* Philadelphia: Lippincott, 1960.

Steele, Richard B. *"Gracious Affection" and "True Virtue" according to Jonathan Edwards and John Wesley.* Metuchen, NJ: Scarecrow, 1994.

Stein, Stephen, J. *The Cambridge Companion to Jonathan Edwards.* New York: Cambridge University Press, 2007.

Stievermann, Jan, and Ryan P. Hoselton, "Spiritual Meaning and Experiential Piety in the Exegesis of Cotton Mather and Jonathan Edwards." In *Jonathan Edwards and Scripture*, edited by David P. Barshinger and Douglas A. Sweeney, 86–105. New York: Oxford University Press, 2018.

Stroumsa, Guy G. *A New Science: The Discovery of Religion in the Age of Reason.* Cambridge, MA: Harvard University Press, 2010.

Sweeney, Douglas A. "Evangelical Tradition in America." In Stein, *Cambridge Companion to Jonathan Edwards*, 217–38.

Swinburne, Richard. *Epistemic Justification.* New York: Oxford University Press, 2001.

———. *The Evolution of the Soul.* Oxford: Clarendon, 1986.

———. *The Existence of God.* 2nd ed. New York: Oxford University Press, 2004.

———. *Is There a God?* Rev. ed. New York: Oxford University Press, 2010.

———. "Phenomenal Conservatism and Religious Experience." In Benton, Hawthorne, and Rabinowitz, *Knowledge, Belief, and God*, 322–38.

Taliaferro, Charles. *Evidence and Faith: Philosophy and Religion since the Seventeenth Century.* New York: Cambridge University Press, 2005.

———. "Explaining Religious Experience." In Schloss and Murray, *Believing Primate*, 200–214.

———. "In Defense of the Numinous." In *Philosophy and the Christian Worldview*, edited by David Werther and Mark D. Linville, 95–108. New York: Continuum, 2012.

———. "The Project of Natural Theology." In Craig and Moreland, *Blackwell Companion to Natural Theology*, 1–23.

Taliaferro, Charles, and Chad Meister. *Contemporary Philosophical Theology.* London: Routledge, 2016.

Taves, Ann. *Fits, Trances, and Visions: Experiencing Religion and Explaining Experience from Wesley to James.* Princeton: Princeton University Press, 1999.

———. "Psychology of Religion Approaches to the Study of Religious Experience." In Moser and Meister, *Cambridge Companion to Religious Experience*, 25–54.

———. "Religious Experience." In Jones, *Encyclopedia of Religion*, 11:7736–50.

———. *Religious Experience Reconsidered.* Princeton: Princeton University Press, 2009.

Taylor, Charles. *A Secular Age.* Cambridge, MA: Harvard University Press, 2007.

————. *Varieties of Religion Today: William James Revisited*. Cambridge, MA: Harvard University Press, 2002.

Taylor, Mark C., ed. *Critical Terms for Religious Studies*. Chicago: University of Chicago Press, 1998.

Teasdale, Wayne. *The Mystic Heart: Discovering a Universal Spirituality in the World's Religions*. Novato, CA: New World Library, 1999.

Thiselton, Anthony C. *Doubt, Faith and Certainty*. Grand Rapids: Eerdmans, 2017.

Thurow, Joshua C. "Religion, 'Religion,' and Tolerance." In *Religion, Intolerance, and Conflict*, edited by Steve Clarke, Russell Powell, and Julian Savulescu, 146–62. New York: Oxford University Press, 2013.

————. "Some Reflections on Cognitive Science, Doubt, and Religious Belief." In Trigg and Barrett, *Roots of Religion*, 189–207.

Toulmin, Stephen. *Cosmopolis: The Hidden Agenda of Modernity*. Chicago: University of Chicago Press, 1990.

Trigg, Roger, and Justin L. Barrett, eds. *The Roots of Religion: Exploring the Cognitive Science of Religion*. London: Routledge, 2016.

Troeltsch, Ernst. "The Place of Christianity among the World Religions." In *Christianity and Other Religions: Selected Readings*, edited by John Hick and Brian Hebblethewaite, 11–31. Philadelphia: Fortress, 1980.

Tucker, Chris. "Seemings and Justification: An Introduction." In Tucker, *Seemings and Justification*, 1–32.

Tucker, Chris, ed. *Seemings and Justification: New Essays on Dogmatism and Phenomenal Conservatism*. New York: Oxford University Press, 2013.

Turner, Edith. "The Reality of Spirits: A Tabooed or Permitted Field of Study." *Anthropology of Consciousness* 4, no. 1 (1993): 9–12.

Tyson, John H. "John Wesley's Conversion at Aldersgate." In Collins and Tyson, *Conversion in the Wesleyan Tradition*, 27–42.

Van Cleve, James. "Why Coherence Is Not Enough: A Defense of Moderate Foundationalism." In *Contemporary Debates in Epistemology*, edited by Matthias Steup and Ernest Sosa, 168–80. Oxford: Blackwell, 2005.

Van der Veer, Peter. *Imperial Encounters: Religion and Modernity in India and Britain*. Princeton: Princeton University Press, 2001.

————. *The Modern Spirit of Asia: The Spiritual and the Secular in China and India*. Princeton: Princeton University Press, 2014.

Van Eyghen, Hans. *Arguing from Cognitive Science of Religion: Is Religious Belief Debunked?* London: Bloomsbury Academic, 2020.

Versluis, Arthur, *American Transcendentalism and Asian Religions*. New York: Oxford University Press, 1993.

Vincett, Giselle, and Linda Woodhead. "Spirituality." In *Religions in the Modern World*, edited by Linda Woodhead, Hiroko Kawanami, and Christopher Partridge, 319–37. 2nd ed. London: Routledge, 2009.

Wainwright, Geoffrey. "Wesley, John and Charles." In *The Oxford Companion to Christian Thought*, edited by Adrian Hastings, 750–51. New York: Oxford University Press, 2000.

Wainwright, William J. "Jonathan Edwards and His Puritan Predecessors." In Gavrilyuk and Coakley, *Spiritual Senses*, 224–40.

———. *Mysticism: A Study of Its Nature, Cognitive Value and Moral Implications.* Madison: University of Wisconsin Press, 1981.

———, ed. *The Oxford Handbook of Philosophy of Religion.* New York: Oxford University Press, 2005.

———. *Philosophy of Religion.* 2nd ed. Belmont, CA: Wadsworth, 1999.

———. *Reason and the Heart: A Prolegomenon to a Critique of Passional Reason.* Ithaca, NY: Cornell University Press, 1995.

———. *Reason, Revelation, and Devotion: Inference and Argument in Religion.* Cambridge: Cambridge University Press, 2016.

———. "Religious Language, Religious Experience, and Religious Pluralism." In Senor, *Rationality of Belief and the Plurality of Faith*, 170–88.

———. "Theistic Proofs, Person Relativity, and the Rationality of Religious Belief." In Clark and VanArragon, *Evidence and Religious Belief*, 77–94.

Walls, Jerry L., and Trent Dougherty, eds. *Two Dozen (or So) Arguments for God: The Plantinga Project.* New York: Oxford University Press, 2018.

Ward, Keith. *Concepts of God: Images of the Divine in Five Faith Traditions.* Oxford: Oneworld, 2009.

———. *Religion in the Modern World: Celebrating Pluralism and Diversity.* Cambridge: Cambridge University Press, 2019.

———. "Truth and the Diversity of Religions." *Religious Studies* 26, no. 1 (March 1990): 2–11.

Warner, Michael, Jonathan VanAntwerpen, and Craig Calhoun, eds. *Varieties of Secularism in a Secular Age.* Cambridge, MA: Harvard University Press, 2010.

Warner, Rob. *Secularization and Its Discontents.* New York: Continuum, 2010.

Warranted Christian Belief symposium. *Philosophia Christi* 3, no. 2 (2001): 327–400.

Webb, Mark Owen. "Meaning and Social Value in Religious Experience." In Moser and Meister, *Cambridge Companion to Religious Experience*, 319–33.

———. "Religious Experience." In *Stanford Encyclopedia of Philosophy.* December 13, 2017. http://plato.stanford.edu/entries/religious-experience/.

Wesley, John. "The Aldersgate Experience." In Outler, *John Wesley*, 51.

———. "A Clear and Concise Demonstration of the Divine Inspiration of the Holy Scriptures." In *The Works of John Wesley*, 11:484. Grand Rapids: Zondervan, 1958.

———. "An Earnest Appeal to Men of Reason and Religion." In Outler, *John Wesley*, 384–424.

———. *Journals and Diaries, 1765–75.* Edited by Reginald Ward and Richard Heitzenrater. Vol. 22 of *The Works of John Wesley.* Nashville: Abingdon, 1993.

———. "A Letter to the Reverend Doctor Conyers Middleton Occasioned by His Late 'Free Inquiry.'" In *The Works of John Wesley*, 10:1–79. Grand Rapids: Zondervan, 1958.

———. "A Letter to the Reverend Dr. Rutherforth, March 28, 1768." In *The Works of John Wesley*, 13:126–40. London: Thomas Cordeux, 1812.

———. "The Marks of the New Birth (John 3:8)." In *The Sermons of John Wesley*, edited by Kenneth J. Collins and Jason E. Vickers, 165–74. Nashville: Abingdon, 2013.

———. "The Nature of Enthusiasm." In *Sermons II, 34–70*, edited by Albert C. Outler, 46–60. Vol. 2 of *The Works of John Wesley*. Nashville: Abingdon, 1985.

———. "The Witness of the Spirit, I." In *Sermons I, 1–33*, edited by Albert C. Outler, 269–84. Vol. 1 of *The Works of John Wesley*. Nashville: Abingdon, 1984.

———. "The Witness of the Spirit, II." In *Sermons I, 1–33*, edited by Albert C. Outler, 285–98. Vol. 1 of *The Works of John Wesley*. Nashville: Abingdon, 1984.

Whitehead, Alfred North. *Religion in the Making*. New York: Macmillan, 1960.

Wiebe, Phillip H. *God and Other Spirits: Intimations of Transcendence in Christian Experience*. New York: Oxford University Press, 2004.

———. "Philosophy of Religion Approaches to the Study of Religious Experience." In Moser and Meister, *Cambridge Companion to Religious Experience*, 55–75.

———. *Visions and Appearances of Jesus*. Abilene, TX: Leafwood, 2014.

———. *Visions of Jesus: Direct Encounters from the New Testament to Today*. New York: Oxford University Press, 1997.

Willard, Dallas. *Hearing God: Developing a Conversational Relationship with God*. Downers Grove, IL: InterVarsity, 2012.

Williams, Paul. *The Unexpected Way: On Converting from Buddhism to Catholicism*. Edinburgh: T&T Clark, 2002.

Winkelman, Michael. "Ethnological and Neurophenomenological Approaches to Religious Experience." In *The Study of Religious Experience: Approaches and Methodologies*, edited by Bettina E. Schmidt, 33–51. Sheffield: Equinox, 2016.

Wittgenstein, Ludwig. *Philosophical Investigations*. Translated by G. E. M. Anscombe. 3rd ed. New York: Macmillan, 1958.

———. *Tractatus Logico-Philosophicus*. Translated by D. F. Pears and B. F. McGuinness. London: Routledge & Kegan Paul, 1961.

Woodberry, J. Dudley, Russell G. Shubin, and G. Marks. "Why Muslims Follow Jesus." *Christianity Today* (October 2007). https://www.christianitytoday.com/ct/2007/october/42.80.html.

Woodward, Kenneth L. *The Book of Miracles: The Meaning of the Miracle Stories in Christianity, Judaism, Buddhism, Hinduism, and Islam*. New York: Touchstone, 2000.

Wuthnow, Robert. *After Heaven: Spirituality in America since the 1950s*. Berkeley: University of California Press, 1998.

———. *America and the Challenges of Religious Diversity*. Princeton: Princeton University Press, 2005.

———. *The God Problem: Expressing Faith and Being Reasonable*. Berkeley: University of California Press, 2012.

Yandell, Keith. *The Epistemology of Religious Experience*. Cambridge: Cambridge University Press, 1993.

———. *Hume's "Inexplicable Mystery": His Views on Religion*. Philadelphia: Temple University Press, 1990.

———. *Philosophy of Religion: A Contemporary Introduction*. 2nd ed. London: Routledge, 2016.

———. "Religious Experience." In Quinn and Taliaferro, *Companion to Philosophy of Religion*, 367–75.

Yong, Amos. *Beyond the Impasse: Toward a Pneumatological Theology of Religions.* Grand Rapids: Baker Academic, 2003.

———. "The Holy Spirit and the World Religions: On the Christian Discernment of Spirit(s) 'after' Buddhism." *Buddhist-Christian Studies* 24 (2004): 191–207.

Zaehner, R. C. *Concordant Discord.* Oxford: Clarendon, 1970.

———. *Mysticism: Sacred and Profane.* London: Oxford University Press, 1961.

Zagzebski, Linda. *Epistemic Authority: A Theory of Trust, Authority, and Autonomy in Belief.* New York: Oxford University Press, 2012.

———. "Epistemic Self-Trust and the *Consensus Gentium* Argument." In Clark and VanArragon, *Evidence and Religious Belief*, 22–36.

———. "Trust, Anti-Trust, and Reasons for Religious Belief." In *Religious Faith and Intellectual Virtue*, edited by Laura Frances Callahan and Timothy O'Connor, 231–45. New York: Oxford University Press, 2014.

Zahl, Simeon. "Experience." In *The Oxford Handbook of Nineteenth Century Christian Thought*, edited by Joel D. S. Rasmussen, Judith Wolfe, and Johannes Zachhuber, 177–94. Oxford: Oxford University Press, 2017.

———. *The Holy Spirit and Christian Experience.* Oxford: Oxford University Press, 2020.

Index

DATE DUE

GAYLORD   PRINTED IN U.S.A.